Nimeiri and the Revolution of Dis-May

Nimeiri and the Revolution of Dis-May

Mansour Khalid

KPI

London, Boston, Melbourne and Henley

First published in 1985 by KPI Limited
14 Leicester Square, London WC2H 7PH, England

Distributed by
Routledge & Kegan Paul plc
14 Leicester Square, London WC2H 7PH, England

Routledge & Kegan Paul Inc
9 Park Street, Boston, Mass. 02108, USA

Routledge & Kegan Paul
464 St Kilda Road, Melbourne,
Victoria 3004, Australia and

Routledge & Kegan Paul plc
Broadway House, Newtown Road,
Henley-on-Thames, Oxon RG9 1EN, England

Produced by Worts-Power Associates

Photoset in Times and printed in Great Britain
by Redwood Burn Limited, Trowbridge, Wiltshire

ISBN 0–7103–0111–1

Contents

DEDICATION

For the Sudan and its suffering people

Introduction

This book has had a rather long genesis. The author was a fellow in the Smithsonian Institution during the years 1978 to 1980. He had then just left the Sudanese political scene after ten years of public service as ambassador, Cabinet Minister and member of the Politburo of the Sudanese Socialist Union (SSU), the only political organization in the country. Like many others, he had become thoroughly disillusioned with the regime's betrayal of its own ideals, a betrayal of a nation and a generation, ours. For Nimeiri's regime, that set out in 1969 to scale the heights of political, economic and social development in a brave new Sudan, has ended less than two decades later, beating the Sudan down to the ground. Sudan is reduced to a country without purpose, its people denuded of spirit and deprived of their faculty for happiness. Nimeiri has failed to reconstruct the Sudan according to the vision of the millions who hailed him in the 'seventies. It is a given fact that this vision has never been articulated by Nimeiri himself; it has always been others, who reflected their own images. This is politics, but the last thing that Sudanese, of whatever political shade, would wish for their country is what they are reeling under now.

For the Sudanese, today's concerns are with neither ideology nor the structure of government, but rather with living and the quality of life. What the country suffers from today is not only bad governance and authoritarianism, but also the prevailing high level of corruption (political and economic) which is the most corrosive element in Sudanese public life. Indeed, it was the author's view of economic corruption that had earlier caused him to leave the Foreign Ministry twice. The emaciation, if not destruction, of institutions, mismanagement and corruption are the main causes of Sudan's tragedy, reflected today in the havoc and the fear that stalk the land.

While at the Smithsonian Institution, the author was engaged in a study tracing the political evolution of modern Sudan. He soon had to set this aside and attend to some topical issues of Sudanese contemporary politics, in response to a challenge by President Nimeiri to people to come out with their views on the regime's crisis. The result was the publication of a series of twenty articles in the journal *Al Ayam*, one of two organs of the Sudanese Socialist Union. These articles dealt with a number of substantial issues, but on the advice of a number of friends the views were toned down. They were meant to excite dialogue rather than add polemics to an already boiling cauldron. At that time too, the author still felt somewhat constrained by a sense of loyalty to a former friend, for Nimeiri had been a close friend of his. Friends or no friends, the errors of rulers with a track record of achievement are often condoned but, when those rulers persist in erring, one day the accumulation of their errors tips the balance against them. Things in the Sudan continue to deteriorate under Nimeiri and that statement will be documented in due course.

So far as the present writer is concerned three major events left their indelible effect: the destruction of the Addis Ababa agreement in 1983, Nimeiri's deviousness in handling the issue of the democratization of the Sudanese Socialist Union in 1978 and confrontation with the Army in 1982. In 1983 Nimeiri, under the guise of administrative decentralization, decided to abolish the regional Government institutions worked out by the Addis Ababa agreement that brought peace to the split country after seventeen years of civil war. The decision was his and his alone. In so doing Nimeiri destroyed, singlehandedly, his most abiding achievement. The reason, which will be elaborated, was simply to concentrate more power in his own hands. Also in 1978, following Nimeiri's calls for national reconciliation in the North, efforts to democratize the SSU and make it more widely based were undertaken. With those efforts I was closely involved and I could see Nimeiri's wily manoeuvres to frustrate them. That in itself belied his claims to democratization and national reconciliation. His future actions proved them hollow.

On the other hand, in 1982 President Nimeiri dismissed twenty-two senior Army officers, some of the best. They included the second man in the regime, First Vice-President General Abdel Magid Hamid Khalil, an able and widely respected soldier's soldier. The Army, led by Khalil, was then facing the President, evidence in hand, with accusations about corruption in high places. None of them challenged his authority, Nimeiri's readiness to protect corruption, even at that cost, said it all. To the author it was the final straw. From then on the contours of authoritarianism and corruption with presidential connivance were set in very bold colours.

The author now firmly believes, and he hopes that the following chapters will convince even the most sceptical reader, that Nimeiri personally is overwhelmingly, though not solely, responsible for the crisis that the Sudan faces today, and that if the country is to come out of its present morass then Nimeiri has to go. Indeed, for the rot to stop he has to go. What the Sudan is witnessing today are symptoms of decline and in politics as well as physics relative decline will one day become absolute decline. These events, more than anything else, have served to purge all emotional reservations. The author has never had any mental reservations.

The almost universal disenchantment with Nimeiri's regime today is in sharp contrast with its early years, when he was greatly admired by many sections of the Sudanese population and by many outsiders. He had then successfully brought the civil war in the country, between the North and the South, to an end; today the civil war rages as never before. He had then successfully clipped the wings of sectarianism, the bane of Sudanese politics for any number of years; today he courts Sufi obscurantists and shocks the world with a welter of political expediency, metaphysical confusion and bureaucratized barbarity. By 1984 the beloved Nimeiri of the 'seventies had become the man whom almost all Sudanese must love to hate.

Why this about-turn? Why have things gone so drastically wrong for the country? Those in the Sudan who claim that it is Nimeiri's mind rather than his policies which need examining have a clue to an answer to this question. But for other Sudanese and for most outsiders, perplexity in the face of recent happenings has been the most common reaction, and it is to them that this book is primarily addressed. It is to be hoped that those who find Nimeiri's motives inscrutable in the contradictory policies he adopts will have a different view at the end of this book.

To analyse Nimeiri's personality is not an easy task. In Nimeiri we do not have a schizophrenic leader with a split personality; his has at least four facets, that of a lofty dreamer, a weak-kneed coward, a megalomaniac and a believer in superstitions. To these is added of late Nimeiri the saint. In order to discern Nimeiri's federation of personalities, or rather unfederated personalities, it is not the author's wish to play the role of a psychiatrist or explore the deep recesses of Nimeiri's soul. Facts in hand, his aim is to demythologize Nimeiri and expose him for whatever he is worth.

Chapter One

The Years of Euphoria and Tension: 1969–1971

Kingly conclaves stern and cold
Where blood with guilt is bought and sold

Shelley, *Prometheus Unbound*

Why they failed

The 25 May revolution was a swift and bloodless affair. The fact that it met with no popular opposition could only be an indication of the lack of enthusiasm for the political parties. The Sudanese stood back and watched the Army return into the political arena less than five years after its removal by a popular revolt. Many have thought that after the unceremonious and almost obscene way in which people dispatched the Army to the barracks on 21 October 1964 the vampire would never rise again. Those who nourished this thought had the shock of their lives five years later. I was not one of them. My articles in the Khartoum daily *Al Ayam*, four months before the event, were evidence of that. Far from being an accomplice, a crystal-gazer or a Cassandra, I was only analysing and predicting.

The ubiquitous apathy and despondency of the people were understandable. Party politics in the period between 21 October 1964 and 25 May 1969 proved to be a re-enactment of the post-independence sectarian and personal battles. The party leaders, like the Bourbons, had learnt nothing and forgotten nothing. Their political record demonstrated that they had learnt very little from the six-year military dictatorship of Abboud, during which all party activity was officially banned. Not even in the period when opposition leaders of all colours were together in prison in Juba (July 1961 to February 1962) was there a serious attempt at introspection and reconciliation of differences. Such differences as existed were personal rather than ideological. Personal ambition, therefore, triumphed over civic responsibility and sectarian loyalty over patriotism.

Party politics in the aftermath of the October revolution were antagonistic in the extreme. The political arena witnessed battles between the traditionalist parties, the Umma and the National Unionist Party (NUP); between the different factions of these parties, e.g. between al Sadiq el Mahdi and his uncle Imam al Hadi el Mahdi inside the Ansar and Ismael el Azhari and the People's Democratic Party (PDP) inside the Khatmiya; and between the Communists and the Muslim Brothers, whose blueprints were incompatible and whose ideologies were mutually exclusive. The Opposition Front which was formed during the military government of General Abboud (1958–64), initially between the Umma and the NUP, symbolized by the meeting of the two leaders Siddiq el Mahdi and Ismael el Azhari to celebrate the 'Id prayer' early in 1960 and later joined by the Communists, was merely a front against Abboud.

The only common denominator was their enmity to his regime. Once Abboud was out of the political arena, the so-called Front collapsed. The traditional parties as such were indistinguishable in their politics. The conflict between them was one between two overlords trapped in the time-warp of old sectarian rivalries. As for the non-traditional parties, the Communists often burned their fingers by overplaying their cards. They were volcanic allies, hardly reassuring to their partners in coalition. The Muslim Brothers, on the other hand, invoked the name of the Lord to justify their worldly aspirations and in the process unleashed among the pious people of the Sudan all manner of misguided zealotry.

The first major political crisis came in December 1965, a year after the demise of the Abboud regime. It demonstrated the lack of both charity of mind and tolerance, two prerequisites for the survival of a pluralistic system. Clashes erupted between the Muslim Brothers and the Communists over the alleged blasphemous statement by a Communist Party member referring to the

Prophet Mohammed's wife. The issue, according to abundant evidence, was laboured by the Muslim Brothers. Parliament decided to ban the Communist Party and a resolution was passed to that effect. This was followed by an amendment of the constitution to enable Parliament to expel its duly elected Communist members. The following month the Communist Party's assets were confiscated and its members in Parliament unseated. Parliamentary democracy proved to be shallow-rooted, as there was no commitment on the part of the parties to the rules of the game. Parliament was just another battlefield.

The political crisis precipitated an institutional one when the Communist Party decided to go to the Supreme Court, which ruled against the constitutionality of Parliament's action. The Government of the day, however, had no intention of abiding by the Court's ruling, forcing the resignation of the Chief Justice, Babiker Awad Allah, who later emerged as Vice-President under Nimeiri and the first Prime Minister after the 25 May coup. His resignation signalled the end of the judiciary as an independent institution endowed with both inherent and express powers to check and control executive action.

The situation was aggravated by yet a third crisis, a constitutional one this time. The Sudan on the morrow of its independence had had no constitution of its own. The dispatch with which independence was proclaimed had not allowed Parliament to promulgate a new constitution. In fact, none of the parties then had a clear idea about the way they wanted to handle the major problems gripping the country: southern Sudan, the role of the two Sayeds (leaders of the two religious sects), the apportionment of power between the different arms of the state, the place of religion in politics etc. All these important issues had to be resolved before a permanent constitution could be devised for the country. Instead Parliament had adopted a modified version of the self-government constitution prepared by Justice Stanley Baker, a British judge of the Khartoum High Court. Baker headed a constitutional commission convened by Governor-General Sir Robert Howe on 19 March 1957. Cosmetic changes to that constitution were introduced by the then Attorney-General A. M. Atabani. This interim constitution was to have been replaced by a permanent one within eighteen months. Nearly twenty-five months elapsed between the declaration of independence (January 1956) and Abboud's intervention (November 1958) with no progress having been made on the constitutional front.

Throughout this period and the one separating the Abboud and Nimeiri eras, Parliament had never got down to an agreement on the real constitutional issues such as the position of the South and the form of government best suited to the realities of Sudan. The failure to do so in the period between 1964 and 1969 was not due to any lack of ideas, for Parliament had at its disposal several drafts and proposals prepared by eminent Sudanese lawyers. In this period, the Sudan witnessed the following constitutions and draft constitutions: the amended Sudan interim constitution 1964 (1, 2, 3, 4 and 5) and the draft Sudan permanent constitution 1968.

Parliament's inaction was due to lack of political will to resolve major issues and problems. Party politicians were more concerned with achieving short-term political ends than settling long-term national issues. It would not be far from true to say that Abboud's regime achieved more in the constitutional sphere than the parties did during their eight years of power tenure, e.g. policies of decentralization culminating in a National Central Council or Parliament. The irony of the matter was that Abboud's decentralization was essentially based on a memorandum prepared by Abdel Rahman 'Ali Taha, Minister of Local Government in the mid-'fifties, during the regime of the parties. The sectarian squabbles made it difficult for the plan to see the light of day; its implementation had to wait for the overthrow of the regime of the parties by Abboud. The plan was refined during Abboud's regime by a commission headed by the then Chief Justice M. A. Abu Ranat.

Perhaps the greatest failure of the regime of the parties was in the South. The civilian government opened a dialogue with the Southerners in March 1965 in which representatives of all major political parties in the North, the major Southern political parties (SANU) and the Southern Front and other Southerners were present as well as observers from seven African nations, including Egypt. The Round Table Conference, as it was called, produced no concrete results.

In its final statement the conference admitted that 'they could not reach a unanimous resolution.' There was abundant evidence that the Northern politicians were not prepared to meet the Southerners half-way. Some, such as the Islamists and the Arabists, were against the granting of any sort of autonomy to the South. Sheikh Ali Abdel Rahman, leading the People's Democratic Party (PDP) almost wrecked the conference by constantly absenting himself from its meetings. The Muslim Brothers, who saw the problem of Southern Sudan only in terms of Islam versus Christianity, missed the whole point though they continued to pay lip service to national unity. Their true colours were shown only when President Nimeiri decided to Islamicize the whole country in 1984. They were the first to rub the issue deep, almost suggesting that if the price of Islamicization is the secession of the South, then let it be so. The rest of the parties were afraid that any concessions they might endorse would be used against them by their political rivals. The only exception was the Communist Party, which, though not having a blueprint ready, came out openly in favour of unity in diversity. Sadiq el Mahdi published his views on the South with heavy religious overtones, only mitigated by the views of William Deng the Southern leader of the Sudan African National Union (SANU), a political ally of Sadiq. The situation in the South was to deteriorate dramatically, as Prime Minister Mahgoub committed the Army further and further. The politicians proved that they had learnt little from past experience in the South, particularly under Abboud. The South, the running sore of Sudanese politics, had contributed directly, more than anything else, to the demise of Abboud. They all knew it. President Nimeiri knows it better than anybcdy else.

By the late 'sixties the Sudanese Army was heavily committed to a war for which it was ill prepared and to which there was no end in sight. The feeling among the officers was that they were suffering because of Khartoum's political bankruptcy. The effect that the war in the South had on Sudanese politics was not dissimilar to the one the Palestine war had on Egyptian politics; both instilled in the Army a resentment of the politicians and a determination to put things right. In fact two of the officers who mutinied in Juba in 1968, holding hostage the acting Minister of Defence, Dr Abdel Hamid Salih, were among the core of officers who led the coup in May: Faroug Osman Hamd Allah and Abul Gasim Mohammed Ibrahim. Nasser's experience in Falouga is to be compared to these young men's experience in Juba and the rest of the South. Some of those very officers and their comrades in arms played an important role in the removal of Abboud by their insubordination to orders to quell the 21 October demonstrations, e.g. Mohammed el Baghir Ahmed, Khalid Hassan Abbas and Zein el Abdin Mohammed Ahmed. General Baghir, who became the first Vice-President under Nimeiri, led the tanks that surrounded the Presidential

Palace, forcing General Abboud to abdicate.

The success of the May revolution was, therefore, largely due to a sense of betrayal by those officers, contrasted with their active involvement in the demise of the Abboud regime, as well as the dissatisfaction of the Sudanese people with the regime of the parties. This mood was symbolized in the unceremonious way in which they bid farewell to the *ancien régime*. These are lessons of history to which President Nimeiri should not turn a blind eye.

Picking the Boss

Since I was not privy to the Free Officers' Movement in the months preceding the May revolution I cannot offer the reader an authoritative picture of what had happened. My only hope is that one day one of the perpetrators will come forward and tell the tale. But, if I cannot point the reader towards an account of the Free Officers' Movement, I can point him away from one particular account: the one put forward by President Nimeiri in his book *The Islamic Way, Why?* That book, written in 1978, sought laboriously to trace Nimeiri's latter-day evangelism to 1969 or before. We are all meant to believe that the May revolution was about Islam from day one, 25 May 1969; that year, as we shall see, was the year when the pilgrimage was to Moscow and Kiev, two improbable Meccas for a fundamentalist defender of the faith. To justify his new Islamicism, therefore, Nimeiri went on to describe in his book how he and his colleagues had piously prayed to Allah before engaging in the coup. Those who knew Nimeiri and his colleagues well dismissed it with smiles. Politicians often make some exaggerations and resort to inexactitudes, not to say lies, in their speeches, but going on record is a different matter altogether. In this particular instance the perpetrators of the coup would tell a completely different story. They were universally drunk that night. Some of them were three sheets in the wind and had the courage and honesty to say so and joke about it.

President Nimeiri, however, portrayed himself in that book as the architect, chief co-ordinator and executor, the Nasser of the coup. In his version, President Nimeiri did not have a single good word for the true perpetrators of the coup; they were all depicted as errand-boys carrying out his orders and directives. He claimed, for instance, that Babiker Awad Allah joined the movement the night before the coup. He did not even mention the role his first Vice-President Mohammed el Baghir Ahmed played in Abboud's demise. It was General Baghir who, as the go-between, eventually prevailed on the General to resign. He also had no word, good or bad, for Omar el Hag Musa's role in Nimeiri's constant protection in the several coup attempts in which he was involved before May 1969. Another such protector, who was not worthy of a mention in the ghost-written book, was Mohamed Abdel Rahman Nugd Allah, the Minister of the Interior (Umma Party) during the Azhari era. Nugd Allah received the added reward of spending some time as a guest in Nimeiri's prisons. When Omar died in January 1977 President Nimeiri, to his *Face the Nation* address, spoke amply of Omar's role in the Free Officers' Movement as an inspirer, protector and intermediary. That was a speech in the air that would soon be dissipated but there is not a word of it in his so-called documented treatise. These are just examples of the deep streak of ingratitude of which we shall see more. In fact Colonel Nimeiri, and this is a matter of common knowledge, was in Gebeit in the Eastern Sudan at the time the preparations were made. He was offered the leadership of the Movement as late as the spring of 1969. It is also a matter of common knowledge that two officers in particular played crucial roles in the mobilization and recruitment of supporters to the coup: Khalid Hassan Abbas and Faroug Osman Hamd Allah. Nimeiri's book has no good word for either, even in his cryptic way of describing events and persons without mentioning names.

Among the names that were being considered for the leadership of the Free Officers' Movement was that of General Ahmed al Sharif al-Habib, Commander of the Southern Region. Al-Habib was loved by his young officers and was well connected; he would have been the Naguib of the Sudan. Another name was that of Omar el Hag Musa, later Minister of Defence. Opposition to al-Habib came mainly from the influential Babiker Awad Allah, who considered him a frivolous man, an opinion he had formed during secondary school. Babiker forgets nothing and threatened that he would not be number two if al-Habib was number one. Omar had close connections with the parties and some officers feared he might hand power back to them; they therefore decided against him, but rewarded him by appointment as the first Minister of Defence in 1969, before moving him to the Ministry of

Information. Another name considered was that of General Baghir. Instead he became Under-Secretary for Defence under Omar and later on he made his way up to be first Vice-President. Nimeiri was chosen to head the movement because nobody had anything against him. He was well connected too and loved by his young fellow officers. It was Faroug Hamd Allah who proposed him, adding that the man had absolutely no commitment to any ideas or ideologies, i.e. he could be sculpted the way the young officers wanted.

Nimeiri indeed, is a very personable character, an excellent public relations man; he has a lot of style but no substance. He always impresses people by presenting the façade of a gentle and humane person. Often he plays the underdog. He has probably never completed reading a book since he left school, though he has written some. He was a ready and indiscriminate drinker, almost to the point of inebriation; young officers enjoyed their drink with him. He had a sense of the people and an ability to relate to them; a simple man of the people. He is endowed with a lot of machismo with an abrasive urge to show it: riding on the top of train wagons, jumping down from cars rather than alighting easily. Young officers liked all that in him. He grew up with all their excesses so it was not difficult for him to identify with them; to them he was the simple and kind, fairly senior officer. With this simplicity and kindness in the end they were all smothered and, certainly, he has outsmarted them all – and many others too.

Military–Civilian Symbiosis

Be that as it may the Army was now brought into the political machine as a matter of course: the perpetrators of the coup with Nimeiri as their co-opted head formed a Revolutionary Command Council (RCC). Nine out of ten members of the RCC were young officers, including the Commissioner of Police, Ali Sadiq, who was brought in by Babiker Awad Allah, a close relation of his. The only civilian member was the ex-Chief Justice Babiker Awad Allah himself, who also became Prime Minister. The RCC was a heterogeneous body comprised of two Communists (Babiker el Nour and Hashim al Atta), two Nasserites of a sort (Babiker Awad Allah and Abul Gasim Hashim), five nationalists (Faroug Osman Hamd

Allah, Abul Gasim Mohammed Ibrahim, Khalid Hassan Abbas, Mamoun Awad Abu Zeid and Zein el Abdin Mohammed Ahmed) and the political chameleon Nimeiri. The RCC endeavoured to dissociate itself from the Abboud legacy. It was not to be viewed as yet another military regime, rather a symbiosis of the army and the civilian political forces with a predominance of elements from the Professional Front of October.

To this end an entirely civilian Cabinet was formed on 26 May comprising over twenty ministers, of whom only seven were members of the Communist Party, five others were so-called fellow travellers, three were members of the National Unionist Party (NUP), and the rest were independent technocrats, avowedly apolitical. There were two Southerners in the Cabinet (Abel Alier and Joseph Garang, the latter a member of the Communist Party) and two ministers were members of the October transitional government (Khalaf Allah Babiker and Abdel Karim Mirghani). I joined that Cabinet by mid-June 1969 as Minister of Youth and Social Affairs.

The new government was meant to offer the Sudanese what they were looking for, a trans-sectarian administration, reflected in this rainbow coalition. In the civilian–military symbiosis the Sudanese were being reassured that the revolution was not a military coup, not a return to Abboud's militarism. The themes and aspirations of May were to be encapsulated in a widely based political organization, the Sudanese Socialist Union (SSU). President Nimeiri announced the intention to form it as early as January 1970. The SSU was to be a forum for political discussions transcending tribal, sectarian, regional and ideological dissension. The Communist Party (CP), whose views on party and class are well known, were vehemently against the idea. The revolution, they claimed, should opt for a united national front comprising the CP and the popular organization: workers, farmers, youth and women, all controlled then by the CP. So while supporting the new regime's onslaught on the parties, and indeed encouraging it, the CP was struggling hard to maintain its own identity as well as the identity and integrity of the pro-Communist Party popular and syndicated organizations. The regime's major response to this trend came in a speech delivered by President Nimeiri in Khartoum North on 26 June 1972.

In that speech the President addressed the question: why have we chosen this organization, the SSU, to be a union in the form of

13

a pact between the working forces of our people rather than a party or a front?

> A party is the tool of a certain class in a society in which class structure has emerged and it usually serves the interests of one class to the exclusion of others. . . . Parties are instruments in the service of conflicting and competing classes, and [therefore] have conflicting interests. The May Socialist revolution came at a time when classes in our country were still in their formative period. Sudan is characteristically a country in which the class situation is not well defined, as opposed to one with clear class structure and interests. The socialist philosophy that our people have [chosen] aims to obliterate the existing differences between different groups and not to consolidate them, making them into conflicting class interests. It is for this reason that we have not chosen to be a party.

Nimeiri was, in effect, associating himself with the Communist view of the class origin of parties but opting for a formula propagated by Nasser, an alliance of the working forces.

One of the immediate tasks entrusted to me after joining the government in mid-June as Minister of Youth was to articulate the policy of the nascent regime, reflected in the different declarations and policy statements made since 25 May 1969. I was also to work for the creation of an organizational framework for youth mobilization. My thinking was clear from the start. Politics worth anything in a developing country will have to be development-oriented. Political organizations worth their salt must be mobilized behind clearly defined development objectives translated into identifiable projects. Some saw in this approach an attempt to dilute 'revolutionarism' but I was not deterred. Ideologization and dilettante pontification were not the order of the day. Quick and direct action was needed.

My creation of the Youth Brigades (Kataeb al Shabab) sprang from this belief. Youths should be given specific tasks: road maintenance, school and hospital construction, etc. The concentration of our efforts should be in the rural Sudan, which needed to be energized. The first of those organizations was created in Kordofan, in western Sudan. Building on an old international connection I went ahead with the creation of youth animation centres, to be engaged in community development, initiation in technology, literacy campaigns etc. UNESCO provided an expert,

Mr M. Inglesi, the secretary-general of the Italian Socialist Youth, and the ILO provided funding and demonstration equipment. Egypt and Algeria provided facilities for the training of trainers. Aware of the role of recreation in enlivening youth, North Korea was approached to help in organizing youth festivals and establishing a youth palace of culture in the Sudan to train the young in music, dancing and indoor sports, for the Koreans are masters of those arts. The experience was, indeed, exhilarating in spite of the tension. The Communist youth organizations were put out of gear; the rules of the game were changed by changing the nature and content of youth mobilization.

In order to weld youth into the regime my approach was functional and recreational, not ideological. Civic and political education would come as a by-product. My proposals for the formation of youth brigades, although vehemently opposed by the CP, which maintained that the only youth organizations that should be allowed were the Communist-dominated existing ones, were supported by all members of the RCC, including Babiker el Nour but not Hashim al Atta. The latter came out against them when we were discussing, at the Council of Ministers, my list of nominees for the higher echelons of the newly created Ministry of Youth. He was energetically supported by the Communist Minister of Health Maurice Sadra. Mahgoub Osman, the Communist Minister of Information and an old friend, rather than siding with al Atta decided to mediate. Other examples can be adduced to show that CP allegiances were mitigated by the typical Sudanese family, tribal, and sometimes sectarian loyalty. One policy or measure would find support from certain elements of the party to be opposed by others.

The Limits of Ideology

Politics in the Sudan, like the rest of the Arab world, has a strong personal flavour, so to speak. Friendships and relationships cut across party divides, commitments to friends and relatives dilute commitments to issues and ideologies. This was as true of the CP as of the traditionalist parties.

Thus we found Babiker el Nour (the Communist) advocating the appointment of Dawood Abdel Latif and Mekkawi Akkrat, two distinguished Sudanese administrators, who are to the right of the

15

political spectrum, as advisers to the newly restructured local government. They happened to be friends of the family.

None the less, ideology was not altogether ignored in my endeavours at the Ministry. I called for an Arab cultural accord (Multaga Fikri) to which all the major schools of thought inside Sudan and the Arab world were invited. This occasioned my first ideological clash with the Communists, who were opposed to the catholicity of the meeting. Slogans like 'the revolution is not for everybody' and 'no place in the revolution for the enemies of the revolution' were raised. The attitude of the CP towards the May revolution was ambivalent. While the party went to great pains to deny that they, as a party, authorized the participation of their members in the government, Communist ministers were very much in the Cabinet and their imprint was left on many of its decisions. Their aversion to the accord was mainly prompted by their desire not to see alternative blueprints challenging the proclaimed Marxist truth. My desire on the other hand was to allow for an intellectual cross-fertilization, so that people should learn from each other's experience. Such interaction would help us in devising our own authentic philosophy. We were not out to borrow prefabricated models. On the other hand, I have always believed that in politics there is no scientific accuracy, and that those who claim so are both pretentious and foolish.

To this end I have never had any mental reservations when it comes to intellectual interactions. Even in structuring the new Ministry I saw to it that top posts were filled with people of all political colours, the rainbow coalition. Our philosophical claims, e.g. widely based participation, should not only be taken seriously in rhetoric but should also be so in practice, were people to trust us and take us seriously. In other words, between rhetoric and practice there should be a zero interval. The May revolution was not an ideological revolution, Marxist or otherwise. It was perpetrated by dissatisfied nationalist officers who had no political commitments. The military–Communist marriage was a political exigency, never ideological. Nimeiri's main opponents when he first came to power, by his own admission, were the traditionalist forces in the country, the Ansar and Khatmiya, the two major religious sects, as well as the Muslim Brothers and their political wing, the Islamic Charter Front. Others may have had their ideological quarrels with the traditionalist forces, not Nimeiri. His was political, rather than ideological; they were bases that should either be domesticated or destroyed.

Attempts were made to placate Sadiq el Mahdi, who was still at large, in view of the position he had taken against sectarianism, denouncing his own uncle the Imam of the Ansar. The negotiations with him, conducted through General al-Fatih Abdoun, whose father was a loyal supporter of the Mahdi family, did not make headway. On the other hand Ismael el Azhari was taken into custody. He was soon to be temporarily released to receive condolences on the death of his brother, who expired when el Azhari was in prison. While mourning his brother el Azhari suffered a heart attack and was taken to hospital. He died shortly thereafter. The way his death was announced in the official media was a source of consternation to many: 'Ismael el Azhari died this morning. He was a teacher in Sudanese schools,' announced Radio Omdurman. The Communists could see in el Azhari then only the man who chased them out of Parliament a few months ago. That was an act of vengeful pettiness. Nations do not demolish their past, for a country with no past will always be a country without a future. In fact, some Communist elements tried to persuade the young officers to ban el Azhari's funeral, under the pretext that it might turn into a hostile demonstration against the regime. Nimeiri called me to a meeting of the RCC where the question was discussed. He briefed me on the issue and asked for my reaction. I then had occasion to listen to Khalid Hassan Abbas who was vehemently against the ban. Khalid was admirably frank. 'How can we ban the Sudanese people from bidding a last farewell to el Azhari when we cannot impose such a ban even on our immediate families. My father spent a sleepless night yesterday crying over el Azhari.' I told the President that not only would the ban be in bad taste, it would also be politically disastrous, a sign of weakness. The government, while taking its precautionary measures, should also associate itself with the Sudanese in mourning one of their heroes. Nobody could deny el Azhari the place due to him as the leader of the Sudanese Graduates' Congress and the man who ushered the Sudan into independence. Faroug Hamd Allah concurred. Nimeiri, with a measure of satisfaction, looked at both Faroug and myself saying, 'Well then, both of you should go to Omdurman as representatives of the RCC and the Council of Ministers to extend our condolences to el Azhari's family.'

Destroy the Ansar

Among the traditional forces, Imam al Hadi el Mahdi (Ansar) and Sharif Hussein el Hindi (NUP) chose to fight. The regime, which had no organized popular base, yet leant more towards the CP and the splinter Arabist groups, Nasserites and Baathists. The political influence of the latter two did not go far beyond the portals of the Khartoum branch of the University of Cairo but all were only too pleased to engage in the demolition of the traditionalist strongholds, each for his own reasons.

In March 1970 relations between the Ansar and Nimeiri reached a climax. Troubles started during Nimeiri's visit to the White Nile and ended in his crushing of the Ansar forces in their stronghold, Aba Island. Accounts of what happened are contradictory; the Ansar tend to exaggerate their losses while authority tends to exaggerate the Ansar armaments. In those days Field-Marshal Nimeiri, as he then was not, engaged in punishing trips all over the country, to places never visited by provincial governors, let alone ruling presidents. People liked him for that. They assembled everywhere to listen to his speeches and craned their necks to have a glimpse of him. He was jostled by demonstrators, men, women and children. There was a lot of hugging and embracing. People were in a collective emotional spasm and Nimeiri was riding high on a wave of adulation. The country was starving for a national hero, their own Nasser or Nehru, for Sudanese leadership had always been partisan. The man was tireless and had a fierce energy. He laboured hard for his job, sitting for long hours and travelling for longer days. Those were the days when he engaged in trips all over the Sudan, unguarded and uncaring. Those were the days when he was not yet cocooned in his security shell. There were no sirens, no motorcades, no legions of bodyguards. He was averse to pomp and circumstance. Nimeiri was reported to have said a few weeks before the coup when he sighted Ismael el Azhari, the then President, driving in his simple car with two motorcycles preceding him, 'the blessed fool with his motorcade does not know what is awaiting him.' For a few years after ascending to power Nimeiri could well afford to decry el Azhari. He was carefree all over the place, guarded at home by an insouciant sentry. Nimeiri now travels in an armoured car and is preceded by sirens, a motorcade of twelve cars and a great host of bodyguards. Absolute power is absolute insecurity.

In the course of those Homeric trips Nimeiri decided to visit the popular base of the Ansar in the White Nile. He was met by hostile demonstrations in Kawa on 23 March and three days later in Kosti Nimeiri broke off his tour and returned to Khartoum. The situation reached a climax. Attempts to defuse it were made by General Ahmed Abdel Wahab, a respected army officer and one-time deputy to General Abboud, and Salah Abdel Salam, a friend of Nimeiri and a relation of Imam al Hadi. These attempts failed. Nimeiri was amenable but some others in the RCC were not. Nor were the Communist elements within the regime. A MIG made a sortie over the island of Aba, where the Ansar leader and hundreds of his armed supporters were ensconced. The authorities delivered an ultimatum to the Imam, while Nimeiri made a radio statement preparing public opinion for the impending measures against the Ansar. He threatened to continue the shelling if defiance continued.

On the 28th there was a leaflet raid on the island, followed by more shelling. The Imam sent a suicide mission across the causeway to engage the troops at Rabak, while enabling him to flee the island. The Imam and some of his followers indeed managed to do so on the 30th but he was reported to have been shot on the 31st near the Ethiopian border. Official reports claimed that he was shot during hot pursuit, while Ansar survivors claimed that he was shot in captivity.

Central to the Mahdiya movement is the person of the Imam who at the same time is both a religious and a political leader. By killing Imam al Hadi and exiling his nephew Sadiq, the ex-president of the Umma party, some elements hoped to demolish the very basis of the Mahdiya movement. In a television statement on 1 April 1970 Nimeiri dwelt on the events leading to the death of the Imam. He accused him of having conspired to topple the progressive regime of May and take Sudan back to the era of party politics, privileges and sectarianism. He was accused of having refused to spare lives by rejecting the ultimatum. More importantly Nimeiri went on to challenge his claim to the Imamate (leadership of the community). An Imam, he argued, would not have fled Aba and abandoned his men.

A man who perpetrates such massacres and sacrifices life and spills blood as he did. And goes on to abandon his island having told his followers that whoever dies defending it would go to heaven. A man who forsakes Aba and its poor inhabitants, those loyal women, children and men who took up arms against the people for his sake, and escapes . . . is such a Hadi fit to be the president of this people? The Mahdi [founder of the Mahdiya movement and ancestor of the deceased Imam], God rest his soul, was a genuine Imam and a great revolutionary leader . . . who led his men in battle after battle never abandoning them until his death. . . . He never fought the Muslims but the colonial power. What al Hadi and some of his sons have committed has nothing to do with the great Imam al Mahdi.

Nimeiri, whose family owes allegiance to the Ansar, refused all attempts by the axe-grinders among the Communists and Arabists to go ahead and destroy Ansarism. In fact, he decided to refurbish the Ansar mosque in Omdurman and resurrect the Mahdi's mosque in Gadir, western Sudan. He also readily agreed to the proposition of Omar el Hag Musa to constitute a reconciliation committee with the Ansar. The committee was to work under my chairmanship and comprised, among others, Dr Gaafer Bakheit, who was then teaching at the University of Khartoum and helping me on a part-time basis at the Ministry of Youth, Karar Ahmed Karar, the secretary-general of the Council of Ministers, and two leading Ansar notables, Mohammed Abdel Rahman Nugd Allah and Hassan Mohammed Dawud. Nimeiri was an exemplary political opportunist and pragmatist. He used the extreme left to destroy his adversaries on the right, then, shunning the left, he looked around for those who could help heal the wounds.

Almost one year after I had joined the Cabinet (August 1970) I decided to leave it in view of a divergence of views with the ideologues and frustration with empty slogans, the emptiness of the slogans only echoing the emptiness of the sloganeers' minds. President Nimeiri, and indeed a number of the members of the RCC, were firmly behind me in my ministerial and political efforts. Surprisingly they included people of divergent views, e.g. Abul Gasim Ibrahim, Babiker Awad Allah and Faroug Osman Hamd Allah. President Nimeiri's support was unflinching; he considered my departure an abdication. I told him that it was a waste of time; revolutions are not about fratricidal battles and settling old scores. I had no desire to burn myself in the furnace of political in-fighting and ideological bludgeoning; let the others fight it out among themselves. There were the Communists versus the renegades, the Arabists versus the Communists, the technocrats warding off the assaults of the sloganeers (alias ideologists) and all looking back in anger, settling old scores. None were looking forward and exploring new frontiers and facing new challenges. The intruders like us, a few, were called contemptibly the *liberali*, i.e. liberals. The *liberali* included some repentant Marxists like Ali el Tom, the Minister of Agrarian Reforms, a resourceful and energetic minister who infuriated few souls. Liberalism was thus a pejorative term in the lexicon of the day and to some it still is. One sometimes wonders how much of political history some of the revolutionaries, set to change the world, have actually read. Abdication was, therefore, not the word. It was not political struggle that one was shunning, rather political gangsterism.

The RCC in all this struggle was fighting with some, aligning with others, distancing themselves from all but in many cases without knowing why. RCC member Zein el Abdin summed it up very well. He was giving me a send-off before my departure; there were only the two of us, he wanted it that way. 'You know, it is all very sad. The first day we received the new Council of Ministers, this distinguished group of intellectuals, all of us in the RCC, without even thinking, stood to attention. There was a feeling of awe, meeting all those big names. Today it is a completely different matter. We know them better.'

I chose to go to the UN as the Ambassador of Sudan, after a short stint as personal representative for the then Director-General of UNESCO (René Maheu) raising funds for UNRWA.

Destroy the Extreme Left

With the removal of the traditionalist threat, Nimeiri felt strong enough to take on his left-wing enemies. He ordered the exile to Egypt of the CP secretary-general Abdel Khalig Mahgoub, ironically accompanied by al Sadiq el Mahdi. In February 1971 he announced that he would destroy the CP. The announcement was followed by the banning, in May, of the students' federation, the women's organization and the youth organization, which were Communist dominated. In the same month Nimeiri declared that the SSU, under his chairmanship, would be the only permitted party in the Sudan. Indeed Nimeiri was very sensitive to claims by

21

the CP, real or imagined, about their role in directing affairs. On 28 October 1969 President Nimeiri had reshuffled his Cabinet, assuming the premiership and replacing Babiker Awad Allah. The change, he said, was needed in order to 'accelerate the revolutionary regime's move towards social justice and socialism and to combat colonialism and imperialism'. The real reason, however, was that Awad Allah was reported to have hailed the role of the CP in the May revolution in the course of an interview he gave in East Germany a few days earlier. Awad Allah was no Communist.

In this battle with the Communists, Nimeiri was assisted by the divisions inside the Communists' ranks. There were, on the one hand, the so-called renegades led by Ahmed Suleiman, the Minister of Foreign Trade, and Muawya Ibrahim, State Minister of Foreign Affairs and later Minister of Labour. This faction tried to outbid the mainstream party in pressing for nationalization. Those measures were almost entirely worked out by Ahmed Suleiman, assisted by the RCC economic adviser Ahmed Mohammed Said al Assad. It was a disastrous bid to outflank the CP.

On 25 May 1970 Sudan's domestic and foreign banks and several foreign-owned firms were nationalized. 'We are at the beginning of socialism. We must show to the world that we can build our country through socialism,' Nimeiri said on the occasion. The following day it was the turn of the insurance industry, and thirty-five foreign companies were transferred to state-owned companies. More nationalization followed. Nimeiri eight years later, in his aforementioned book, blamed it all on the Communists, meaning by that the Party. The nationalization and confiscation measures were concocted in haste with no prior studies, economic analysis, nor even a policy document explaining the rationale behind them. Nationalization included restaurants, cinema houses and drapers; even the Bolshevik revolution was more selective. There was also discrimination against certain groups. Many of the nationalized persons were either naturalized Sudanese or Sudanese by birth with non-Sudanese ancestry. Nimeiri who is always infatuated with novel ideas particularly when they make a sensation, jumped at the occasion. He supported the measures whole-heartedly: they were the punch statement in his May anniversary speech, and he was proud of it.

The renegades decided to co-operate with Nimeiri as they envisaged a leading role for themselves inside the SSU. The mainstream party led by the veteran Communist Mahgoub favoured the retention of the CP's identity and independence and maintained that co-operation with Nimeiri would only make a more formidable enemy of him, a Sa'Lazar as Mahgoub put it. The anti-party group, now well settled in power, had the lethal information by which they could destroy their erstwhile comrades. They did it with relish. The final showdown between Nimeiri and the Communists took place in July 1971 when Hashim al Atta staged a coup. Nimeiri and the rest of the RCC members were arrested and a new seven-member RCC was announced in which Faroug Osman Hamd Allah was included, and the ban on Communist organizations was lifted. The rebellion was thwarted by the NCOs led by a corporal, Hamad Iheimir, whom we shall meet four years later. He made history twice in the life of Nimeiri. It was a counter-revolt from the bottom.

Nimeiri's revenge was severe and clinical. Major Atta and the other coup perpetrators were summarily executed. Nimeiri ordered the arrest of everybody suspected of having participated in the planning of the coup. On the 26th the two ex-members of the RCC, Babiker el Nour Osman, who would have replaced Nimeiri, and Faroug Osman, were executed. Their plane was forced to land in Libya, the two were arrested and handed over to the Sudanese authorities. Faroug was no Communist; he had been lumped with them ever since Nimeiri dismissed him, together with al Atta and el Nour, from the RCC in October 1970. The latter two were Communists. Nimeiri, in his book on Islam, chose to call el Nour a Communist informer, i.e. he reported the minutes of the RCC to the CP. The reason for the dismissal of Faroug was entirely personal. He had, as Minister of the Interior, cultivated the jealousy of Mamoun Awad Abu Zeid (head of Security) on account of Faroug's criticism, not without justification, of the security high-handedness. Abu Zeid was throughout supported by Khalid Hassan Abbas. The label that had come to be attached to Faroug suited Nimeiri's purposes and enabled him to put him out of the way. Nimeiri resented the man for his popularity, intelligence and energetic nature; he saw in him a potential challenger. He had been happy to play Abu Zeid's game and dismiss him from the RCC. Faroug, we recall, was the man who had proposed Nimeiri for the chairmanship of the RCC.

Faroug's presence on board el Nour's plane and his inclusion in the new RCC did not help. Faroug, Nimeiri told me after the execution, requested that Abul Gasim Ibrahim and myself testify that he was not a Communist nor could he have been a party to the July plot. For Nimeiri, that was too late. He was ready to tolerate Atta but not Faroug. In effect it is very revealing to compare the lauda-tory language in which he described Atta to the very disparaging references to Nour and Faroug, in his aforementioned book.

Nimeiri's account of his being taken captive and his escape is very telling. He shamelessly recounted in a world-wide press con-ference 'Not only was I arrested in the bedroom of my presidential house but a number of weapons were placed at my throat and I was made to hold my hands above my head for over an hour. Then I was marched out in my night clothes barefoot.' He did not have the courage to insist that he be allowed to don his military uniform, the way General Khawad the Commander-in-Chief of the Army in 1969 did when he was arrested following Nimeiri's coup. He too was in his night clothes. 'I am the Commander-in-Chief and this is how I shall emerge from my house,' he said. Nimeiri's fear for his life increased as the counter-rebellion forces approached the palace; he pleaded with his captors to go outside and 'face the tanks firing on us ... because if this continues we shall all die.' At first they ignored him but eventually he persuaded one of the rebels to go outside the front door of the palace and wave a white towel. Those were his own words (*African Diary*, p. 5609). This aspect of Nimeiri's character could have been treated as an aberration. The following chapters reveal that that was the real Nimeiri all through, another layer of the character, the weak-kneed one.

Also telling was the way Nimeiri treated the captive secretary-general of the CP, Abdel Khalig Mahgoub. Mahgoub was brought to the army HQ in his *gallabiyah* or national dress, with his hands tied together with his own turban. Abul Gasim Hashim, Omar el Hag Musa and myself were present. We were waiting for a call from Cairo from Yahia Abdel Magid to confirm his acceptance of the offer made to him to assume the Irrigation portfolio. Yahia, a distinguished irrigation engineer, joined the Cabinet a few days later. Abul Gasim, always composed, questioned Abdel Khalig coolly and politely about the reason behind the coup. The two were talking when Mamoun Abu Zeid (head of Security) came in. Abu Zeid, on discovering that the secretary-general of the CP had been arrested, was exhilarated and started shouting 'We've got him.' There was nothing personal; it was the jubilation of a security man who has made a coup. Maghoub was tired, worn out, with his lips cracking. He asked for water and Omar poured him a glass, two,

24

three. With the man hand-cuffed, Omar had to hold the glass for him to drink. Having quenched his thirst, Mahgoub asked me for a cigarette. I obliged by lighting one for him, placing it between his lips. Abul Gasim Hashim continued his cool discussion, asking him why he perpetrated the coup. Mahgoub said something to the effect that he had done his bit for the Sudan's independence. 'You don't know me . . . but ask Omar who is my peer. Ask Mansour who knows me well.' Abul Gasim, still collected and dignified, asked why his party had voted against the Anglo-Egyptian agreement. Abdel Khalig asked for a second cigarette. He got it. At this point, Nimeiri and Abul Gasim Ibrahim showed up. Nimeiri gazed at the hand-cuffed man, clenched his teeth and said nothing. Then he impulsively picked up the half-full glass of water and emptied it on Abdel Khalig's face. Abul Gasim Ibrahim, wishing to outdo his President, pulled the cigarette from his mouth. Omar el Hag Musa stopped Nimeiri from displaying other traits of his vindictive nature by requesting that Mahgoub be taken away. The incident is striking for here were two officers (Abul Gasim Hashim and Mamoun Abu Zeid) who suffered the same humiliation Nimeiri had gone through. And there was a third, Omar, the quintessential staff officer. Mamoun's reaction was human, Abul Gasim's dignified and Omar's humane. It could not be the heartlessness of the military. Omar and Abul Gasim did not display it. It could not be the reaction of the humiliated. Mamoun did not show it. There must be something deeper. Great men show generosity and grace in victory. Talleyrand was reported to have said of Napoleon: 'How can such a great man be so badly brought up?' Maybe in that lies the answer.

A year later the failure of the Communist coup was celebrated and Nimeiri took the salute in the Martyrs' Square. We both went back after the commemoration to Nimeiri's office. Nimeiri was sobbing during the celebration. I asked him what was wrong with him; I was curious. He answered that somehow he felt responsible for all the lives of those who died . . . our friends as well as our adversaries. Even Nimeiri, it seemed, was capable of compassion. 'Human beings are very contradictory creatures' said Svetlana Alliluyeva, Stalin's daughter, to the *Observer* (26 March 1984). She had been asked whether people who do a great deal of evil are also capable of being affectionate. Nimeiri's character has at least five layers, we said, and there is no lack of evidence to show more, like this relapse into compassion.

Chapter Two

The Years of Promise: 1971–1975

It was the best of times, it was the worst of times; it was the age of wisdom, it was the age of foolishness, it was the epoch of belief, it was the epoch of incredulity, it was the season of Light, it was the season of Darkness, it was the Spring of hope, it was the Winter of despair.

Charles Dickens, *A Tale of Two Cities.*

With the tension generated by ideological cleavages behind him after July Nimeiri made his ascent to an almost unassailable plateau. Nimeiri and his newly formed Cabinet got down to business: institutionalization, nation-building and development. The Nimeiri we shall meet in this chapter is the lofty dreamer, the man who wants to make history. We shall attempt to describe the main achievements of the May regime from 1971 to 1975; the latter year is a bench-mark in the history of the regime. Our purpose is not to proffer an exhaustive picture nor an appraisal of these achievements, but rather to give the reader an idea of what was, and what could have been, realized. Later chapters will reveal how Nimeiri and his cronies not only halted the process that was started, but also worked towards the unmaking of these achievements. Nimeiri was elected President for six years in 1971 and undertook to uphold and abide by the will of the people; now he sees himself an Imam, combining both spiritual and temporal power and imbuing people with faith. It is important that we dwell on the way he viewed his powers, privileges and duties during this early phrase, quoting him *in extenso*.

The July coup and counter-coup led to and accelerated the progress of many a project. On the Southern front there was the replacement of Joseph Garang by Abel Alier. There was also a major change in foreign policy reflected in the improvement of relations with the West and the conservative Arab states, all of which helped solve the seventeen-year-old Southern problem. The solution of the Southern Sudan problem made it easy to fill the constitutional hiatus: a constitution was promulgated in 1973. The change in foreign policy opened the door for massive foreign economic aid and investment, which helped finance an ambitious development programme. Upon his reinstatement Nimeiri passed various decrees reorganizing the executive and Dr Gaafer Bakheit's local government decentralization programme was adopted. Early in 1972 the SSU was launched. The period was above all one of promises, promises for sweeping reforms, major restructuring of institutions and rethinking of policies. Unlike the regime of the parties, we thought, the May regime was promising action through clearly set programmes. Describing this era of promise Nimeiri said in his speech to the nation on 11 November 1972 that:

> Until 24 May this country was on the ground and in crisis . . .
> its energies exhausted . . . its national unity dispersed . . . and
> its image of itself distorted . . . its capacities lost or wasted . . .
> and then came May to lift the giant from his fall, restore the
> glitter to his image and make his national unity a reality and to
> remove once and for all party divisiveness, the authority of
> tribalism and the predominance of sectarianism. It was to
> build in theory and in practice . . . a new society, populist in
> origin and revolutionary in organization and practice.

Revolutionary Purity: Setting the Standard

Before dwelling on these subjects, it will be appropriate to look back to a very important phase in the early days of the May revolution (1960–70), the purification of public life. The slogan of the day, then, was purging public life of the corruption allegedly implanted by the regime of the parties. Public officers from now on should be guided by revolutionary purity. The symbols of corruption in the regime of the parties were a few ministers and public servants. All of them were tried before special revolutionary courts presided over by members of the RCC. The trials were open and the accused were allowed to defend themselves. It was all meant to be a public show to discredit the *ancien régime* for its misdeeds. The trials have also, or should be presumed to have, set standards for the uprightness of holders of public office.

It is of great relevance to give the reader an idea of the sort of charges that were brought against those ministers, the severity of the punishments meted out and the standard of 'revolutionary purity' that was established. The first of these ministers, Ahmed al Sayyid Hamad, ex-Minister of Commerce and Supplies was tried in September 1969 under the 1969 Political Corruption Act. The charges brought against him relate to favouritism in issuing import licences to ineligible traders, all members or supporters of his political party (NUP). The court's verdict was:

1. Imprisonment for a period of six years.
2. Deprivation of political rights, i.e. voting, standing for elections etc.
3. A fine of £S30,000 (or alternatively three years' internment).
4. Prohibition from holding civil service offices or membership of boards of directors of publicly owned companies.

The second, Ahmed Zein al Abdeen, was brought before the revolutionary courts in November 1969. He had served as Health Minister in the pre-revolutionary government and was a well-known lawyer and a member of the NUP. He was accused of having used his office to secure personal gains. The court decided on:

1. Imprisonment for ten years.
2. Deprivation of political rights.
3. Confiscation of 5000 shares he had owned in a certain company which, the prosecution maintained, were acquired illegally.
4. A fine of £S5,000.
5. Prohibition from membership of the boards of directors of public companies.

The third, Clement M'boro, a leading Southern politician and ex-Minister of Industry was tried in May 1970. He received a sentence of four years' imprisonment and was deprived of his political rights for ten years. Clement was convicted of giving an approved enterprise licence to industries that did not qualify under the laws of the land and regulations of the Ministry. In question was the authorization for Mazda (the Japanese motor company) to establish an assembly plant under the guise of an approved industry, enjoying all the privileges given to such industries.

The fourth, Abdel Majid Abu Hassabo, ex-Minister of Guidance was brought before the court in July 1970. He was accused of 'immorality and political corruption'. The prosecutor accused him of:

1. Spending government resources on Sudanese and foreign journalists who had not rendered any services to the government.
2. Using government funds to finance extravagant parties. (The party in question was given for the legendary Egyptian singer Um Kalsoum.)
3. Using government funds to build a house at a cost of £S45,000 and the embezzlement of £S14,442, a charge on which he was acquitted, while he was convicted and sentenced for the first two charges.

In addition to these revolutionary courts, an investigation committee was set up in June 1969 in order to look into malpractices in the Presidential palace from 1965 to 1969, particularly as far as finance was concerned. In its final report to the Minister for Presidential Affairs the committee wrote: 'Investigations have disclosed that huge raises in salaries had taken place during the last four years. They have also revealed blatant overspending in some areas reaching ten times the stipulated figures.' Examples given for such overspending were: the cost of el Azhari's visit abroad was in excess of £S100,000 and the palace has spent £S4,860 on musical instruments. It is worth adding here that all the visits undertaken by Ismael el Azhari were publicly announced official visits, none of them were escapades or holidays. The report went on to say that 'members of the Council of State granted themselves raises in excess of the sum total of their salaries (i.e. a raise of more than one hundred per cent).' The report gave details of el Azhari's visits and other palace expenditures ranging from the minting of medals to musical instruments to cutlery to telephone bills etc. All this, needless to say, was disclosed to the public; after all, it was meant for public consumption.

In order to underline the theme of revolutionary purity further,

29

Nimeiri recalled the Sudanese ambassador to Lebanon, Mustafa Medani, for making a gift of cigarettes (two cartons) to a member of the RCC (Abdul Gasim Ibrahim) who was visiting Beirut. 'Do not spoil these young men,' Nimeiri told the ambassador. 'They are a different breed from the Ministers of the past.' With the travels of the previous President denounced for having cost £S100,000, frugal and pure Nimeiri could not countenance proposals for chartering a plane from Egyptair at £S20,000 to fly him and a Sudanese delegation to China. He wanted to use commercial airlines. That was the level of purity and the height of the standards set by the May revolution, and it is by those very standards that the actions and inactions of its leadership should be judged.

Take me at my Word

The dissolution of the RCC and the holding of a plebiscite represented a major step towards institutionalization and legitimization of the May regime. It was Khalid Hassan Abbas who put forward the idea of dissolving the RCC and nominating Nimeiri for the presidency on 12 August 1971. Not all the members of the RCC were in favour, for some wanted a rotational Presidency, e.g. Zein el Abdin Mohammed Ahmed. However, Nimeiri's immediate reaction was to ask for a plebiscite, 'I shall accept to shoulder the task if the people want me.' The future revealed that he was only seeking the weapon of the people and popular will to use against his rivals inside the RCC and the government.

Before its dissolution the RCC promulgated Republican Order No. 5, which became Sudan's interim constitution pending the formulation of a permanent one. Under article 15 of the Republican Order the SSU was to nominate a sole candidate for the presidency who would be approved or disapproved by a plebiscite. The first President would be nominated by the RCC, as the SSU was not yet established. Nimeiri was the choice of the RCC for President, Zein's pleading for a rotation having been submerged in the overwhelming support of the other members of the council for a sole candidate. We suggested that Nimeiri should present the nation with a manifesto and seek elections on the basis of a political programme. The reader might consider such an exercise futile, indeed silly, since Nimeiri was the only candidate. It was Nimeiri we were concerned with when we insisted on a manifesto; we wanted to impress on him the idea of a mandate, of a programme of action and of accountability.

Facing the nation on 14 August 1971 in one of the largest mass demonstrations seen in Khartoum Nimeiri solemnly declared:

> I make God the witness as I renew the trust and reaffirm the pact . . . that I shall continue to be for them [the people] and with them a loyal soldier and a faithful servant. Not as a despotic ruler, or a defiant overlord . . . I shall grant your wishes all of my attention and effort and set my heart on your love. . . . I struggle under your banner, safeguarding your unity, fortifying your will and harnessing your energies. . . . I shall remain faithful to your banner; honouring it for I should rather become a martyr than let it fall. . . . We shall continue along the difficult path until we achieve real victory.
>
> Because of all this, my free compatriots, I have accepted the RCC's decision to nominate me for the Presidency of the Sudan. I would not have accepted it [the nomination] had it not been made contingent upon a referendum. [This referendum] will not only be an expression of your acceptance but also of your readiness to deploy your vast capacities and hearts in the service of the principles and goals of the revolution, for I, and here I speak truthfully to you, cannot alone carry the responsibility.

A month later Nimeiri introduced his manifesto saying: 'I consider it my duty towards you . . . and your right . . . that I should present you with my book [manifesto], so that you might be enlightened as you decide [cast votes]. The era of inherited rights has gone . . . and that of blind support and rule by mandate has passed away.' (President's speech before the election, 9 September 1971.)

Once again Nimeiri was setting new standards. Nimeiri, the loyal servant of the people, was solemnly declaring his submission to the will of the people, the only source of legitimacy. Unlike his predecessors who sought blind support, he was urging them to judge him on the basis of his commitment to certain ideals, strategies and modes of operation. In other words rulers were not to be judged by their taking power but by what they did with power once they had it. The support Nimeiri was seeking was not support for his person, rather for the 'principles and goals of the revolution' a revolution sparked in 1969 by a small group of men, and articulated later by many. It was not a one-man affair, though less than a decade later the President, by his word and action, made it so.

The President was unflattering in his references to the sectarian leadership. They treated the Sudan, or seemed to be treating it, as their personal estate. Not Nimeiri, he was not a hereditary overlord. The Sudan had then two Imams. They were the religious overlords Nimeiri referred to when vaunting his humble origins in 1971. A new dawn has therefore opened. Men in politics would no longer be sanctified. Between the two discredited Imams people had a freedom of choice, and both of them were subjected to humbling experiences; attacks in the press, criticism in Parliament etc. They could even be totally rejected by the fringe, the lunatic and the sober. A decade later Nimeiri became the one and only Imam of the Sudan, and disagreement with him became high treason. Under the new Imam, the choice is not even take it or leave it; it is take it or pack up.

Reorganization and Devolution of Authority

After his swearing-in Nimeiri undertook a major reorganization of the executive. In a restructured government the Ministries were grouped on a functional basis with a clearly defined line of command with the President at the top. Various new Ministries were created, notably one for Public Service and Administrative Reform. The reorganization of the administration was not a shot in the dark, it was meant to be a lasting process. The new Ministry had an important role to play in this regard in job classification, training, codification of personnel regulations etc.

In introducing this reorganization the President declared:

Our term has started . . . by specifying the tasks and goals of the different organs and ministries. Most of these State organs had functioned without control and within no specified limits which caused a great deal of chaos and harm. The new reorganization was not an extempore act concocted overnight but the result of a study which lasted for two months; for a modern state cannot be built on hatched-up laws. The reorganization of the ministries aimed at rationalizing their performance. The creation of the posts of Vice Ministers was not an extempore decision either. It was an exigency, which has transpired from my investigations of the records of some ministries and personal knowledge of their needs, especially since the workloads of these ministries have increased. (Presidential address to the new Cabinet on 16 December 1971.)

In May 1973 Nimeiri issued decrees defining the functions, duties and goals of every branch of the executive in great detail. Presidential Decree No. 3 defines the functions, duties and prerogatives of the offices of the President, the Prime Minister (articles 20–3), the Ministers (27–8) Ministerial Councils (24–6), Parliamentary Deputy Minister (27–8), General Secretaries of the Government (29–33) and the Civil Service (34–41). Presidential Decree No. 4 (9 May 1973) superseding Presidential Decrees Nos. 5 and 6 (12 October 1971) enumerated fourteen ministries and went on to specify the goals, functions and internal composition of each of the ministries.

More importantly, Presidential Decree No. 6 created an institution for central planning, a high council for planning and overseeing development planning, headed by the President. Its membership comprised the Vice-Presidents, the Prime Minister and a host of other central government and regional government ministers. The presidency, at the summit, of this administrative pyramid would equally function in an institutional manner. That did not escape Nimeiri's mind and he drew his ministers' attention to the themes of co-ordination, planning and well-researched measures. He invoked those themes in explaining his actions and justifying the new reorganization:

The era of extempore decision has gone. In order to achieve full co-ordination I have appointed two Ministers for Presidential Affairs and Cabinet Affairs to act as my right hand and to help make sure that a degree of order exists in the minister's performance. Experience has taught me that decisions which are not accompanied by in-depth studies and preceded by consultation with every concerned party only cause harm and create more problems than they would have sought to solve. The *ancien régime* relied on the ministry as a basic independent unit for both making and implementing policy

> . . . this turned the ministries into a collection of independent
> entities each with its own ever-present personnel. . . . The
> Presidential Republic, in its new form, seeks, first and
> foremost, the removal of all vestiges of government within
> government and [is] against inertia and lack of global vision.

So in Nimeiri's words, government was to be institutionalized and
streamlined and the decision-making process based on well
thought out and researched studies.

The most significant institutional change of this period,
however, was the implementation of the 1971 People's Local
Government Act. The Act entailed a large measure of devolution
of administrative power away from Khartoum to the nine provinces
of Equatoria, Bahr al Ghazal, Kordofan, Upper Nile, Blue Nile,
Geziera, Kassala, Khartoum Northern and Darfur. It also entailed
the idea of local popular participation in the administration of the
Sudan. That system was later enshrined in article 6 of the Constitution.

The People's Local Government (PLG) system was a pyramid of
People's Provincial Councils, People's Rural and Town Councils.
Below the Rural Councils were Village Councils, these being the
first to be elected. In all Councils twenty-five per cent of the elected
members were by law to be women. Members from the village and
neighbourhood councils, as they were called in urban areas, sat on
Rural and Town Councils and members from these on the Provincial Councils. Popular and syndicated organizations, i.e. workers,
farmers, national capitalists, professionals and the army, were also
represented. The Provincial Council administers all the services in
the province, including agriculture, health, roads, housing and
town planning, community development and the police.

The objective of the various reforms at local and provincial
levels was two-fold:

1. Removal of the powers of the traditional tribal leadership.
2. Linking local administration with the SSU.

In other words, in addition to its administrative functions, the PLG
had a political one, to promote and explain the objectives and
actions of the SSU. The Province Commissioner was to be appointed by the President himself, to whom the Commissioner was
responsible through the Minister of Local Government.

To acquaint the Sudanese with the new reorganization of the state an energetic campaign was undertaken in the media and different forums of public expression. A small booklet entitled *The Building of a Modern State* was issued by the SSU. On decentralization, that booklet lists the following priorities:

1. Consolidation of the PLG, making it into an executive instrument in the hands of the people while providing it with the needed infrastructure: trained personnel, organs for local planning etc.
2. Co-ordination of financial aspects between the different units of the PLG and central government along new lines which will give the former more freedom of action on a clearly defined basis.
3. Increasing the resources of PLG organizations enabling them to meet ever increasing demands. The programme also calls for an improvement in the general level of services throughout the Sudan, giving a list of priorities, while underlining the importance of popular mobilization of human resources (women, youth and professionals) to supplement financial inadequacies in the system.

While the new arrangement was, *prima facie*, a devolution of power away from Khartoum, in reality it increased the power of the President by placing him at the top of a pyramid with its base in villages and neighbourhoods. The President was meant to be a patron of local government; however, patronage to Nimeiri meant effective personal control. Nimeiri's concern with local government was not where that concern should apply, i.e. alleviating the lot of the people and maintaining public services and amenities. His concern was more with increasing the area of patronage and using the system to produce lavish spoils. As a result there was a carousel of gubernatorial appointments. For example, in the course of six years (1971–8) Khartoum Province had six governors; so did Geziera. None of them stayed long enough to see his plans through. In this respect Nimeiri the lofty dreamer was betrayed by Nimeiri the manipulator. Local government could easily have been an effective tool of management of remote rural areas as well as problematic urban ones; instead it became window-dressing for the hegemony of (his) central power. Such considerations could not have escaped Nimeiri, and now he justified the new system.

The creation of the posts of Province Commissioners was
dictated by the new perception of local government which is
against the imposition of central rule by the central Ministries
which thwart initiative and violate all the tenets of
decentralization. The new system, besides achieving true
decentralization, will bring about unity in administration;
something which State organs and organisations have always
lacked.

This is only the theory and Nimeiri knew it. The reality as far he
was concerned was something else. On the other hand Dr Bakheit,
the founding father of the PLG, did not waste an opportunity to
recite the virtues of decentralization. He was not only the Minister
of, but also the educator on, Local Government. His fight was not
limited to the centrists who, jealous of losing their power and authority, were putting up road-blocks against the march of decentralization. There was also the SSU with its basic role of mobilizing
human resources in order to make up for the inadequacies of the
system. People were to make up for them through self-help, but in
place of self-help there was only lip service. Bakheit wrote several
guide-lines, manuals and directives as to how that integration
could take place. Abu Gasim Ibrahim, as secretary-general
of the SSU in later days, tried to energize the process in his own
fashion. He did not survive in his post long enough to see his
plans through.

In addition Bakheit had to fight with the sycophants and he never
hesitated to give them a piece of his mind. In 1971 when a new
bridge was inaugurated by the President at the Blue Nile (Kober),
the Governor of Khartoum declared that the bridge would be
named after Nimeiri. The President was full of smiles. Bakheit rose
up, put his prepared address aside and charged, addressing the
crowd, the Governor and the smiling President, 'We create institutions to function and laws to be applied. The Governor has committed a big error. The authority to name bridges rests neither with
him, with me the local government Minister nor with the President
of the Republic. It is for the Khartoum People's Local Council to
call this bridge what it pleases.' Naming a bridge is a matter of no
great significance, but in a system where the ruler is prone to megalomania such reminders are important on two counts. Firstly they
serve as a humbling experience for the ruler and secondly they

encourage faith in the doubting institutions. Institutions are not window-dressing; they are meant to exercise authority.

Beside the restructuring of the executive, plans were drawn for reshaping the security forces. The revision was to be in aim as well as organization. The call in these sectors was for greater co-ordination, accountability, better delivery and the upholding and protection of the principles of the May revolution. In this regard Nimeiri was clear and sharp:

> In my election manifesto I assert that I do not want them [security forces] to become a tool of terror and subjugation but a vigilant guardian and a watchful superintendent. There is nothing more injurious to the citizen's integrity than taking away from him his security and sowing fear in its place. These organs must, therefore, organize themselves and co-ordinate their efforts. For competition between security organs only victimizes truth and freedom. For these reasons I have created an organ [attached] to the Presidency which should provide me with a clear picture of the security situation enabling me to follow up events, in order to prevent deviation and oppression. (16 October 1971)

In the course of the years that followed, it was not Nimeiri who was warding off the excesses of security; exactly the contrary. Those who claim that the Sudan was saved from the prospect of an Amin-type brutality only thanks to its institutions got it right. In the following chapters we shall come across many incidents substantiating this contention. The Sudanese security services, like all security services, may have had a few excesses, but they have never degenerated into unscrupulous henchmen of the regime, for their actions were always tempered by Sudanese family and clan affinities. The barbarity under which the country is reeling today, far from being the work of institutions, is rather the end of the road in Nimeiri's battle with the institutions, all ignored, emaciated and completely destroyed.

SSU: Guide, Mobilize and Educate

1972 was the year of the SSU. It was launched in January. We have dwelt in chapter 1 on the divisive nature of party politics prior to the May revolution and on how the SSU was envisaged as a union of forces, an organ transcending tribal, sectarian and racial divides. All parties of the pre-revolutionary era represented such grouping, with the exception perhaps of the Communist Party which was trans-sectarian, although it tended to be a party of the urban middle class. Parliamentary multi-party systems always led to one of these sectarian parties dominating Parliament.

The SSU was also envisaged as a policy-making organ and a tool of popular mobilization behind clearly defined programmes. As a policy-making machine it had to complement the activities of government and not compete with it. The two had to work hand in hand and to this end channels of communication between the two were established. It is of paramount importance in a one-party system, such as the one we have chosen, to guard against such an eventuality, i.e. competition rather than co-operation. Nimeiri, the consummate manipulator, used this innate tendency and played one against the other. The destruction of both institutions was, therefore, a foregone conclusion.

The SSU had to guide, mobilize and educate. To guide it needed its think tank; the specialized committees of the central committee were created for that end. Mass support and mobilization would be secured through modern channels of communication without discounting the old channels of family and clan. Policy-making would become a national science of cause and effect in its own right. Our intention was to break away from the politics of clubism and slogans. Heralding this era of purposeful politics, Nimeiri announced at the first SSU Congress that:

> We have established special committees which would strive to guide political action [basing] it on research and examination and supplying it with useful information to enable it to come up with solutions to problems based on an in-depth study of the problems themselves.

With this understanding in mind, the first Central Committee adopted action plans which were a result of intensive studies in which ministers, university professors, technicians from all professions, as well as representatives of the workers' trade unions took part. These plans were the guiding light for the government in its development drive in the early 'seventies. Popular organizations,

which participated actively through their representatives in the formulation of these plans, were readily mobilized behind these
policies, playing an effective role in their implementation. But for
the SSU to deliver the goods it was expected to deliver, indeed for
it to function at all, it had to be democratic. Political parties are
normally born out of political convulsion. Those created from the
top are apt to disintegrate if they are not broadly based, democratic
and able to build a consensus. Consensus presupposes dialogue and
debate, for democracy is a transaction not a linear action. This was
almost an article of faith and a commitment, asserted by the Constituent Congress of the SSU in 1972 and enshrined in the first basic
rules adopted. Not only should the minority abide by the will of the
majority, but also the latter should respect the right of the former
in expressing their views. Without such a process of open and free
dialogue democracy would never take root, nor would the SSU be
an organ of veritable mobilization. It would turn, as it did, into a
party of patronage run by cheer-leaders. As for the democratization of the process of political promotion, we aimed in the forma-
tive years for gradual democratization. The first draft of the basic
rules of the SSU provided that the Politburo be composed of ex-
members of the RCC in addition to nominees of the President.
Two years later during the deliberations of the first National
Congress (February 1974) we agreed on a gradual process of
democratization at the end of which all members of the Politburo
should be freely elected by the Central Committee. It seemed
natural that the first Politburo should include all members of the
RCC; they were after all the perpetrators of the revolution and
their goodwill was necessary if the whole thing was not to falter.
The process of democratization initiated in 1971 should have been
carried to its logical conclusion, if words meant what they said. To
this end we maintained that the second Politburo (1974) should
reflect a step forward towards that goal: all names, including those
of the ex-members of the RCC, should be subjected to a vote.

Naturally enough, battle cries were raised by some of the ex-
members of the RCC. We stood our ground; there was no room for
inheritance in a republic, especially not in one which purports to be
both revolutionary and progressive. If national heroes were to
govern the country *ad infinitum* el Azhari should be brought back.
The ex-members of the RCC were indeed the perpetrators of the
revolution but that should not entitle them to membership of the
Politburo in perpetuity. Such a contention defeats the very aim and

objects of the revolution. The man who fully appreciated this was Abul Gasim Hashim. He played a great role in pursuading his colleagues of the merits of our arguments. Nimeiri for his part supported our proposal not on principle, i.e. for what it entailed in terms of greater democracy and better representation, but because he saw in it a diminution of power of the RCC ex-members and their claim to enjoyment of the spoils of the revolution. He wanted all the spoils for himself.

The first step towards democratization was that the President should present his list of nominees for the Politburo to the Central Committee for ratification. The list was to be accepted or rejected in its entirety by the Central Committee, his first list was in fact rejected by ten members of the Committee, with the votes openly taken. Among those who came out against the list was Abdel Wahab Ibrahim, head of Security. The fact that he could oppose the President and retain his job for some years showed that there was a measure of democracy and some acceptance on the part of Nimeiri of the rules of the game. Abdel Wahab made it clear later that he was against three names in the Presidential list and he felt so strongly about it that he chose to say no. In the second National Congress the Politburo was elected by the Central Committee from a list of thirty put forward by Nimeiri; there were no nominated members. Some of the nominees who were not elected were close friends of Nimeiri and he would have liked to see them elected. The list of the nominees produced by the President increased to fifty names in the third Congress, therefore increasing the range of choice. The process initiated in 1972 was working and should have been allowed to go to its logical conclusion. It was soon aborted. Nimeiri had laboured hard to reverse the process to the extent of proposing in 1984 the abolition of the SSU itself.

Continuing his assault on democracy within the SSU Nimeiri, rather than encouraging or tolerating dissent, scotched it. In fact he did more, dispensing with dissenters, always acting against the basic rules. Those rules stipulated that members accused of contravening the policies or rules of the SSU should be presented to a disciplinary committee where charges against them were made, evidence adduced and opportunities for rebuttal afforded. But in the course of the five years following the election of the first Politburo (1974–9), as we shall discuss later, Nimeiri dismissed nearly ten elected members of the Politburo acting *ultra vires* of the basic rules. In one particular case disagreement with him in the Executive

[Cabinet] resulted in the deposition of the disobedient Minister from his elective position in the Politburo. The Minister in question (Mohammed Hashim Awad) took exception to the President's decision on tax increases and tendered his resignation from his Cabinet post (Ministry of Commerce). To Nimeiri that disobedience could be punished not only by removing the Minister from the Cabinet; he had to be politically disavowed also.

So with the systematic removal of the nay-sayers the President ended by surrounding himself increasingly with yes-men, sycophants, unsuspecting political oddities and make-believers. By 1980 the SSU, as we shall see, had signed its own death warrant. It had committed political suicide and was entombed in Khartoum in February of that year. The concensus-building, broadly based, policy-making organization thought of in 1971 by Nimeiri the intrepid explorer of new horizons (the lofty dreamer), was by 1979 destroyed by its very architect. By that year, the SSU had glaringly failed in mastering the architecture of power, so it had to turn into refining the choreography of power, its role no longer that of policy-making but of political folklore. But even in this unseemly endeavour its success is doubtful, for today many, many Sudanese would tell you that the SSU is the longest-running farce on Sudan's political stage.

A Farewell to Arms

1972 was also the year of the Addis Ababa agreement which put and end to the seventeen-year-old internecine strife. The 9 June declaration which the Free Officers made after coming to power and in which they recognized the right of the Southerners to some measure of autonomy was not followed by any concrete measures. The tension and dissension in the North was not conducive to such action. Nimeiri's high-handedness did not help either. We shall have occasion later to talk about the role that foreign diplomacy played in the solution of the problem, by way of obtaining the goodwill and assistance of Western countries, church organizations and African leaders. That helped in creating new channels of communication between the North and the Southern rebel movements and eventually convincing them of our seriousness.

Delegations from the North and South had in fact been

conducting secret negotiations since May 1971 through the good offices of the World Council of Churches. Concomitant discussions were also opened with some dissident Southern elements living in self-exile in Britain. Ambassador Abdin Ismael, Professor Mohammed Omar Beshir and Barbara Haq played an important role in that exercise. The government sought to convince the Southerners that they were prepared to settle for some degree of regional autonomy. A detailed law defining the constitutional position of the South within a united Sudan was passed. This went a great way to convincing the Southerners that the new government meant business.

The conference which led to an agreement being signed on 27 February 1972 met in Ethiopia, with Addis Ababa as the venue and Haile Selassie the mediator. The Emperor offered his country's capital, his own prestige and his government's facilities. The agreement took place against opposition from two directions: the Arabists and Islamicists, within and outside government. They were both opposed to the granting of regional autonomy to the South.

In the eyes of the Arabists, regional autonomy for the South and African involvement in the settlement, i.e. the Emperor and the All-Africa Conference of Churches (AACC) vitiated Sudan's Arab image and orientation. What the Arabists failed to realize was that a strong, united Sudan would only be an addition to, and not a derogation from, a wider Arab community. On the other hand, the unity of the Sudan is the unity of Africa, the Sudan being a microcosm of the continent. For the Islamicists the problem of the South was the creation of Christian missionary activity, which instilled in the Southerners a feeling of separateness from their Muslim neighbours. To grant them autonomy was to compromise Islam's position in the Sudanese state. There were also a few other accusations as to how should we meet with national rebels outside the Sudan and how we should tolerate their calling themselves the Southern Sudan Liberation Movement. Some of those elements were waiting for our return from Addis Ababa, not to hail our success but to bury us as traitors. A few others were waiting to gloat over our failure; negotiated peace, they thought, was a chimera. The Addis Ababa agreement was a saga of its own deserving a separate book, a book on the play within the play. There were many villains of the piece and few heroes. Two of those heroes were Dr Gaafer Bakheit and the Reverend Canon Burges Carr, the secretary-general of the AACC. We could not have done much without them, not only because of their lucidity and resourcefulness, but also because of their patience and ability to suffer fools gladly. There were fools on both sides. Bakheit and Carr had the fantastic ability to listen to all manner of clownish nonsense, yet pretend that they were giving their ears to distilled wisdom.

The Addis Ababa agreement grouped the provinces of Bahr al Ghazal, Equatoria and Upper Nile into a self-governing Southern Region with Juba as the capital. The region would have its own People's Assembly and High Executive Council. It gave the regional government control over education, health, agriculture and forests, the police forces etc., leaving control of defence, foreign affairs, the Army, communications and national economic planning in the hands of the national government.

The weight that Nimeiri exerted against the Islamicists and Arabists was of paramount importance for the resolution of the problem. One ought at this juncture to consider Nimeiri's reasons and motives for supporting the peace process as he did. The fact that nearly two years had elapsed between his June declaration and the Addis Ababa conference, during which period more spoken promises and only a high-handed approach to the problem were seen, shows that principles – such as the belief that the Southerners were ethnically and culturally distinct and entitled to some degree of autonomy – were not the motives. One arrives at such conclusions with the benefit of hindsight, particularly after the unmaking of the Addis agreement nine years after its conclusion. Internal problems such as the struggle with the Ansar and the Communists are more likely to have figured in Nimeiri's thinking than principles. A friendly South within a united Sudan would be an invaluable political asset; this much events were soon to prove. And another asset would be the political prestige both inside and outside the Sudan that such a resolution would bring him.

The agreement signed and ratified in Addis was later a subject of intensive discussion in the Politburo, but was eventually adopted unanimously. Our insistence on having the agreement discussed and adopted by the Politburo was prompted by the desire to have a universal commitment to it, particularly from the doubting and the suspicious. The whole regime had to be mobilized behind the agreement, if the peace effort were to succeed. Suspicion and doubts should be nipped in the bud. All the time, however, we were aware that if things ever went wrong, there would always be somebody who would say 'we told you so'. That we never minded. When things went right, on the other hand, there were a hundred fathers of the achievement. None the less there were still a few elements within the regime who continued to harbour suspicions. Silly whispers were heard about a secret agreement, as if we were dealing with a foreign power. The whispers continued even after the agreement was translated into law, becoming part of the law of the land. Suspicions and fears were not only limited to the Khartoum folk. Joseph Lagu, who led the Southern delegation for the ratification, was also not sufficiently convinced to make it back to Khartoum with us. He asked for a guarantee for his safety from Emperor Haile Selassie. In those days all that was to be expected and we understood it well. We asked the Emperor to allay his fears, which he gladly did.

On arrival in Khartoum we, both delegations, were rushed to meet the President. Abel Alier was in tears. The President's reception was cordial and disarming. Nimeiri excels in chats and off-the-cuff remarks. He reminisced about his days in the South. He joked and laughed breezily. Then, not wasting time on more courtesies, he went on to business. He had already received my brief on the misgivings expressed by our Southern brothers and the potential powderkegs in the agreement. One of the most thorny issues was the integration of the rebel armed forces into the national Army. 'Your boys were good courageous fighters; I am happy that you have reached an agreement to integrate them in the Armed Forces,' Nimeiri said to Lagu. Without a pause he went on to ask Lagu that, before embarking on the process of integration, he should select 200 of his best men to be included in the Republican Guard, Nimeiri's. Nothing could have been more reassuring and disarming. We thought it was a master-stroke. A day later Lagu was appointed major-general in the Army which he left a few years ago as a major. The title must have meant a lot to Lagu, a soldier. To the cynical Nimeiri what was there in adding a word? The major was now a major-general.

Lagu, therefore, did not become what everybody else was expecting him to be, the first president of the regional government. That was Abel's lot. Abel, whom many people would call the best President Sudan never had, and probably never will have, is a humble, judicious and accommodating man; all the qualities needed for ruling a country as split apart as the Sudan. On hearing of Lagu's appointment Abel urged me to convince the President to nominate Hilary Lugali as southern president. The southern president should come from a minor tribe, he thought. It took both modesty and wisdom to think in those terms. The President thought otherwise and maybe he was right at that juncture. Abel's words, however, were prophetic, as we shall see later.

After seventeen years peace had been restored. It was farewell to arms and on with nation-building and development. But it was only through mutual comprehension and purposeful policy that unity could be stitched together. The Addis Ababa agreement was but a start, though a significant one. It had to be integrated in the basic law, the constitution. And so it was, in 1973, as an organic law of the constitution, only to be amended according to the procedures established in it. More action was needed to set up the new government in Juba, equip the region with the basic infrastructure, integrate the rebel forces in the army, rehabilitate the refugees and create political and administrative mechanisms for ironing out differences that were sure to ensue. In a couple of years all that was achieved with a large measure of success, given the goodwill and support the agreement received both within and outside the Sudan. The latter will be dealt with later on.

On the other hand, erasing the ugly memories of seventeen years of conflict was not an easy thing, so an extensive public relations campaign was undertaken in the whole country, including the South itself, to allay fears and explain the purport of the Addis Ababa agreement. In that connection, Nimeiri made a goodwill tour of the South, covering all provinces. While in Juba, the new capital of the southern region, he celebrated a peace Mass in Juba Cathedral. He also attended the wedding of a leading Southern politician in the same cathedral. That gesture alone left a great impression on many of the Southerners. The sight of a North Muslim leader in a Christian place of worship in the heart of the South left an indelible mark on the minds of the worshippers. And this was the same Nimeiri that will come back, ten years later, to impose a false conception – his own – of Shari'a on them, animists and Christians alike.

Government by Laws not Men

The Addis Ababa agreement paved the way for the resolution of the long-standing constitutional problem. A constituent Assembly was convoked, including both elected and nominated members. All political shades, though not all organizations, were represented. Professor Nazir Dafaa Allah, a former Vice-Chancellor of the University of Khartoum, and a scientist of renown, was appointed as Speaker. In addition to his many personal and professional qualities Nazir had also been the chairman of the round table conference on Southern Sudan in 1965. That involvement with the Southern problem tipped the balance in his favour.

The Assembly had before it several drafts on different aspects of the constitution presented by members. The main draft, however, was authored by Dr Gaafer Bakheit, with substantial contributions from Badr el Din Suleiman and myself. In this endeavour we used as our starting-point the draft constitution prepared under the regime of the parties that was never adopted, as well as the criticisms levelled against it in the constituent Assembly at that time. We also went through different constitutions, particularly those of the French Fifth Republic, India, Tanzania, Algeria, Tunisia and Egypt. Those constitutions were perused for guidance rather than copying in striving to enshrine in the constitution the basic social and economic tenets of the regime's ideology. So far as the apportionment of power and the reflection of Sudan's cultural realities in the constitution were concerned, our attention centred on five areas:

1. The question of Southern Sudan and constitutional guarantees against tampering with the Addis Ababa agreement.
2. Religion: how to specify in the constitution a role for Islam as the religion of the majority while recognizing other religions and spiritual beliefs professed by citizens.
3. The balance between a strong Presidential regime and a system of accountability ensuring discipline in the exercise of power.
4. Safeguarding the rights of the individual in a one-party state where the classical concepts of basic rights would seem irreconcilable if not irrelevant.
5. Decentralization of government and devolution of authority.

These drafts and counter-drafts were the subject of an energetic debate both at committee and plenary levels. The debate was open and broadcast live. Citizens were urged to put across their views both directly to the Assembly and through the media. However, the very issues that threatened the peace process proved to be the major hurdles in the way of promulgating a new constitution, namely, national identity and the role of religion. The Islamicists led by Ali Suleiman wanted a constitution that enshrined Sudan's Islamic identity with a stipulation that Islam is the official religion of the state. The constitution that was eventually promulgated in May 1973 was more accommodating: article 1 of the Constitution describes the Sudan as a 'unitary, democratic, socialist and sovereign republic, and a part of both the Arab and African entities'. On the question of the role of religion, article 16 states:

a. In the Democratic Republic of the Sudan, Islam is the religion and society shall be guided by Islam being the religion of the majority of its people and the state shall endeavour to express its values.

b. Christianity is the religion in the Democratic Republic of the Sudan being professed by a large number of its citizens who are guided by Christianity and the State shall endeavour to express its values.

c. Heavenly religions and the noble aspects of spiritual beliefs shall not be abused or held in contempt.

d. The State shall treat followers of religions and noble spiritual beliefs without discrimination as to the rights and freedoms guaranteed to them as citizens by this Constitution. The State shall not impose any restrictions on citizens or communities on the grounds of religious faith.

e. The abuse of religious and noble spiritual beliefs for political exploitation is forbidden. Any act which is intended or is likely to promote feelings of hatred, enmity or discord among religious communities shall be contrary to this Constitution and punishable by law.

As to the issue of an official state religion Dr Bakheit, the Leader of the Assembly, made charges against what he called hypocritical sloganism. The state should endeavour to uphold the values of Islam and should consider Shari'a as a main source of legislation.

Anything else would be demagogy if we did not mean it and a contradiction of the letter and spirit of the constitution if we did, said the Leader. In saying that we had things like the place of women in society and the rights of Christian citizens in our minds. Classical (historical) Islam propagated by the Sudanese fundamentalists does not recognize their right of governance over Muslims. This view is challenged by other Moslem schools of thought, to which Sudanese fundamentalists do not subscribe. However those very fundamentalists are outwardly committed to provisions in the constitution prohibiting discrimination on the basis of sex or religion. And therein lies the contradiction.

In effect even today the self-professed true Muslims, are evading issues like the ones mentioned above. Islam has to be applied in its entirety, they say, meaning by that flogging, the amputation of hands and the stoning of adulterers to death. But its entirety, according to their reading of Shari'a (flawed by many others), should also mean that Christians should not rule over Muslims. This is hardly in consonance with the principle of non-discrimination on the basis of sex or religion (article 38) of the constitution. Those Muslims would have to go through cumbersome mental gymnastics to justify a place for the Abdel Aliers and Joseph Lagus in the higher echelons of the government of the Islamic Republic of the Sudan or for the host of women ministers and judges were they to apply their own version of Islam and continue to pay lip service to article 38. This is one issue on which the fundamentalists remain dubiously vague and that was precisely what we warned against in 1973, calling it by its real name: hypocrisy.

The powers the constitution accords to the President of the Republic fall into three categories: executive, legislative and symbolic. Article 80 describes the President of the Republic as the head of the state and continues, 'In him vests the executive powers and he participates in making laws. He acts on a direct mandate of the people through a plebiscite prescribed by law. The President shall be nominated by the Sudanese Socialist Union in accordance with its basic rules.' Although the aforementioned article vests executive powers in the President several articles in the constitution provide for the creation of institutions through which executive power is to be exercised, e.g. article 90 states that 'the President of the Republic shall appoint Ministers to run the ministries assigned to them by a Presidential Order.' Chapter 7 also deals with the people's local government and the devolution of executive authority. The executive powers vested in the President therefore do not go beyond similar powers invested in heads of state in presidential systems, the President being an institution not an individual. On the other hand, as we shall see later, a seemingly nebulous amendment of the articles relating to the President, introduced in September 1975, proved to be of great harm to Sudan's constitutional evolution.

That President Nimeiri was conscious of the institutional nature of the Presidency is not a matter of conjecture. In his speech on the occasion of the third anniversary of the May revolution (1972), a year baptized as the year of the constitution, Nimeiri solemnly pledged that the new constitution would reflect:

1. National unity.
2. Striving for the establishment of a socialist society based on sufficiency and social justice.
3. Restructuring of social and economic relationships.
4. Stability of government through institutions, laws, and replacing loyalty to individuals by loyalty to the nation.

We shall come to more such affirmations by the President, all underlining the theme of institutional authority and denouncing loyalty to individuals. Individuals meant the religious chiefs and political leaders of the regime of the parties who had personalized power, e.g. Azhari.

As to the legislative powers of the President and the Assembly article 118 states: 'The legislative power shall vest in the People's Assembly together with the President.' The President's power, in general, is that of any head of state, i.e. giving his assent to the laws before they are promulgated. The overriding authority in legislation rests with the Assembly. According to article 118: 'The People's Assembly shall approve the general plan for development, pass the general Budget and exercise supervision and control over the executive in accordance with the provisions of this Constitution.' But while the constitution gives the Assembly the power to monitor the activities of the executive (headed by the President) it also gives (in article 106) the President the right to issue Provisional Republican Orders having the force of law 'when the People's Assembly is not in session or in cases of importance and urgency.' The article adds an important proviso to the effect that

> Such Provisional Orders . . . be submitted to the People's
> Assembly within fifteen days from the date of issue if the
> People's Assembly is in session, or at the first meeting in case
> of dissolution or prorogation and end of session. If such
> Provisional Orders are not submitted as prescribed above or
> submitted but not passed by the People's Assembly they shall
> cease to be law without retrospective effect.

It is evident from the letter and spirit of the constitution that
legislation by Parliament (People's Assembly) is the rule, and legislation by the President the exception. Hence it is called provisional
and subjected to rigorous limitations. Up to 1981 the Assembly had
considered 194 Bills presented by the executive and duly enacted
them after intensive discussion, while it passed in the same period
244 Provisional Orders issued by the President. In few of these
cases was there enough urgency to warrant a Provisional Order.
The tendency towards such gross departure from constitutional
norms has been more evident since 1977. Needless to say this
cascade of Provisional Orders confiscated the right of the
Assembly to legislate, particularly when the choice before the
Assembly is either to adopt or reject the Order in its entirety. Only
two of the 244 Provisional Orders were rejected by the Assembly in
1976: the Employees' Discipline Act and the Judiciary Act. None
of the successive Speakers has challenged the President's high-
handed way in legislation, although the President's attention was
drawn in 1979 by his new Attorney-General, Dr Hassan Turabi, to
the unconstitutionality of this procedure. Laws must be properly
vetted by the Council of Ministers and presented to the Assembly
as Bills. Came 1983, Dr Turabi himself was leading the chorus
hailing the most far-reaching Provisional Orders passed by Nimeiri
in the course of his fourteen-year reign, the Islamicization laws.
Some of these laws were in flagrant contradiction of the constitution, and they still are.

In exercising his power of assent to laws article 107 empowers the
President to object to a Bill passed by the People's Assembly but
requires him to

> send it back together with reasons of his objection within thirty
> days from the date it has been presented to him. If such a bill
> [the article continues] is not sent back within the

aforementioned period or if it were sent within the period above mentioned and the Assembly passed it again with a two-thirds majority of its members it shall become law.

By the same token the President's power to dissolve the Assembly is not a constitutional anomaly. Several constitutions in both presidential (e.g. France) or parliamentary (e.g. India) systems empower heads of state, with clearly delineated limitations, to dissolve the Assembly when its existence becomes non-conducive to the good functioning of government, e.g. constant frustration of governance or where there is evidence that members have lost the support of their constituencies. Article 108 of the constitution stipulates that such action should be undertaken in consultation with the Speaker. Consultation, in constitutional parlance, means advice and consent, not information. The article also provides that an election of a new Assembly must take place within sixty days of the date of dissolution, with a clear proviso that the new Assembly shall not be dissolved till it completes a session. Later we shall give examples of Nimeiri's complete disdain of constitutional limitations insofar as Parliament's dissolution is concerned, and always with no objection from the Speaker, with whom consultation is to be sought. In only one instance (1977) was the President challenged by both members of the Assembly and the secretary-general of the SSU and he backed down. That experience should not have escaped the attention of the complacent speakers. Later on we shall see how this complete docility has led Nimeiri to encroach even on the Southern Regional Assembly, dissolving it at will. This time it was not without a fight. Speaker Clement M'boro launched a valiant campaign and went to prison for it.

President Nimeiri tried to dissolve the first Assembly in January 1977 before it had completed its four-year term. The Assembly was convened on 24 May 1974. There was no obvious political reason for its dissolution except for the fact that the Assembly had started to tread on dangerous zones, debating issues that the President thought should rather be left untouched (see chapter 5). Several people advised the President against that, foremost among whom was Dr Zaki Mustafa, whose views were sought by the President. In view of the President's adamantine position and the support given to him by the Speaker, who chose not to make an issue of the question, we were forced to bring Abul Gasim Mohammed Ibrahim, secretary-general of the SSU, into the wrangle. With a

51

lot of gusto Ibrahim convened a meeting for a large number of the Assembly members in the course of the SSU General Congress, made one of his interminable speeches and assured the members that the dissolution was simply not on. The President, to make sure that Ibrahim should not get away with all the applause (indeed none of it), passed the word that he had never thought of a dissolution. That Assembly was dissolved only after it had completed its term (December 1977), to allow for electing the third Assembly that was convoked on 13 March 1978. So apart from the first Assembly (held from 12 October 1972 to May 1973) and the second Assembly referred to above, no subsequent Parliaments were allowed to survive the period prescribed by the constitution, and all were dissolved without an objection by the members and Speakers. The third Assembly lasted for two years and the fourth for only one year.

The constitution also empowers the head of state, in a not untypical situation, to

declare a state of emergency and take necessary measures . . . which may include the suspension of all or any of the freedoms and rights guaranteed by the constitution, [whenever the President of the Republic] is satisfied that an imminent danger is threatening the independence of the country or the integrity and safety of its territory, or its economy, or the republican organs of the state and its constitutional institutions or the fulfilment of its international obligations in the achievements of the people.

As in the case of article 107 the exercise of power here is subject to an important proviso, namely that the people's 'right to resort to the courts shall not be suspended' and that

the President of the Republic shall submit the declaration of a state of emergency and the measures taken pursuant to it to the People's Assembly within fifteen days from the date of its issue and if the Assembly is not in session the President shall convene it within thirty days to deliberate upon the matter. If the Assembly is dissolved the matter shall be laid before the new Assembly at its first meeting. . . . [In any case] the state of emergency shall not continue for more than thirty days, and except when the People's Assembly is dissolved the President shall not renew or extend the aforementioned period save with the assent of the Assembly.

All this goes to show that the exercise of Presidential authority, within the meaning of the constitution, is not meant to be a licence for the President to act at will. The legislative power is mainly vested in the People's Assembly, with the President's role limited and circumscribed. Executive power is presumed to be institutionalized, and in certain cases subjected to clearly defined limitations, e.g. a state of emergency. Nimeiri's actions demonstrate his complete obliviousness of all those limitations, and not without reason. He was capable of getting away with it only because of the shyness of the institutions which are equally empowered by the constitution to check, control or reject (partly understandable).

Constitutional checks on the Presidential exercise of power are not only restricted to the balancing limitations provided for in articles 106, 107, 111 and 118. The Assembly also has the right to challenge the President's policies if they deem such policies contrary to public interest or not supported by public opinion. Article 109 of the constitution provides that 'The People's Assembly may, by a two-thirds majority of its members, request the President of the Republic to refer to a public referendum his policy in several matters or in a particular matter if the Assembly is of the opinion that such policy is against the public interest or is not supported by public opinion. The President shall accede to such a request within sixty days from the date of the request presented to him.' This article was never invoked by the Assembly even in situations when there was a universal disenchantment with serious decisions taken personally by the President and against the advice of both political and administrative institutions, e.g. the decisions on Southern Sudan which led to civil war.

Furthermore the constitution also empowers the Assembly to impeach the President. Article 115 stipulates that 'The President is immune and shall not be charged with an offence, except on a motion by one-third of the members of the People's Assembly and supported by two-thirds of members of the same Assembly in a meeting held *in camera*. He shall be tried before a special court constituted according to law.' So while the President is immune from action in normal courts, on charges relating to offences committed by him, such charges can be formulated by the Assembly according to the procedure prescribed by the constitution. The

President, however, shall not be criminally liable for acts done in the course of his duty except in cases of high treason. The Assembly, therefore, is empowered to bring charges against the President both for offences committed by him against the laws and the constitution, though he is not criminally liable for them before normal courts if they involve such a liability, save for high treason. It is also empowered to undertake his impeachment notwithstanding appearance before the normal courts for acts of high treason. The President's repeated breaches of the constitution to which he has sworn an oath of allegiance and his constant frustration of the due process of law certainly amount to political offences under the first part of Article 115. Some of those offences amount to treasonable acts under the constitution. Article 220 provides that 'any act intended to wreck the constitution ... shall be high treason punishable by law.' Nimeiri's onslaught on the Addis Ababa agreement is one such act. Not only does it contravene article 8 (Southern Sudan autonomy) but Nimeiri's wholesale Islamicization measures and their indiscriminate application to non-Muslims is in flagrant contradiction of article 16 of the constitution if not also of the spirit of true Islam. They should have been ruled unconstitutional as long as the constitution was valid. Equally his exercise of legislative power in contradiction of article 106 completely incapacitates the main legislative organ (Parliament). And if all those acts do not wreck the constitution, God knows what will. Other political offences, for which the President could have been impeached, may be traced in his constant attempts to frustrate the work of the Assembly, particularly in exposing corruption, examples of which will be dealt with later. Such acts are not only in flagrant contradiction of article 152 of the constitution: 'No court or any other authority shall interfere with the work of the People's Assembly', but also, and more important, with the all-embracing oath to respect the law, to work honestly and uphold the principles of the May revolution. Purity is one of those principles, and it was Nimeiri's courts that punished Ministers of the regime of the parties for their breach. The punishment meted out to the convicted Ministers included the deprivation of all political rights and privileges.

The same applies to the President's constant deviations from the strategies set by the supreme political organization, the SSU. It is from that institution that the President draws his legitimacy, for in the first place a person may be a candidate for the presidency of the republic only by virtue of his being elected by the SSU General Congress as its President. To that position he is elected on the basis of a commitment to a strategy. The role of presidents elected on strategies is to see to it that the actions and policies of government are consistent with those strategies, not to change strategies at a whim. In this connection the role of the Parliamentary party (Hayaat al Majlis) is precisely to ensure that the strategies of the political organization they represent are respected, checking departures from them from whatever organ that departure comes. They are the link between the SSU and the People's Assembly rather than between the President and the Assembly.

President Nimeiri was not unfamiliar with those constitutional limitations and checks and balances. We made sure that his commitment to them was not only limited to the oath of allegiance to the constitution that he also swore before the Assembly. We also made sure that his commitment to institutions should go beyond the measures he has taken for government reorganization, essentially meant to institutionalize the presidential republic. The best indication of Nimeiri's preparedness to accept his new constitutional role was his *Face the Nation* programme. Facing the whole nation on 11 March 1974 the President had with him three of his aides, Dr Zaki Mustafa, the Attorney-General, Dr Gaafer Bakheit, the author of the constitution, and myself, in view of my contribution to that constitution. Among the various questions that Nimeiri put forward to us was one on the interpretation of article 115 of the constitution and another on the meaning and implications of a presidential republic. We were supposed to be Nimeiri's mouthpiece.

Dr Mustafa observed that it is clear from the text (article 115) that it has not given the President of the Republic anything like absolute immunity, for it states that the President enjoys an immunity (but) then goes on to limit that immunity. It further states that the People's Assembly can meet and look into the matter. If two-thirds of the members decide to adopt a motion put forward by one-third of the Assembly, a charge could be levelled against the President forming the subject-matter of a trial. This trial is to be conducted by a special court instituted according to law. In other words, Mustafa continued, immunity is limited, beyond which limitation the President will be called to account before the institution empowered by law for that purpose. It is clear from the text that the President is not criminally liable for acts done in the course of his duties.... The limit that has been laid down for this [immunity] against criminalization is high treason. If a President is accused of high treason according to the definition [given] by the Constitution immunity is lifted, even over acts perpetrated in the execution of his duties.

Dr Bakheit went on to remark that by comparison with other presidents the Sudanese President enjoys little immunity. In fact article 115 was a refined version of the article relating to the same subject in the draft constitution that was before the constituent Assembly of the regime of the parties (1968).

On the meaning of the Presidential Republic, responding to Nimeiri's question as to his powers under articles 80, 81, 82, 99 and 100, I made the point that the presidency is an institution rather than a person, an institution headed by the President. The President, according to articles 89 and 90 of the constitution is assisted in the discharge of his executive duties by Ministers. In presidential systems, I emphasized, Ministers do not form an independent body from the presidency, giving the example of the US where they form the President's Cabinet. In France, I said, despite the fact that the constitution talks about a Council of Ministers and a government, article 9 of the French constitution makes the President the head of this body and gives him the responsibility of leading and supervising the executive. I also made references to presidential powers in several other constitutions, namely Cameroun, Guinea, Tanzania, Ivory Coast and India. The emphasis was, therefore, on the fact that the presidency was an institution and that the President and Ministers should work hand in hand. Nimeiri agreed, adding, 'Dear citizens, you now see that we are governed by institutions.' In other words, the permanent constitution has created a government of laws and institutions, not men.

Evidently, what we strove for was a system of an effective institutionalized government where power is disciplined, organs are accountable and authority is harmonized. By these ideals we have set great store and to them we were all committed, the President included. More than anybody else the President's active commitment was not only demonstrated in his oath of allegiance to the constitution but was also solemnly reasserted in his declarations before God and the people. But texts are one thing, practice quite another. Only practice and application help to ingrain ideas and ideals into the calcium of the system's bones. If the whole constitution was diligently respected and religiously followed and it still failed, its failure would have been an intellectual one. On the other hand, when institutions, political and legislative, authorized by the constitution and the basic rules to exercise control and checks, abdicate their authority and responsibility for lack of moral courage, leading to the failure of the system, then that failure must be deemed to be a moral one.

The degeneration of constitutional presidential rule in Sudan into an autocracy is bound to be attributed (and in fact is being attributed) to the constitution itself by two groups: first, Western observers and so many Sudanese opposers of the regime who might deem the powers that our 1973 constitution gave the President to be excessive and injudicious and, secondly, what we might call the hangers-on, the spineless technocrats and the guardians of the faith who had decided to survive it rather than fight it out. One can almost hear this latter group saying: 'Nimeiri is simply exercising powers bestowed upon him by the constitution.'

Our answer to the first group falls in two parts: firstly, the powers that were given to the President were not excessive and we have argued that our constitution, like many others, provided for means of checking the presidential powers and rendering the person of the President accountable. The powers in question, furthermore are, broadly speaking, the same as those enjoyed by, for instance, the Presidents of Tunisia, Tanzania and Algeria, three one-party African and Arab states. In all those countries the heads of state, though authoritarian, still worked within a certain constitutional framework which as we have said, is not necessarily more restrictive than our own. One thing is sure: the exercise of presidential power, in those countries, has not degenerated to the level which it has reached in Sudan. The degeneration of the presidential system into an autocratic one is due to Nimeiri's innate autocracy, to the negative role played by Parliament, in failing to exercise the powers granted to it by the constitution aimed at keeping the President in his place, and to the failure of the party (SSU) which in a one-party system has a vital role to play checking the executive powers of the President and monitoring the working of the executive arm of the state. Whatever one might think of the one-party systems of eastern Europe, one cannot deny the fact that they fulfil this role with clinical efficiency by dictating policy (in fact, this is the very reason why a one-party system is distasteful to the Westerner) and by wielding tremendous power *vis à vis* the leadership of the party and the Presidency of the Republic. Witness, for instance, the fate of Malenkov, Khrushchev and Podgorny in the

USSR and the Gang of Four and Liu Shau Shi in China.

Secondly, we ought to remind our reader that constitutions on their own are no guarantee against tyranny and autocracy, for two reasons:

1. They stand in need of interpretation and in the absence of a long constitutional history and powerful constitutional organs Presidents can abuse the constitution, twisting the meaning of its text and flouting its spirit.
2. They can be amended by the head of state if he happens to have a sufficiently docile political organization and pliant Parliament.

Nimeiri, as we shall show, did both. And the more the institutions were emaciated, the more he became the fulcrum of power, with those very institutions competing for his favour rather than playing their role of supervision and control. Consequently, the success of the constitutional experiment depends upon the commitment of the powers that be to the spirit of the constitution. The incumbent President, in particular, should act against the tendency to deify himself, so strong in the third world, and should not take advantage of the shyness and moral laxness of the various institutions. A constitution is a living organ which evolves through interpretation and exegesis.

To our second group of critics, we say flatly: failure to exercise the powers prescribed by the constitution cannot be expunged by blaming the constitution itself. They are shirking the issue. They shied away from their task of checking these powers of the President (indeed some of them waged a war against those who took their responsibilities seriously, accusing them of sinning against the President) and the President took advantage of this, like all Presidents who lack a sense of history and proportion. Those who tried to act responsibly fell victims to the President and his sycophants while the Presidential system fell victim to an autocrat, a timid party and an unwilling Parliament. In fact, no President in the history of Sudan needed such checks and constraints more than Nimeiri, if anything because of his innate autocratic nature and utter cynicism of which we shall learn through many examples. General Abboud, for example, who ruled Sudan as a military dictator (1958–1964) with no populist claims, no party to account to and no Parliament with which to share power, showed more sensitivity towards the will of the people. Abboud's constitution bestowed all executive and legislative powers upon the Supreme Council of the Armed Forces. That council, by decree, delegated all its powers to its President, General Abboud. However when the absolute dictator sensed that people no longer wanted him, he abdicated, not in fear but having recognized that he had outlived his usefulness. He acted as any traditional Sudanese politician would have acted.

On 14 April 1974 all the latter-day critics of the constitution, having been decorated by President Nimeiri for their new 'achievement', the constitution, were listening attentively and applauding heartily the following message:

THE UNITED REPUBLIC OF TANZANIA

My Dear Brother,
On behalf of the Government and People of Tanzania I should like to extend to you and to the Government and People of the Sudan my sincere congratulations for the great effort you have made to enable the Sudan to get a new constitution. The new constitution for the Sudan coming as it has, after the end of the civil war in the South, is a happy victory not only for the Sudan but for the whole of Africa. It is a victory that has been made possible through your honesty, sense of realism, and above all through your untiring efforts to deal with the challenges of the leadership of the largest territory on the African continent. We in Tanzania would like to share with you this moment of happiness and joy with the knowledge and hope that the people of the Sudan and you in particular can now get down to the crucial tasks of national reconstruction and development. Accept Dear Brother the renewed assurances of my highest consideration.

J. K. NYERERE
PRESIDENT

It was not Nyerere alone who was overjoyed with Sudan's constitution. All the assembled Sudanese leadership and its coterie were full of joy and self-congratulation on yet another achievement of the May revolution (*cinjaz* is the word). But Nyerere's message was of great significance not only because it came from a prestigious African President; there was another reason too. As early as June 1969 several goodwill missions were sent around Africa and the Arab world to explain the motives and objectives of the new regime. Wherever they went, they were received politely but with differing degrees of enthusiasm. Tanzania was the exception; the reception was cold and almost discourteous. Nyerere is always suspicious of soldiers in politics. He often gives the impression of treating them almost like a lesser breed. But those who were delegated by the May revolution to go to Tanzania were not soldiers, they were professionals, some of them well known in East Africa, e.g. Murtada Ahmed Ibrahim, the Minister of Irrigation. But even the presence of people highly respected in East Africa, like him, was not a good enough saving grace. Nyerere's stand-offish attitude towards Sudan's new regime changed only after the Addis Ababa agreement, for those who resort to peaceful settlement of disputes could hardly be a jackbooted dictatorship. Nyerere, as well as many other African leaders, contributed a lot towards the consolidation of the peace process. The constitution, to him, was yet another step towards democratization. Indeed, all of us viewed the constitution in this light, including the joyful coterie. The experience has sadly proved a moral failure.

The Philosopher King

President Nimeiri, who later emerged as an Islamic Imam, preacher and philosopher, was a different man indeed in the years of promise. He was not only conscious of his modest origins, he had no ideological nor intellectual pretensions and never cared about admitting it. Nimeiri, in those years, did not see himself as a philosopher king or religious sage, rather a political leader responding to the needs and problems of the Sudan with an open mind. He was never ideologically predisposed to any line of action. When the secretary-general of the government, Ahmed Babiker Eisa, spoke of Nimeirism as a philosophy of action, Nimeiri was outraged. In a *Face the Nation* programme on 9 September 1974 he dissociated himself from the allegation, attacked its author and emphasized his lack of commitment to an ideology, his open-mindedness and political pragmatism. He started by referring to the conference at which Eisa spoke of Nimeirism, saying that he had to come out against it lest his silence be interpreted as acquiescence or approval.

Nimeiri was in a fit of outrage, not so uncommon. Lambasting his Minister, the President said:

> I disown any political system ascribed to me. I do not belong to any school of thought. This revolution was a war on ready-made moulds and preconceived solutions; a war on things copied out of books or arrived at by speculation. Sudan is free to go along any path and embark upon any experiment; there are no obligations save the preservation of its independence, self-esteem, heritage and values. I do not profess, or wish anybody to profess on my behalf, a philosophical system which determines Sudanese national politics. Political action in the Sudan is governed by the will of the Sudanese people. I am always keen to reiterate a belief of mine which I shall never forsake; that I am constantly learning from the people and following their intuition. I do not stand in lofty towers professing wisdom and preaching it. I have always got enough courage to admit errors and go back on them. For I know that he who works must pay a price.

Nimeiri went on to point out that he had enlisted the expertise of men of science and letters to help him with his task.

> The leading posts, as you already know, are occupied by a specialized team of scientists, university professors and those who have attained the highest scholastic degrees. . . . Some of them have furthermore had experience in the international scene. . . . Some have gained this experience in the context of their academic work. We have elected to invest their achievements in development at the national level.

That was Nimeiri of 1974, a mortal like us all, learning from others, erring and modest enough to admit his errors, seeking counsel and advice from those who knew, selecting his advisers on the basis of their scholastic and professional attainments and, of all things, dis-owning claims that he was Sudan's philosopher king. Came 1978, a different Nimeiri had emerged: Nimeiri the author on Islam, imparting his teachings to the Sudanese on matters of their religion and beyond these, charting the path for a rejuvenated Islam all over the universe. Only six years later (1984) we see Nimeiri the author transformed into Nimeiri the Imam, making his way to mosque pulpits every Friday and preaching to the faithful on matters of this life and the life hereafter. Religious authors and the Imams are inspired, so the counsel sought is by now discounted.

The Promises of the Economy

In his all-encompassing address to the Cabinet in October 1971 President Nimeiri paid special attention to the state of the economy which was 'suffering from lack of direction, misallocation of resources and not well thought decisions'. He declared that review plans were already under way.

Sudan, the largest country in Africa (2.5 million square kilometres) is endowed with a great potential for agricultural development. Only one tenth of its arable land is under active utilization, the carrying capacity of the land therefore hardly used. The country does not suffer from the population pressures known to other developing countries, with about eight persons per square kilometre (compared to twenty-five in Ethiopia and 560 in Bangladesh, for example). This figure does not reflect the whole reality since it should be viewed in the light of the fact that the majority of Sudanese live on the banks of the Nile, a situation that leads to imbalances of both population distribution and development efforts. One factor that strongly militates against the development of this great potential is the inadequacy of transport and communications. In this respect even the longest natural highway in the country, the Nile, is hardly utilized.

The Sudan has known development planning since independence, but the fractious party politics did not make it possible for any plan to be carried through. General Abboud's regime, free from partisan dissensions, made an impressive initial attempt on development, e.g. railways, irrigation and agricultural expansion, industrialization etc. The dissent-ridden regime of the parties that succeeded Abboud did not take off from where the military regime had stopped, in spite of all the cries for change, modernization and development voiced in October. The priorities of the parties were completely elsewhere, outfoxing the adversaries in order to capture power. What to do with power was immaterial. Nimeiri's government in 1971 had also inherited the disastrous effects of the amateurish confiscations and nationalizations of 1970 that had almost pulled the Sudanese economy from its hinges. Those who carried out the nationalization had no further plans for what lay beyond. Against this background President Nimeiri's government got down to business: pick up the pieces, restructure the economy and set the future goals.

In August 1972 Nimeiri ordered the return of some thirty companies, which had been expropriated in 1970, to their former owners. In the same year a Development and Promotion of Industrial Investment Act, which aimed at encouraging Sudanese and foreign private investment, was passed. A clear indication of the regime's new orientation was the statement made by the National Economy Minister, Ibrahim Mansour, 'Development cannot be shouldered by the state alone; it would mean postponing the prosperity of present generations to give the public sector time to generate capital and train managers.' So while Sudan was committed to a socialist economy led by the public sector (controlling the commanding heights), there was also a significant place for the private and mixed sectors. Sudan was to look increasingly to countries from which the capital flow needed for development would be safeguarded, e.g. industrial countries of the North and the rich Arab states. As a gesture of goodwill at the end of his state visit to Britain (March 1973) Nimeiri agreed to compensate some British companies whose assets had been expropriated in 1970 (the majority of the nationalized companies were British). In a press conference in London he declared that Sudan welcomed foreign private investment and that guarantees for such investment would be provided for under the rubric of Sudanese law (*Financial Times*, 31 March 1973).

A five-year plan was drawn up in 1972. It laid down economic goals and set priorities. The main target was to bring the country to a level of self-sustained growth. This would entail basic changes in socio-economic structure, production relations, full mobilization of human resources, optimal use of financial as well as natural resources with due regard to the protection of the environment. Development priorities were defined as agriculture (the leading sector with which other sectors should be interlinked and interlocked), transportation, industry (as a complement to agriculture, e.g. agriculture-related industry and import substitutes) and the upgrading of social services, particularly health and education. The plan was to achieve some immediate results within a specific time frame, e.g. food self-sufficiency, increasing employment opportunities and increasingly generating a surplus for export to help improve the balance of payments. The plan was adopted by the SSU and on the basis of the plan short-term programmes of action were also formulated and adopted by the SSU.

At the functional level the success of the plan depended on the close co-operation of the Minister of Finance and National Economy (in allocating funds and observing respect of priorities), the technical Ministries, e.g. Industry, Agriculture, Transport and Communication and Irrigation (in planning the different projects and supervising their execution) and the Ministry of Foreign Affairs (in deploying diplomacy for development, i.e. attracting foreign investment and capital flow). One important piece of legislation that stands on its own is Legislative Order 27 of 2 March 1972. That Order provides *inter alia* that no foreign financial commitment shall be undertaken without the prior authorization of the Minister of Finance, both as to content and procedure. The development plan formed an integrated whole, so that any departures from it would start a chain reaction. A delay in the execution or completion of a certain project would upset the finances by increasing the cost of the execution bill and by delaying the date of the start of production, generally the bench-mark for the commencement of repaying debts and interest, i.e. upsetting debt servicing in accordance with amortization schedules. On the other hand, the plan's success depended, at the political level, on popular mobilization, i.e. self-help. To underscore the importance of this aspect self-reliance was enshrined in the constitution as a national policy (article 17). That article states that 'Self-help emanating from the people's free will is an innate characteristic of the Sudanese society and shall be consolidated and co-ordinated by the state.' An unprecedented effort in this connection had been undertaken by the SSU through rural development committees engaged in exploiting rural potential to improve the lot of the rural populace and broaden Sudanese rural economy. Achievements were registered in areas such as school and hospital construction, road maintenance, water supply etc.

With the objectives clearly set, priorities established, human and material resources fairly though not optimally utilized and diplomacy mobilized to help achieve the set goals, the Sudan had every opportunity of going forward. To translate the plan into well articulated and feasible projects several in-depth studies were undertaken, e.g. a master plan for transportation (rail and road), a twenty-five-year plan for agricultural development, sectional plans for industry, a plan for storage and a plan for river transportation. All these plans were financed through technical assistance from Kuwait, the Federal Republic of Germany and other countries. Most important among these plans are the master plans for agricultural development and the one on transportation. The former was the greatest achievement of development-oriented diplomacy, which will be discussed more fully in the chapter on diplomacy. The plan, financed by the Arab Fund for Economic and Social Development (AFESD) envisaged a $6 billion investment in twenty-five years. In its first phase (1976–85) over a hundred projects were envisaged with an estimated investment of $2.3 billion. The project covered agriculture, livestock and agriculture-related industries. The details of the AFESD plan were worked out by a number of Sudanese experts to whom the job was subcontracted by the Fund. The experts were led by Hamza Mirghani (a former Finance Minister) and Kamal Agabawi, who later became Minister of Agriculture under Nimeiri. The failure of this extremely ambitious though realistic plan was entirely due to the disruptive policies pursued by the President, which resulted in dissipating the goodwill towards the Sudan generated in the early 'seventies. These policies, many examples of which we shall later come across, had discouraged even the most enthusiastic among Sudan's friends on the other side of the Red Sea. The failure of the agricultural development plan was destined to have its repercussions on all other plans, agriculture being the lead sector of the economy.

The agricultural master plan apart, the years of promise registered an impressive record of achievement in agriculture. The area under crops increased by three-and-a-half million acres and major agricultural projects, of which some had been on the drawing-board for years (Rahad), were executed. Those projects included the Rahad scheme, which involved three provinces and brought 300,000 acres into cultivation (cotton and ground-nuts) along a fifty-mile-long canal linking the Blue Nile and the Rahad River. The £180 million project was financed by the International Development Agency, the Arab Fund for Economic and Social Development, the Kuwaiti, Saudi, Sudanese and US governments. The scheme included plans to accommodate some 14,000 families and provided employment for 90,000 workers.

Another major scheme of the same period was the Kenana sugar project near Kosti. Alarmed at the cost of imported sugar and attracted by the prospect of increasing its foreign currency reserves, the government authorized the British company Lonrho to undertake a feasibility study. Plans were drawn for the world's largest sugar plantation irrigated by a complex canal system. The scheme included a refinery to yield some 300,000 tons of sugar a year, expanding its capacity to one million tons, enough to satisfy much of the Middle East market.

The Jongeli Canal scheme represented another major project intended to bring together western technology and expertise and Arab money to exploit Sudan's natural wealth. The proposed canal would drain the Sudd creating an initial 200,000 acres in the south and semi-nomadic tribes would be settled on the reclaimed land. An agreement was reached with Egypt on the sharing of the water which would become available because of decreased evaporation. In effect Jongeli was one of the more important factors in the emergence of the new format of co-operation between Egypt and Sudan: economic integration. More will come of that.

In other areas of activities the industrial value added rose from £S67 million to £S143 by 1975. Several industrial projects interlinked with agriculture were either initiated or completed, mainly sugar and textiles. On the other hand, with priorities set and transport projects integrated into the fabric of the general plan, that sector too had seen remarkable accomplishments. The completed roads by the end of the plan years have tripled in length the existing network, as the decade opened with only 330 kilometres of macadamized road in the whole country. Over 300 kilometres of inherited trunk roads were all completed under Abboud with US (AID) assistance: 187 km (Khartoum–Wad Medani), 29 km (Khartoum North–Khoglab), 35 km (Khartoum–Jebel Aulia) and 32 km (Omdurman–Wadi Seidna). A much more ambitious network was envisaged in the master plan and a few sections were initiated. The road network included the completion of the Medani–Sannar–Kosti road and the Port Sudan–Khartoum road to pass through Kassala. In addition work was initiated, according to the master plan, in the West, White Nile, Blue Nile and the Southern Gelabat on the Ethiopian–Sudanese borders. A joint technical committee representing both countries had gone a long way in this regard in co-operation with the ECA. The Sudan railways also received a lot of attention, effort and money. The Sudan railway, one of the oldest in Africa (1905), was the only effective transport network linking the different parts of the country, nearly 6,000 kilometres of railroad. The railway system had increasingly deteriorated in the late 'sixties and after, for a host of reasons: outmoded methods of operation, lack of maintenance, ill-defined worker–management relations etc. The only extensions that had been introduced in the system since independence were carried out in the Abboud era, including the first railway linkage between the North and the South, i.e. Babanoosa–Nyala (Western Sudan) in 1959, Sennar–Damazin (Blue Nile) in 1958, Babanoosa–Wau (South West) in 1962 and Girba–New Halfa (Eastern Sudan) 1962.

The five-year plan, however, was more concerned with the consolidation of the railway system and improving its operational efficiency than extending it, stepping up utilization of existing rolling-stock to carry a larger volume of freight and a greater number of passengers. The plan targets were nearly met in passenger transportation (94 per cent) but not in the freight aspect. The failure in this connection was compounded by the fact that the construction of the Port Sudan–Khartoum 810-kilometre pipeline financed by Kuwait relieved 30 per cent of the railway capacity, making it available for the transportation of non-petroleum commodities.

This period also witnessed a complete revolution in the field of telecommunications. A microwave network was established to link the different parts of the extensive Sudan, with a view to integrating it with the African telecommunication system. The network within the Sudan extended from Khartoum to Sannar via Madani, to continue at a later stage (after 1975) to Kassala. Another one stretched from Khartoum to Port Sudan via Atbara, to be extended to Halfa and eventually to be linked to Aswan-Cairo. A third network was to go out from Khartoum to the Southern Sudan thus linking the Arab and African worlds. In addition a satellite station was completed in 1974, linking Sudan with the outside world, and other satellite stations were constructed in all the main cities of the Sudan, helping to improve both telephone communications and TV transmission.

In order to finance this ambitious development plan, the May regime had up to 1975 borrowed nearly $300 million, 42 per cent of which came from Arab countries. The rest came from the World Bank group, western and eastern European countries, and the African Development Bank. The short-term borrowing in this period, however, amounted to $75 million, the bulk of which came from the Kuwait Foreign Trading and Investment Company, the Bank of America and UBAF (Arab French Banking Union). According to the UN General Assembly statistics the net disbursement of concessionary financing to the Sudan has gone up from $25.9 million in 1970 to $298.9 million in 1975. It is remarkable that in this period support from the socialist countries (other than China) was on the increase in spite of the events of July 1971. Sudan was out looking for development partners irrespective of creed as long as there were no strings attached to their aid. It is also remarkable that Arab concessional aid, that was on the rise up to 1976, dwindled sharply thereafter. Chapter 4 may give one clue to the reasons for this decline.

Table 2.1 *Concessional Assistance (OAD) to Sudan Net Disbursement in millions of $ US*

	1973	1974	1975	1976	1977	1978
Western Europe	42.6	54.4	110.3	115.6	109.2	224.2
OPEC (Arab)	3.3	80.0	188.2	253.2	111.3	71.7
Socialist countries (East Europe)	8.8	10.9	−2.0	−6.2	−6.1	−3.3
China	7.6	9.2	3.4	2.8	2.7	—

The projects referred to above, while not wholly successful, represented a great step forward (there were few misbegotten endeavours). They would, however, have been more successful had it not been for the President's disruptive interventions with which we shall deal in chapter 4, and his engagement in meretricious projects. In effect, no major economic accomplishment has been recorded by the regime since the mid or late 'seventies. Nimeiri is still living on past achievements and is self-congratulatory about feats of which he, as we shall illustrate, has contributed more than anybody else to frustration and eventual destruction. Unable to relate cause and effect, or unwilling to admit error and change course, he looked for salvation elsewhere. This is one reason why the Nimeiri of 1984 has increasingly engaged in sermons exhorting people to forget earthly pursuits and strive for a place in heaven, the final abode of the righteous. But even then Nimeiri will not let go; he will be the one to shepherd the Sudanese into the heavenly paradise, for the earthly paradise is not worth the trouble after all.

Sudan's attempt at rapid development and industrialization was fraught with difficulties, the very same human and non-human problems which faced the countries which started out on the road of development before us and after us. Attempts at change from above present one not only with a most difficult problem of macro-economics but with a host of political, geographical and sociological problems. We made no claim that we had managed to solve these problems; it is doubtful whether they will be ever solved completely. The terrain remains as treacherous as ever and one has no accurate maps and charts to go by.

All very nice

In conclusion while one should avoid having an inflated view of accomplishments in the years of promise, the inescapable fact remains that whatever achievements Nimeiri's regime was able to vaunt were mainly his successes in the years of promise. What Sudan witnesses today is nothing but a breach of a promise and an extinction of hope. 1971–75 were the years of relative achievement and motivation. They were also years of many a promise; promises of better things to come. The political mobilization, the economic realizations, the image of seriousness of both the leader and his government, all enhanced the regime's prestige and augmented the base of its support, both within and outside the Sudan. We, then, had every reason to be euphoric and exhilarated; a dream had come true. Maybe we were too involved in our musings and ruminations about futures, to have time for self-doubt. Failure – 'the possibility does not exist'. None of us, unfortunately, had the intuitive self-doubt of Napoleon's mother who was reported to have said on the coronation of her son, 'It is all very nice, if it lasts.'

Chapter Three

Sorcerer, Apprentice and the Ayatollahs of Socialism: the Genesis of Authoritarianism

He who makes another powerful ruins himself, for he makes the other so either by shrewdness or force, and both of these qualities are feared by the one who became powerful.

Machiavelli, *The Prince*
(trs. Bergen Evans)

Doers, Cheer-leaders and Equerries

Apart from the members of the RCC President Nimeiri, in the early 'seventies, was surrounded by three groups. There were the technocrats, politicized and apolitical, who had been chosen for their academic and technical skills. They were engaged in the execution of policies, sometimes devising policies in their respective departments. They were a multicoloured group, for President Nimeiri had cast his net wide to engage Sudanese talent of all political hues to participate in the building of their country. They were all grateful to him for that. To them it was a dream come true after years of frustration over party bickerings between October 1964 and May 1969. Because of the nature of their work and their ability to deliver the goods this group assumed a commanding role inside the state machinery. They were held in high esteem both internally and externally, being, so to speak, the jewels in Nimeiri's crown. Their achievements are abiding: the solution of the Southern Sudan problem, major irrigation and agricultural projects (Rahad, Kenana, Jongeli etc.) which gave credence to Sudan's claim of being the bread-basket of the Arab world, an unprecedented road and telecommunication network, a far-reaching government decentralization based on popular mobilization, reform and re-organization of public service, law reform and codification involving Sudanese and expatriate talents, industrial expansion far beyond what was achieved under Abboud, who ushered Sudan into industrialization, and a calculated exploitation of all these achievements to win respectability and sympathy abroad.

The second group, though not all of them possessed the professional credentials of the first, comprised some able, high-minded and dedicated men engaged in political mobilization within the SSU. They have laboured hard to give the political organization a measure of credibility, building on the political and functional successes of the regime. The whole system was based on the complementarity of managerial politics and political sensitization and mobilization. Nimeiri was indeed sculpted by these two groups from the very ordinary clay he was. In addition to those competent politicos, within the second group there was also a host of cheer-leaders occupied in emotive rhetoric, delivering nothing and claiming more than their entitlement in the system. Slogans are one thing; action is another. They too were still political animals though, however naively set to change the world, through shibboleths and battle cries.

The third group, the palace equerries and place-men, were neither here nor there. They were in the business neither of delivering the goods nor of political mobilization; rather they used their special position inside the palace to promote their personal interests. In the process, they saw to it that the President's kith and kin were engulfed with them; the typical blackmailers' approach. Their stock in trade was their access to the President. They would work through no institutions and indeed persuaded the President that institutions were only power centres bent on subverting his authority. President Nimeiri needed no persuasion because he is viscerally anti-institution. This group was led by Dr Idris, Beeby, Mr 007, the last appellation earned because of his unrelenting effort in discovering plots against the President, all figments of his rich imagination. In latter days he established, with South Korean help, an intricate communication network with audio-visual devices to monitor the President's office. Remember Watergate and Nixon's wire tapping? Dr Idris was a Lecturer in zoology in the University of Khartoum. He was made to resign in the mid-'sixties for conduct unbecoming his profession, divulging the zoology examination papers to a girl student who was reported to have become his second wife more than a decade later: a true 'lover's progress' to 'the true end of love' in the best tradition of John Donne. Dr Idris' university episode was investigated by a disciplinary board comprising the Dean of Agriculture, Professor Amin Karib, the Dean of Law, Professor Mohammed Ibrahim Khalil, and the University Registrar, A. M. Gubara. The board recommended to the Dean of Science that, in view of the nature of the charge, Dr Idris should be advised to resign his university post. After a short period in the lurch Idris was picked up by Dr Samani Yacoub, secretary-general of the National Council of Scientific Research, as his assistant for administration. The Council was chaired by the President who had then shown an interest in the work of the Council. A rapport was soon established between Nimeiri and Idris; the President was attracted by the doctor's servile demeanour. However, in spite of the badge of infamy Nimeiri was not deterred from appointing him as Minister for 'Special Affairs' – the dubious title itself was very telling. Dr Idris, because of special talents, survived all ministerial reshuffles despite the strong opposition to him from different quarters including the Army.

As early as October 1972, prior to President Nimeiri's major Cabinet reshuffle following his inauguration, Omar el Hag Musa, Minister of Information and Culture and I went to the President to tell him that the nomination of Idris shamed the Cabinet. We dwelt on the odious university incident. Nimeiri played possum as he always did when he was not interested in the subject. We insisted and Nimeiri retorted:

'Why should you be bothered by the man? I need him as an errand boy.'

Omar, a soldier talking to a soldier, answered: 'Mr President, what you need is a staff officer. Why don't you consider somebody from the Army?'

There was no nod or wink. Omar looked at me and muttered: 'The President must have seen in Idris what we couldn't see.' Taking me by the arm, Omar bade farewell to the President and said: 'It is late and I have a bridge to cross,' for Omar lived on the other side of the Nile.

'Indeed, from now on we all have a very long bridge to cross,' I said to myself with a sense of foreboding.

The university incident was haunting Dr Idris. He wanted it erased, so on the appointment of Ahmed Suleiman as Minister of Justice he raised the matter with him, hoping that the affable Ahmed would be amenable to his request. Idris could not have raised it with the former Minister of Justice, Vice-President Babiker Awad Allah for Babiker was allergic to Idris. Ahmed found no trace of the record of the case in his Ministry. He was ill-advised to look there in the first place. The action was a disciplinary one taken by the University. He called the Vice-Chancellor, Professor Mustafa Hassan Ishag, who was inflamed with wrath. Mustafa called on me as a friend at the Foreign Ministry. I have always had a lot of respect for the man's intellectual honesty, humility and moral courage. Mustafa blew his top and declared: 'Over my dead body. I shall make a hundred copies of the investigation report, just in case somebody wants to destroy the record of this infamy.' He then cooled down and mused: 'Perhaps we should have kept him in the University. Only the pittance we spend on fish and toads for the Zoology Department would have then been at stake. Now, it is the country's exchequer that is in jeopardy.' And how right he was.

Be that as it may, these three groups around the President were strange bedfellows: the doers in both the political and executive branches; the gallery of cheer-leaders aspiring to office; and the presidential shop-lifters. There was a lot of jealousy and misconceptions among these groups. Those in the executive branch, by the nature of their work and achievements, were the centre of much publicity at home and abroad. The President identified with them, or, rather, with their accomplishments. The others were involved in less glamorous work in the SSU. Cabinet offices are not without flourishes in a country like the Sudan where officialdom is the be-all and end-all. On the other hand some of the SSU politicos viewed the supremacy of the party as a licence for intervention in the daily management of government, a matter resisted by those in the executive branch, many of whom were also members of the higher ranks of the SSU. As to the third group, conflicts were apt to erupt between them and the institutionalists of the executive, the law-makers and the law-breakers.

Sudan's Watergate: a Farce

The first major confrontation between the group of the institutionalists and the palace shop-lifters came in the second half of January

1975. The target was the Finance Minister, Mr Ibrahim Moneim Mansour, who had been unrelenting in his denunciation of their activities. Mansour never knuckled under in spite of all the cajoling and intimidation. The assault on him followed his granting of a licence, with the knowledge and assent of the President, to a joint-stock company to undertake the import and export of government and other supplies. The story of this company (Nile Valley Overseas Ltd) dates back to 1970, following the nationalization of all foreign companies involved in import-export. At that time a leading Sudanese businessman, Mohammed el Hassan Abdalla Yassin, applied for the registration of a Sudanese private company to undertake this type of business. The company was to be based in London. The matter was processed by the technical department and approved in principle by the then Minister of Foreign Trade. The Bank of Sudan authorized in 1971 the transfer of £5,000 to London to help meet the expenses of registration there.

By 1972 when Mansour assumed overall responsibility for finance and trade the matter was again brought to his attention for final incorporation. He advised Yassin, the main promoter, to go public and include the government in the operation. Yassin agreed and the company was restructured to include seven leading Sudanese entrepreneurs owning 60 per cent of the shares, with 40 per cent left for the government. Nobody cared to look into the facts or trace the background; it was the Minister's head they were after. To ensure that the attack on the Minister was clad in ideological garb the palace valets sought to enlist the support of the ideologues and cheer-leaders of the SSU. The link between the cabal and the ideologues was Faisal Abdel Rahman, who was at the time Minister of State in the palace.

But all this was a pretext, and pretexts are not motives. The motive of some of the SSU politicos was misguided ideological intransigence, of others jealousy, but that of the palace cabal was to remove the vigilantes who were checking their rapacious exploits. Mansour prepared a lengthy memorandum to the President explaining the genesis of the overblown story. Rahman intercepted the memorandum and routed it to the SSU for 'ideological vetting'. Ministerial memoranda to the President were always analysed and summarized by the Cabinet Office, not the SSU. By a strange coincidence, the dossier of the company disappeared mysteriously the same day from Mansour's Ministry to land in the SSU. The plotters wanted to disarm the Minister of all evidence he needed to explain the facts and exonerate himself. By now the plot hatched in the palace was complete. The SSU was brought into it as a fellow-traveller in sin. By then the SSU was no longer a political organization where differences of opinion were tolerated and conflicts composed through debate; it had now been turned into a fractious coalition of factions plotting against each other, an animal farm where rat eats rat.

The ideologues were the first to give the conflict an ideological dressing, accusing the Minister of departing from and violating the principles of the May revolution. They had various slogans at their disposal; in the words of the trade: deviation, revisionism and betrayal. The Minister's 'unrevolutionary' conduct, they claimed, was exemplified in granting an import monopoly to a certain company (Nile Valley Overseas Ltd) on 5 December 1974. Terms like revolution and socialism are very fuzzy in the absence of a clearly defined ideology. They are also very comfortable tools for both mystification and denigration. If monopoly was what they were against, it was the height of demagogy to treat the issue as one of socialist ideology and betrayal of the SSU's socialist faith. Even in America monopolies are closely scrutinized and guarded against by anti-trust laws. On the other hand, if monopoly there was, it may have been a serious infringement of free trade and equal opportunities. The Minister, however, was not allowed to put his case forward.

So the SSU, only three years after its creation as a unifying political engine, became not only organizationally fissiparous; it had also become, insofar as ideology was concerned, a system of colliding antitheses. The thesis was obscure, the synthesis wanting. Mansour was never invited by the competent sections of the SSU to explain his thesis. Instead the matter was hastily sent to the National Assembly with the backwoodsmen mobilized and the cheerleaders lined up to malign, discredit and eventually slay the Minister. The National Assembly became a battleground, with all the odds stacked against the Minister of Finance. Opening the debate the Controller of the Assembly, Badr el Din Suleiman, charged that the company had been granted a monopoly over all exports and imports, in the public as well as the private sector. The Controller within the SSU scheme of things is the counterpart of the leader of the Assembly, the nearest thing to the leader of the opposition in a multi-party system; his role is to focus and articulate the other point of view, i.e. the views of those taking exception to government policy. What was serious about this act, the Controller added, was that it had placed the whole of the public sector at the mercy of seven people (the private persons who held 60 per cent of the shares of the company). In his opinion this was a departure from socialist principles and those of equal opportunity and free competition. An imaginative member compared the episode to Watergate. They all asked for the dismissal of the Minister.

When Mansour was called upon to speak he was terse and in fine fettle for a fight. In giving the background to his decision he noted that it was approved by previous Ministers as early as 1971 and by the President himself in 1973. He was immediately admonished on a point of order by the Controller, and in a ruling by the Speaker, and asked not to mention the name of the President in this affair. Mansour, in fact, was not trying to shovel responsibility onto others, since he declared that he should be held totally responsible for the decision, asking members of the Assembly to cease referring to the Minister of State and the Under-Secretary of his Ministry. The Minister went on to say that the company had been registered according to the laws of the land, which did not stipulate that the government should be a major shareholder in such joint enterprises. The company, he explained, did no harm to the public sector; on the contrary, it opened up new markets for it. There was neither monopoly nor curtailment of equal opportunities, he added. He demanded that, in view of the seriousness of the charge, he should be put on trial and that the matter be brought before the special courts which were instituted by the revolution for this purpose. The basic rules of the SSU provide for the disciplinary procedure to be followed when a member violates the principles or policies of the organization. Mansour continued, to no avail, demanding that he be put on trial several months after his removal.

The whole debate was rehearsed and orchestrated. It was the parting shot in the SSU civil war. The Assembly passed a motion calling for the withdrawal of the monopoly granted by the Minister of Finance. The Leader of the House, Ahmed Abdel Halim, made it clear that the Assembly should not interfere in the affairs of the executive; it was only to make recommendations to the President. In his capacity as Leader he was there to explain and defend government action. He chose to abstain. He neither called for a Cabinet meeting to reassure himself of the legitimacy of Mansour's decision, which was approved by the President and several Ministers before him, nor requested that the matter be investigated by the competent authorities of the SSU to ensure the nature of the deviation from 'socialist' ethics, before overexposing it in Parliament.

The Speaker, too, made a big show of the occasion. Addressing the Assembly he quoted President Nimeiri: 'I want this Assembly to exercise courageously and responsibly its authority, inspired by the spirit of the revolution and the will of the people.' He then turned to the Minister and said: 'The Minister . . . and our brothers in the executive branch must well understand the meaning of those guidelines. They must well understand that, when institutions question them and bring them to account, it does so fully aware of its role in monitoring and reprimanding as well as in building a new society.' The words were noble, inveighing against corruption and asserting that nobody is above the law, a refrain in all Nimeiri's speeches. Our institutions were not meant to be paper tigers, so we were told. The future alone would tell!

The whole spectacle was palpably surreal, a strange marriage of convenience under the guise of socialist purity. There was the palace cabal led by Dr Idris, who does not mind his p's and q's in politics, let alone raise the banner of socialism. There were the ego-ridden cheer-leaders paying lip service to revolutionary socialist causes and chanting, like a Greek chorus, praise for achievements they have contributed precious little to. And there were the odd-men-out in this coalition of convenience; the ideologues led by Badr el Din Suleiman, who were blinded by ideological intransigence. Badr el Din, otherwise an able man of integrity, was a reborn realist, when he took over the Ministry of Finance some years later. Not only did he desocialize many institutions but he also conducted the biggest economic liberalization policy since May 1970.

He was justified in a fair number of those decisions. Ministers of Finance always know better in office. Pragmatism is the name of the game, they would say, on facing the stark realities.

The Saturday of the Long Knives

President Nimeiri was rubbing his hands in glee, watching this spectacle. He enjoys nothing more than playing one against the other, friend and foe alike. In the process the country went to pieces. He liked Mansour and was appreciative of his abilities (Mansour was rehabilitated six years later, ironically to replace Badr el Din as Minister of Finance). But by 25 January 1975 President Nimeiri's relationship with his Minister was soured. On that date Mansour tendered his resignation, just a few days after the debate in the Assembly. In spite of the urgings of the First Vice-President, General Baghir, Mansour was adamant. Baghir was adept in calming people and healing wounds. Nimeiri, on the other hand, fuelled conflict, looked for cracks and devised means to widen them. Mansour claimed in his letter of resignation that there was a conspiracy against him and that President Nimeiri was aware of it, implying his connivance. Mansour is not only a man of talent, he also has unflinching courage. His letter of resignation was bold and iconoclastic. It read:

Mr President of the Republic
Greetings and respects,

Intrigues have reached, in my opinion, a state which threatens the safety of the Sudan and what has taken place is not the first of its kind . . . and will not be the last.

Your Excellency is fully aware of what has happened and what is taking place as well as of those who perpetrate such acts. I was brought into government to participate in a lofty task. Instead of attending to the responsibility vested in me now I find myself involved in repelling conspiracies. The choice before me now is either to be engulfed with the conspiratorial cliques or to distance myself, looking for a job through which I might render service to my people.

I have opted for the latter.

That is why I am tendering my resignation from the office of Minister of Finance and National Economy from 26 January 1975.

My remaining in service from 2 o'clock of 22 January 1975 until today 25 January 1975 was meant to give you the opportunity – as you have always asked me to – to take appropriate measures. The day the country starts to reap the fruits of what I have planted – a process which has, in fact already started – will be the day of my happiness.

I bid you farewell and assure you that:
I have not broken the oath I swore to serve this country.
I have not entered into conspiracies.

May I also ask you to keep whatever men you have . . . for they are few.

May God take the country, yourself and myself into his protecting hands. For there has never been a period – since your assumption of the leadership – more serious than the period we are in now where people conspire against each other from 'within'

The Faithful
Ibrahim Moneim Mansour
25 January 1975

The President could not countenance such an accusation nor accept such 'defiance'. He had always said, 'I do not permit any of my ministers to resign.' He was the one who made and broke appointments. So President Nimeiri decided, typically, to play the game of the palace cabal. The SSU, we said, was only a fellow-traveller in sin. From that day Nimeiri's Sudan was never the same again.

The palace cabal, encouraged by their success against Mansour, or rather against probity in public affairs, because that was what the feuds were about, as we shall see in the next chapter, now turned to the others who supported institutionalism and public probity. Among this group was the Minister of Industry, Belal, and myself. Zaki Mustafa, the Attorney-General, was saved because he was preparing the way for resigning in May 1975. He too did not endear himself to the palace cabal by his constant references to legality. Yahia Abdel Magid, the very competent Minister of Irrigation, was paving the way for an exit to the United Nations. He had not much time for the political oddities of the palace. In the meantime the palace cabal was impressing on the President that the trio – of Finance, Industry and Foreign Affairs – was part of a power centre. 'Power centre' is an expression borrowed from President Sadat. He used it to describe Nasserite strongholds, within the government and the party, who posed a challenge to his authority. To President Nimeiri it had a different connotation. Power centres were those aides who reminded him, often unobtrusively, of his constitutional limitations or drew his attention to the need for rational and well-considered judgment in government action. This should apply more to governments claiming to be standard-bearers of 'revolutionary purity'. None of these Ministers shouted their criticism of presidential action from roof tops. But none of them could keep silent either, lest the law of unintended consequences might apply. The President thought otherwise. He often referred to the urgings of these Ministers as attempts to usurp or share his authority.

Against this background came the fateful Saturday of the long knives (26 January 1975). The President decided to make a clean sweep. Everybody who was thought to have agreed with, or nodded approval to, the actions of this trio was now ready for Nimeiri's political abattoir. So out went Omar el Hag Musa from Information, Gaafer Bakheit from Local Government, Wadie Habashi from Agriculture, Sir el Khatim Khalifa from Education etc. Omar was not only Nimeiri's saviour in many attempted coups, as we have described earlier, he was almost his father confessor after 'May'. Nimeiri offered him the Embassy in Bonn and Omar refused. 'I would rather go to Shambat [where his home was]. I have children to raise.' Nimeiri decided to shift him to the SSU as assistant secretary-general. Bakheit, the founding father of the people's local government institutions, was removed with his agenda half completed. Bakheit was not only the founding father of the people's local government, he was its mainframe computer; you pushed a button and all the facts and figures oozed out. He too went to the SSU. That was, indeed, a masterpiece of surrealism out of Buñuel. The power centre accused of the betrayal of socialism was now ensconced in the citadel of socialism, the SSU. From then onwards the SSU was run and managed by Omar and was intellectually fed on Bakheit's diet. When he died a few years later the system suffered intellectual anaemia.

The Ministry of Finance, on the other hand, rather than being entrusted to the socialist 'radicals' went to Mamoun Beheiry, an economist with recognized credentials, both inside and outside the Sudan, but hardly a firebrand socialist. Pretexts are not motives, as we said before. And these are the ways of Nimeiri.

I went to Education, replacing Sir el Khatim, and Habashi went to the National Council of Scientific Research. Musa, the Minister of Industry, like Mansour was completely out. He was the *bête noire* of the palace group. He knew his department well, was quite at home with details and very lucid. His adamantine position not to go along with shady deals sponsored by the palace brought him the wrath of the President. He refused to budge, no 'coward soul' was his in Sudan's 'storm-troubled sphere'. A few Ministers who identified with this group, like Abdel Rahman Abdalla, Minister of

Public Service, were left out because they did not pose a direct threat to the interests of the palace middlemen; their departments did not issue licences or approve deals. The outgoing Ministers who had set their shoulders to the wheel for four eventful years were now paying the price of their success and hard labour to inspire an unworthy master.

Nimeiri decided to bid farewell to the parting Ministers in his own style. It was not only Mansour who deserved a scurrilous Presidential send-off; he had had more than his share in the People's Assembly. It was, indeed, a requiem for all those who made life impossible for the palace cabal and deserved the sack, demotion or banishment to the SSU, the Siberia of Sudanese politics. Nobody believed in Nimeiri's eulogies of the SSU. His future actions proved the doubts correct. The requiem was a lengthy speech, full of innuendo. The President (or rather the speech-writer) almost accused the parting Ministers of inefficiency. Nimeiri's reproaches of his Ministers degenerated into repudiation of the achievements of his own regime. He described development projects as fictitious, Ministers as intellectuals living in ivory towers, and claimed that whatever achievement there was, was the work of the SSU. From then on notice was served that the SSU was the be-all and end-all, a matter that nobody had challenged before; nor did Nimeiri mean it seriously.

The Requiem

Like most autocrats Nimeiri is only restrained in his dealings with others by an innate insecurity and a half-appreciation of his weaknesses and deficiencies. With the moral support that the palace cabal and his new friends were giving him and the confidence they instilled in him, he was emboldened to come out and speak his mind. The monumental new friends we shall meet again in the next chapter.

Hitherto Nimeiri had been inhibited in his dealings with his Ministers. He never verbally abused them; if anything, he was too shy to criticize them. Nimeiri always gave his Ministers reasons for their dismissal, or, as was more often the case, for their reappointment. He used to call ministerial reshuffles the interchanging of positions of the revolutionaries. His speeches during this period were free of invective, being written by serious and responsible members of his government. Omar el Hag Musa monitored his *Face the Nation* programme, removing all that did not befit a head of state. The rest of his speeches were written by Ahmed Abdel Halim, Gaafer Bakheit, Badr el Din Suleiman, Abu Bakr Osman, Mahdi Mustafa and myself. Department speeches addressed to political meetings were written by the various Departments and came under the scrutiny of one or the other of the above.

Enter onto the scene Mohammed Mahgoub, born and raised in Egypt. He was brought in by Dr Idris to help him in preparing briefs for the President. He ended by being entrusted with the composition of Nimeiri's speeches and, later, books. The speeches aimed to demonstrate Nimeiri's independence of his Ministers by heaping abuse and insults on them. Mahgoub, who had started as a prison officer before joining the Guidance Division in the armed forces, and then became editor of the armed forces newspaper, was spotted by Dr Bahaa for his 'special' talents. Mahgoub, were it not for his position as Nimeiri's new inspirer, would have been too trivial to be penned down. Within the Sudanese political landscape, increasingly inhabited by weird creatures, Mahgoub is the nearest thing to the nasties of the underworld of Cicero, Illinois in the bad old days. No other person than this duo (Idris and Mahgoub) have brought the whole system into more disrepute. In the beginning the zoologist was the sorcerer, the prison officer the apprentice. A few years later the monsters destroyed the Frankenstein that had created them.

Mahgoub's first major work was Nimeiri's address to the Council of Ministers on 28 January, the requiem. In this speech he told the newly constituted Council of how he had been 'monitoring' and 'observing' the activities of certain Ministers for a long time, as if it was the role of presidents to observe, not to rule. The terms 'monitor' and 'observe' became increasingly used either as a pretext or sometimes an alibi to absolve the President from responsibility when things went wrong. Nimeiri went on to say that he had overlooked certain incidents, hoping that these Ministers would go back on their error. 'However, certain Ministers in the previous Council have missed all these opportunities.' He claimed that his main concerns during this period were development and unity. Nimeiri did not pause to say by whom and through what media national unity and development were achieved.

'I decided,' Nimeiri continued, 'to wait until they hit bottom.'

This patience was interpreted by some as ignorance of what was going on. 'I was well aware,' he continued, 'of what was taking place and its repercussions inside and outside the country. I watched the attempts of some Ministers to create isolated empires, claiming sovereignty over the ministries. I watched how they claimed that they were power centres and the source of power and the decision-makers in our country.' The next chapter will throw some light on the distorting prism through which the President was watching. The watchful President would not relent. 'I watched how they were only nominal members of the SSU, at a time when it was the only political organ in the country.' The disgraced Ministers were all members of the highest ranks of the SSU. Some of them composed its literature, laid down its rules, and mapped out its programmes of action. Others were the planners and executors of whatever achievements there were and which the watchful President not only vaunted then but continues to vaunt today.

Then came the telling remarks; the motive for all the venomous attack.

'I watched how they were issuing directives contrary to those of the President, and how they attempted to delay the execution of his directives. I followed the attempts of some to abort the initiatives of the President, especially in the field of development. They had their ways and means of doing this, such as deliberate procrastination in preparing studies on the various projects. This meant that on more than one occasion the project was executed at a higher cost because of the mad rate at which international prices rose.'

In fact, that was the only statement in Nimeiri's speech that was in register with reality. What he did not say was what the Nimeiri Ministers were 'disobeying' was not His Excellency the President of Sudan, rather the salesman of a big conglomerate labouring hard to mortgage the country. Nimeiri then turned, using innuendo, to his *bête noire*, the Minister of Industry.

'What is strange in the case of these is that they had been at all times in the front row when the foundation stones were laid for all these projects.' That was an unjustifiably cutting indictment of his Minister of Industry. President Nimeiri in all his addresses does not name persons, he only accuses. The parting Minister of Industry was the one under whose superintendence all the major industry projects, with all their failings, were either executed or launched. Up to the last May anniversary (1984) Nimeiri had no industrial achievements to flaunt other than those projects. Even in the fields of mining and petroleum exploration which became the highlights of Nimeiri's speeches the Minister's imprint is there. Oil exploration is a result neither of flukes of geography nor accidents of geology, rather a serious review and plan for the exploration and exploitation of the country's mineral wealth. Musa Belal, taking over from Musa el Mubarak, was very much at the helm. For as early as 1971 there was a growing suspicion among Sudanese that claims by oil companies of the lack of interesting sedimentary areas in Sudan, except in the Red Sea strip, did not reflect the whole truth. There was also an increasing realization that the Petroleum Resources Development Act of 1958 and the Petroleum Resources Development Regulations made under the Act were not sufficiently encouraging for investors. The Act and Regulations provided for 50–70 per cent share profits for the government. Only a few companies showed interest in investing under those Regulations, e.g. Agip a subsidiary of ENI Continental Oil Co., Shell and BP, the latter receiving a five-month permit in September 1959. Steps to review the Act were undertaken in 1972 and 1973. The modified Regulations encouraged a number of companies. The 1973 oil crisis provided an added impetus to oil explorers. As a result concessions were signed in February 1974 with Ball and Collins (Oil and Gas Limited) covering a total area of 13,600 sq. km. on-shore and offshore in the Red Sea, Pacific International covering 2,400 sq. km., Oceanic Exploration covering 14,400 sq. km. Chevron Oil Company (Sudan) a subsidiary of Standard Oil of California (SOCAL) was granted 39 licences covering 28,301 sq. km. of the Red Sea in October 1974 with an additional 516,000 sq. km. in the South Central part of Sudan in November 1974.

Turning his eyes to his Foreign Minister, Nimeiri went on to read:

'I watched how their duties which involved journeying abroad increased. Some of these did not require such trips; the exchange of letters and memoranda would have sufficed. Then there were the various consecutive conferences which for some members of the previous Council were more of the nature of holiday rather than business trips. For the reports emerging from these revealed that they were conferences on the level of Ambassadors and not Ministers.'

The said Foreign Minister, of all Nimeiri's Ministers, was the most on record with daily, monthly and annual reports, the latter published by Khartoum University Press and available in bookstores in Khartoum. All these reports reflected activities both inside and outside the Sudan; the President did not have to look far for evidence. Many of the Foreign Minister's travels abroad were with the President himself, excepting the presidential escapades, of which we shall see a lot in the following chapter. But those who seek to sully a reputation do not bother with ascertaining facts; indeed, they shun facts.

The speech, like all accusatory utterances by Nimeiri, was a monologue, not followed by a debate or discussion. Nimeiri is averse to confrontation. However, after this spurt of aggression the President sought to make amends by arguing that the reshuffle was in the nature of a policy reorganization and not a settlement of old scores.

All ... Licking the Dust

Nimeiri, having finished his speech, ordered it not to be broadcast as if he was reading it for the first time. Five minutes later the order was changed. Two Ministers went to the President to tell him that his was an epoch-making speech, his greatest ever. Wadie Habashi, the elderly Minister of Agriculture and a fiercely proud and upright man was almost in tears. He thought it a bit tedious to be the subject of a lecture by somebody who could have been his son and to be commanded by a man who knew next to nothing of what we were all doing. The week after, Nimeiri's speech was adopted by the People's Assembly as a historic document, and historic it was. For in the whole of Nimeiri's reign 26 January 1974 was not only an entry in the chronology. It was a climactic date.

Nimeiri continued to be haunted by his speech and kept coming back to it time and again. One of these occasions was his monthly *Face the Nation* programme of 10 February 1975. He admitted that there were many eyebrows raised because of the reshuffle, observing that many questions had been raised about it, the reasons behind it and whether it was connected with the Nile Valley Company affair and the criticisms he had made of certain Ministers. He started by claiming that the recent government changes were not mere reshuffles but constituted a reorganization of government along new lines. He claimed, furthermore, that he had been working on this new system for some time. He went on to deny any connection between the Nile Valley Company affair and the changes. The decision of the Assembly to remove the concessions granted to the company, he alleged, only accelerated the process of reorganization, for it was not possible 'to delay the dismissal of someone (Mansour) from the Cabinet pending the change in a few weeks; as it was impossible to dismiss a few and retain others for a short period.' As to the question whether the 'reshuffle was made in support of the role of the SSU and whether this served to emphasize its position as a power above all powers', Nimeiri said, 'It is sufficient to say that this [SSU's supremacy] is an incontestable fact; furthermore, this has been our position throughout.' The 'incontestable fact' was still much in doubt by August 1979 when Nimeiri humiliated the SSU; and in January 1982 he massacred it.

When Gaafer Bakheit died a few months later Nimeiri came back again to the events of January 1974, possibly through a feeling of guilt. He said in his *Face the Nation* programme (April 1976) that he was well aware of Bakheit's ill-health and that was the reason he removed him from the Ministry of Local Government. Nothing was farther from the truth, for the assiduous Bakheit was encumbered with the leadership of the National Assembly, the chief editorship of *al Sahafa* and the assistant secretaryship of the SSU. Bakheit, in fact, died writing his daily article; a very heroic death for a cerebral giant.

The only beneficiaries of the SSU's attack on the institutionalists were the palace cabal. The defenders of the faith rather than finding cause with the institutionalists fighting corruption had, unwittingly, entrenched corruption and corruptors. They were party to the demise of the institutions that could have checked Nimeiri and curbed the influence of Dr Idris and company. The banner under which the ayatollahs of socialism waged their war against the executive was 'the supremacy of the party' (*Hakimiyyat al Tanzim*). The untranslatable Arabic is not as forthright as the English might suggest. Parliament, on the other hand, by lauding the President's rudeness in dealing with his Ministers, whom he had treated with deference till then, had encouraged an unwholesome trend. In the course of the years, Nimeiri has overreached himself, becoming ruder and more proud of it. In the end all were licking the dust, not excepting the SSU and Parliament. The turn of each of those institutions came when they had become an encumbrance on the President. They were all destroyed equally unceremoniously.

The drollness of the reshuffle was that Bakheit, who was dismissed for 'ideological' reasons, went on to assume responsibility for ideology in the SSU. So it fell to the discredited Bakheit to tutor people on the supremacy of the SSU. Dr Bakheit produced the main working paper for the SSU Central Committee (March 1975) explaining the concept of *Hakimiyyat al Tanzim*, arguing that the SSU did not govern or rule but planned and supervised the executive on implementation of policy. That concept, which was a far cry from Nimeiri's speech, was adopted by the Central Committee with the President sitting in the chair.

As for Parliament, because of the role it had played in the Nile Valley Company affair, it earned the appellation by the President of 'the eye that sees and the ear that hears for me'. Like many of Nimeiri's utterances, rhetoric always gets the better of practice. The same Parliament was dissolved only two years later on account of its exercising its faculties of seeing and hearing in an 'undesirable fashion'. We shall have occasion later to give examples of how Nimeiri attempted to silence Parliament, or rather, completely emasculate it.

The noble words from the chair which were heard during the Nile Valley Company episode were no longer uttered. In their stead there were corridor whispers and arm-twisting to dissuade Assembly members, who were thinking of the unthinkable, pointing an accusatory finger at those close to the President.

At the same time Nimeiri was taking measures aimed at strengthening his position within the SSU itself. He thus sought to amend article 16 of the rules of the SSU giving himself powers to take decisions in the absence of the Politburo and Central Committee of the party. Two months after the reshuffle (March 1975) Ahmed Babiker Eisa, rather prophetically, questioned the proposed amendment arguing that it would emaciate the Politburo, since it gave the President the power to dismiss it at his will. Badr el Din Suleiman defended the proposal, as he saw it, saying that the President did not intend to use the amendment for this purpose but for taking urgent decisions in the absence of the Politburo. He also added that the Politburo would be empowered to review such decisions. Nimeiri agreed. As we shall show later, article 16 was to be invoked regularly as justification for measures which were only designed to concentrate power in Nimeiri's hands. We say that Eisa's words were prophetic, because despite Nimeiri's promises he went on to do exactly what was feared, to dismiss members of the Politburo of the Central Committee who stood in his way, such as Mohammed Hashim Awad and Lawrence Wol Wol. Encouraged by the bovine docility of the Politburo, as well as the Central Committee that elected it, Nimeiri later on, in 1982, dissolved both bodies, in one of his greatest political massacres, far beyond that of 1975. And following the gruesome carnage President Nimeiri, using the same speech-writer, denounced the SSU, highlighted its futility, not its utility, and ordered his Ministers to keep at arm's length from it. We shall tell more of that in due course.

I opened this chapter by saying that, apart from members of the RCC groups around Nimeiri, the RCC members, or whoever remained from them, were only conspicuous by their absence in all this conflict. They chose to remain in its outer rings. As we have seen earlier, the RCC was a heterogeneous body comprised of the Communists, Nasserites, nationalists, and the political chameleon Nimeiri. In the first chapter, we described the circumstances in which el Nour, al Atta and Hamd Allah were executed and, in the second chapter, how the RCC was dissolved soon after. The remaining members of the dissolved Council were given various portfolios in government and the SSU. In fact, they were all made, *ex officio*, members of the Politburo.

In Sudan, as in the rest of the third world, independence figures became pillars of the establishment. Their fight against the colonial power earned them respectability and prestige and put them on a par with feudal lords and religious leaders. Some of these independent figures challenged, with a large measure of success, rooted religious leaders. A Sudanese example of this was Azhari's fight with el Mirghan. It was these leaders and their male heirs who inherited the Sudan (the biggest country in Africa) in 1956 and governed it for thirteen years, until the May revolution. Revolutions are carried out in the name of the oppressed and dispossessed (namely, the people) to do away with inherited rights and rule by mandate, as Nimeiri put it. Power belongs to the people, he said.

Invariably, revolutions only manage to substitute one oligarchy for another; the RCC members themselves became pillars of the new faith. They governed in the name of the revolution, socialism and various other 'isms. The RCC in Sudan, however, was an exception. It committed suicide as a body at a very early age. We have seen how Khalid Hassan Abbas, exhilarated by the triumphant return of 22 July, managed to persuade his comrades in arms, with few recalcitrant ones among them, to abdicate and hand over the reins of power to Nimeiri. Khalid's action may be considered, at least by some, as a high-minded one. Others attribute it to a sense of resignation resulting from the murder of his young brother (an officer) during the Communists' coup. The RCC had no hereditary rights over the Sudan and, were the revolution to be loyal to its ideals, people should be given the right to assert their will and choose their leader. Hence came the decision to present Nimeiri's candidature on the basis of a defined programme of action, for popular adjudication. To many of us this was the logic of that noble decision by the RCC. With this understanding we got down to business, creating a widely based and open-ended political organization that would enshrine the sovereign popular will, mapping out a programme of action as a political platform for the Presidential candidate and eventually promulgating a constitution which disciplines the exercise of authority through checks and balances and well articulated provisions for accountability. In this context we proposed that the collective leadership of the SSU, i.e. the Central Committee and the Politburo, would have to be progressively elective. By necessity this entailed the avoidance of turning the RCC members into life peers of the realm, i.e. *ex officio* members of the Politburo. Nimeiri gave his whole-hearted support. To us it was a matter of principle, to him it meant removing the last vestiges of RCC authority.

Typically, Nimeiri proceeded to discard the RCC members one after the other. The first three to go were Babiker Awad Allah and Mamoun Abu Zeid and, ironically enough, Khalid Hassan Abbas, who was the person behind the dissolution of the RCC and the making of Nimeiri into a President. Babiker resigned from his prestigious yet powerless post of First Vice-President. Active and opinionated as he was, he was also incensed at the lack of consultation on the part of Nimeiri. Mamoun Abu Zeid, whom Nimeiri had supported against Faroug Hamd Allah, was soon dismissed as secretary-general of the SSU for a clash of style and personality rather than more substantial reasons. The subject-matter of the conflict between Nimeiri and Khalid was the organization of the Army. The latter was Minister of Defence under Nimeiri; Abbas, foolishly enough, offered his resignation thinking that he would bring pressure to bear upon the President. Nimeiri accepted the resignation without further ado.

Under the pretext of wanting technocrats and experts to do the jobs of planning and transport, Abul Gasim Hashim and Zein el Abdin were dismissed. Zein was replaced by Dr Abbadi in the Ministry of Transport and Hashim by the Southerner Lawrence Wol Wol in Planning. Only Abul Gasim Ibrahim was left. His turn came when Nimeiri got rid of him, not without the latter putting up a fierce challenge and a fierce fight. For the time being, however, Nimeiri needed him for symbolic reasons. All the RCC members were later resuscitated, though subdued and docile. Those of them who managed to survive longer than the others have done this only by saying nothing and saying it very well.

But the long and short of it is that members of the RCC have certainly betrayed their own revolution by keeping mute. Out of deference in the face of Nimeiri's constitutional transgression and political deviation, they also have done themselves an injustice by being highly unconcerned with intellectual self-improvement, and without such improvement they have remained tentative leaders. Some of them have pinned their colours, unquestioningly, to Nimeiri's mast, and in the process, they have become tools for his invidious politics. In fairness to them all, however, none of them has been entrapped in the corruption circuit; that they left for the boss. If anything, some of them were highly sensitive to it and they showed it. For example, when Abul Gasim Ibrahim's brother was accused of embezzling funds from Sudan Airways, he immediately went to the First Vice-President, General Baghir (Nimeiri was away then), and told him, in tears, that he was resigning from his job. The accusation of his brother might be damaging to the regime, he thought. Baghir insisted that Ibrahim should retain his job, as his brother's behaviour did not reflect on him. Baghir, however, maintained that the matter must be left for the judicial authorities without interference. The case went to the Attorney-General who investigated it and took it to court. The brother was convicted and sentenced. The court's verdict was twice appealed by the Attorney-General, claiming that the sentence meted out was insufficient. That incident said a lot about the way institutions were functioning and the way many of us wanted them to function. The political sensitivity of Abul Gasim and Baghir's respect for the rule of law, as well as the Attorney-General's integrity, were things to be proud of. Nimeiri was making it known that the due process of the law should be respected. We shall have occasion later to see how the President reacted when accusations were made against his own brother. In Nimeiri's justice we are equal before the law, but some are more equal than others. At the end of the day, with all their pros and cons, the RCC members who had started in May 1969 hoping to write the history of a new Sudan, ended by being a footnote in that history.

Chapter Four

The Unholy Trinity and the Genesis of Economic Corruption

Here is a man of splendid abilities but utterly corrupt. He shines and stinks like a rotten mackerel by moonlight.

John Randolph

The Unholy Trinity

'The Khashoggi that everyone knows today is a man who made it with my help,' Soraya Khashoggi told a journalist. 'I wasn't a Muslim wife in a veil who sat meekly out of sight. I was his full business partner and he took advice from me' (*Sunday Times*, 16 December 1974). That was why she was suing him for the largest alimony award ever made, £1,135,000,000. Notwithstanding Soraya, the Khashoggi that everybody knows today is a man who made it with the help of many friends and admirers. One of those helping friends is the President of the Democratic Republic of Sudan, whatever the worth of his help. The public relations manager of this operation was Dr Idris, who served as State Minister for Special Affairs. Under the purview of this Ministry fell nothing and yet everything. Nothing, because it served no identifiable governmental function; everything, because Dr Idris, with the express or tacit approval of Nimeiri, acted as the President's *alter ego*.

The People's Palace, as the Presidential Palace came to be known, was the stage for a grotesque drama. The actors of the piece in this palace drama included, beside Adnan Khashoggi and Dr Idris, a Salim Eisa who did Sudan the disservice of bringing in

Adnan, supposedly to exploit its potential for development. In this chapter we shall recount the lurid details of this drama, while attempting to shed some light on the dysfunctional role that this trio has played in frustrating Sudan's development plans and de-institutionalizing the country's organs. The chapter will also reveal Nimeiri's role in aiding, abetting and conniving with this unholy trinity.

The Minister of Special Affairs was entrusted with supervising tourism, which came under the range of authority of the Council of Ministers since there was no specific departmental Minister responsible for it. In that capacity he sent Abdel Rahman Kibeida, Director of Tourism, to Beirut with the task of obtaining ideas on tourism and how best to develop Sudan's tourist industry. Kibeida was to meet accidentally a dubious journalist who owned a tourism bureau, Salim Eisa. Salim told Kibeida that he could introduce him to someone who knew a lot about the industry and who would be interested in investing in Sudan. The offer was conveyed to Dr Idris, who extended an invitation to the two in the name of the President. The man in question was Adnan Khashoggi, the larger-than-life wheeler-dealer. Adnan and Salim arrived in Khartoum and were taken to the South to assess the potential of the savannah. Kibeida, having done his bit, was removed. From then on it was not the smaller fry but the sharks who went into business.

Nimeiri warned about the Man who surpassed Zaharoff

The time was not very propitious, for these were the days when Adnan's handling of military sales to Saudi Arabia was being investigated by the Senate Foreign Relations Sub-committee on Multinational Corporations. The hearings of the Sub-committee together with the Northrop and Lockheed papers released to it revealed 'only a fragment of the truth because they did not cast any light upon the practice of padding contracts with large sums that would accrue to those with the power to decide whether or not projects should be given the go-ahead' (*The House of Saud*, p. 562). Enough, however, was revealed to make any government thinking of engaging Khashoggi or accepting his 'help' think twice, for news of the investigation was all over the place. The Sudanese Ambassador to the United States, Abdel Aziz al Nasri, wrote extensively to Khartoum on the Lockheed affair. Files on Adnan and particularly Salim were compiled by Ali Nimeiri, head of Sudanese security and no relation to President Nimeiri. The President was not impressed. What he did not like to hear was presumed non-existent; his was government by amnesia. On one occasion he told the secretary-general of the Council of Ministers that he was tired of seeing those reports on Adnan and Salim; the directive was duly reported to the security chief. Ali Nimeiri responded angrily that it was not the duty of the security agencies to please the President. They were to keep him briefed on everything that endangered national interests; what he did with the information was his own responsibility. Ali Nimeiri viewed the role of an intelligence agency as that of providing the government with information not only on the plans and motives of opponents but also on all matters that might, in one way or another, infringe the national interest. Ali continued sending his reports to the President none the less. They sat there dusty and unmolested with all their excruciating revelations inside them. Later episodes reveal how Nimeiri was always averse to what he did not want to hear, many times dismissing the messenger if he did not like the message.

Adnan opened an office for his company (TRIAD) in Khartoum, employing a number of lawyers and professors from the University of Khartoum on a temporary basis to compile and analyse relevant information and data on the Sudan. His vital information, however, came from inside; he got to know about government projects, planned or under consideration. TRIAD, therefore, became better placed to come up with offers for all government projects. Dr Idris and the other minions did the rest.

Khashoggi's greatest asset, however, was the friendship of the President; a friendship which did not cost much either. There were no payments to election campaigns, which in the case of Nixon's was to the tune of $50,000 by his own admission to the Watergate prosecutors (*Arms Bazaar*, p. 195), for when he met him, Nimeiri was already a President and well on his way to becoming a President for life. Nimeiri, furthermore, had no daughters to please (one of Nixon's daughters received a $30,000 bracelet from Soraya Khashoggi which she revealed in December 1979 (*The Daily Telegraph*, 20 December 1979)). Khashoggi got off very cheaply; the President's price was a few trips aboard the 727 and DC9 (fuelled at the Treasury's expense) and some cruises in his yacht, the 'Nabeela' (after his daughter).

Khashoggi's success in Sudan, as in other places, was due to his making sure that the right 'players', as he called them, 'had their requirements satisfied in order to get the contracts signed' (*Arms Bazaar*, p. 198). Khashoggi's success was also due to his ability to manipulate people, to reassure the doubting, the sceptic and the scrupulous and to impress the impressionable. Nimeiri, in fact, had been impressed by Khashoggi particularly after he met him; for he was the know-all, can-all person, the one who knew the 'high-ups' in Saudi Arabia, Europe and the US. Khashoggi's statements and his debonair style reinforced this belief. He was, therefore, able to take Nimeiri for a long ride, metaphorically speaking. While resentment against Khashoggi in Saudi Arabia was mounting and when the King's disapproval of the man became known, Nimeiri nevertheless continued to have blind faith in him; indeed, he brazenly challenged Saudi officialdom on many issues about which they knew better, if only because these came within their professional domain. In the end Nimeiri reaped the whirlwind, having, on Khashoggi's advice, sown the wind.

The Onerous Debt and the Missing Six Millions

Adnan's first move came after Saudi Arabia agreed to give to Sudan a guarantee for a $200,000,000 loan. The deal had been negotiated by the competent Sudanese authorities with the Saudi Foreign Minister Omar Sakkaf and Finance Minister Mohammed Aba al Khail, with a view to bolstering Sudan's foreign currency reserves. Saudi Arabia had been providing long-term interest-free loans to the Sudan government by way of budget support. The transactions were carried out through the Saudi Arabian Monetary Authority (SAMA); $26,760,000 in 1972 and $21,420,000 in 1973, Algemen Bank: $15,000,000 in 1972, and $15,000,000 in 1973, the Saudi National Commercial Bank: SR40,000,000 in 1974. All these loans were negotiated and concluded through the established bilateral mechanism. Similar arrangements were concluded with Kuwait through the recognized bilateral channels, e.g. deposits of KD5,000,000 in 1971 by the government of Kuwait and KD5,000,000 in 1973 by the Kuwait Industrial Bank.

News of the guarantee was conveyed to Adnan who immediately came in with a diabolical idea. If he was allowed to raise and manage the $200,000,000 he would be able to attract $1,000,000,000 for the Sudan. To that end he put forward a plan for using the funds to establish a development corporation. Adnan was taken at face value by President Nimeiri for what he said and entrusted with raising the money. From then on the deal was no longer the one conceived and negotiated by the institutions as a matter of course, rather a secretive matter handled by the unholy trinity and the President. The competent departments were asked to keep their hands off because 'this was the way the Saudi high-ups wanted it.' It was Nimeiri, not Adnan, speaking.

Adnan went on to negotiate a loan syndicated by no fewer than thirty-one European banks and carrying a high fluctuating rate of interest. In one year it reached 16 per cent. The loan was to be repaid in seven years with a three-year period of grace, a total of ten years. The conditions for repayment included a commitment charge on the undisbursed amount of a half per cent, a semi-annual interest rate of three-quarter per cent in addition to the average prevailing rate in Euro-dollar loans. Accordingly the service charges on the first tranche was $10\frac{7}{8}$ per cent and on the second $12\frac{7}{8}$ per cent. Add to that a 2 per cent commission received by Adnan, i.e. $4,000,000. All the aforementioned facilities made available to Sudan by Saudi Arabia in 1971–3 were very soft loans (2 per cent service charge repayable in fifteen years and more). This was hardly a way to finance development; exorbitant interest rates and short repayment terms. Besides, the erratic fluctuations in interest rates would not be conducive to forward planning by the Sudanese financial authorities for the allocation of resources to meet repayment schedules; resources were limited and the demands on them numerous. Given our past experience with Saudi Arabia and the world money market, the loan could have been secured on a fixed interest rate with longer grace and repayment periods, if the money were to be used in bolstering the reserves of the central bank. This was much more so if the money was to be used for development projects, as indeed it was. Repayment in such a case would have to take into account the realistic time needed for the gestation of and returns from the development projects. And after all the loan could have been raised through normal channels at a much lower fixed rate of interest, for the Saudi guarantee was as good as cash. The affair infuriated the Saudi establishment. Anwar Ali, the President of the Saudi Arabian Monetary Agency (SAMA) conveyed that much to the

Sudanese Minister of Finance during the fall meeting of the IMF in 1974. What infuriated them most were the whispers emanating from the palace that somebody on the other side of the Red Sea was having his slice of the cake. Omar Sakkaf conveyed to Nimeiri, in a meeting arranged on the sidelines of the Islamic Conference in Lahore, his surprise at the onerous terms on which the loan, guaranteed by SAMA, was obtained. Sakkaf, who was certainly not speaking for himself, told Nimeiri circumspectly that he (Nimeiri) did not need to commute between Jeddah and Khartoum and indeed around the world in Adnan's private plane. Nimeiri, in those days, was making use of Adnan's plane in his different trips, including that to the Islamic summit in Lahore. The Kingdom would provide for the President of Sudan the necessary means of conveyance, if he so desired, added Sakkaf. In fact Nimeiri took up the Saudi offer seven years later in the form of a presidential Boeing 707 given by the Saudi King.

The World Bank was not too happy with the deal either. Sudan by that time had resumed discussions with the IBRD for the reinstatement of the Sudan Consultative Group, comprising a number of donor countries taking interest in supporting the development of the country. Robert McNamara, the President of the World Bank, like many others was appreciative of Sudan's achievement in reestablishing peace in the South and wanted to extend a helping hand. On a government invitation he visited the country soon after the Addis Ababa agreement and declared his intention of increasing IDA support for the Sudan. However, following the *débâcle* of the Saudi-guaranteed loan he had second thoughts. In the course of a visit to him in the spring of 1974, McNamara intimated to me that the way the deal was concluded and the astronomical interest rate accepted by the Sudan implied either one of two things, mismanagement and the squandering of assets or suspected corruption. In either case, McNamara said, Sudan could not expect to draw upon IDA funds. People who squander money like this should be very rich. He proposed, furthermore, that the IBRD was ready to assume responsibility for the loan and use the Saudi guarantee for raising the loan at a fixed concessional price, at a certain percentage below the prevailing rate and with no service charge or commission. He suggested an approach, for that end, to any bank nominated by SAMA. McNamara repeated the same thing to the Sudanese Minister of Finance who stopped in Washington en route to Sudan from Jamaica, where he attended the ACP-EEC meeting. That meeting was attended by the Sudanese IBRD Executive Director Misbah el Makki.

The matter was brought to the attention of Nimeiri on my return. It was also conveyed to him by the Minister of Finance. He was informed of the onerous nature of the deal and the damage it would do to the country's economy. Sudan could not afford to discount the views of the World Bank or those of the man who should be presumed to speak authoritatively on behalf of the Saudis (Omar Sakkaf). The matter was not left at that. Sakkaf, who was aware of the IBRD offer, proposed that if we were not enthusiastic about the World Bank's offer we should consider going directly to the world money markets. He mentioned Chase Manhattan and Algemen as examples. The Saudis would help in the initial contacts.

Knowing my President, I decided to approach him not only with the information but also with an alternative plan. I suggested that he give his green light for the Minister of Finance, the Attorney-General and myself to start negotiations with Chase, since I was going to meet with them in the fall anyway, to arrange a loan for financing the purchase of the Sudan Ambassador's residence in New York. The President pretended to have given his assent. I thought we had won the day, not against the palace cabal but for the Sudan. A meeting was arranged in New York soon after with the chairman of Chase, David Rockefeller. Mansour, the Finance Minister, Zaki Mustafa, the Attorney-General, and I discussed the financial and legal implications of the restructured deal. Zaki proceeded to Caracas for the Law of the Sea Conference, leaving it for Mansour, Jamal Ahmed and myself to meet with Chase. In that meeting an agreement was soon reached on restructuring the loan at a 5 per cent fixed rate interest, i.e. less than half the rate obtained by Adnan, and again with no commission.

An invitation was extended to Rockefeller to visit the Sudan and conclude the deal. He arrived on 22 January 1975, a few days before the Cabinet reshuffle in which the Minister of Finance was relieved of his functions and I was moved to Education. Indeed, it was the same day that Mansour was facing the National Assembly on the Nile Valley farce. I accompanied him to the President's house; Mansour was there. Nimeiri's reception was warm and cordial. That was the first time he met Rockefeller, who must have been highly impressed with the President's simplicity and empathy. Nimeiri is wonderful in relating to people, provided you do not have to work with him; this was the way he carried everybody in his confidence before he showed his real colours.

Mansour immediately went to business in a corner of the President's living-room, with its spartan simplicity only adorned with photographs of his early school days, as well as those of President Nasser and Abul Gasim Mohammed Ibrahim. Abul Gasim's photograph was removed a few years later when he fell from grace, and the same thing happened to one of the other members of the RCC, which was the centre-piece of Nimeiri's mementoes. Nimeiri's displeasure is always expressed visibly, a sign of an uncouth rather than a refined temperament. Next to Mansour on a modest sofa sat Rockefeller's personal assistant Robert Hoen. Nimeiri was then proud of the modest furnishings he used to have when he was a colonel and continued to use them thereafter. The Minister of Finance was discussing with Hoen the implementation programme of the restructured deal; the period of grace, the schedule of repayments etc. Rockefeller, on the other hand, was busy with the banal courtesies of protocol. Eventually he went direct to the subject, telling the President how happy he was to be able to help the Sudan in restructuring the $200,000,000 loan.

Nimeiri who has a fantastic ability to freeze his emotions, except when he is faced with danger to his life, showed a perfunctory concern for the whole matter. Then came the shocker: 'I know nothing of what you are talking about.' Rockefeller murmured deferentially, and went on talking about Sudan's potential for development. That was an outrage and the statement was galling, according to the later statement of Jamal Ahmed, State Minister for Foreign Affairs, who was privy to the whole story. Adnan and not the Sudan had won the day. The episode was as embarrassing as it was painful.

In effect Adnan had tried to frustrate the Chase deal long before Rockefeller's visit. He got wind of our contacts with Chase through his presidential public relations managers. Not knowing the exact nature of the deal and wishing to remain on the scene, he contacted Chase Manhattan asking them to join him in managing the $200,000,000 through the proposed Sudanese Development Corporation (SDC). He was already assuming that he would be responsible for running the SDC. Adnan was by now deciding, if with the support of the President, how the country's economy should be run. However, since Sudanese officialdom decided to stick to their guns and frustrate Adnan's plan for managing the Development

Corporation he decided to create a parallel financial institution in which the government, through the SDC, would be an equity shareholder. Chase was to manage that one too.

Chase responded by sending Wayne Fredericks, its Director of International Relations, Africa and the Middle East. Dr Idris, and not the Minister of Finance, received Fredericks and sent him to see the Governor of the Bank of Sudan. The Governor wrote on 17 March 1974 asking for directives from the State Minister for Commerce, Hassan Beleil, whose written reaction was 'I know nothing of what they are talking about', passing the buck to Mansour. Minister Mansour was infuriated with the matter. He wrote on 20 March asking for an explanation from Dr Idris, only to receive a flat denial of any knowledge of the affair. The whole affair not only smacked of corruption but was also naive and infantile. Governments keep records, records being the institutional memory of the system. Fredericks, in fact, met the Governor of the Bank of Sudan on the express instructions of Idris. On his return to New York he wrote to Jamal Ahmed enclosing a copy of his letter to Dr Idris regarding the question at issue. In that letter to Idris dated 20 April 1974 Fredericks wrote:

> David Buckman and I would like to express our great appreciation for the very nice warm reception and cooperation extended to us during our trip to Khartoum in March in connection with the proposal of the Triad Group to form a joint venture bank. As you are now aware, the Chase Manhattan Bank declined the offer of Mr Khoshoggi and since you were so helpful to us, we feel we should explain the reasons for our decision.

TRIAD, using President Nimeiri's trusted errand-boy, was wooing Chase to join them in the formation of an international private bank with 25 per cent equity holding and responsibility for management. Chase maintained that the holding was not sufficient to justify the substantial commitment of human resources required to manage the operation. Chase, however, confirmed its faith in the Sudanese economy. Its refusal of Adnan's offer did not reflect a lack of confidence in that economy. 'On the contrary, the study we made confirmed our opinion that the Sudan is entering a phase of dynamic growth promising far reaching economic benefits for its citizens as well as for the neighbouring countries,' wrote Fredericks to Idris. He concluded: 'Mr David Rockefeller conveyed much of the foregoing information to the Foreign Minister, Dr Mansour Khalid and Ambassador Jamal Mohammed Ahmed during the course of a meeting here at the Bank on April 16 and assured them of the Bank's continued interest in the Sudan.'

It was evident that TRIAD was trying to use Chase as window-dressing while exercising control of the operation. It was also evident that the presidential Minister for Special Affairs was negotiating the deal, not on behalf of the Sudan, but on behalf of TRIAD. He was in no way concerned with the potential in Chase's declared willingness to participate in the development of the country. But when he was caught *in flagrante delicto* he naively denied knowledge of the whole affair. Dr Idris had yet to learn the risks of working with bureaucratic institutions. They keep records and they have channels of communication. The Governor of the Bank of Sudan, Ibrahim Nimir, who is too much of an organization man, brought his Ministers in.

Notwithstanding the administrative irregularities the most serious thing in the Adnan/Chase operation was the question of policy involved. All banks, we recall, had been nationalized in the course of the disastrous blanket confiscations and nationalizations of 1970. If there was one nationalization decision on which there was universal agreement, within the May regime committed to central planning, it was the nationalization of banks, banks being the most important tool for controlling monetary policies. The creation of a private bank represented a departure from the regime's policies and a transgression of the country's existing laws. For such a major departure from established socialist policies to come from the very man (President Nimeiri) who accused and punished his Minister of Finance only a few months later of a breach of socialist faith reflected not only hypocrisy but also immorality on stilts.

Idris was not acting on his own. In fact on 27 September 1974 he signed, on behalf of the Sudan Government, an agreement with 'Triad Capital Management Holding Corporation', a Luxembourg corporation with its principal offices at Gefinor Centre, Beirut. Adnan signed for that corporation. In the first paragraph of its preamble the agreement begins 'Whereas the Sudan has reached a decision to establish in the Sudan a new financial institution to engage in merchant banking, commercial banking, trade and other related activities, in connection with foreign interests...'

Decisions in the Sudan are reached through the deliberations of competent political, executive and legislative organs, much more so when those decisions entail departures from established policies. Neither the SSU nor the Council of Ministers had reversed government policy on banks at that time.

The agreement stipulated further that the Sudan government would subscribe up to 25 per cent of the equity capital of the Bank while TRIAD and its *selected* partners would control the rest, i.e. 75 per cent.

Adnan, with the benign protection of Nimeiri, went on to borrow money guaranteed by Saudi Arabia at twice the interest rate offered by others. To add insult to injury, he came up with his plans for the deployment of the funds. To start with, and under the pretext of protecting the revolution abroad and 'greasing Saudi machinery' (those were the words used) $10,000,000 was deposited abroad. Adnan was entitled to a 2 per cent commission on the operation, i.e. $4,000,000 over and above the exorbitant interest rate, and exorbitant it was, for the Saudi guarantee's real value was in inducing preferential borrowing terms. As for the rest of the money ($6,000,000) only God knew, and only Adnan and President Nimeiri would be able to account for it. In fact the chairman of the SDC Mohammed Abdel Magid Ahmed who was to receive $200,000,000 as capital for the SDC received only $190,000,000. The incorruptible Magid would not keep mum. As early as mid-1975 he drew the attention of the Minister of Finance to this gap and decided to reflect it in his books as a loan to the government. When Mamoun Beheiry assumed the portfolio of Finance, replacing Mansour, he was faced with this dilemma. He left the Ministry a few years later, still unable to solve the riddle.

As if all this was not enough for AK, as Adnan is known, he came up with a further idea that the Sudan Development Corporation should be run by a board headed by Nimeiri himself and including Dr Idris and two non-Sudanese, i.e. himself and Salim Eisa, as if the Sudan was up for grabs. Mansour came out strongly against these plans. He told Nimeiri that it was unprecedented for a President to sit on the board of a company and that there was no shortage of indigenous skills and no need for foreign participation in the running of Sudan. Even on the eve of independence, Mansour pointed out, suggestions that the IMF should manage the newly formed Bank of Sudan were dropped and the Sudanese assumed the management of the institution themselves, albeit with some foreign advice provided by the IMF. Mamoun Beheiry was the first Governor.

Dr Idris on the other hand was busy preparing drafts for the establishment of the Corporation. Sure enough, it was not the Attorney-General of Sudan who was involved: it was Daniel G. Zerfas, an attorney nominated by AK. On 21 February 1974 Zerfas proposed not only the legal instruments of the loan but the procedure to be followed by the competent Sudanese authorities in finalizing the loan operation, including a draft of the decree to be signed by the President. A memorandum to this effect was sent to Dr Idris, reading:

MEMORANDUM

TO   His Excellency
Dr Bahaa El Din Mohamed Idris
State Minister for Special Affairs
At the Presidency

FROM   DANIEL G. ZERFAS

DATE   21 February 1974

In order to obtain the first $50,000,000 under the Loan Agreement by the 15th of March 1974, it is imperative that the following matters be accomplished on or before the dates set forth:

ACTION	DATE
Issuance of Presidential Decree authorizing loan.	2 March 1974
Issuance of Presidential Decree creating SUDAN NATIONAL DEVELOPMENT CORPORATION (SNDC)	2 March 1974
Meeting the Board of Governors of SNDC in Khartoum to authorize trust agreement and commencement of operations	4 March 1974

Execution of Loan Agreement trust agreement and related documents in Khartoum	7 March 1974

Completion of establishment of bank accounts, issuance of instructions to banks in New York and Paris relating to placement of $50,000,000 etc.	12 March 1974

In addition to these very important matters, there are many mechanical details requiring signatures and deliveries that will take many days lead time because of the distances and numerous parties involved. I am sure you appreciate the complexity of the transaction and tight time schedule involved, and therefore, that any significant changes in the documentation after 2 March (the Presidential Decrees, SNDC charter, etc.) will result in serious time delays

Respectfully

The draft of the decree did not make less depressing reading.

To make sure that the situation did not get out of hand they saw to it that the President entrusted the whole matter of the Presidential Decree to Dr Idris. The President did better; he issued a blanket authorization to Dr Idris prepared by AK's lawyers and signed by Nimeiri on 1 August 1974. The authorization read:

I, GAAFAR MOHAMED NUMERIE, President of the Democratic Republic of the Republic of Sudan, hereby designate Dr. Bahaa El Dien Mohamed Idris, State Minister for Special Affairs at the Presidency of Government, as the authorized representative of the Government of the Democratic Republic of the Sudan for the purpose of negotiating and executing, in the name of the Government, such documents and agreements as are required in connection with development projects of the Democratic Republic of the Sudan. This authority includes the execution of all contracts and required financial and credit agreements for the said development projects.

Done in Khartoum this 1st. day of August 1973.

GAFAAR MOHAMED NUMERIE
PRESIDENT,
DEMOCRATIC REPUBLIC OF THE SUDAN.

One thing that intrigued me in the authorization was the way the President's name was spelt, with a U and not an I. A few months before the President refused to receive the letters of credence of the Ambassador of Zaire because the President's name was mis-spelled in those documents. The unfortunate Ambassador had to wait for over a month for the documents to be sent back to Kinshasa, corrected and returned. This fastidiousness in protocol was absent in the case of the monumental authorization not only read but signed by Nimeiri. From then on Dr Idris, with impunity, played havoc with the Sudanese economy.

Mansour refused to budge on the question of the Sudan Development Corporation (SDC). I persisted with him. Nimeiri had no option but to give in on the issue of foreign management of the Corporation, as well as the personal participation of the President in such management. Mansour also succeeded in including the Ministry of Finance in the Board of Management, although AK's draft excluded it. But while agreeing to these changes, Nimeiri lay in wait. He was sharpening his knives for the fateful Saturday.

Adnan tried all manner of tricks with Mansour, cajoling, intimidation and eventually bribery. Early in 1974, at a meeting with the President attended by AK, and at the Council of Ministers, Mansour repeated his worn-out argument that institutions should be involved in all financial deals. AK told the President how proud he should be with Ministers like Mansour who were both courageous and knowledgeable. The Minister, while making his case, told AK that the doors of the Ministry of Finance were always open to him. AK missed the point.

After that meeting AK asked the Minister to join with 'them' in their Sudan operations. 'There are three of us and you will be the fourth,' he told the Minister. 'Your share will be one fourth of all gains made and I will take care of your interest in all previous operations out of my own share,' he added. AK went on whispering conspiratorially, 'And by the way, where is your private bank account abroad?' Mansour, who is as good as Nimeiri in freezing his emotions, rushed to the President and told him of the audacity that defied all convention. The Minister expected the President to fume with rage, order the arrest of AK, suspend the operations, whatever. None of that happened. The President, with a cultivated sense of astonishment, remarked 'I never expected him to do a thing like that with my Ministers' (really!) 'but sure enough I am not the THIRD MAN!' Even Graham Greene could not have produced one like this. Nimeiri that very night was wining and dining with AK at the presidential guest house officially allotted to him. The house was not to be used by anybody else; even its servants and attendants were hand-picked by Idris.

The Fuel Crisis and the Fictitious Refinery

In the early 'seventies Sudan's daily consumption of oil was in the region of 30,000 barrels. Most of this was supplied by a Shell/BP refinery in Port Sudan. The Shell/BP (Sudan) company was formed in November 1962. The refinery started operation in October 1964 with a capacity of 20,000 barrels a day increased later to its present capacity of 30,000 barrels a day. In the wake of the 1973 energy crisis it was decided that the Sudan should take direct control of our energy supplies. While on a visit to Iran on behalf of the Arab Foreign Ministers meeting in New York to mobilize world public opinion after the October war, I received a telex from Mansour requesting me to discuss with the Shah the possibility of direct crude oil purchase for the Shell refinery. Iran was then the traditional supplier of that refinery. Mansour also asked me to discuss on my way back, with both Kuwait and Saudi Arabia, the idea of energy support for the poor Arab countries severely hit by the oil-price hikes. The Shah was more than helpful. He promised to provide Sudan with its needs of crude oil and extend a medium-term credit of $60,000,000 on a 6 per cent fixed-term interest for that purpose. That was the first time such an energy aid was received by the Sudan.

After the completion of my Iranian mission I proceeded to Saudi Arabia to discuss the possibility of securing constant supplies of crude oil. In the absence of Ahmed Zaki Yamani, the Minister of Oil, I met with Prince Saud al Faisal, presently Saudi Foreign Minister. He was then Under-Secretary for the Ministry of Petroleum. With the Prince I discussed both crude oil supplies to the Sudan and the position of the refinery in Port Sudan. Discussions on the latter subject were initiated earlier by Musa Belal, Minister of Industry and Mining, who fully briefed me on Sudan's stand in increasing the capacity of that refinery to meet the new requirements generated by our development drive. The Saudis showed interest in helping. Prince Saud confirmed the Kingdom's willingness to assist and suggested that the matter be discussed by technicians from both sides.

As a follow-up to these discussions a technical mission from both the Ministries of Finance and Industry, led by Hamad Satti, undertook a visit to Saudi Arabia between 12 and 21 February 1974 to discuss the question of crude oil supplies. As to the refinery, Minister Belal struck a deal with his Saudi counterpart involving a joint venture to establish a second small refinery on the Red Sea with a capacity of 30,000 barrels a day. The Saudis would also consider participating in the equity of the existing refinery owned by Shell/BP were the Sudan to acquire title over it, as indeed it did under Badr el Din Suleiman, who succeeded Belal in Industry. It went without saying that either one or two refineries, once partly owned by Saudi Arabia, would be ensured of Saudi crude supply. The two refineries, it was envisaged, would produce over 50,000 barrels a day creating a surplus of 20,000 barrels which would have paved the way for further industrial and agricultural expansion.

AK got to know about the project from his known sources. He parachuted in. Rather typically he came up with a grandiose plan for the building of a mammoth refinery five times the capacity of the proposed one. He claimed that this would not only enable Sudan to satisfy its own needs, but also those of much of East Africa. 'You are not only a Sudanese, you are an African leader and such a refinery will enhance your prestige and influence in East Africa,' said AK to Nimeiri. Adnan knew how to massage Nimeiri's ego, already oversized. The President sottishly believed what he said. AK stated furthermore that the project had the backing of the Saudis who, he claimed, would finance the project and supply the refinery with crude at concessionary prices. I told the President not to pay heed to these will-o'-the-wisp ideas, and that we were better advised to proceed with the small project, conceived and agreed to by the institutions in both countries. There was no reason why the Saudis should agree to such a grandiose plan and, after all, we were not in the business of selling oil. All that the Sudan needed was to satisfy its own requirements. The President would not listen; he was already living in his dreams, inspired by AK.

The Saudis in fact had indicated to me their thinking on the grandiose plan, so I was not guessing. In the course of the meetings of the UN General Assembly special session on the new International Economic Order (NIEO) Dr A. Z. Yamani, who was leading his country's delegation, pointed out that the Saudis themselves were building a refinery at Yaubu across the Red Sea. There was also no question of concessionary prices for oil, since the Kingdom was bound by international agreements on pricing. If the Kingdom were to give concessionary prices at all, this would have to be done only through a subsidy from the Saudi Ministry of Finance to Petromin, said AZY, as Dr Yamani is known. And if the Kingdom were to do this, why bother with a refinery? Why should it not pay the subsidy directly as budget support to Sudan? That made sense. The refinery was important, however, not for the Sudan, but for whoever was going to procure it and get a commission in the process. That was the rub. The Sudanese national interest and the predicament of the country (fuel supply needed by ongoing development projects and those that were already on the drawing-board) were not the issue. I entreated AZY to come to Khartoum and tell Nimeiri of the official Saudi position. I wanted the President to hear the story from the horse's mouth, as he had disbelieved what I told him just as he disbelieved what Sakkaf told him on the $200,000,000 loan. Yamani obliged.

A meeting was organized in the late summer of 1974 for the signature in Khartoum of the agreement on the Saudi–Sudan exploitation of the Red Sea resources by Yamani and myself. The matter had been under negotiation between the two countries for the past year. On the same day that we were to sign the agreement Dr Yamani called on the President. I advised the President that they should meet tête-à-tête. The meeting was as depressing as it was embarrassing for, though a private meeting was arranged between the President and AZY, at which I deliberately chose not to be present, the omnipresent Adnan and Salim Eisa appeared on Nimeiri's invitation. Nimeiri repeated AK's arguments on the refinery to AZY, and AK concurred. Nimeiri was playing the role of the salesman. AZY, on the other hand, reiterated his views on concessionary prices. He added that the Sudan needed a refinery to meet its own requirements of fuel and that the Kingdom was willing to help with that. At this point Salim, brash and disrespectful of convention, intervened, making a derogatory remark to AZY by saying, 'The matter of financing the refinery and the cheap crude is going to be settled by people high up in the Saudi hierarchy.'

AZY, an urbane and polite man, was dumbfounded. His reaction was silence. Later on he remarked, 'We are brought up differently. We are taught to speak politely in the presence of our elders.' There were several delicate shades of meaning in AZY's words. The President of Sudan had not only allowed such an important guest to be insulted in his presence, he had indeed demeaned his office and his country by allowing a non-Sudanese to insult a friend of the Sudan and a representative of a trusted sisterly country.

On 27 September 1974, after the meeting with AZY, Dr Idris signed, on behalf of the Sudan, an agreement with TRIAD Naft Company SA, a Panama company with its principal offices at Gefinor Centre, Beirut, for the establishment of the refinery, on the basis of a fifty-fifty equity participation. TRIAD was to commission and contract out the preparation of the feasibility study for the project, the cost of the study being shared by the two contracting parties. Marubeni Corporation of Japan was mentioned as a possibility. In the meantime TRIAD already had in hand a report on the refinery prepared by Beicip, an affiliate of Institut Français de Petrole (IFP) under a contract signed in February 1974. The report discussed the establishment of a refinery with a capacity of 140,000 barrels a day to be boosted to 200,000 barrels a day.

AK, equipped with this report and the 27 September agreement, and fortified by the President's support, went on shopping around the world for the mammoth refinery. Top of his list was Romania. AK was certainly briefed about the discussions that took place between the Sudan and that country for the construction of the small Saudi-Sudanese refinery on the Red Sea. The matter was reflected in the protocols signed between the two countries. One of his main contacts was de Chambrun, a Harvard-educated French politician who served under General de Gaulle as Minister for External Trade. AK's network was wide and influential. We continued telling the President *ad nauseam* that we believed in the veracity of what Saudi institutions told him and us. After the meeting with AZY he should have realized that the game was up. Saudi Arabia is not the desert kingdom some people want to think it. In dealing with other governments the King works through his men, not intermediaries.

Nimeiri refused to budge and had a few unkind words for the Saudi establishment, ranging from accusations of jealousy of AK to personal interest. Nimeiri could not see, in spite of all the abundant evidence before him, that all that AK was interested in was selling a refinery to the Sudan, getting his commission, and leaving the scrap for the country to grapple with. The errand-boys in the palace had no time for national interests and concerns; they were only waiting for their share of the crumbs falling from AK's table. The results of all these exploits were disastrously predictable to whoever wanted to see. The Sudanese planners were concerned neither with prestigious white elephants nor supremacy over Africa. Their eyes were riveted on fuelling their engine of development on the basis of well conceived and calculated plans.

Despite all the warnings and advice Nimeiri went on and ceremoniously laid the foundation stone of the 140,000-barrel refinery in May 1974. To date the stone stands on its own, for neither the mammoth nor the more modest refinery agreed upon by the institutions in both countries was built.

Sudan development projects and endeavours, in all areas of activity, were the outcome of serious studies and planning, not fiction. They were the result of the lucubrations of many Ministers and technicians, as indeed they were followed up and carried out by the toil and sweat of many workers who had the leadership to look up to. Science fiction took the lead when presidential judgment became contaminated by wishful thinking, induced by cheats. Realities were ignored and in their stead the decision-maker was sustained only by make-believe. The Port Sudan mammoth refinery was one of these decisions.

King Faisal Enraged

Incensed by Nimeiri's remarks on Sakkaf and AZY I decided to go straight to the higher-ups in Saudi Arabia. To this end a visit to Saudi Arabia was undertaken by Musa Belal and myself under the guise of discussing the Red Sea joint exploitation programme. Sakkaf organized a meeting with King Faisal in Taif. Sakkaf insisted that I should see the King alone. He told the King so and withdrew, taking along with him Belal and Dr Rashad Faroun, the King's Counsellor who normally attended all meetings with him.

I told the King of our predicament, adding that all that AK was doing purported to be done because he, the King, wanted it that way; the 'higher-ups', beyond ministerial institutions, could only be presumed to be the King. I particularly mentioned the $200,000,000 dollar loan and the refinery. The King was enraged by these allegations. His words on AK were harsh; Sakkaf told me later that these were not from the King's usual vocabulary. To show the measure of his anger the King banned AK from the Kingdom.

The Saudi guarantee and refinery affairs exposed AK for those who were willing to see. Nimeiri chose to be blind to these revelations, deaf to his Ministers' advice and oblivious of the promises he had made both to Saudi and international personalities. AK is never to blame. He is in the business of making money through whatever means. He said so often; no 'revolutionary purist' is he, nor did he claim to be one. He was proud to see himself filmed as the 'pirate'. It is the man who, more than any other Sudanese leader before him, injected elements of morality into politics, that is to blame.

The 'revolutionary purist', instead of putting an end to his deals with AK, now that he was banished from his own country, chose to intercede on his behalf with King Faisal. The action was embarrassing for the Saudis, especially Faisal, and humiliating for the Sudanese. On a state visit to Saudi Arabia Nimeiri asked the welcoming King if he would do him a favour. Like a true Arab host, Faisal gave an unconditional yes. The favour was the forgiving of AK, whom Nimeiri had brought with him in his own plane, i.e. Adnan's. AK stepped into the country he was banished from to the amusement of the Saudis. The King could not go back on his word.

111

A Page for Page

With Nimeiri sinking lower and lower in murky waters, the government too was dragged more and more into sleazy operations. It was now the turn of telecommunications and Kuwait's money. Successive Ministers of Communication were aware of the need to improve Sudan's link with the world. With Sudan's increasing exposure to the outside world in the early 'seventies that need became more urgent than ever. A satellite project had been conceived in the late 'sixties and was the work of various government departments. The project was shelved at the very last moment because of a scandal that had erupted when it became apparent that, out of two offers, the more expensive one was preferred. Bashir Abbadi, the Minister of Communications under Nimeiri, decided to revive the project. An approach was made to the Kuwait government (Kuwait Development Fund) to finance it. The Kuwaiti Fund undertook to meet most of the cost of the project and the gap in financing was to be bridged by Ex-Im Bank, which meant that the Sudan should buy American. Both the technical work and the financial negotiations were undertaken by Sudan government institutions.

It was now Salim Eisa's turn to suck at the bloodstream of the Sudanese economy. He got in touch with Don Hughes, Page Engineers' representative in Beirut, offering to secure the contract for them if he was made their middle man. As usual he caught wind of the project from 'special' duties, which turned out to be shopping around government departments for projects for TRIAD and its nominees. Page is a respectable US systems engineering business. The matter could have been negotiated normally between that firm and the technical departments, but Salim dealt only with the 'high-ups'. Hughes was taken to see Dr Idris, where an agreement was signed by the phenomenal doctor on behalf of the Sudan government on 2 August 1973, using the blanket authority bestowed upon him by the President one day earlier. As a witness to his signature, for a matter of such great moment to Sudan, was affixed the name of Sid Ahmed Mohammed Rahma, a junior secretary in Dr Idris' office.

The signed contract reflected a price inflated by one million dollars from what was estimated by both the technical and financial

Sudanese authorities. Eisa's intervention was not for nothing. Sudan officialdom was furious. The Under-Secretary for Communications, Mustafa Allam, wrote to his counterpart in Planning, Dr Nasr el Din Mubarak, protesting. Planning was in the dark, came the answer. Dr Abbadi would not have it. He took a tough stance against the improper conclusion of the contract and the million dollars extorted through Dr Idris' 'good offices'. Page, on Abbadi's suggestion, accepted a reduction of the price by half a million dollars to be used towards the installation of a telex network. Abbadi was not satisfied and insisted on the retrieval of the other half million. Nimeiri, who was in the know all the time, decided to intervene in the tug of war which ensued, not, however, on the side of legitimacy but as a conciliator. As if the squabble was over a piece of cake, Nimeiri's verdict came: a quarter of a million from you and a quarter of a million from you. The interests of the palace cabal had to be safeguarded. It had never dawned on the 'revolutionary purist' that a contract relating to the same subject-matter had caused a national scandal and almost brought down the government during the discredited regime of the parties.

Swakin and the Saudi-German Connection

The Sudan, the largest country in Africa, is almost land-locked. Port Sudan, the only port on the Red Sea, was taxed beyond its capacity especially after the re-opening of the Suez canal. Adequate port facilities were essential for the success of the development programme. It was out of this realization that plans for rennovating Port Sudan and rehabilitating the traditional port of Swakin were drawn. Swakin, a quaint dilapidated haven, was used by the Ottomans during their occupation of the Sudan in the nineteenth century. Port Sudan harbour, lying on a natural coral bay on the Red Sea, dates back to 1909. It was developed over seventy years to its present capacity, 200 linear metres of quay with a total of fourteen berths. Nearly a thousand ships call annually and the number is expected to increase in view of the planned agricultural expansion, entailing a growth in both the export of agricultural goods and the import of capital goods. As in the case of the refinery, the plans for Port Sudan/Swakin were conceived as an integral part of a whole. You cannot talk of agricultural and industrial production without providing for energy supplies and you cannot envisage an export drive without catering for port facilities. The road transport network and the Port Sudan–Khartoum pipeline financed by Kuwait, catering for the transport of 600,000 tons per year of oil products from Port Sudan refinery, were a part of this grand design. With all this in mind the Sudan began identifying sources of financing for yet another major project. In the winter of 1973 I visited Copenhagen, as part of an Arab delegation, to expound the Arab point of view on the energy crisis to the EEC summit. I undertook that mission jointly with Ministers Abdel Aziz Bouteflika (Algeria), Mohammed Massmoudi (Tunisia), and Adnan Bajahji (United Arab Emirates). Bajahji and I were to continue the trip to Bonn to meet the German authorities and media. In the course of that mission we spoke extensively on the new vistas for trilateral co-operation involving petroleum surplus money, European money and technology and the development potential in the Arab developing countries. On the margin of these meetings I met Egon Bahr, secretary-general of the SDP and discussed with him the possibilities for trilateral co-operation in the Sudan. On his becoming Minister of Co-operation, Bahr decided to make the first trip under his new mantle to the Sudan. He wanted to make Sudan a show-piece for trilateral co-operation. Bahr arrived in Khartoum accompanied by the Sudanese Ambassador to Bonn, and travelled across the country to the Gezria and Southern Sudan.

On his return to Khartoum Bahr shouted '*Eureka*.' He declared his intention to concentrate German aid on two areas, agriculture and transportation. That was indeed the way we had set our priorities in the development plan. He also offered to help with hydro-electric power generation at the Biden falls (Southern Sudan). Bahr was sweating hard during his meeting with the Southern Regional Government in Juba, the battling ceiling fans having ground to a halt as a result of a power-cut lasting for hours. The contagion of power-cuts has now travelled downstream to Khartoum, the national capital.

It was within this overall framework that Bahr picked on the Swakin port project. He was enthused with it. Right there and then he declared that the German government was prepared to allocate DM72,000,000 to the project as a first tranche. The project was to be undertaken jointly with Saudi Arabia. He suggested flying directly to Riyadh to discuss the matter with the Saudi authorities. We requested him to leave the Saudis for our established bilateral mechanism. President Nimeiri was kept abreast of all those developments by both the Planning and Foreign Ministries. Bahr, on the other hand, was true to his word. By November 1975 the German Agency for Technical Cooperation Ltd, on Bahr's instructions, appointed the German firm Rhin-Ruhr to undertake a study of the new port while reviewing the existing port facilities in Port Sudan. Rhin-Ruhr completed its study and delivered it to the Sudanese authorities by October 1976. Germany had done her share of the job and was waiting. Not a word from the Sudan or the Saudis, and for 'good' reasons.

AK was informed of the project and the negotiations with Bahr by Dr. . . . .; you guessed it right. He was not slow in parachuting in on this one too. AK put on his Saudi hat and claimed that the Saudi Ministry of Defence would provide the finance for the Swakin project provided he himself was in charge. He wasted no time. He got in touch with a German construction company operating on the Port Sudan–Hya Road near Swakin. The choice of the company (Strabag) was not fortuitous, for giving the contract to a German company, AK thought, would forestall German objections to the absence of fair bidding.

AK's troubles, however, were two-pronged; not only did the Germans insist on fair bidding but they also queried the figures quoted by Strabag which they deemed to be 30 to 40 per cent higher than they should have been. The figures that Strabag was quoting, it turned out, had been fixed by TRIAD. The German figures were worked out by a special consultant to the Sudan Port Authority Corporation, recruited under German technical assistance, to help review the project costing. Dr Abbadi, the Minister of Transport, called in the Strabag representative and admonished him. The man, rather than crying *mea culpa*, told the Minister that he had nothing to do with pricing. The contract was signed by President Nimeiri personally and the figures were given by TRIAD. Abbadi took up the matter with the President, who tried to explain away the inexplicable. 'The Saudis wanted it that way,' the President told his Ministers. 'They conceived the project as an integral part of the defence of the Red Sea and it would be financed by the Saudi Ministry of Defence,' he added. In other words he was telling the minister, 'Shut up and hands off.' Future events proved that all this was sham.

The agreement itself, signed by the President, was a national insult. Finance for the project would be provided by Saudi Arabia, said the article on financial arrangements in the said agreement. The signatory, we recall, was not the Saudi Finance Minister but the President of the Republic of Sudan. There was no dearth of legal talent in the country to advise the President that he had no right to sign a contract with a foreign company, committing a foreign government. The German government, however, did not swallow the bait and insisted on the normal procedures of German aid, i.e. fair bidding among eligible companies. They also added that if the Saudis wanted to carry out the project without going through these procedures then the operation should be split into two parts, a matter unacceptable to both the Planning and Technical Departments of the Sudan. The project was devised as an integrated whole and should be implemented as such. The tug of war continued with no progress made.

By November 1976 I had another opportunity to be involved in the project, having been re-instated in the Foreign Ministry. In the course of an official visit to Saudi Arabia with the then Prime Minister Rashid el Tahir, we opened the subject again, this time with Prince Fahd, as he then was. Prince Fahd instructed the competent Ministers to conduct negotiations with their Sudanese counterparts on the questions raised. Saudi officialdom denied any knowledge of the involvement of the Ministry of Defence in the project. They added that the Kingdom was only too willing to consider financing Swakin through the Saudi development fund, provided the Sudan gave it the necessary priority in the long list of projects sent to them. That was what the President was told all the way by his advisers in Planning, Transport and Foreign Affairs. Dr Idris, who was with us in that mission, claimed that he knew better than the Saudi Foreign and Finance Ministers. His sources, he claimed, still confirmed that the project would be financed by Defence, the usual cock and bull story. There were all those dubious telephone calls made by the indomitable Idris, in which nobody knew who was briefing whom. Idris, however, ceased to talk of the 'higher-ups' on this occasion. The Prime Minister of Sudan had already discussed the matter with Prince Fahd and there was no one 'higher up' than him, King Khalid having entrusted his brother, the Crown Prince, with the conduct of government business.

We came back empty-handed, in spite of all the suspect telephone calls by Idris with his 'sources'. Almost a year later the President, accompanied by a king-size delegation, went to Saudi Arabia to discuss economic co-operation. His then Minister of Finance had a long list of projects and requirements, among which was Swakin. The Saudis confirmed the position they had taken all the time. Swakin would be financed by the Saudi development fund if it was given priority by the Sudan. At long last Nimeiri gave way. The project was not launched until 1978. One would have presumed the innocence of the Sudanese President, having been taken for a ride for four years by AK and his public relations men in Nimeiri's palace, were it not for what has followed. The President, instead of punishing those who had thwarted such an important project, instructed Nasr el Din Mustafa, the Minister leading the delegation of Sudan to Bonn, to discuss the new German aid protocol which included Swakin and to insist on Strabag.

That proposal was rebuffed not only by the Germans but also by the head of the Saudi delegation, Khalid al Masoud. The Saudis were present for the first time in a joint Saudi-German negotiation over Swakin. The Minister asked that the meeting's record should indicate that he (the Minister) had done his best on behalf of Strabag.

The Floating Cement Factory

The Sudan development drive entailed, by necessity, massive construction work. The cement industry is basic to the construction industry. The Sudan has two cement factories, one on the White Nile at Rabak and the other in Northern Sudan at Atbara. In the early 'seventies the combined rate capacity of both factories did not exceed 200,000 tons annually. Local cement supply, therefore, did not keep pace with demand. Many important projects, such as the Kenana sugar one, were given permission to import their own cement.

For this reason the Ministry of Industry and Mining has undertaken several studies in both the North (Red Sea) and South (Kapoeta) to determine potential areas for cement production. One of the major areas identified for such production is Marsa Ara

117

Kiyai on the Red Sea. It has the largest deposits in the country with enough reserves for the cement industry for a hundred years at the annual rate of 500,000 tons a year. At the same time negotiations were under way with the Kuwait Cement Company and Kuwait Foreign Trading, leading an Arab consortium, to establish another factory in the Red Sea area at Durdeib. Guest, Keen and Nettlefold of the UK were to undertake the works for the plant, with an initial capacity of 500,000 tons rising to 2,000,000 tons a year.

AK's trusted informers divulged to him plans for constructing a cement factory in that area of the Red Sea. No sooner had the information passed to him than he came with another one of his fanciful projects. This time he was to sell to the Sudanese government a second-hand factory. He proposed to buy and dismantle a factory in California provided that he managed the reassembled factory himself. Objections were raised against AK's scheme by the usual vigilantes. It was Musa Belal's turn again. He maintained that the price proposed for the used factory was exorbitant, that, even if the Sudan agreed to buy the factory, it would have to be inspected and that there was no question of TRIAD managing the factory. The Sudan had been running its own cement factories for over a decade. AK responded that the factory had been ordered and was already on the sea so there was no way to inspect it; the process was irreversible. The Sudan was to buy a pig in a poke. As far as the cost and financing were concerned, Belal told AK that the matter would have to be discussed with the country's financial authorities, who would have to determine the terms of financing and the competitiveness of the offer.

The Minister of Industry's inability to countenance such deals cost him his job; he was dismissed for his constant 'disobedience' on 25 January 1974. The new Minister of Industry, Badr el Din Suleiman, was not, however, of AK's mettle; he had Sudan's interest at heart. Suleiman came up with an ingenious way of curbing Adnan. Since the latter was not interested in enterprise, in the sense of investing capital in profitable business, but rather in mediating deals, often at exorbitant prices, he decided to call his bluff by giving him the choice of financing the project himself and taking the risks. Badr el Din signed a licence for AK and told him to go on with the project at his own peril. The government would be only too happy to see the factory running and producing. AK, of course, pretended that he was happy and went out with his licence in March 1975. The floating factory has yet to reach its port of call in the Sudan and be reassembled. At the same time every stalling tactic in the book was used by the palace cabal to frustrate the Kuwaiti project, and, like the case of the refinery, the Sudan got neither Adnan's nor the Kuwaitis'. In fact, Adnan's licence was withdrawn five years later because of his inability to live up to his obligations. The affair should have done much harm to Nimeiri's image, since, following the granting of the licence to AK, he had decided to stick his neck out and promise the people, in his *Face the Nation* programme, that cement shortages would be solved within six months. But Nimeiri always counts on people's short memory and lack of inside information.

Arms and the Man

Selling arms is AK's *métier*. The Sudanese Army is too modest for AK's exploits. One of the main things to which President Nimeiri and his colleagues addressed themselves after the coup, as was to be expected, was the re-organization and modernization of the Army. Not much progress was achieved in the years of tension. After 1972 Nimeiri and his successor in the Ministry of Defence, General Awad Khalaf Allah, an Air Force officer, went ahead with revamping the Army – unable to meet its basic function in defending the country's territorial integrity and the achievements of the May revolution – and helping in development. There was no intention of creating a *grande armée*. The rationale often given for the solution of the Southern Sudan problem was: you cannot have war and development at the same time. The country's resources were to be pooled and mobilized for one thing, development.

In this sense the Army establishment had a clear idea about the way the Sudanese armed forces should be developed. They had a clear vision of their needs and requirements of arms and *matériel*. What AK had in stock, however, did not match the Army's needs. The Army's established list of priorities was worked out on the basis of plans well studied within the country's global strategies. The list included communication networks, early warning and air defence installations and transportation for rapid deployment. AK did his best to influence the Army establishment. He failed. He then turned to the Supreme Commander, Nimeiri, who was more amenable. If the country's development plans could go to hell, the Army's did not deserve a better fate. Dr Idris, who was often rebuffed by the vigilant soldiers, avoided addressing them directly as he did with his civilian colleagues, for soldiers carry guns. In this case it was Nimeiri himself who did the arm-twisting.

AK sought to appease the new Commander-in-Chief, Khalaf Allah, the Air Force man, by making available to the army four used helicopters. The General declined the offer. It was demeaning to the Sudanese Army to accept outmoded equipment which it had not asked for nor inspected to verify its suitability, Khalaf Allah said. Adding insult to injury, Dr Idris told the General that the helicopters were already paid for. By whom? On whose instructions? For what use? These questions remained unanswered. The General's final word was 'No' to the helicopters, which are still lying in the desert under the scorching sun of Khartoum for all to see as a stigma of corruption.

Now that the helicopter appetizer had been aborted by General Khalaf Allah, Dr Idris and his mentors came with another bribe. On 16 May 1974 a certain Mr Louis Lauler visited the Assistant Military Attaché, Colonel Mohammed Tewfik Khalil, with a letter from Dr Idris dated 14 May. The letter read:

Col. Mohammed Tewfik Khalil,
Military Attaché,
Embassy of The Democratic Republic of
The Sudan,
London.

Dear Sir,

This is to introduce Mr. Louis J. Lauler. Please issue two documents as per the attached samples or slight variations thereof, as will be requested of you by Mr. Lauler. Mr. Lauler will also specify verbally to whom each of the documents has to be addressed. The documents are: a) a purchase order for a quantity of 3000 G–3 type rifles and b) an end-use certificate for this material.

Kindly assist Mr. Lauler in carrying out this mission without delay as the material has to be in Khartoum before May 23, 1974

Yours faithfully,

DR. B.E.M. IDRIS
STATE MINISTER FOR SPECIAL AFFAIRS
AT THE PRESIDENCY OF GOVERNMENT

The whole thing looked suspect to the vigilant Colonel. In the best tradition of Dr Idris everything was shrouded in secrecy. Questions such as to whom the purchase order and the end-use certificate were to be addressed and by whom the payment was to be made would be answered verbally as if it was a Cosa Nostra deal. Governments keep records and documents, particularly when deals relate to combustible issues. What was even more surprising was that in all those dealings there was never a mention of the Sudanese Ministries of Defence and Finance, the Bank of Sudan, or even the Ambassador under whom the Military Attaché worked. Mr Louis Lauler happened to be the managing director of Triad Capital Management International Ltd. Payment was to be made by a certain Perco Establishment of Geneva. This could not be the way institutionalized governments work; it did not look legitimate. The Colonel did the right and courageous thing. He told his visitors that he would have nothing to do with them and reported the matter to Army HQ, with a copy to his Ambassador who reported it, in turn, to Khartoum. Nimeiri was informed on the strength of the Ambassador's report, and his nonchalant reaction was: 'I know.'

The helicopter deal was but a bait and the G3 rifles but a starter for what was coming. The Saudi Ministry of Defence, as a sign of goodwill, offered a grant to the Sudanese armed forces, financial assistance to the tune of $40,000,000. No strings were attached. Typically, the palace cabal claimed that the Saudis wanted this money to go towards a certain end, purchasing Magirus trucks. The Magirus trucks were an old story. As early as 18 October 1973 Dr Idris signed, on behalf of the government, a contract with Klockner Humboldt Deutz (KHD) of Cologne, represented by Dr H. Zimmerman and Dr P. Kyd von Renburg. The government, under that

121

contract, was to purchase 150 trucks. The deal was to be financed by KHD on terms set out in paragraphs 2 and 3 of the contract. Both parties agreed that an additional 200 trucks would 'be completely covered by the German Commodity Aid for the fiscal year 1974.' The contract went on to say that 'the foreseeable aim is the importation of about 1000 heavy trucks from KHD.'

The Sudan under President Nimeiri, had made almost a fetish of a centrally planned economy. Development plans and action programmes were mapped out and were to be financed from identifiable finite resources. A special government department, the National Council for Planning, was entrusted with the allocation of those resources. Planning, understandably, had other urgent priorities for the German commodity aid which was now to be lavished, through presidential largesse, on KHD Magirus trucks. Finance, on the other hand, was not happy with the deal, for they said procedures for purchasing and procurement should be followed. There was almost a consensus that the trucks were unfit for the Sudan's arid climate. The President would not agree and had to be persuaded that the matter should be referred to those who knew better.

To this end a delegation led by Mohammed Bedri, representing the Ministry of Agriculture, the Mechanical Transport Department and the Sudan Mint, visited Germany to inspect Magirus trucks and tractors. KHD was not only seeking to sell trucks; they were also offering to establish an assembly plant for trucks and tractors in Port Sudan. The report of the mission was negative. On the other hand the Minister for Industry argued that the proposed plant would not meet his Ministry's requirements for licensing; 45 per cent of the parts should be manufactured in the Sudan for an industry to qualify for such licensing. He drew attention to the case of Clement M'boro, Minister of Industry during the regime of the parties, who was tried and convicted by the revolutionary courts for, *inter alia*, having granted a similar licence to Mazda, the Japanese car manufacturers.

KHD which had a long-standing representative in the Sudan, had now decided to look for a more influential intermediary. Dr Idris was the most eligible; he proved it by signing the agreement. Sure enough he brought in TRIAD but wanted the blessing of the President. The President obligingly called in his recalcitrant Minister of Industry, in the presence of AK, who unabashedly requested that a letter be sent, in the name of the President, requesting KHD to grant him 50 per cent of the equity in their proposed plant in the Sudan. The Minister reiterated his technical views on the unsuitability of the project, adding that he considered AK's proposition regarding the President's intervention with KHD improper. 'It is not for us to tell them who should do business with them and the President is a President.' Belal was concerned with the dignity of the office and person of the President, but dignity cannot be thrust on people. AK, faking admiration of the Minister's courage, told Nimeiri, 'You should be proud that you have such competent and candid Ministers.' He said the same thing of Mansour. The comment was only beguiling talk to lure the Minister into the quagmire of corruption. He too could have had his share of the cake. The Minister, unimpressed, told Adnan that his only concern was with industry, and the importation of trucks was a matter that fell within the purview of the authority of the Ministers of Commerce and Finance. Evidently AK was not so much concerned with industry; it was the commission he was after.

AK and Idris were indefatigable when it came to making money. So AK went ahead with the procurement deal for the Army, notwithstanding the report of the three-man mission and the views of the Army. In fact, Nimeiri himself, when he was told by his officers that their preference went to Mercedes if they had to buy German, concurred, recalling his experience in the South with Mercedes trucks. But then business is business. None the less the deal with the Magirus was struck. AK got his commission and he paved the way for a new agent with a magic name, Mustafa Nimeiri, the President's only brother, of whom we shall see a lot soon. Mustafa is chairman of a corporation bearing the same magical name: Wad Nimeiri Cooperative. That says it all.

KHD, encouraged by the ability of their influential new intermediaries, sought to go ahead with financing the rest of the deal through German commodity aid. The Sudan Ambassador to Bonn, Muzzamil Ghandour, was called by Dr Idris and informed of the 'Presidential wish' in this regard. The President, who could not care less for the counsel of his military and technical advisers, would not be bothered either with the priorities set by his own Ministry of Planning for the allocation for foreign aid. A sizable part of that German commodity aid was already earmarked for the Khartoum and Khartoum North sewage system. To the palace, the political powerhouse of the regime, plans and action programmes were only rhetoric.

In agreement with the Minister of Finance, I decided to lead the Sudanese delegation to Bonn on my way to the UN General Assembly. The new German aid protocol was being negotiated. It was a one-day affair. The Germans needed no prompting or explanation. Dr Eppler, the German Minister of Co-operation, expressed his surprise on learning that German government money would go to finance a deal with a private company. I told him, in no uncertain terms, that the Sudan priorities were set by the Ministry of Planning and those were the only priorities I was aware of. No sooner had I reached New York than I received a message from the President which was both rude and crude. In effect it said I was hereby instructed to undo what I had done in Bonn. My response was cool: 'I shall take the appropriate action and discuss the matter with Your Excellency in Khartoum.' The climax was to follow.

The Flying Home

AK's headquarters were divided between Paris, London, Beirut and California; his real home, however, was his Boeing 727. Among the useful tools he carried aboard his plane were two closets – one for Arab and one for Western clothes.

His wife Soraya was another important asset. She first came to Sudan because she was preparing a supplement for *Vogue* magazine on the Sudan. She was accompanied by a few models. The photographic session took place late in 1973. During this period Madame Khashoggi received VIP treatment. She was met at her husband's plane by a presidential limousine and stayed in the presidential guest house. She made four or five trips, always receiving the same VIP treatment.

As official photographer to Nimeiri, the new-found job, she travelled with him around the country. On one particular tour, the President and his photographer spent a few days in Port Sudan in the east of the country. Nimeiri's photographer soon assumed another role, in charge of his public relations. Her main duty became to keep journalists, particularly women journalists, at arm's length from the President. (These included Huda al Husseini of the Beirut daily *Al Anwar* and May Gandour of the Beirut women's journal *Al Shargya*.)

124

Private Lives

As a matter of principle people have no business focusing their attention on other people's private lives, be they Presidents or otherwise. But Nimeiri is not 'others'. He is the first Sudanese President to consider the private lives of his Ministers and aides a public domain; so should his be. In fact, because of the standards he has set for others, he should be exposed remorselessly to the public gaze. Nimeiri is avowedly a 'revolutionary purist' and purists, revolutionary or otherwise, have no business wallowing in sybaritic splendour. Now, as a latter-day evangelist, he is ordering innocent unwed men and women who dare be seen together in public to be flogged, locked up and publicly humiliated as adulterers; Nimeiri's commandments obey no legal or religious convention. In view of all this Nimeiri's conduct, past and present, cannot escape being part of the public domain. On the other hand, one would assume that, of all Sudanese people, the over-indulgent President Nimeiri of Mogadishu should be the last to be enraged by people drinking and womanizing. Maybe, with Allah's help he has turned into a contrite sinner but, with the help of Allah too, there will come a day in the years of our Lord, when the rest of sinful humanity in the Sudan will also atone to save their souls. They do not have to be dragged into penitence kicking and screaming.

President Nimeiri was now in the middle of a vice circuit. Even the symbolic May revolution celebrations were engulfed in it. Salim Eisa became its master of ceremonies. He organized two world-famous Arab singers, Farid Al Atrash and Warda al Gezairya, to come to the occasion. In their trail came a troop of girls few of whom were received at the presidential guest house. Five years after the socialist revolution the regime was celebrating its anniversary in the fashion which it had denounced in 1969 as lavish and wasteful – the charges made against Abdel Majid Abu Hassabo, Minister of Information during the regime of the parties. The lavishness for which Abu Hassabo was indicted was giving a party for Um Kalsoum, the legendary Egyptian singer, on which £7,000 were spent. Information Minister, Omar el Hag Musa kept at arm's length from this aspect of the celebrations, saying, 'I do not want to be the Abu Hassabo of the next people's courts.' Invitations for such theatrical and artistic functions always came from the Minister of Information. Not for this one. Omar saw to it that invitations for the Eisa entertainment group went out in the name of HE the President of the Republic.

Nimeiri became increasingly entrapped by his valets. Temperance and discretion had never been among his attributes; in politics as well as pleasure he always over-indulged. The outings organized for him by AK meant that he spent even less time in his office. On one such outing to Geneva he enjoyed the facilities of the Griffin Club, hardly visited by heads of state. Others took the form of cruises around the Mediterranean in AK's yacht. On one visit to Nice, Nimeiri did not bother to inform the Sudanese Ambassador of his presence. Travelling incognito was much more enjoyable and AK could take care of organizational matters. The Ambassador got to know about his President's presence only after French security got in touch with him, enquiring about security arrangements for Nimeiri.

Nimeiri was gradually distancing himself from the league of revolutionary leaders with whom he was initially identifying himself, such as Nasser and Boumedienne. He now belongs, according to his deeds, with the Bokassas of the world.

Dabbling in Diplomacy

Dr Idris's naivety in dealing with bureaucrats was more than matched by his deviousness in dealings with diplomats. Frustrated by my constant efforts to call his bluff and heartened by presidential protection of his lawlessness he decided artlessly to go over the head of the Foreign Ministry, as if the Ministry was a person, not an institution. His direct communication with the Military Attaché in London was only one example. On 7 November 1973 President Nimeiri decided to appoint Salim Eisa as an adviser and in that capacity to provide him with a Sudanese diplomatic passport. Diplomatic passports are issued to a host of persons at presidential will, to Sudanese and non-Sudanese. Dr Idris, instead of addressing himself to his Cabinet colleagues in the Foreign Ministry, chose to send stealthily a handwritten note to the Ministry's executive office, conveying the President's order to issue a diplomatic passport for Eisa. As if Idris was ashamed of the presidential decision, Eisa's passport application form reflected that he was born in Dongola, the ancestral home of the President. Dr Idris did not have to create a fictitious Sudanese birthplace for a foreign holder of a Sudanese diplomatic passport; the President, as we said, is empowered to issue those passports irrespective of nationality. Several diplomatic passports were issued to notables who helped the Sudan or played a heroic role in the region, e.g. Myriam Makeba, the African freedom fighter and the star of many an African summit was provided with such a passport without having to pretend that she was born in Khartoum.

Equipped with his diplomatic passport Salim bombarded Sudanese missions and legations in Beirut, London and Cairo asking for VIP treatment to himself and his boss, a treatment those diplomats only extend for limited categories of their own citizens holding diplomatic passports. My instructions to the embassies were clear: no such facilities for the Saudi and Lebanese. If they were to have VIP treatment at all, they should seek it from their own embassies. We were already the laughing stock of Arab diplomatic circles.

There was more than laughing, for highly respected Sudanese diplomats were disconcerted at criticism bordering on loathing coming from some Arab circles. For example, President Nimeiri in the spring of 1975 went to Iraq on an official visit. He sent Salim Eisa as an advance party to prepare the economic (read business) aspects of the visit, notwithstanding that Nimeiri was accompanied on that visit by all the staff generals of the economy, led by Badr el Din Suleiman. The Iraqis could not take this. They slammed their doors in the face of the pushy Lebanese, conveying their disdain to Omar Adeel, a former Sudanese Ambassador and the Resident Representative of the United Nations Development Programme in Baghdad. Adeel was a close friend of President Ahmed Hassan al Bakr and indeed the whole of the Iraqi establishment. There should have been no doubt as to the source of his information. Adeel also had no ulterior motive, for he did not know Salim from Adam. Without mincing his words, he conveyed the Iraqi displeasure to the President, in the course of a dinner given in his honour by the Sudan Ambassador in Baghdad. Nothing could have infuriated Nimeiri more than exposing his Achilles' heel. So there came the typical reaction: either me or this man stays at the party. Adeel, 'this man', left and whatever he or the Iraqis had thought before of Salim's relationship with Nimeiri was now confirmed.

Idris persisted in his diplomatic blunders. In mid-1974 he

127

instructed the Sudanese Ambassador in London, Ahmed
Suleiman, to contact his American counterpart requesting him to
urge the Ex-Im bank in Washington concerning the financing of
pumps for Kenana Sugar. Kenana is an independent entity empowered, by the laws constituting it, to deal and transact without
governmental intervention. Where such intervention was required
it was generally done by the Ministers of Industry and Finance, as
indeed the latter was doing in the case of Ex-Im. That incident,
however, enraged not only Sudanese officialdom. It also provoked
the Americans. The presidential Minister, having taken our own
institutions for granted, was naively seeking now to take other
governments for a ride. The American Ambassador in Khartoum,
who was certainly briefed by his colleague in London, called me on
21 June 1974 to express his dismay. I asked him to address himself
in writing to the appropriate authority within my Ministry. A few
hours later came his letter to the Under-Secretary of Foreign
Affairs.

EMBASSY OF THE
UNITED STATES OF AMERICA

June 21, 1974

His Excellency
Fadl Obeid
Under Secretary
Ministry of Foreign Affairs
Khartoum

Dear Fadl:

I have just learned to my surprise that officers of our Embassy
in London were recently asked by the Sudanese Ambassador
there to call regarding a pending Sudanese Export/Import
Bank application. The Sudanese Ambassador described the
approach as being 'on instructions from Khartoum'.

Without wishing to make this a matter of official record, I
thought I should let you know on a personal basis that such
procedure can only be found puzzling by officials of my
Government in Washington. Equally, it would appear hardly

likely to strike a responsive chord with officials of the Export/ Import Bank. As you, of course, know, I and my Embassy are ready at any time to serve as a channel between your Government and the people at EXIM as, I am sure, is your estimable Ambassador Hamza and his staff in Washington. *The possibility that private businessmen may occasionally take actions which muddy the waters would seem also to suggest the desirability that our official channels be kept clear.* In this way we can assist our common objective of assuring optimum consideration for your country's priority financial needs.

With warmest regards,

Sincerely,

Bill

William D. Brewer

The US Ambassador got it right. No Minister working for an institutionalized government would seek such a tortuous and awkward channel of communication. It should be presumed to be an action of private businessmen muddying the waters between states.

Needless to say, the Minister of Planning in Khartoum, who was handling the matter, was completely in the dark about both the uncalled-for presidential intervention and the circuitous dealing of the presidential Minister. The acting Foreign Minister (Dr Idris was in the habit of doing those things when I was out of town) wrote on 1 June 1974 to his colleague in Planning, pursuant to a report he received from our Ambassador in London, advising him of the incident. To that letter the Minister of Planning replied on 15 June, affirming that the action was unnecessary since his Ministry was handling the matter through the appropriate channels, adding that such acts were not only reprehensible but also detrimental to the name of the Sudan abroad.

Unholy Trinity and Holy Father

Adnan wanted to use Nimeiri to score not only material but also

129

diplomatic gains for himself. He rather fancied himself in the company of kings, presidents and other dignitaries. He already knew a lot of them. Nimeiri, a President, would be his conduit for meetings and poses with more of such people. He came up with an idea with Jerusalem at its centre, knowing the great sentimental value of the city for the Saudis, especially King Faisal. He proposed the sending of a delegation of Muslims and Christians to the Vatican to secure the Pope's support for the internationalization of the city. Nimeiri would emerge from this mission as a viable Muslim leader. (Nimeiri did better later; he emerged as an Imam.) Remember the story of the refinery and, through it, earning prominence in Africa. The whole idea was naive.

The fact that the Jerusalem problem could now be reduced to one of religious denominations did not escape the wily Adnan, but the solution of the problem was not his prime consideration. Rather, he wanted to enlarge the basis of his diplomatic contacts and please King Faisal, who lived and breathed Jerusalem. Adnan claimed, however, that he was undertaking this mission on behalf of the Saudi authorities. Without informing me, his Foreign Minister, Nimeiri sent a message to Emperor Haile Selassie to accompany him. The matter was brought to my attention in Addis Ababa by both the Ethiopian Foreign Minister, Dr Menassie Haile, and the Sudanese Ambassador, Mustafa Medani. I opened the matter with the President on my return to Khartoum. Unashamedly he claimed that he thought that the Ambassador would inform me anyway. In fact he told the Ambassador to handle this matter without communicating with the Ministry headquarters, i.e. the Minister. His message to Addis was carried by Dr Idris. The President must have been nursing some compromising secrets and did not want a confrontation with me. It later transpired that he was. Nimeiri insisted that the initiative was taken by King Faisal. 'But why aren't the Saudis participating?' I asked. He said they would. I then proposed that a Christian African delegation to the Pope should include a Catholic, and possibly other denominations. The President grunted. Having by now accumulated enough experience in deciphering the inscrutable mutterings of the President I said 'So let us invite Kenneth Kaunda a Catholic and William Tolbert a Protestant.' Nimeiri agreed and out went the telexes. Both responded in the affirmative, with Kaunda sending his Foreign Minister, Vernon Mwanga, and Tolbert sending the Vice-President.

Of all these preparations and communications Saudi officialdom knew nothing. So much was told to me by Sakkaf, whom I made a point of asking, and that was what Nimeiri was afraid of all the way. Nimeiri continued, however, to confirm that a Saudi delegation would participate in the talks, even after discussions in the Holy Sea, had been long in progress. Finally the delegation emerged; the Kingdom of Saudi Arabia was represented by AK and Salim Eisa. Luckily they arrived after the meeting with the Holy Father, but in good time to pose for a photo with him outside the Vatican Palace.

It was attempts like these to frustrate their schemes that set the two looking for ways and means to get rid of me. They seized upon an interview of mine published in the Lebanese weekly *Al Hawadith* entitled: 'Foreign Minister of Sudan to *Al Hawadith*: Iranian aid to Sudan equals the sum total of Arab aid' (*Al Hawadith*, 13 December 1974). Apparently they told Nimeiri that the article had caused great consternation in the Arab world. Wanting independent confirmation of their story they turned to our Ambassador in London, whom they invited to the Dorchester, asking him to write to Nimeiri to tell him that Arab Ambassadors in London had conveyed the displeasure of their governments to him. The article itself was a good example of journalistic sensationalism; I made no such statements. All I said, after enumerating the countries that were financing Sudan development, was that Iran was helping us too and that the Iranian contribution for 1974 (the $60,000,000 for oil) was more than the total Arab aid for that particular year. In fact the Kuwaiti Ambassador in Beirut, Sheikh Adsani, who later on became Speaker of the Kuwaiti Parliament, on reading the sensational headline, contacted in alarm his Sudanese counterpart, who referred him to the middle of the page. There was a long recital of the worthy contribution of Kuwait to Sudan's development.

Nimeiri was well aware of the role the Foreign Ministry was playing in mobilizing Arab resources for development, for diplomacy for development was more than a slogan. He was aware of the role undertaken by his Foreign Minister with Sheikh Sabah al Ahmed of Kuwait, Omar Sakkaf of Saudi Arabia and Mohammed ben Mubarak of Bahrain in the strategy for Arab food security and the place of Sudan within that strategy. In fact, the last briefed the President when he stopped at Bahrain, *en route* from an official visit to Iran, about the decision of his government to allocate a million dinars for the preparation of the master plan for the project. That effort was laboriously carried to its conclusion in the fateful 1974, with the creation of the Arab Authority for Agricultural Development. He was also aware of the role of his Minister as chairman of the OAU six-man ministerial committee charged with laying the grounds for Afro–Arab economic co-operation. The committee entrusted its chairman with pleading, explaining and negotiating the framework for that co-operation. That effort culminated in the creation of the Arab Bank for African Development based in Khartoum, also in 1974. Nimeiri had in his hands the record of failures and achievements. He did not have to listen to the suspect whispers coming out of the Dorchester in London. But he did so for his own good reasons, or rather their own good reasons. The news of the reshuffle of 26 January 1974 was already circulating in Khartoum two days before. The tale-bearer was Salim Eisa who arrived from Beirut by Middle East Airlines on the evening of Thursday 24 January.

TRIAD and the Super-planners

Adnan found the whole process, whereby Ministers and technocrats would draw up plans for projects which would then be divulged to him by his sources in Nimeiri's palace, to be too tedious and cumbersome. Things could be much simpler if a team of his did our job and decided what the 'real' needs of Sudan were. Such a team would have, furthermore, access to some vital information and data on how to maximize the profits of TRIAD. The country should be run from the offices of TRIAD. Adnan brought a team of economic experts, allegedly from Stanford University, to take the economy into their hands. The Minister of Finance and I were invited to a tea-party at the Presidential palace and presented with a *fait accompli*; we were introduced to the people who would do our jobs better. Adnan was present. Two-thirds of Nimeiri's Cabinet and a large number of his technicians received their education in the most prestigious American universities, not to mention others. They have distinguished themselves in both academic and practical fields. And they all knew without intermediaries the way to Stanford, which happens to be about nine thousand kilometres to the right of Nimeiri's socialist Sudan.

The palace tea-party was a social gathering where everybody was introduced to everybody, exchanging banalities. Two days later (23 April 1974) a letter signed by Dr Idris was received by the Minister of Finance referring to the palace 'meeting' and submitting the Stanford proposals. Stanford, through TRIAD, would undertake a study in order to determine which areas of the economy required immediate attention and propose the remedies. They would also draw up medium- and long-term development plans and follow up and supervise their implementation. The project would have cost over half a million pounds and involved 190 man/months of work.

The Finance Minister's response was curt and loaded. He noted that he knew of no palace meeting; he had been invited to a tea-party. He added that he had noticed the absence of the Commissioner-General of Planning at the so-called meeting. Decision-making has its processes. Driving the nail home the Minister sent copies of his letter to both the Commissioner of Planning and the secretary-general of the Council of Ministers. Then came some of the home truths:

1. General policies and planning targets are matters of sovereign policy. They have been determined by the competent political organs.
2. Agricultural development was now a subject of in-depth study by the Arab Fund for Economic and Social Development within the Arab food security strategy. Stanford could offer its services to the Fund.
3. Storage as an economic service was fully studied by the Canadian firm Howe, with Kuwaiti financing, and negotiations were under way to secure French co-operation in implementation.
4. Transport planning was also completed by ADAR (Pennsylvania), financed by Kuwait.

The Minister went on to enumerate the efforts of the government in sector planning, through Arab and international help covering, industry, manpower and training, mining etc. So once again an attempt by the leader to mortgage his country to a corporation was frustrated.

The Frontal Attack

The time comes when silence becomes acquiescence and connivance. I felt that the time had come to call a spade a spade. What was happening was blundering on a magisterial scale and broad daylight robbery. The Sudan does not belong to one man and many of us have a big stake in upholding the achievements of the regime. Besides, there were our claims of pure morality, the revolutionary courts, the public humiliation of the officers of the *ancien régime*, the high standards we claimed to set for public office-holders. Was it all rhetoric and clichés? Were we to be passive witnesses of a corruption never known on such a scale? Some may have thought that moral deviations would be shrouded in the mendacity of revolutionary rhetoric without realizing that, in the end, people become part of what they condone. What was worse was that condoning corruption makes a habit of it. Eventually it did. There was also the moral imperative of regimes set to change the world; never lose sight of the fact that there is an irreconcilable contradiction between right and wrong. The wrecking of our development plans also did not escape our minds. The cluster of all that disruptive interference was destined to lead to the collapse of the development plan. Neither did we want to see our regime dismantled nor, indeed, the idol discredited. In spite of the ambient gloom and creeping suspicions many of us were still hoping against hope that the man was good, and the trouble came only from those around him. It was a case of central good and satellite evil. There were many explanations traded; the man wanted to change the Sudan overnight, he was impatient, he had no realistic sense of how much and how long it would take to change a country like the Sudan. The soldiers of fortune were playing on all those weaknesses, it was often said. These explanations were not completely off the mark. In addition there was the overriding consideration: people thought that the Nimeiri who achieved unity, development, respectability for the Sudan was incorruptible. This thought had insulated their minds from even contemplating the possibility. What people did not realize then was that Nimeiri's character has many layers, and one of them is prone to corruption. With the benefit of hindsight we can now say that as early as 1973 Nimeiri was ostensibly presiding over the Sudan, but in reality he was presiding over the moral decline of his own regime.

Incensed with Nimeiri's telex on the German aid I went to see him on my return from New York with abundant evidence in hand. The meeting was crisp. I gave an oral report on my mission at the UN, as I have always done, then went straight on to the German aid story. The President was impassive, the face impenetrably opaque. I immediately realized that he was fuming with anger from within. I decided to continue.

'Mr President, I understand your noble desire to change the country overnight.'

He did not allow me to finish, but pulled me up short, saying 'I would have preferred to change it yesterday.' Very noble words indeed, if he only meant them. I persisted, depicting a gloomy picture of what our friends across the Red Sea and on the other side of the Atlantic think of us, narrating the catalogue of infamies and misdeeds in which the members of the palace cabal were involved.

There was first their incessant interference in the economy, signing contracts and burdening the country with financial obligations without consulting the appropriate Ministers, sometimes acting against their advice. Indeed, six years later (1980), when Nimeiri, through the strictures of the IMF and the prodding of his Finance Ministers, Osman Hashim Abdel Salem and Badr el Din Suleiman, finally succumbed to the disciplining hand of the Bank of Sudan and the Ministry of Finance (not for long though), the government had to hire a special adviser, Morgan Grenfell, to identify the size of the total indebtedness of the country. There was no record in the Bank of Sudan of obligations undertaken by the palace. Morgan Grenfell sent out telexes to all Sudan creditors asking for details. This could hardly be the country whose elite was described by Hammarskjöld in 1956 as the Prussians of Africa. The country had become by that time (1980) a house of woe, run by ignoramuses. The Prussians were no longer running for office, they ran to the borders instead, voting against Nimeiri with their feet. The many contracts concluded by the palace cabal, encumbering the country with debt, were not even vetted by our legal authorities; they were prepared by lawyers nominated by the contractors and certainly tailored to their needs. All of them were signed in complete secrecy by Idris, with his secretaries Kaltoum el Obeid and El Sheikh Rahama acting as witnesses.

Nimeiri's reaction was to deny that Dr Idris had ever signed a contract, doing nothing more than exchanging letters of intent with various companies. That answer did not square with the facts.

What Nimeiri did not know was that copies of all the agreements signed by Dr Idris were shown to me by friends of Sudan in international governmental and private financial institutions who were increasingly alarmed at the state of the Sudanese economy. Some of those contracts were making the rounds in the international money markets, released by the so-called investors shopping around for money for the Sudan. Those investors, in spite of their billions, were not in the business of investing their own money. The agreements, all duly signed, included: a contract with Klockner Humboldt Deutz AG, Cologne, West Germany, for the purchase of Magirus trucks signed on 18 October 1973; an agreement with Triad Naft Company SA for the establishment of a petroleum product refinery and petrochemical plant signed on 27 September 1973; an agreement with Triad Natural Resources SA, a Luxembourg holding company, for the construction and establishment of a textile complex signed on 10 February 1974; an agreement with Triad Natural Resources SA for the establishment of an integrated livestock raising and processing complex signed on 10 February 1974; an agreement with Triad Capital Management Holding Corporation, a Luxembourg corporation, for the establishment of a financial institution engaged in merchant banking, commercial banking and trade etc. signed on 27 September 1973. In other words the Sudan had been auctioned to one conglomerate, the auctioneer being, of all the Presidents of Sudan since independence, the only one who claimed to be the saviour of the country's body and soul from feudalism, capitalism, parasitism and whatever other -ism there was in the lexicon of demagogy. Should you tell your President that he was a liar or should you assume that the man was still not in the know? The unholy trinity were doing all this behind his back. In November 1974 I opted for the latter, thinking that if he did not know he would not be long in finding out. The Nimeiri of the early 'seventies was too modest for us to assume the former or indeed for anybody to believe us if we did.

Continuing with my charge sheet I went on telling the President that AK was using government agencies to further his own ends. Despite his billions he was not prepared to invest a single penny in the Sudan, rather he was making unearned increments using information supplied to him by one in our midst. At an advantage he kept parachuting into development projects conceived and prepared by the Sudan and financed, through the interventions of our institutions, by friendly governments. The only cost that

Adnan incurred, I continued, was his aeroplane.

Then came the question of the $200,000,000 guarantee, the astronomical interest rate and the anger of the Saudi establishment over the way it was concluded. The President could take no more. He was visibly angry, retorting 'I do not want to hear anything about this. This is money which we are not going to repay. Adnan promised so and he knows the Saudis better than you do.' He was genuinely, it seemed then, under the impression that the loan was on a never-never basis. It did not dawn on His Excellency that, had it been at all like that, why should SAMA issue a guarantee rather than dole out the money directly from their own coffers to the Sudanese exchequer. 'Your friends are bidding for their own gains,' he added. The friends he was referring to were the Sakkafs.

Nimeiri would have tossed me through the window if he could. It was characteristic of Nimeiri to see things in very personal terms; people were friends or enemies, outsiders or insiders. He sees only primary colours. Disagreement with him is enmity or defiance, concerted action by his Ministers conspiracy, and criticism of policies he espoused, even when they are blatantly wrong, is an attack on his person and a challenge to his authority. None of his Ministers ever claimed that their authority is on a par with his. Few of them, however, have refused to accept the thesis that obeisance to him should go to the extent of submission to corruption.

For those who are asking what has gone wrong with the Sudan development plan, why the country's economy is in a shambles and why the country that was destined to become the bread-basket of the Arab world is importing grain and dried milk the answer was given above. The Sudan economic plan, like any plan, is an organic whole; tamper with any part and you unleash a chain reaction, tamper with more than one and the whole thing collapses. So, if the Sudan had continued, through its bilateral mechanism, monetary co-operation with Saudi Arabia it would not have been in the dire straits it is in today. By mid-1978 Saudi Arabia, not without reason, decided that budget support to the Sudan would only be made on the basis of a certificate of good health from the IMF. The Sudan did not need the IMF mediation with the Saudis, who had been extending budget support to the country and its Central Bank to help bolster its reserves as early as the mid-'sixties. It was a government dealing with a government. Came 1974 and it was the revolutionary pure government of the Sudan that opted for dealing with its Saudi partners through the sullied hands of intermediaries.

The rest of the story need not be retold.

On the other hand, had the refinery been constructed as planned, production would have started in 1976, meeting Sudan's need for fuel. Shortage of fuel was the major debilitating factor that shattered industry, destroyed agriculture and almost brought transportation to a halt. Sudan would have been able to realize its dreams for food export or at least meet its set targets of self-sufficiency. The fiasco of Swakin also meant the choking of the economy; available agricultural produce could not be exported and capital goods for development could not be unloaded in time to meet programmed targets. In sum the deleterious effect of those decisions became deep and lasting. Nimeiri and his cronies, by those actions, had denied Sudan future sources of income that would have put the country in better economic stead in terms of favourable trade balance and self-sufficiency in food. The Sudan development plan has not failed; it was aborted, and it was aborted by the very man who stood to benefit most from its implementation if he was seeking a place for himself in history. But the man who had wanted hard and striven harder to be number one never knew, at any point of time, why he wanted to be number one.

In attributing the failure of our development programme and the collapse of our economy to the dysfunctional role played by Nimeiri and his clique, we are not claiming that our planning and the execution of the projects cannot be faulted nor that we are beyond criticism. Far from it; Nimeiri or no Nimeiri, we have to admit serious errors were made. Some of these are excusable because at the time we did not know any better, e.g. absence of sufficient data, while others are clearly the result of misjudgment and miscalculation. One might mention in this context the Malut sugar project and the textile industry, to which we shall come in chapter 7. Having said that, however, the sad truth remains that most of the projects and plans were aborted too soon to enable us to exercise the self-criticism and thus learn the necessary lessons.

Chapter Five

The Shocker and its Aftermath: 1975–1979

In friendship false, implacable in hate:
Resolv'd to ruin or to rule the state.

Dryden, *Absalom and Achitophel*

Guided Leadership, Witchcraft and the Perukes

Deluded by the momentum of his success, Nimeiri decided to draw on his reserves of political support and prestige. These had been won by his, or rather his government's, achievements in solving the Southern problem, the re-organization and rationalization of the state machinery and whatever development projects were under way. This generated a measure of legitimacy at home and respectability abroad. After 1975, Nimeiri felt strong enough to go it alone. In arriving at this decision he was greatly influenced by his advisers Adnan and Eisa. He was also encouraged by the coalition of convenience between the palace cabal and various elements inside the regime, who gave him for the first time a taste of personal power. The original SSU basic rules never recognized such power, and the constitution laid down all manner of checks and balances against the abuse of power by the different state organs, including the presidency. Reminders of those checks and balances, as we have seen, had not been lacking.

But while President Nimeiri, or rather, the palace master-minds of the 1975 events, knew what they wanted to do with the concentration of power in the President's hands, the others did not. The palace placemen were blundering, under the President's benign unconcern, and they wanted to continue gamely their illicit exploits, with his express support. On the other hand, neither the

139

ayatollahs of socialism nor the revolutionary *poseurs* of the National Assembly got down to business, after all the row they had kicked up about socialism and revolutionary purity, in order to delineate the bounds of this socialism, change course away from the unrevolutionary path or indeed carry their assault on corruption to the power centres where purification was needed most. In fact, the socialist battle cries soon became a distant echo; the closer they were to the core of the malignancy, the more timorous they became. Beheiry, the new Minister of Finance, seeking a firm financial policy, began to introduce into the economy an element of fiscal sobriety. The IMF, hardly a socialist institution, was now looking into the books more closely than ever. The IBRD, with the help of a number of Sudanese experts, was earnestly reviewing the performance of public enterprises, surely not with a view to strengthening socialism but rather to underscore the inadequacies of public ownership in the Sudan. Beheiry never had before him a new blueprint on socialism and the jubilant socialists never sat down to articulate their desired brand of socialism, nor did they review and redress the so-called unrevolutionary plans. In fact the revolutionary *poseurs* continued afterwards with the same sloganeering to hail the very internal and external achievements inherited from the discredited era, be they institutions, policies, blueprints or projects. The People's Assembly, Nimeiri's 'eyes and ears,' deliberated for a few months on the Nile Valley Company farce, eventually exonerating Mansour. Few members, however, cared to raise the issue of the monumental corruption and betrayal of the May ideals perpetrated by the palace, which was mentioned only in furtive whispers.

Nimeiri's spirituality (the understanding of which is of paramount importance in analysing the recent Islamicization measures) is an incongruous mixture of Islam, superstition and belief in witchcraft and magic. Dr Idris – the natural scientist – was the first to be engaged in recruiting witchdoctors to peer into the future in order to see what was awaiting the socalist leader, and the patron of the Sudan National Council for Scientific Research.

The Speaker, Rashid el Tahir, inadvertently introduced Nimeiri to his father-in-law, a pious man in his own right, probably responding to Nimeiri's call. Nimeiri was seeking to endear himself to religious sages. Nimeiri could not see the scholar in the religious sage, only his ability to dispense benison. The sage was to be, from then on, Nimeiri's protector. That he has done by giving Nimeiri a ring and a walking stick. By wearing the one and carrying the other he is assured of protection until Gabriel blows his trumpet.

Nimeiri, of course, found it convenient to forget not only about the planners, the scientific researchers and the modern institutions but also the guards, armed to the teeth, without whose protection, stick or no stick, he could not have escaped many attacks on his life. And it was convenient because he would owe nothing to anybody; it was all divine protection. Idris knew better and, since he was paying the piper, he called the tunes. Thus the divinely inspired messages were more often than not dictated by the zoologist Idris. Charlatanism is his *métier par excellence*.' Already in 1974, he introduced a well-known impostor from Obeid by the name of Sharif Abdalla who was supposed to be a magician. That man became the *mufti* of the palace and was regularly given VIP treatment, living in a Presidential villa in Kober on the outskirts of Khartoum. The Holy Man was caught at Khartoum airport smuggling a large number of perukes. The airport customs officer, Mohi al Din Sabir, insisted that the merchandise be confiscated until an import licence was produced and customs duty paid. Nimeiri ordered the man dismissed and the perukes released. He threatened to go himself to the airport to secure their release. The customs officer was suspended pending investigation. As for the merchandise, the Minister of Finance, brought into this fairy-tale by the President, contended that neither he nor the President had authority over customs, for the powers of the Director of Customs were enshrined in the laws. The Minister could only secure the release of the merchandise by paying the duty. It was agreed that the amount be charged to the palace. Sabir's death in a car accident was to Nimeiri very portentous; he was convinced more than ever of Abdalla's magic powers.

It was at this period that Nimeiri sent a circular around the Ministries entitled *Guided Leadership* (the word 'guided' is very significant), in which he asked Ministers and senior officials to swear an oath to him, undertaking not to drink alcohol. Having had more than his share, Nimeiri decided to abstain from drinking. One revealing aspect of Nimeiri's character is the pain he feels on seeing people enjoying what he does not enjoy. The circular was a source of sarcasm; few people paid heed to it and Nimeiri knew it. It was, however, a useful tool for blackmail, to be used, in case of need, to discredit and scandalize. Nimeiri has a voracious appetite for scandal and slander. For example, in 1979 the new assistant secretary-general for the SSU, Yahia Abdel Magid, called on the President to tell him that he had come across several cases of misappropriation of public funds: money dispensed by the SSU for private use, e.g. wedding presents, holiday travel, furnishing private homes etc. Nimeiri gave one of his sly smiles, a foot wide, and told Yahia, a disciplined and honest technocrat, that his drawers were full of such incriminating documents. Never mind, he said. Obviously the President was not so much interested in the probity of those working with him as much as he was interested in having incriminating evidence against them to be used when needed. Yahia assumed his new function in the wake of a major shake-up of the SSU with a view to making it more effective in pursuing the ideals of the May revolution, the very ideals to which Nimeiri solemnly committed himself in October 1971, and on the basis of which old politicians were purged.

The first persons to be affected by this misconceived religiosity were an Ambassador to Cairo and a senior officer in the Medical Corps. The Ambassador was a victim of Mahgoub, the speechwriter. Failing to influence the Ambassador to extend undue privilege to him, he reported him as an alcoholic. Nimeiri wrote to his Ambassador, asking whether he was in the habit of drinking. The honest Ambassador wrote back saying that he took a drink or two for reasons of health. Nimeiri summoned the Prime Minister, Rashid el Tahir, and myself and told us he wanted to sack the Ambassador. I told Nimeiri that he was not the only person not observing the ban on alcohol – although he was one of the few who admitted it. He was a very able man and his dismissal and public humiliation would be a big blow to his family. My appraisal of his abilities was supported by the Under-Secretary, Mohammed Mirghani, who was called to the meeting, on my advice, in absence of the Foreign Minister, Mahgoub Mekkawi. Tahir took Nimeiri's side arguing that the Ambassador should be made an example. Both the President and the Prime Minister knew only too well that closer to home the higher echelons of government were studded with inebriates, but it was of these relatively uninfluential people that Nimeiri chose to make examples. In effect, when some people tried, unjustifiably, to make a hullabaloo about the appearance on TV, allegedly drunk, of two of Nimeiri's friends (as they then were) Abul Gasim Mohammed Ibrahim, the Secretary-General of the SSU and Zein el Abdin Mohammed Ahmed, the President came out strongly in their defence. The defence was revealing; while clearing them of the charge of drunkenness, he added that they were young with all the excesses of their age, and whatever those excesses were the Sudanese should never forget their leading role in the revolution. Two years later, when Abul Gasim fell from grace, it was those very excesses of the young who should be allowed to live their age that were highlighted in the indictment order. It is not only Nimeiri's mind; his moral standards too are always selective. Faults are not to be corrected, some penalized, others justified, but all the time monitored and recorded to be used when needed.

The Disenchantment of Iheimir

While Nimeiri was soldiering on, dividing the ranks of his friends and adversaries, contaminating political judgment with super-stition and condoning high-level corruption, the country was being torn asunder. There were morbid signs of disintegration all over, not excepting the Army. In September 1975, a young Colonel, Hassan Hussein, attempted a *coup d'état*. The Muslim Brothers were thought to have been behind that coup, but there were few of their imprints in it. Among those who took part in this attempt were elements that played a role in re-instating Nimeiri in July 1971, such as Hamad Iheimir, who led the NCOs and stormed the palace to release Nimeiri. That Iheimir should be among the leaders of the coup against Nimeiri, only four years after he had fought for his life, was an indication of the level of disenchantment in some quarters of the Army.

The majority of those who participated in the coup attempt came from western Sudan (including Iheimir himself). Western Sudanese looked with envy on the South's autonomous status and the fact that it was the recipient of government and international aid, while the West remained as underdeveloped as ever, especially the Nuba Mountains. The coup was callously dismissed as a racist-inspired movement. In fact, even some of the senior pol-itical officers of the regime, originating from the depressed areas of the Sudan, were being vocal about their disenchantment with the way those areas were ruled from Khartoum. The South was an example to be emulated. One of these officers was the Governor of Kordofan (western Sudan) Mahmoud Hasseib, who came from the same region as Iheimir. Hasseib maintained in his official address to the SSU General Congress in January 1977 that regionalization was the only solution to the problems of those areas. He was shouted down by Nimeiri. The sycophants, to a man, followed Nimeiri in denouncing the racist tendencies in Hasseib's call for regionalization. Three years later, failing to grapple with the problems of the regions, particularly amenities and social services, the President announced his policy of regionalization (January 1980) as the only lasting solution to the problems of administration in the Sudan. Unashamedly the same chorus of sycophants, again to a man, hailed the declaration as yet another success of the May revolution, a new presidential revelation.

Going back to the September coup, news reached the Head of Security, Mohammed Yahia, that a coup was under way, organized by the Paratroopers in collusion with the Tanks Division. Yahia got in touch with Brigadier Yusuf Ahmed Yusuf (Commander of the Paratroopers), asking him to report immediately to Army Headquarters. Yusuf decided instead to inspect his forces before reporting to Army Headquarters, as any responsible officer would have done. On arrival there he was surprised to find out that the lights were off in the barracks of the night patrol. Upon enquiring he was told that there was a black-out but, as it turned out, these were the very soldiers that would attempt the coup. Realizing that their plot had been discovered, they decided to advance their zero hour. They moved and took control of part of the HQ before Yusuf reached it, immobilizing troops that could have been used against them.

Yusuf went to HQ for consultation, then moved to mobilize his forces, not knowing that the camp had already fallen into the hands of the rebels. He was arrested along with the Commander of the Tanks Division, General Taj al Sir al Maghoul, and the Deputy Chief of Staff, Mohammed Osman Hashim. Instead of moving to arrest the other officers in HQ the rebels tried to persuade Yusuf, whom they respected and admired, to join their cause. It was all over, the rebels told Yusuf; the President was under house arrest. Nimeiri had a rest-house outside Khartoum and was in the habit of spending Thursday nights there; not this Thursday, however. The rebels had surrounded the rest-house while Nimeiri was in his official residence inside the Army barracks. Yusuf managed to slip a message to the two senior officers still at Army HQ, Mohammed Yahia and el Sir Mohammed Ahmed. Both of them found their way stealthily to Nimeiri's residence and told him the news. One would have expected the President to want to go either to Army HQ or the Presidential palace or some other Army command post where he could monitor (he always monitored) and organize an anti-rebel operation. Nimeiri did nothing of the sort. He ordered his bodyguard Hussein Salih to hurry himself and his wife in Hussein's Volkswagen to the house of a friend of his, Mohammed Babatot, in Gereif, outside Khartoum. Al Hadi el Mahdi, we recall, was castigated by Nimeiri for abandoning Aba island. The President was abandoning his Aba for a safe haven in a friend's house, leaving it to the generals, the brigadiers and his former colleagues in the RCC to mobilize the forces, dislodge the rebels and re-instate authority. Many Presidents exercise their authority to the hilt and beyond. Nimeiri does this and more. He, more than any other President I know of, wastes no opportunity in asserting, in almost every speech he makes, the powers bestowed upon him by the constitution, as he misreads it, the power to lead and command in politics, diplomacy, the economy, administration etc. It was, however, only in the one area where Nimeiri is supposedly proficient, the Army, that this command was always abdicated when it was needed most. And it is in situations like these that we encounter another layer of Nimeiri's personality, the weak-kneed one. July 1971 might have been an aberration, we said. September 1975 could be nothing but a disgrace and an example of more of the kind to come. The disgrace was compounded by the way Nimeiri dealt later with his saviours, all unceremoniously cashiered. In that Nimeiri showed yet another layer of his complex personality: ingratitude.

The events of September 1975, brought into the light other facets of Nimeiri's character: not only Nimeiri the weak, who fled Khartoum and left his officers to fight the rebels and crush the insurrection, but also Nimeiri the superstitious, who believed that the survival of his regime was due to divine intervention. Nimeiri would not relate cause to effect; this is partly why he never felt that he owed anything to the officers who battled and risked their lives to keep him in power. They were simply the tools of divine intervention. That is, of course, a charitable explanation. Another ingratitude could be seen in his reluctance to give people their due. There is also the fear generated by his own inadequacy and humiliation. The divine is innocuous; it has no stakes in the game of power.

The September experience led Nimeiri to concentrate more power in his hands. Article 82 of the permanent constitution reads: 'The President of the Republic is the symbol of sovereignty and national unity and a representative of the people's will.' This piece of constitutional symbolism is saying that the institution of the Presidency symbolizes sovereignty because it is the highest authority in the land, national unity because it transcends the North–South regional divide, and should represent the will of the people, the only source of legitimacy. Nimeiri read it differently: firstly, for him the presidency is a person and not an institution; and secondly, he equated his will with that of the people; he does not act upon the people's will, for he is the people: *le peuple, c'est moi.*

Article 81 provides that the President is responsible for maintaining the constitution, protection of the country's independence, the safety of its territory and territorial integrity and the proper conduct of public authorities. Articles 5 and 6 (title 11) of the French constitution, for example, provide that the President ensures respect for the constitution, regular functioning of public authorities, the continuity of the state, and protects the independence of the nation, the integrity of its territories and its respect for treaties. These, of course, are institutional functions. They cannot be, nor is it feasible for them to be, carried out by a person. President Nimeiri, however, with the help of some, saw these powers as personal ones and acted accordingly, rambling into all areas of political, executive and legislative power.

We shall show later how Nimeiri would, time and again, come back to those two articles, arguing that whatever he was doing was in line with the constitution because he was expressing the will of the people. Notwithstanding this gross misreading of articles 82 and 81, Nimeiri wanted to add another clause to those two articles which would give him the right to issue decrees with the aim of protecting sovereignty, national unity etc. and which, furthermore, would have the force of law. Bakheit, the author of the constitution had been vehemently opposed to that amendment which blatantly contradicted the spirit of the constitution. Bakheit had called on me at the Ministry of Education. He was an Assembly member; I was not. He had told me of the desire of Security to have the constitution changed to allow for preventive detention without limitation. (Preventive detention could be exercised subject to time limitations provided for in law.) Preventive detention is very controversial issue. Many see in it a restriction of a fundamental right:

freedom of movement. Critics, however, while underlining human rights imperatives, often overlook the exigencies of public order, peace and tranquillity. Sudan's preventive detention law was issued with due regard to article 41 of the constitution: 'Freedom of movement and residence shall be guaranteed for all citizens, except for reasons of security and public health as prescribed by law, provided that the period and extent of any restriction thereon shall be fixed.' The law itself was borrowed from that of India and Tanzania.

The Indian experience deserves a special attention in view of that country's deep-rooted constitutional traditions. Also, since many of the critics of such laws in the Sudan are supporters of a pluralistic system, Indian experience becomes relevant. The issue of preventive detention was hotly debated in the Indian Constituent Assembly in 1947. The Assembly was then considering a bill of rights based on the US Constitution Fifth Amendment (no deprivation of life, liberty or property without due process of law). The assiduous and learned Constitutional adviser to the Assembly B. N. Rau played an important role in influencing the final outcome. Rau undertook a few trips to Europe and the USA to consult with constitutionalists including a visit to Justice Frakfurther of the US Supreme Court. That visit helped tone down many of Rau's propositions. Preventive detention has been known in India since the India Defence Act and even before (Bengal State Prisoners Regulations of 1818). These laws were originally meant to control dangerous persons whose presence at large threaten public peace and safety, e.g. smuggling, inciting communal and religious conflicts etc., but they were often used to incarcerate political opponents. Some of the members of the 1947 Constituent Assembly themselves had been subjected to those abuses. Despite their personal misfortune, however, those members could see the necessity for having such a law to safeguard the unity, integrity and economic wellbeing of the newly independent state. The overriding reason for the Assembly's decision in favour of the law was that courts made of immovable judges were less sensitive to the social and economic needs of the public than the representatives of the people who were periodically checked and elected by the people (Parliament and government). However, to guard against government abuse, the Indian laws provide that preventive detention of individuals beyond a prescribed period should be subjected to review by an advisory board consisting of judges or people qualified to be judges. That in itself was not enough guarantee since those laws were abused by Mrs Gandhi during the emergency. She could not, however, get away with it: not only was she checked by the judiciary but also by the people. She was thrown out of office by the people who 'periodically check and elect' Parliaments.

We were aware from the start both of the need to have appropriate laws and of the possibility that those laws might be abused. So under our legal set-up people held in preventive detention have to be reviewed periodically by the National Security Council and must be released on completion of the period prescribed by the law. Attempts to frustrate this procedure were rejected by the Attorney-General, Zaki Mustafa, as being unconstitutional. The President had consistently agreed with the advice of his then Attorney-General. Security, none the less, was able to go, deviously, around the law, e.g. releasing the detained person on completion of the period prescribed by the law and then immediately arresting them again.

I told Bakheit that the positive thing about all that was that the constitution, by and large, was working and being respected. Both Nimeiri and National Security realized that there were constitutional limitations to their powers and they were seeking to remove those limitations through constitutional means. In a sense they were seeking the easy way out, doing their job uninhibited by the constitution rather than fighting their way through the legal thicket. With the benefit of hindsight one can see now that the Indian model could only work within a system where people are supreme; they can make and unmake governments. Pluralism by itself is not the guarantee; it is the respect of the actors for the rule of the game that matters. We had seen examples during the regime of the parties in Sudan of disregard of the judiciary (in the case of the Communist members of Parliament). There were also examples where a dominant party in Parliament could abuse, with impunity, not only laws but the constitution itself (expulsion of elected Communist members of Parliament). So the problem in the end would be one of careful balancing between the right of the government to govern, e.g. establish law and order, and the right of the individual to enjoy his liberty within the law.

Bakheit continued talking, often gazing wonderingly: 'What about our claim that the Permanent Constitution was a result of serious deliberations? For months we have reviewed all types of constitutions, including the draft constitution prepared by the regime of the parties, to come out with something durable. Were this Constitution to be changed simply because there was an aborted coup, the whole exercise would have been futile. It could hardly be a permanent constitution. We would have no credibility.' He went on talking and debating.

However, while Security's preoccupation was with preventive detention, Nimeiri's was with quite a different matter. He was more concerned with the consolidation of his personal power, a power to legislate uninhibited by Parliament, issuing decrees that would have the force of law. He also wanted the constitution to stipulate that abuse to his person was a treasonable act. The President was persuaded to drop the latter. One should have asked how long it would take before abusing Nimeiri became high treason? In fact, it did not take long. Nimeiri did exactly that in his proposals to amend the constitution in July 1984. Eventually both Nimeiri and Security got away with the amendments relating to articles 81, 82 and preventive detention. Thus Nimeiri achieved another victory in his battle to concentrate power in his hands, the first step towards undoing the constitution. In fact, it was those very amendments introduced in September 1975 that Nimeiri agreed to remove in order to enable the opposition to join the ranks of the SSU; of that more shall follow. The Speaker of the Assembly and the First Secretary of the SSU, Badr el Din Suleiman, disagreed with Bakheit. They thought, perhaps sincerely, that the President was to be trusted. To them he was the bulwark against opposition forces.

Since September 1975 the constitution we had promulgated two years before was never the same again, not because of preventive detention, but because of the very nebulous addition to articles 81 and 82 which turned out to be pretexts for undoing the constitution itself. Bakheit fought to the end, tooth and nail, to no avail; the man with all his apparent simplicity concealed a ferocious steely will, always sharpened by challenge. He died in March 1976 overworked, despondent and disillusioned. Nimeiri, after his own fashion, came up with an obituary for Bakheit to which we referred earlier. He praised the man's achievements, the most important of which (the constitution) he had flouted. The turn of two others, the Addis Ababa agreement and local government, would come.

We have quoted Nimeiri's tirade against his Ministers, the last but not least part of which was devoted to his Foreign Minister, who travelled around the globe, attending conferences and cocktail parties. This same voluble and carefree Minister was called upon to organize and accompany Nimeiri on his trips to Europe and the USA and to help negotiate bilateral arrangements with the new administration in Ethiopia. These negotiations were meant as a follow-up to the Ethio-Sudanese Boundaries Agreement concluded in 1974, putting an end to a problem that had bedevilled the relations between the two neighbours for seventy-five years. The solution of that problem had eluded successive Sudanese governments since independence. In fact, that visit achieved more than was expected from it, an agreement by the Ethiopian authorities entrusting the Sudan with mediation in the Eritrean issue. Dr Gaafer Bakheit was named by the President as mediator. Ali el Nasri Hamza was chosen by Bakheit as *rapporteur*, while Obeid was chosen as the venue for secret discussions. Neither Bakheit nor the Ethiopian Head of State behind the initiative, General Aman Andoum, survived to see the outcome of this endeavour. As for the US and European trip the carefree Minister was charged by the President with the preparation of a trip that had lasted for seven weeks, abandoning his Ministry (Education), at the most crucial time as far as schools and universities were concerned. The President should have realized, by then, that travelling was not avoidable after all, in the trade of diplomacy, even for non-diplomats.

Who is in Command?

That trip was a fateful one. It was followed by a shock, the aborted July invasion. It was a shock because it reminded Nimeiri of his vulnerability and the shakiness of the regime. The architects of the 2 July 1976 coup were Sadiq el Mahdi and Sharif Hussein el Hindi, leaders of the Opposition Front. Libyan involvement in that attempt was exposed during the trials that took place later in Khartoum and Omdurman. Two thousand men trained in Libya had been infiltrated into the country during the year preceding the coup. The coup was planned to coincide with Nimeiri's return from an official trip to the USA and France. Nimeiri and his Ministers, of whom I was one, escaped death by arriving half an hour earlier than expected. Nimeiri decided to leave an hour before the scheduled departure time. Time has again confirmed Nimeiri's belief in the powers of his magicians. The rebels captured many targets speedily, and the Army HQ in Khartoum was put under siege. The Muslim Brothers were very much involved, and they managed to capture the central telephone exchange in Khartoum. The rebellion was crushed, thanks to the role played by some senior Army officers. The conspirators failed because they challenged and antagonized the Army. For the Army the crushing of the rebellion was a question of honour and pride rather than an affirmation of a commitment to a man or to a regime. No Army would have accepted humiliation by a gang of armed civilians.

Nimeiri was met at the airport by, among others, Generals Baghir (the First Vice-President) and Mohammed Osman Hashim (Deputy Chief of Staff). In addition to a host of Ministers receiving the President there was also the Head of Military Security, Mohammed Yahia. Ali Nimeiri, the Head of National Security, who flew with us from Paris, was also on the scene. When the news of the coup was broken to Nimeiri he looked nervous and frightened, no longer the usual façade. He was sadly worried and so preoccupied with his personal safety that he wasted no time in discussing the situation with his Ministers or making arrangements for his guest, Ahmed Mochtar M'Bow, director-general of UNESCO, who flew with him from Paris to accompany him to the African summit in Mauritius. It was my lot to see that the man and his wife were cleared before leaving the airport. General Hashim arranged for them to be taken to the official guest house while Ministers, with shells already whizzing about their heads, were left to make arrangements for themselves. On the advice of Ali Nimeiri and Mohammed Yahia, the President was hurried to a hiding-place (Ali Nimeiri's brother's house) in Khartoum Extension. There he remained until it was safe for him to return to his palace, playing absolutely no part in the measures that allowed his triumphant return.

By contrast General Baghir was serene, confident and imposing. There was no question at five o'clock on the morning of 2 July 1976, or indeed for the two days that followed, as to who was in command, articles 81 and 82 of the constitution notwithstanding. The old bull had taken charge and he would continue the fight to the death in order to save the regime. Baghir has always had an unruffled concept of leadership and command. Leaders are to lead, and especially to lead effectively in time of crisis.

Nimeiri's reproach of Imam al Hadi comes back again willy nilly to one's mind. Hadi was neither a soldier nor had he an Army under his command. President Nimeiri's incessant references to his authority as commander, protector, guide and omnipresent leader of the Sudanese also come to mind. The General's life was spared because of his courage; Khalid Hassan Abbas had advised him to use the military barracks in Omdurman, not knowing that these had already fallen to the rebels. Khalid's was the reaction of impulse. Soldiers assess situations before they plunge into action. Baghir discounted Khalid's advice and decided instead to do the logical thing a Commander-in-Chief would do: go to his command post. So both of them went to the Presidential palace to direct the resistance operation. That was the place from which command should emanate, Baghir told Khalid. Had they gone to Omdurman they would have met the fate of Hussein Shelali, commander of the Medical Corps, who courageously left the airport after meeting Nimeiri to report to his unit. Shelali was shot dead on the White Nile bridge on his way to Omdurman. He was one of many military exemplars who paid the price, with their lives, for commitment to duty. Baghir was able to use the official exchange, which had not been affected, to get in touch with, and mobilize, key units, including the one in Wadi Seidna, north of Omdurman. He was also able to mobilize forces under the command of Fatih Bishara, stationed in the Military School of Physical Education. From his command post Baghir also co-ordinated with Brigadier Mohammed Yahia, who played a big role in lifting the siege of the HQ in Khartoum, and with General Yusuf Ahmed Yusuf, who fought valiantly with his limited resources inside the besieged HQ.

At the same time there was Bona Malwal's attempt to establish links with the outside world. Bona, too, left the airport for his Ministry, to help pick up the pieces. That was where I joined him twenty-four hours later. And had it not been for him neither communication with the Army posts around the country nor with the outside world could have been maintained. Using the offices of the Sudan News Agency (SUNA) and with the help of foot messengers Bona was able to communicate with the Egyptian Ambassador in order to alert the Sudanese forces stationed in Suez. And through the network of SUNA he managed to relay his messages to the outside world via Juba and Nairobi. SUNA was also used to pass messages from General Baghir to the commanders of Army units across the country. The official telephone exchange linking Ministers had remained intact, allowing contact between the General and the Minister of Information. Bona was made to resign two years later, reinstated a year thereafter, only to be apprehended again and put under house arrest for nearly a year because of his disagreement with Nimeiri on Southern policy.

Army officers such as Baghir could have capitalized on their success in containing the incursion. Instead, we found the selfless Baghir triumphantly emerging to tell the Sudanese in a statement that was read on his behalf that their President would soon address them. The President was leading the resistance from his alternative command post, said the faithful General. He wanted to cover up for the shameless abdication of the leader.

Back to Institutionalization

The storm subsiding, Nimeiri emerged from his hiding-place with mixed feelings. There was his realization of the limitations of his power, popularity and vulnerability. There was also the appreciation of the role that his friends and supporters played in saving his regime, indeed his life. This never amounted to gratitude or a feeling of indebtedness to the selfless and infinitely more courageous officers; again Nimeiri's view of events was distorted by his peculiar spiritualism. For Nimeiri, his arrival before the scheduled time was not a coincidence; he had a presentiment, one which could only have been implanted by God, who wanted to save Nimeiri and deliver Sudan. Concurrent with this, and perhaps because of it, there was a feeling of bitterness and humiliation, a feeling which would rather efface memories of the whole affair than face their causes. For the time being, Nimeiri accepted, grudgingly, the need to share power. He gave the premiership to Rashid el Tahir, Abul Gasim Mohammed Ibrahim became secretary-general of the SSU, while Beshir Mohammed Ali, the Army Chief of Staff, became Commander-in-Chief of the Armed Forces and Minister of Defence.

In addition an office of Prime Ministerial rank – that of Presidential Assistant for co-ordination – was created in order to deal with matters not falling within the purview of the Prime Minister's activities. That post was entrusted to me. Nowhere in government was there a greater need for co-ordination and discipline than in the Presidential palace. The palace, as we have shown earlier, was a shambles. Naively I thought that at long last there had been a change of heart, and Nimeiri had come to realize the virtue of disciplining authority. I say naively because in all probability, and his future action bore this out, he was only scheming to have a counterweight to the very Prime Minister he appointed, scattering banana skins on his footpath.

Our concern with the institutionalization of the Presidency dates back to 1971, long before the promulgation of the constitution in 1973. The Presidency is not a man, we thought; it is an institution. To this end no sooner had the President been inaugurated in 1971 than he proceeded to issue two very important orders, Decrees 2 and 3, both dated 12 October 1971. Decree 1 dealt with the appointments of Babiker Awad Allah as First Vice-President and Khalid Hassan Abbas and Abel Alier as Vice-Presidents. Decree 2 provided for the creation of the post of a Minister of State within the palace, supported by several specialized departments in the fields of economics, national security, social affairs and legal affairs, as well as the President's private office, e.g. personal secretariat. The idea was to recruit the best talent available within the civil service to feed the political powerhouse of the regime with the input necessary for enlightened decision-making. The departments were to be of an advisory, not an executive nature, e.g. preparing background studies, briefs, analysis etc. Alongside those departments Decree 3 created four national advisory councils to help focus and articulate policies on the basis of decisions taken by the competent political and legislative organs. These councils were

1. The Council of Economic Advisers.
2. The Council on Rural Development.
3. The Council on Urban Development and City Planning.
4. The Council of Science and Technology.

The President, who shuns institutionalization saw to it that none of this was carried out, concentrating more and more power in the only auxiliary office within this establishment: the President's personal secretariat. Part of the havoc played by that secretariat was related earlier, all of it under the President's eye and with his express or tacit blessing.

Having been entrusted with this co-ordination post I seized the opportunity to instil an element of discipline and organization into the office of the Presidency, one of the main causes of economic, managerial and political turmoil. A comprehensive report was produced to this effect, dealing with every conceivable aspect of the Presidency. The report concentrated on all the areas of activities that constitutionalists call the reserved domain of the head of state. The President's executive functions were already delegated to the Council of Ministers. My endeavour was to make the Presidency an institution with defined functions and duties, an institution which could be managed by any President.

The function was made easy by the Presidential Decree creating the Council of Ministers in August 1976. Under that decree a number of areas of activity were excluded, e.g. relations with Southern Sudan, the judiciary, the Auditor-General, universities, defence and national security and foreign affairs. The Council of Ministers was to attend to the management of government, dealing with development projects, budget and finance, the civil service, social services, information, general education etc. They were also to prepare bills for the National Assembly and draft agreements with foreign powers and institutions.

Top of the list of my priorities was the question of co-ordination between the central and regional governments. The absence of a mechanism for co-ordination between these two organs played an important role in the conflicts that erupted between central government and regional government ministers on the apportionment of power in the years 1975–6. A council entrusted with the task of co-ordination was created on 10 May 1973, in the wake of the Addis Ababa agreement, but was abolished in the so-called reorganization of February 1975, which demolished all institutions without reflecting on the rationale behind their creation, let alone consulting and perusing the preparatory work and literature relating to them. The council, created by decree in May 1973, was presided over by General Baghir, the First Vice-President, a man with great authority and prestige in both North and South. It included in its membership Ministers like Gaafer Bakheit and Abdel Rahman Abdalla, Minister of Administrative Reform. Its *rapporteur* was a Minister from the South, Andrew Weiu. More than a wailing wall, that council had done admirably well in ironing out conflicts between government agencies in both the North and South.

Conscious of this situation we first hastened to work out a blanket law issued by an interim order in June 1977, covering nearly forty laws in which the powers of central government Ministries were delegated to their counterparts in the South. Earlier

(29 April 1977), a technical committee was formed by Presidential Decree 118 to review, from an administrative point of view, the experiences of both the People's Local Government in the whole country and the Regional Government in the South. The committee was presided over by Kamil Mohammed Saeed (Province Governor) and comprised Mohammed Ali Nadim (Province Governor) and Mohammed Ibrahim Abu Salim (Director of Sudan's Archives). On the strength of their technical report a high-powered commission was formed soon thereafter by Presidential Decree 187 to review the organization and, if necessary, propose the redivision of the different regions. The ten-man commission was presided over by Abdel Rahman Abdalla, a former administrator and later Minister of Administrative Reform in successive Nimeiri Cabinets. Six out of the ten members came from Southern Sudan, including the *rapporteur*, Dr Toby Madot. The heavy Southern representation in that commission was a deliberate policy decision. It is noteworthy that the President in issuing his decree creating that commission was acting on the strength of authority bestowed upon him by article 81 of the constitution, to which reference was made earlier. We shall have occasion later to see how the President, invoking the same article, decided personally and without prior studies or advice to redivide the whole South and suspend Regional Government institutions. That decision, with its serious political and constitutional implications, was simply drawn out of a hat. The calamities that have ensued from Nimeiri's foible are now a matter of common knowledge.

In addition to co-ordination with Southern Sudan a systematic approach was needed for Presidential decision-making relating to the SSU, the universities, the judiciary etc. The President, within the present Sudanese constitutional set-up, is the only link between the political and executive organs. This is the rationale behind his assumption of the presidency of both. Policy decisions from the SSU need to be classified, synthesized and translated into executive orders to the appropriate government agencies, executive, legislative, judicial and regional. On the other hand reports from the different regional SSU secretariats are meant to reflect the successes and shortcomings of the system, its ability to deliver and live up to its ideals. These inputs, together with the national security reports, the records of the National Assembly etc. should be the primary sources from which briefings are made to the President, keeping him abreast of the state of the nation.

For the universities the responsibility of the President is more in the nature of patronage. Under the Higher Education Act, the President is empowered to appoint both chancellors and vice-chancellors of universities on the recommendation of the chairman of the Higher Education Council. In making these appointments the President would need to have both the tools and information necessary for an objective decision, a system whereby the views of professors, students and other educators could be ascertained. In order to co-ordinate all these functions small units were created at the Presidency, headed by a Minister of State. Dr Hassan Abdin, a man highly respected by his peers both in the university and the SSU, was appointed to the job.

Several other persons were named to head the other specialized units: legal, diplomatic, administrative etc. More important was the creation of an integrated information system and a documentation and information centre. Dr Hassan Abasher el Tayeb, an able Sudanese management expert, had a lot to do with this exercise. Gone were the days of walking files with claims of indispensability. Moreover, information centres need no Mercedes cars nor do they have pensions and extended families to be sent to London on vacation at government expense. Presidential decisions should no longer be based on hearsay, whim or personal predilection. The salient facts of all cases should first be made available to the decision-maker, the President, in order that he might make informed judgments.

In addition to my co-ordination functions I was also named Presidential Adviser on Foreign Affairs. Here again a line of demarcation was drawn between foreign policy planning and day-to-day management of diplomacy, the latter being left for the Foreign Minister (Mahgoub Mekkawi) and his diplomats. Using both the Foreign Ministry and outside resources we engaged in a wide attempt at forcasting and policy planning on issues of immediate importance to Sudan's security and relations with the outside world, e.g. studies of the Gulf (long before the coming of the ayatollahs); the North/South dialogue, its impediments and prospects; the future of Arab/Israeli relations, war or peace; the neutralization of the Red Sea and the Horn of Africa; Africa and the arms race; Sudan and boundary agreements; Kenya after Kenyatta (Jomo was still alive); southern Africa after the independence of Rhodesia (negotiations on the independence of Zimbabwe were under way but a successful conclusion was not yet around the corner) etc. All these studies were prepared by teams drawn from the Foreign Ministry, universities and other relevant government departments. At the centre of all these studies was Sudan's role and the different options open to it. The President, I thought, needed to have before him well thought-out alternatives, on the basis of which he could formulate policy decisions to be discussed and adopted by the competent political organs.

With the economic situation deteriorating, as a result of the lawlessness of the palace cabal exacerbated by the energy crisis, the economy could not escape the President's mind. The management of the economy, according to the new government restructuring, was left to the Council of Ministers. However, there were some nagging problems, on which the President's attention had to be riveted, such as the accumulation of public debts. In this regard a position paper was prepared by a respected Sudanese economist, Professor Ali Mohammed el Hassan of the University of Khartoum. At the same time, marking his concern with this problem, the President declared in opening the second session of the National Assembly in 1976 that he would sponsor a high-powered international workshop to discuss problems of development finance in the Sudan, a euphemism for the debt crisis which was looming large on the horizon. Our aim in organizing the meeting was to attract to Khartoum Sudan's major creditors and development partners, in order to acquaint them with the country's investment potential and pick their brains as to the best way to handle the country's increasing debt profile. That important meeting took place in January 1977. The way it was handled by the uppermost authorities was revealing in so far as both government management and civic sense were concerned.

My assumption of these new responsibilities inside the palace created, as was to be expected, a great deal of ill feeling on the part of the palace cabal. They did not waste time in making mischief with the Prime Minister, persuading him that a parallel government was already installed in the palace and was impinging on his powers. This in-fighting was probably what Nimeiri had hoped for in the first place. The cabal was more alarmed by the streamlining of decision-making and the quality of personnel introduced into the palace. None of those new officers would hesitate to call a spade a spade.

Immediately following the Presidential announcement in the National Assembly I requested the Prime Minister to delegate the

State Minister in the Cabinet, Izz el Din Hamid, to work with me on the preparation of the meeting, using whatever links I had outside the Sudan to assemble an impressive group that would make the *Who's Who* of the Sudan creditors' league. The non-Sudanese participants included Dr Ahmed Mohammed Ali (President of the Islamic Bank in Jeddah), Mr Gerol G. Watterson (Commission of European Communities), Dr Hassan Abbas Zaki (President of the Abu Dhabi Fund for Economic Development), Mr P Henley (Export Credits Guarantee Department, London), Sheikh Ibrahim Abdel Karim al Ibrahim (Deputy Chairman and Managing Director, Arab Investment Company), Mr Z. G. Patel (Deputy Administrator of the UN Development Programme), Mr John Goodridge (Vice-President of the First National City Bank, New York), Mr Khosh Kish (President of Iran Central Bank), Dr Mahsoon Jalal (Vice-President of the Saudi Development Fund), Mr Paul Marc Henry (Director of OECD Development Centre) and Mr Stanley Please (of the World Bank). The Sudanese private sector was represented by Abdel Salam Abul Ela and Fatah el Rahman Beshir and the government was represented by Finance Minister Mamoun Beheiry, leading Ministers in the economic sector.

Beheiry presided over the meeting though he had the grace to request me to take the chair in view of my role in organizing it. I declined to tell Beheiry that the meeting was a functional workshop and as such it should be run by our economic shop steward. Hamid, the State Minister at the Prime Ministers' office, was the *rapporteur*. The workshop, entitled 'workshop on development financing and promotion of foreign investment in Sudan', was indeed an occasion for these financiers to discuss Sudan's debts with Sudanese ministers and managers of financial institutions in order to arrive at a solution to this chronic problem which was both satisfactory to the creditors and not detrimental to Sudan's development plans. The meeting addressed itself to the following problems: (1) growing government expenditure and insufficiency of domestic resources to meet them; (2) a high and growing foreign debt service and (3) cash imbalances of a rather severe magnitude.

Needless to say all this was not to the valets' liking; it was anathema to those who thrived in chaos and made fortunes out of non-accountability. Given Nimeiri's bitterness generated by the July 1976 coup, his aversion to power-sharing and his valets' resentment at the new inhibiting arrangements, the *modus vivendi* established after the July coup was destined to collapse.

The Resurrection of the Demons

The first clear indication on the part of Nimeiri that, as far as he was concerned, the institutional changes which had been brought about were only cosmetic, was his stance over the question of the Tourism Corporation. The National Assembly, which Nimeiri had urged to expose corruption, was about to discuss a matter raised by the performance of the above corporation. The question concerned the performance of the Tourist Corporation and several of its deals, including one concluded between the Corporation and an hotel chain in which bribes were allegedly paid. Reports of this particular deal were compiled by Ali Nimeiri (Head of Security). The President intervened and removed on 29 May 1977 the Corporation from the purview of the authority of the Council of Ministers. So in addition to foreign policy, defence, Southern Sudan etc. tourism now became an area of paramount importance to be retained within the domain reserved for the President.

The reason given by the President for the amendment was that tourism needed his personal attention, though development or education did not. The decision was also telling in that the President was now of the belief that even his exercise of executive functions was immune from the Assembly's supervision. Luckily Nimeiri, who assumed the portfolio of Finance a year later, did not hold it for long, for the budget too would then have been excluded from Parliamentary scrutiny. This misreading of the constitution was undoubtedly strengthened by those who maintained that the President's name should never be invoked in Parliamentary debate, even when it touched on executive decisions he had made. Nimeiri, by placing tourism under his own responsibility, sought to immunize the actions of Dr Idris, for accusations levelled against him would be accusations against Nimeiri's person. Dr Idris could thus work undisturbed under the President's cloak. Nimeiri made nonsense of his calls for Parliament to probe the executive, 'my eye that sees and my ear that listens'.

The palace cabal was now back in business. Indeed they had never relented in their attempts to frustrate, bypass and ignore institutional limitations, as the master was doing with the constitutional ones. Dr Idris, with the help of AK, was now joining hands with a new partner, Chairman Kim of Dawoo, a South Korean conglomerate. Kim is an astute business man, an AK of the Far East. Like him he also has a taste for politics, associating with the high and mighty and influencing decisions in favour of his country, a real patriot. For years Kim was trying to persuade the Sudan, which had excellent relations with North Korea, to have similar relations with the South. Of this we shall have occasion to see more in the chapter on diplomacy.

The South Koreans, however, promised that, as the price of such recognition, they would open their coffers for the Sudan. On the strength of this promise President Nimeiri went on the air to talk, in his *Face the Nation* programme, of the hundreds of millions South Korea was about to make available for development in the Sudan. He mentioned roads, agriculture, industry, you name it. Kim, as a sign of goodwill, opened offices for Dawoo in Khartoum, mainly engaged in construction. He had his reasons.

The South Koreans put forward plans for building a cultural centre in Khartoum. China had already built a similar complex named the Friendship Hall. The Koreans were not to be outdone by the Chinese. They decided to call theirs the Friendship Palace. They also promised to match the Chinese in providing a local component of the cost for the project, as the Chinese had done. China, who made available to the Sudan the foreign component needed for the execution of all their projects on very soft terms (a seventy-year repayment period and a nominal service charge) had also provided, on the same terms, a local component through the proceeds of the sale of Chinese commodities. They knew of the constraints on government to make local money, of a large magnitude, available for such big projects. These operations were entirely left by the Chinese to the competent government departments. In the case of the Koreans, however, according to Dr Idris, the importation of Korean commodities would have to be entrusted to certain traders; all, of course, friends of the Doctor.

The matter came before Harun al Awad, Minister of Commerce, who raised all manner of objections to this *modus operandi*, arguing that imports should be advertised to allow all eligible traders to apply for licences and leaving it to the Ministry to decide according to its established procedures. He conveyed his objections to the Prime Minister, who in turn briefed me. This occasioned the first major clash between Nimeiri and myself after the

161

July coup. Nimeiri insisted that the Koreans wanted it that way, i.e. that certain persons be given the right to import the Korean commodities. He also told me that if his Prime Minister would not instruct the Minister to give the go-ahead he would do it himself. Once again the President was not only obstructing his own government's procedures, he was flouting the moral standards his own regime had set as early as 1971. In fact the first Minister of the old regime to be tried, convicted and sentenced, Ahmed al Sayyid Hamad, was accused of exactly this. In the case of Ahmed, however, it was partisan favouritism, favouring members of his party in the issuing of licences. They were all Sudanese. In Nimeiri's case it was obeisance to the will of a foreign government, worse still a foreign company. Of course nobody believed that the Koreans cared a hoot as to who would be importing and trading in their commodities in the Sudan. But then it was the President who said it.

The Korean Palace project went through different phases. At first it was meant to be luxury flats to be ready for the OAU summit scheduled to meet in Khartoum in the summer of 1978. Then it was decided to turn it into an hotel, which brought it more within Idris' departmental authority. The Minister of State for Finance handling the project, Osman Hashim Abdel Salam, was vigorously against it. It was not one of our priorities and the financial terms were onerous, he told both the President and Dr Idris. On the other hand the Minister of Public Works, Mustafa Osman, on the strength of the advice of his technicians, ruled that the project be reviewed since the prices were jacked up by about 40 per cent. The President insisted on the project, notwithstanding the advice of his technicians and Ministers. Osman courageously held his ground and told Dr Idris that he would only give the go-ahead if a letter was sent to him from the palace to the effect that the project should go on even if it was not on the planning priority list. This was a matter of principle, Abdel Salam said. In an act of the utmost cynicism a letter to that effect was sent to Abdel Salam, signed and sealed from the palace. The Minister of Public Works also stuck to his guns. A meeting was arranged by Dr Idris for negotiations with the Koreans at the Ministry of Public Works. One hour, two, three passed with no Koreans in sight. On calling the palace to enquire, the Minister was told not to worry; the contract with Dawoo had already been signed by Idris. A few years later, when many of the Sudanese creditors were clamouring for the repayment of debt instalments, Dawoo was given priority, thanks to Presidential intervention. They were being repaid in commodities, mainly cotton. Among the creditors bypassed were Arab Development Funds who already had new lines of credit available to the Sudan, which could only be released on the settlement of accruing debts.

With this mode of operation the economy was apt to continue declining. The rate at which the Sudanese economy was sinking into debt accelerated. The Minister of Finance, Beheiry, became more worried and frustrated. He wanted to keep the President informed on a regular basis about the degenerating situation. Beheiry prepared a detailed memorandum in which he reviewed the state of the economy, dealing with public debts and uncontrollable expenditure. He suggested measures to deal with the situation and asked the Governor of the Bank of Sudan to produce a periodic report on the foreign currency situation. The report was to go to the President with copies to the Prime Minister and myself. Nimeiri's reaction was less than favourable. He viewed the process of keeping him in touch by supplying him with data as harassment on the part of the Finance Minister and an attempt to impose his ideas upon him. Nimeiri asked Beheiry to tell 'his' Governor not to send him any more reports. Beheiry and the Governor wanted to present the raw facts of the economy, hoping that they would do their work on the thinking and action of the President. 'Tell him that those figures would not frighten me,' the uninhibited Nimeiri said to Beheiry. All the economic revelations were not enough to fray his nerves. Only shocks like the ones of September and July did.

Nimeiri was to be confronted with more truths. While I was on a visit to Saudi Arabia for the joint Saudi-Sudan Commission, headed by the Foreign Ministers on both sides, I had a long brief with me. Among the things to be discussed was a request for the Saudis to assume responsibility for the repayment of the $200,000,000 loan guaranteed by Saudi Arabia, as well as the interest that had accrued on it. It was an irony, for this was the very loan which the President claimed was given to us on a never-never basis.

The Saudi Foreign Minister, Prince Saud al Faisal, unhesitatingly told me that the Kingdom, as a big lender, could not do this. It would set a precedent. The accumulated interest by then was equal to the principal. The matter, he said, should be looked into by the technicians to consider possible refinancing for the repayment of the loan. It was the lot of the Governor of the Bank of Sudan, Ibrahim Nimir, to do this. A few months later an agreement was reached through the IMF, as a part of the economic stabilization programme, whereby Saudi Arabia would take charge of the principal but not the interest. It was our own doing and the Saudis were not prepared to bail Sudan out of problems of its own making. They were ready to finance, and finance generously, Sudan's development programme but not to pay the bills of its government's mismanagement and corruption.

This much was conveyed to Nimeiri who had always maintained that the Saudis had no intention of reclaiming their money. Sudan went on paying interest which by that time had exceeded the principal. Nimeiri was chillingly unembarrassed when I told him all that. 'It doesn't matter how, as long as it is going to be repaid,' he said. His statement was mind-boggling. This could not be the same man who claimed that the Saudis wanted it that way. It could not be the proud President of the Sudan who would not see the disgrace in the fact that our most trusted partners in development were now dealing with us through the good offices of others, the IMF. And certainly it could not be the leader of a poor country going deeper and deeper into debt who could not see the criminality of making his country pay unnecessarily over $100,000,000 in interest (the difference between what was obtained by AK and what was offered by Chase).

But Nimeiri's most effective way to deal with truths and revelations like this was to brush them aside. He lives in his own world of make-believe. But even make-believe has a limit. You can hang a hundred lemons on a pole, but that would not make the pole a lemon tree. To Nimeiri it would. Beheiry was dismissed in a minor reshuffle in February 1977, a month after he had presided over the meeting on development financing and the promotion of foreign investment, to be replaced by Sharif el Khatim as Minister of Finance. In that reshuffle I was appointed to assume, in addition to my functions in the palace, the portfolio of Foreign Affairs, the first step towards easing me out of the palace. Four months later (29 May 1977) the President undertook his major reshuffle which put an end to institutionalization and resurrected the demons.

By Republican Order 156 (29 May 1977) the Tourism Corporation was removed from the authority of the Prime Minister, as indicated earlier. Dr Idris was rewarded for his services to the republic by being promoted to full Minister status. Mohammed

Mahgoub, the author of the requiem, was made Minister of State. Ali Nimeiri, the man who gave refuge to the President in his brother's house, was relieved of his functions to be replaced by General Omar el Tayeb. His presence was an annoying reminder of a shameful episode in which the President's ego was bruised and his pride bloodied. Ali was made Ambassador to Teheran, shortly before the arrival of the real Ayatollah. The other saviours of Nimeiri were soon to follow: General Baghir, General Beshir Mohammed Ali, General Yusuf Ahmed Yusuf. Brigadier Mohammed Yahia, the Head of Military Intelligence, was saved from the humiliation of unceremonious dismissal by his death on 2 July, fighting to defend Nimeiri's regime.

A month after the February minor reshuffle the President addressed the nation, presenting the political platform for his re-election for a second term. In that speech he solemnly declared, 'Whoever of my aides and assistants gives me good advice and proves to be faithful and efficient, I shall draw him closer to myself and shall honour him and raise his standing.' The President went on to quote a saying of the Prophet: 'If God wishes a Prince to fare well he gives him a good minister, who if the Prince forgets reminds him . . . and if God wishes him ill he gives him a bad minister, who when the Prince forgets, fails to remind him.' In that address he also promised that if he were elected he would devote part of his second-term presidency to preparing his successor. That solemn declaration was as good as the lies in it. Six years latter (1983), Nimeiri was re-elected for a third term only to propose a year later an amendment to the constitution making him President for life. As for the good Ministers, we have met a fair sample of them in the May reshuffle. The rest of the bungling, inept helpers would come later. Nimeiri, entrapped within his palace cabal, also suffered another great loss, the death of Omar el Hag Musa, his father confessor. Omar died in February 1977 after having nominated the President as SSU President for a second term. In his own way, he used to have a great influence in taming the President.

Nimeiri never had a good grasp of economic issues nor did he care for details. His reaction to the report of the Governor of the Central Bank abundantly proved that. He generally left his Ministers to grapple with problems, many of which were of his own creation. The economic Ministers, rather than attend to the country's overwhelming problems, often found themselves busy putting out fires kindled by the palace in the first place. The economy was thus in deserved tatters. To Nimeiri the easiest way out of the mess he created was through visiting the results of his own mistakes on others, looking for scapegoats. In the course of his fifteen years in office the Sudan has gone through eleven Ministers of Finance. Nimeiri was always out to save his neck rather than remedy the ills of the economy. This vortex of ministerial changes has sapped vitality and frustrated planning, for planning presupposes continuity.

So out went Beheiry and in came el Khatim. The new Minister, like his predecessors, had to deal with figures rather than fiction. And his turn had come to bring some home truths to the presidential ear. Khatim presented a lengthy memorandum to the Council of Ministers, the salient points of which were prepared by Osman Hashim Abdel Salam and the dismissed Mamoun Beheiry. The memorandum painted a gloomy picture of both the economic and fiscal situations and impressed upon the Council the need for economic stabilization and the implementation of sweeping austerity measures. Khatim particularly drew attention to Legislation 27 of 2 March 1972 relating to the procedure to be applied in contracting outside obligations that have financial implications.

The Council was divided. There were those to whom figures meant little and who hardly did their homework. They disposed of the issues in a spirit of cavalier persiflage. Some were shouting slogans about development being the road to salvation, as if they were addressing a public gathering, not a decision-making body. They could not see that development without the necessary financial backing would only backfire and sink Sudan yet deeper into the red. Only a few others wanted to break out of the vicious circle of debt, interest and more debt. They voiced their concern about the mismanagement of the economy, the deteriorating productivity, the negative role played by the palace valets and the larcenous waste resulting from the intervention of foreign elements in the affairs of the Sudan. I was one of this group, a mere handful.

For Nimeiri this was a stab in the back. When I went to see him about an impending trip to Norway, a return call to the visit made to Khartoum earlier in the year by Knud Freydlund, the Norwegian Foreign Minister, Nimeiri told me, 'You could have told me privately instead of raising the matter inside the Council of Ministers. . . . Unlike anybody else my door is open to you. You could have told me all you wanted to tell.' He was referring to the debate in the Council of Ministers. The remark told me a lot about what

Nimeiri thought of his Ministerial Council. It was a hostile force to be reckoned with, not a decision-making organ to formulate policies and to be consulted. To Nimeiri's mind offices are favours bestowed on friends who should show their gratitude by their silence if not their outright connivance. The more important the office, the greater the gratitude of the beneficiary should be. To him my criticism of our economic performance was downright ingratitude. He also wanted friendship maintained his way; I wanted it mine. As a result I was removed once again from the Foreign Ministry, and out went Khatim, the Minister of Finance. The Prime Minister, Rashid el Tahir, was made Foreign Minister and Nimeiri assumed the portfolio of Finance, claiming that the situation required his own personal supervision.

Nimeiri always endeavours to give ministerial reshuffles fundamental rather than personal reasons, such as policy reorientation. When Nicola Sayqali of the Beirut weekly *Al Sayyad* asked him, 'What are the reasons behind the two fundamental changes in the new Cabinet: your assumption of the Premiership and the Finance Ministry and the dismissal of the Foreign Minister and the appointment of the former Prime Minister in his place?' Nimeiri gave a preposterous answer:

In view of the fact that Sudan has assumed a bigger role in the world because of its influence in world affairs, it was necessary to entrust the Foreign portfolio to someone at the level of Vice-President. . . . Apart from that, foreign policy is a concern of the President. It cannot be shaped by personal whims. While acknowledging that Mansour Khalid is a capable minister, his personal opinions were not cemented to the people. I have given him two opportunities and he failed. The foreign policy that I want is the policy of development and not of cocktail parties. It might be *necessary* to attend such parties but it cannot be sufficient. I am confident that al Rashid el Tahir will *execute* the foreign policy I dictate *to the letter* (*Al Sayyad*, 6–13 October 1977).

The statement was telling in many ways. For one thing, the President did not mention a single word about his assumption of the portfolio of Finance, the economic crisis and how he would through personal supervision, deal with it. Some observers tried to read in

167

Nimeiri's reshuffle an attempt to pave the way for the two leaders of the Opposition. He was holding the premiership for Sadiq el Mahdi and Finance for el Hindi, they thought. These were the very posts the two held before the May revolution. That was, of course, too rational an analysis. Experts in Nimeirology knew better. Nimeiri's decisions can never be subjected to rational analysis; they are always alibis and personal vendettas. In September 1977 things came to the boil. The economic malady was properly diagnosed by successive Ministers, and the remedy, though bitter, was prescribed. Nimeiri, however, was not so much concerned with saving the patient as with absolving himself from responsibility. He therefore looked for scapegoats. Khatim was yet another scapegoat in a long and endless list. As to his 'ungrateful' friend, the Foreign Minister, there were enough reasons for a personal vendetta and by now the reader must have seen a lot of them.

Nimeiri's humourless statement about cocktail parties was made four years before his prohibition laws, though a couple of years after his 'guided leadership' circular, which prohibited Ministers from drinking and cocktail parties, necessary or not necessary. Adlai Stevenson, with his refined sense of humour, may have put it better. 'Diplomacy,' he is reported to have said, 'is alcohol, protocol and vitriol.' But, cocktail parties aside, what Nimeiri was after was something else. The chapter on diplomacy will throw some light on Nimeiri's brand. His reference to his Vice-President and new Foreign Minister was demeaning, saying he would carry out his master's policy to the letter. 1978 and beyond gave us a taste of those policies.

Ministerial reshuffles, as we have said before, are also occasions for settling old scores. Nimeiri dismissed the Minister of Public Works, Mustafa Osman, whose views on the South Korean affair were well known, and a year later the Minister of Defence, General Beshir Mohammed Ali. The latter was on a trip to the flooded Gezira district, where the Army was undertaking relief operations, when he was told of his dismissal. Nimeiri would not listen to Information Minister Bona Malwal who suggested waiting for the General to come back from his mission before the news was announced. The General learned of his dismissal from his car radio on the way back to Khartoum. He stopped the car, removed the flag and drove home. The only conceivable reason for his removal from office, to be replaced by Nimeiri himself, was the fact that he was a reminder of a past better forgotten; a reminder to him that he owes his continuance at the helm to the courage and altruism of certain officers dismissed *sans cérémonie*.

The scandalous way the General was dismissed was not an exception but almost a rule. In 1978 Nimeiri dismissed Foreign Minister Jamal Mohammed Ahmed while he was on an official visit to Belgium. In 1979 Minister of Finance Osman Hashim Abdel Salam received the news of his dismissal through the wires of the IMF. He was in Washington negotiating Sudan's economic stabilization programme. And in April 1984 the Minister of Commerce, Ahmed Salim, got the sack while he was leading his country's delegation to the EEC–ACP negotiations in Fiji. He was the spokesman for the whole of the ACP group. Ingratitude you may call it, but it is also utter lack of sensitivity.

General Baghir, the commander of the July operation, was soon to resign his post for 'health reasons'. That was his way of saying that he was sick of it. He was replaced by the former RCC member Abul Gasim Mohammed Ibrahim, who was till then the blue-eyed boy of Nimeiri. Shortly thereafter the love was lost. The Minister who is 'not cemented to the people' (myself) was entrusted with the editorship of *Al Sahafa*, one of two SSU organs, as well as the assistant secretary-generalship of the SSU in charge of ieology, a most improbable place. From then on I was meant to articulate and propagate policies and ideologies that I was, supposedly, unwedded to.

A few friends might ask the question: why did you stay after August 1977? The same question could have been asked: why did you stay after February 1975? The latter question we answered in chapter 4. We thought that it was a case of central good, satellite evil, so one had to dig in and fight. In politics battles are fought and lost before they are fought and won. As to the former question the answer is more difficult. One should have done it; 'should have' is a very unfortunate expression in any language. However, there was a lot at stake and one was dealing with a devious man ... so one had to 'answer a fool according to his folly lest he be wise in his own conceit.' Accusations like derision of the SSU (by refusing an office within the party secretariat), opposition to the national reconciliation (which was the issue of the day) etc. could have been levelled, with absolutely no opportunity to answer back. Nimeiri's monopoly of the media has put people in a vulnerable position in relation to him. By having access to the media of *Al Sahafa* and the SSU, one would have at least a forum in which ideas could be expressed. Within the bounds of the possible this forum was fully used, sometimes to call Nimeiri's bluffs as we shall see later.

Divide and Misrule

Institutionalization having failed and public discontent over the state of the economy growing stronger by the day, Nimeiri aware of the threat that the opposition National Front continued to pose, launched a programme of 'national reconciliation'. His commitment to this 'national reconciliation' with the different parties in the North, was as disingenuous as his commitment to unity at large between the South and North. Nimeiri never wasted time on good causes for their own sake; they were good only if they could help entrench him in power. The South was to be won not for the sake of national unity, but as a countervailing force against the North, still divided in its support of the regime in the early 'seventies. The patriotic considerations that had motivated the architects of the unity agreement, both in the North and South, and the many Sudanese who hailed the agreement, were a different matter. In the same vein, what Nimeiri aimed at in national reconciliation was simply to defuse the time bomb represented by the opposition in exile. It was a cynical ruse to manipulate the opposition.

Nimeiri had in fact asked Ali Nimeiri (Head of Security) to put together a hit squad and eliminate the leaders of the opposition, el Hindi and el Mahdi. Ali Nimeiri refused. He was a Muslim, he told the President, and furthermore, many members of his family were Ansar, i.e. followers of the Mahdi. Such an act, Ali said, would be a stigma for life on himself, his children and his family. 'The job of Security is not to eliminate the President's enemies,' Ali continued, 'but to provide him with information on the actions and motives of adversaries.' Nimeiri told the unbending security man that he knew how to do it as he had his parallel security agency, meaning by that the feeble palace cabal and possibly their mentors abroad. Ali was sacked in 1977.

With this new device of national reconciliation Nimeiri could not only eradicate opposition but also use elements of the National Front (the outside opposition front led by Sadiq el Mahdi and Sharif el Hindi) to counterbalance internal elements. Already, as he was making overtures to the opposition he was castigating SSU elements for being against national reconciliation and for attempting to halt the process. They were after the protection of their own positions, he claimed.

Nimeiri met Sadiq el Mahdi in Port Sudan on 7 July 1977. That meeting was preceded by one organized by a leading Sudanese businessman, Fatah el Rahman Beshir, and held at President Nimeiri's house in Liverpool (the President had become a summer Liverpudlian since the late mid-'seventies). The meeting was an icy one, interrupted by statements like 'If you think that you are the Imam of the Ansar, I am the leader of the whole Sudan. You are welcome to come and conquer power.' It was the bully in Nimeiri that was speaking. In fact this imamate issue must have been bothering Nimeiri a lot, and it is certainly one of many reasons that influenced his future decisions on religion and the state. By the middle of 1977 there was a thaw. Nimeiri welcomed Sadiq with the news that, as a token of his goodwill and as a sign of appreciation for the trust Sadiq had placed in him by meeting him (what a view to have of oneself!), he had decided to grant an amnesty to all political prisoners. Sadiq went on to enumerate the reasons which prompted him to take this step: fear of Soviet designs, fear for the South, the need for stability and unity in order to attract Arab money. There must have been a few other reasons that Sadiq chose not to mention. But, as was to be expected, Sadiq told Nimeiri that he was encouraged by the President's statements of late, displaying a commitment to the tenets of Islam ('We have been hearing new things about you . . . you are guided by Islam'). Nimeiri clapped in jubilation. Somebody was believing him.

Sadiq agreed that conditions in the Sudan did not favour a multi-party system and that one party or one integrated political organization was more suitable. Nimeiri, at this point, started to praise the SSU and its achievements in an attempt to convince Sadiq that it was the desired organ. He could not, he said, in view of the popular support it wielded, do away with it in order to satisfy a minority. (Seven years later, as we shall see, Nimeiri proposed the abolition of the SSU which 'wields great popular support'.) Sadiq disagreed, claiming that he wanted a more open, more representative and more effective party. At this point Nimeiri said, 'I do not say that the SSU is a revealed organization; in fact, there is ample room for improvement and you have the right to call for it.' (Sadiq was invited to put his views to the Central Committee of the SSU later on.) Sadiq went on to talk about a democratic constitution and

Islamic legislation. Here again Nimeiri retorted with an ingeniously non-committal statement:

> 'Our state of affairs was not "revealed" but is capable of being reformed. And whereas I do not agree with your request for a democratic constitution, for the present constitution, to my mind, is democratic, there is no harm in a constitution with "more" democracy and Islamicism in it.'

The two interlocutors went on to discuss foreign affairs. Nimeiri mentioned Ethiopia and the success of the Eritrean revolution against the 'bloody regime'. 'As for Libya,' he continued, 'I must, in retaliation for what happened in Khartoum last year, launch a similar movement in Tripoli.' Sadiq argued that it would be best not to interfere in Ethiopia's internal affairs. 'Good neighbourly relations,' he said, 'are necessary because we have long borders with them and we are fed by the same river.' As to the Libyans, Sadiq said that they had nothing to do with the July movement and that the responsibility for what had happened rested with Sudanese exiles. He expressed his hope that a reconciliation would be affected with the Libyans. Nimeiri welcomed the idea and charged Sadiq with the task of opening talks with Gaddafi. Sadiq did that and his mission was hailed in the Sudanese local media. Probing the extent of Sadiq's commitment to his alliance with Sharif el Hindi, Nimeiri suddenly interposed

> 'I must remind you that I am meeting you in the capacity that I know and not as a representative of others. Others should not brag about this meeting, especially not el Hindi. This man is a devil and he is very greedy. Unlike you he has accounts in various banks. He had asked King Faisal (God rest his soul) in 1972 to arrange for a meeting with me in Jeddah. In fact we met and talked. He made claims through the media that I had negotiated with him on this and that, which made it imperative for me to repudiate his allegations thus closing the door.'

In a sense that was all that Nimeiri was after, to drive a wedge between Sadiq and el Hindi. In fact, I was a witness in Jeddah of Nimeiri's first meeting ever with el Hindi, and his last. It was an amusing spectacle. Nimeiri resorted to one of his common tricks, that of playing the underdog, the one who knew nothing and was responsible for nothing: the beguiled. He surprised me by lauding el Hindi for his courage and resolution in Aba. He said the rebel forces fought very well and that the government forces could easily have lost the war. That should have completely disarmed el Hindi. He pretended he was. If he really was then it would have been a masterpiece of public relations, disarming your arch-enemy in the first encounter. Nimeiri is an excellent actor and in Jeddah he had occasion to show his talent. The reality, however, always came out earlier than expected. That was why el Hindi, a consummate actor himself, never fell into the trap. El Hindi started by saying that with the Communist Party out of the way the prospects for national reconciliation were better. He also said that he was no longer interested in politics; he wanted to return to Sudan and take part in its development. He added that he had good relations with Prince Mohammed al Faisal, who was looking forward to investing in the Sudan. Hindi insisted that the process of reconciliation be launched immediately. He also wanted a declaration to that effect. Nimeiri promised that he would make such a declaration immediately he returned to Khartoum. This was never done.

To go back to Nimeiri's meeting with Sadiq in Port Sudan, Sadiq asserted that he was talking on behalf of his other colleagues. So for the time being Nimeiri failed to divide the Front. He told Sadiq, however, that he was free to make the contacts he wanted within the country. On that note of accord ended the Port Sudan meeting. Sadiq had swallowed the bait. For all of us a process of national reconciliation had begun; some of us decided to take it seriously. The Sudan does not belong to us nor does it belong to the opposition. However, in the course of the years from 1969 to 1977 we had achieved many things that we were proud of and able and ready to defend. On the other hand there was a lot to improve upon within our system. Those who went through and fought constitutional transgression, economic blunders and discrepancies between text and action should be the first to admit that. There was no sediment of doubt in my mind as to where I would stand on both issues.

Others within the SSU were averse to criticism, particularly when it came from outsiders. Such criticism was suspect even when it touched on brazenly obvious shortcomings. What those SSU elements did not know, or did not care to know, was that the objective critiques of Sadiq would, if anything, strengthen the regime. On the other hand even his unsubstantiated castigations, while inadmissible, would not pose as much danger to the system as would our condoning of the President's continuous violation of the laws and deviation from the ideals set by the regime. To make confusion worse confounded these same elements continued to recite chapter and verse, both the constitution and the National Charter, while passively watching their Bible being trampled on. In the circumstances, their aversion to the criticism emanating from the newcomers was indeed suspect.

After his meeting with Sadiq, Nimeiri decided to give him a taste of power, of things to come, paving the way for his becoming a member of the Politburo. He was invited to address the Central Committee. Sadiq spoke about the changes he would want to see, including changes in the name and organization of the SSU. He also spoke strongly against the idea of the alliance of 'popular working forces'. In the following weeks prisoners were released and some rehabilitated in their former jobs. Many of Sadiq's supporters were brought back to the civil service. Sadiq himself returned in September. This followed a general amnesty announced by Nimeiri. Abdel Wahab Ibrahim, Minister of the Interior and State Security, pleaded in the National Security Council that the measures should include the Communists. He argued that since the government was releasing the extreme right (Muslim Brothers), it would show a balanced judgment if the extreme left (the Communists) were also included. A large number of Communists received amnesty and many of those Communists who were living in exile returned then.

Sadiq's nomination to the SSU resulted in some friction between himself and his erstwhile supporters. By late 1977 Sadiq had become isolated inside his camp. Nimeiri had managed to buy time for himself at the price of a few hundred political prisoners. At the same time Nimeiri sent a delegation headed by the Speaker of the Assembly, Abul Gasim Hashim, to London to talk to el Hindi, the 'devil'. After seven days of talks between el Hindi's representative and the Nimeiri government an agreement was reached. A press conference was held in London at the Sudan Embassy on 22 April 1978, in which el Hindi announced his support for Nimeiri's national reconciliation programme and the agreement was read.

The agreement was a give and take: what Nimeiri wanted was an undertaking by el Hindi that he would resume political activity inside the Sudan, and would not work on the unmaking of the Addis Ababa agreement (Nimeiri reserved this task for himself).

El Hindi wanted a democratic SSU and guarantees of unions' rights and freedom. El Hindi, like el Mahdi, accepted the idea of a one-party system but stipulated that 'its ranks be opened to all the sons and daughters of the Sudan and that all its ranks, from the base to the leadership, be elected'. He also expressed support for the Addis Ababa agreement and the solution of the Southern problem which 'had squandered the material and human resources of the country for seventeen years'.

Article one of the agreement with Hindi stated that the permanent constitution was the basic law of the land and underlined the fact that the third part of the constitution

> guarantees basic freedom and rights to citizens including the right to participate in public life and to conduct elections for public offices . . . the freedom of belief and worship and the performing of religious ceremonies . . . the freedom of expression and of the press . . . the right to assemble peacefully and organize and participate in demonstrations. . . . This chapter although allowing the suspension of these rights and the enforcement of emergency measures in exceptional circumstances stipulates that these measures shall be lifted as soon as the exceptional circumstances which make such measures necessary cease to exist.

In article six of the agreement el Hindi maintained that the 'foreign policy of the Sudan [shall be] based on the principle of positive neutrality in Arab affairs especially during this critical period' (i.e. Nimeiri should withdraw his support for the Camp David agreement). The agreement ended by calling for the dissolution of the National Front and provided for the return of its members, especially fighters, the disbanding of the training camps and the handing-over of weaponry inside and outside the country to the armed forces. The declaration stated that those returning would be able 'to enjoy all rights and have all duties that the Sudanese people enjoyed,' therefore 'putting an end to the era of disagreement, conflict and disunity so that the opposition could come back home with all its men'.

The original draft agreement sent to Nimeiri, though containing the main points of the adopted one, also contained classical references to the separation of powers, as if drawn from

175

Montesquieu's treatise. The President passed the draft to Badr el Din Suleiman and myself for comment. We both discussed it, in the light of constitutional provisions and Suleiman drafted the amendments making the text more in consonance with the constitution, allowing for future modifications that would spell out or consolidate the chapter on the rule of law. It was intriguing, however, that el Hindi in his handwritten letter to Nimeiri has insisted on only one thing, the insertion of the words 'the Sudanese opposition', in reference to his group. Nimeiri unquestioningly agreed, saying, what was there in a word? Despite the fact that the last paragraph of the agreement mentions 'our belief in the sincerity of good intentions of the President' el Hindi had no illusions about Nimeiri; he remained in exile.

Sadiq, on the other hand, was completely outmanoeuvred by Nimeiri. His appointment to the SSU Politburo gave him illusions of power, but he was never to attain real power. Nimeiri had clasped Sadiq in a deadly embrace and almost choked him to political death. Sadiq, however, was able to wriggle free, putting up a fight over Nimeiri's single-handed support of Sadat's visit to Israel. On the other hand, by opening negotiations with el Hindi and signing the declaration of April 1978 Nimeiri was strengthening el Hindi's political platform at the expense of Sadiq's, as the former came to be seen as the real leader of the opposition in exile, and perhaps that was why el Hindi insisted on using the word 'opposition' in reference to his faction.

By February of 1980 the national reconciliation programme had broken down in all but words. Sadiq stayed out of the country when preparations for regional and national elections were being made. In a *Face the Nation* television broadcast, Nimeiri spoke of continual close communication between himself and Sadiq. He added, 'I can now confirm that Sadiq el Mahdi fulfilled all he had promised, loyal to his homeland, to which he is devoting all his efforts and capabilities.' He could also have added 'and very useful to me'. Nimeiri's eulogy meant nothing. The same Sadiq was described two years later as a foreign agent.

The incorporation of elements of the Opposition Front (chiefly Sadiq) had served two purposes: it enabled Nimeiri to contain Sadiq and introduced an element of conflict in the SSU itself, between the newcomers (Sadiq and the Islamicists) and the old guard. In dealing with the Islamicists Nimeiri put his SSU hat on, reaffirming all the time his commitment to the SSU, the National

Charter, the constitution etc. With the SSU he wore his national reconciliation hat, repeating his commitment to the process of incorporating all elements of the Sudanese polity into the SSU. It was amazing to listen to Nimeiri, wearing his SSU hat, lambasting sectarianism while at the same time allowing for all the old sectarian configurations to re-emerge nearly a decade after May 1969. The inclusion of Sadiq el Mahdi, his uncle Ahmed el Mahdi, and Ahmed al Mirghani (Khatmiya sect) as members of the Politburo of the SSU at one time or another was only one piece of evidence of that. It was equally amazing to listen to the same President, and indeed to many unsuspecting underlings of the SSU, telling the world that sectarianism was dead and buried, in spite of all the symbolism reflected in the presence of sectarian leaders in the higher echelons of the SSU.

With his agreement with Hindi, and that with Sadiq before it, Nimeiri could have been a consensus President. He was already hailed in the foreign press as the man who brought peace to the South and unity to the whole of Sudan, the wise and magnanimous leader. But Nimeiri, with a cynical lack of a sense of history and proportion, wanted to rule the Sudan on his own terms, oscillating left and right but still always right. The President missed the chance to achieve what no other leader had achieved. The ego-ridden President who had conquered the South was now only seeking to have the Mahdi, the Mirghani and the Hindi under his feet in order to dominate the very air people breathed in the North. Both the opposition outside and many within were ready to live with a reformed Nimeiri; after all there was a ten-year investment in him. Nimeiri, however, wanted something else; his stratagem was to divide and misrule. Nimeiri's basic premise, not without reason, was that the day the Mahdi and Mirghani sincerely agreed on something, water would flow uphill. He acted accordingly.

The Best People in the Sudan

From the Foreign Ministry I went to *Al Sahafa* and the SSU. I took national reconciliation seriously and decided to engage in a national debate that went beyond the slogans: the philosophy behind our institutions, economic and constitutional achievements, religion and its place in our scheme of things. *Al Sahafa* was a good medium. Sadiq el Mahdi was the first to respond to my invitation. He wrote several articles on the economic situation. A debate was organized on public freedoms, to which people of different political shades were invited, including some renowned rejectionists. I also initiated another public debate through a series of articles addressed to both the Marxists and the Islamicists. Some thought that the exercise was tedious and pedantic; it was more comfortable to trade in slogans.

It was also during this period that I endeavoured to put my views on the democratization of the SSU. The opportunity made itself available when the Central Committee of the SSU, in response to Sadiq's appeal, entrusted the Politburo, in the wake of the reconciliation, with reviewing the structure, policies and modes of operation of the SSU. On 23 March 1978 the Politburo selected a committee to undertake this task, under the chairmanship of Abul Gasim Ibrahim. I was made *rapporteur* to that committee. The newcomers were represented on that committee by Dr Hassan Turabi (Muslim Brothers). Other members included, *inter alia*, Badr el Din Suleiman and Bona Malwal. Turabi and I had done more than our share in the preparation of the committee's report. Suleiman was honest enough to take exception and present his own dissenting report.

I presented that report to the Politburo within six weeks. The report proposed certain measures to rejuvenate the SSU, its vitality already sapped and its muscles atrophied. The SSU was becoming more and more directionless and purposeless. Nimeiri himself said even worse about it a year later (August 1979) though he gave the wrong reasons for failure and visited responsibility for it on the least responsible. Regimes with revolutionary claims, always need rejuvenation lest they lose their momentum and eventual credibility. 'God forbid we should ever be twenty years without rebellion,' Thomas Jefferson said. He was as revolutionary as they came and he knew the pitfalls. The report underscored three basic themes: collective leadership, effective political supremacy through an energetic role in policy planning and supervision of the execution of plans and integration rather than subordination of trade unions and the media to the SSU.

The salient points of the report presented to the Politburo were:

1. That democratization meant first and foremost that elections should be held for all posts on the Central

Committee and the Politburo, including the SSU secretary-general.

2. No appointments to the Politburo should be made by the President, except for a few office-holders who would become *ex officio* members, i.e. Speakers of the National and Regional Assemblies, Vice-Presidents, and the Army Commander-in-Chief.
3. That both the Central Committee and Politburo should be reduced in size and made trimmer, giving examples from other one-party systems in both eastern Europe and Africa.
4. That ultimate authority, in all policy decisions, would rest with the Politburo when the Central Committee was not in session, i.e. the President only acting as a head among equals.
5. All policies and programmes to be voted upon.
6. That the President in exercising his constitutional prerogatives as head of state, e.g. appointing Members of Parliament, should seek the advice of the Politburo.
7. That unions should not be domesticated but allowed to act freely, according to a prescribed programme within the framework of the national charter. The same should apply to the national press.
8. That the specialized committees of the Central Committee should address themselves to specific functions and work on drawing up programmes of action rather than waiting for government departments to submit programmes for approval.
9. That the SSU should be self-sufficient and should by 1981 depend totally on its own resources.
10. That the SSU bureaucracy should be reduced and selected on the basis of stringent criteria and that the General Secretariat be limited to three assistant secretaries-general.

In fact, the report included some fifty pages in which about forty specific proposals were made.

Nimeiri was evasive. He started by arguing that the measures would entail an amendment of the constitution, forgetting all his statements in 1975 about the omnipotence of the SSU. A few speakers took off from his leading statement and began disparaging the memorandum. Some of those speakers were members of the committee that prepared the report and hardly uttered a word against it at the committee stage. A few others joined in the castigation. Rashid el Tahir, for example, argued that there was nothing new in the proposed measures, for the problem with the SSU was not in the highest echelons. (My word!) Badr el Din Suleiman, on the other hand, maintained that the proposed measures would turn the SSU into a ubiquitous and omnipotent machine. Omnipotence, in the end, became a one-man privilege. A third group, who would normally have shared my thinking, proposed referring the matter to another committee; their way of saying 'Count us out, Jack' this time. Their reasons, confided in me later, were that they were suspicious of Turabi's blessing and defence of the report. Of these men, very few have survived long enough to pray to God with Nimeiri as the Imam and Turabi as the Muezzin. With the help of Dr Turabi (for his own reasons) we managed to demolish the many feeble arguments advanced at the meeting. Turabi was right in saying that this was the first time one had heard of a political leadership shying away from assuming authority that theoretically belonged to them in the first place. I recalled the President's statements on the supremacy of the SSU, his 'requiem' of February 1975 among others. I also recalled Dr Bakheit's memorandum, adopted by the Central Committee in March 1975 on the same subject: *Hakimiyyat al Tanzim*. One of the highlights of that memorandum which I stressed was the paragraph defining SSU authority. That document asserted:

1. The hegemony of the SSU in national action.
2. Hegemony does not mean licence to do what we please; it is action within prescribed constitutional, political and legal limitations.
3. The SSU is not the party bureaucrats, whatever their positions are within in the hierarchy.
4. Hierarchy in the SSU is popular hierarchy, which means that the individual, the President of the SSU, comes at the bottom of the pyramid.

That document, as I said, was read by its author, discussed by the Central Committee and adopted unamended. Nimeiri was then in the chair all through. The President who normally dreads confrontation (that is why he always addresses his decision-making organs in monologues) surprised all those who wanted to be more royalist than the king. 'I am a democratic President and whatever you decide I shall abide by. In the exercise of my duties as President I have always sought the advice of the Politburo and acted upon it.' That was the final Presidential verdict. Certainly he did not mean it, and was happy to see the Politburo deciding, not on the basis of Nimeiri's declared verdict, rather on that of his unspoken inner feeling.

Bona Malwal, with his caustic sense of humour, summed it up very aptly. 'If I were in the place of the *rapporteur*, I would not have produced such a report. My report would have been much more concise. It is all milk and honey, there is nothing to improve upon and we are the best people in the Sudan,' said Bona. Having listened to all that my decision was final and unequivocal. I surely do not belong to the 'best people in Sudan'.

It was, therefore, time to say goodbye. My tolerance had cracked. I was disgusted and never cared to conceal my disgust. It was no longer political differences; the issue was by now one of self-respect. However could any man witness with his own eyes all this treacherous betrayal of ideals and desecration of institutions without murmuring an objection, if such ideals and institutions mean anything at all to him? However could any man see all those ideals demolished and still go on acting virtues that were no longer there? However could any man identify himself with all these monstrosities while unashamedly bending over backwards to denounce them in the privacy of his home and the homes of his friends? At times, some leading lights of the regime would tell you that all was well when you knew that they were saying the opposite the day before. Alarmingly, some of them were even honest about it, the only justification for their optimism being that Nimeiri was full of smiles in this morning session with them. That, in a sense, summed it all up. The May revolution is what Nimeiri does. Those who believed in this were welcome to their beliefs. Not me. However, when the same people mumble chapter and verse about the charter, the constitution, revolutionary purity, then their attitude should be called something else. There are several names in the book for such attitudes: careerism, opportunism, arrivism, moral cowardice, naivety – all despicable. All the slogans in the world would be too thin to conceal the moral bankruptcy of these attitudes. Opposition to Nimeiri, even on points of procedure, had by now become phenomenal. It could have been made routine if men knew how to summon up courage and put the man in his place, to say no when the answer could be nothing but in the negative. Some of these blessed souls spoke three languages but never knew how to say no in any of them; deference and respect are one thing, subservience quite a different thing.

I decided to take a short leave of absence to prepare for my exit, advising the SSU secretary-general, Abul Gasim Ibrahim. On my return Nimeiri called me. He was quivering with rage. 'Do you think that there is no boss here,' was the overture. 'I needed you for the preparations for the African summit.' (That was a few months after his relieving me of the Foreign Ministry.)

I was bemused, shocked and, indeed, amused in a morbid sense. However could big men act like this? 'I deal with an institution,' I told the President. 'The secretary-general was informed.' Abul Gasim was watching the spectacle and obviously pained. Between us there is a mutual respect and empathy. I owe him a lot. Continuing, I went on to say that the President had too many important occupations to be able to attend to granting leaves.

At that point Nimeiri retorted: 'Seemingly you no longer want to work with us and maybe I should consider relieving you of your duties after the African summit.' He went on to say that he would like to do this in a manner that would not ruin my future. More than ever, I was then convinced that the man was completely off his rocker.

Nimeiri was in the habit of dismissing people, leaving them in the cold, only to pick them up later more subdued and obedient. Some were left out there to freeze to death. I have always known that there was this love/hate relationship between us. July 1978 was a hate season, although his love was demonstrated in that he wanted me to leave without damaging my future. The way he went about it was too much. Nimeiri was, by now, thinking that he was HE the President of the World, but even megalomania has its limits. He thought that his dismissing me would shut all doors before me, so he kindly wanted to save me from such a prospect. I stood up, thanked the President and told him that I knew what I was going to do; I wanted to relax and write. Nothing distresses Nimeiri more than dealing with people who give the impression of self-sufficiency. He has laboured hard to establish a dependency relationship, not only between himself and his political colleagues, but also with the whole Sudanese elite. His attitude towards them is very ambivalent. He knows that he needs them and he has an inherent respect for those who can deliver. But he also knows that they have an edge over him; they know better. For a megalomaniac this is highly intolerable, so they must be bribed, corrupted, humiliated, all amounting to the same thing. The hard nuts to crack must be destroyed. In this unworthy endeavour Nimeiri was helped, to a large extent, by the frivolousness of a not so small section of the elite, ablaze with apathy and devouring gossip. Nimeiri, the consummate manipulator, knew how to feed that gossip with his deliberate incessant talk of change, meaning by that Cabinet re-shuffles, the ministerial carousel. Nothing pleases more the ego-ridden aspirants (the people in the cold) and the other political hitch-hikers who are waiting for a ride. In addition, there are also those waiting to gloat over the discomfiture of their political or professional competitors. In the face of all that, gleeful Nimeiri carried many a day. Nimeiri's attitude towards Sudanese intellectuals, though not reminiscent of that of Goering ('Whenever I hear the word intellectual I reach for my gun') has some similarities. 'Keep the beasts on their toes' might be his motto. The beasts were indeed frightened. Conventional wisdom has it that the pen is mightier than the sword; the machine-gun is, of course, a different matter. Nimeiri's bullying of the intellectuals reflected both his wickedness and weakness, the weakness always emerging when the bully's bluff was called. In two instances, as we shall see later (the cases of the lawyers and doctors), Nimeiri's bluff was called and, sensing the changing tide, he was made to bend ignominiously to the wind.

As far as I am concerned, three hours after my meeting with Nimeiri, I handed an unsealed letter of resignation to the secretary-general of the SSU, Abul Gasim Ibrahim. He was not at all over-joyed when he read the letter addressed to the President. His eyes were soon riveted on a quotation from an Arab poet praying that things would not fall into the hands of the wicked.

'Am I one of them?' Abul Gasim asked.

'Far from it,' I said.

The decision to relieve me was taken a few weeks later and I made my way to the Smithsonian Institution. Short of stopping me from leaving the country HE the President of the World would have been hard put to it to undo that one. To me the decision to quit was a source of solace; there were no second thoughts. In politics as in love, it is always less painful when you are the one who took the parting decision. You always keep hoping against hope (man's capacity for make-believe is infinite). Then one day the Rubicon has to be crossed. For years I had been arguing, persuading, dissuading and defying from within, hoping to achieve the desired ends. When I had reached the end of my tether I was left with no choice but to resort to the ultimate defiance in the circumstances, quitting. Men should not endure what they cannot alter. The other alternative left for a rejectionist would be plotting from inside to destabilize. That is not me. I would rather confront from the other side of the fence.

Oil, Sugar and the Yemeni Connection

One of the often cited phrases in the SSU national charter is the reference to workers and peasants as the people with the most genuine interest in the May revolution, and certainly they should have been. But more and more evidence has accumulated to show that the real beneficiaries, the people with the most 'genuine' interest in the May regime, were those in the palace cabal. So while politicians were feuding over the economy, national reconciliation, the democratization of the SSU, etc., the cabal was busy doing its own thing, making money and consolidating it to make more money, with thoughtless and insatiable greed. The period under review (1975–9) has witnessed yet more of the multicoloured corruption of the palace cabal and its cronies.

Nimeiri assumed the portfolio of Finance to attend personally to the deepening economic crisis. He did nothing and a few months later he decided to promote the Minister of State at Finance to full ministerial rank. He was doing the job all the way anyhow. So it was not el Hindi who took over Finance from Nimeiri but Osman Hashim Abdel Salam on 22 March 1978. It was Osman's lot to see to it that the economic stabilization measures were implemented. Broadly speaking, these measures aimed at curbing government expenditure and borrowing and encouraging production. Osman's remedy was no different from what his predecessors prescribed. Nimeiri could have adopted these measures under Khatim were it not for the confrontation at the Council of Ministers. He could have espoused them, made them his own and boasted about them to his *Face the Nation* programme. Nimeiri had not yet met an economic plan which he did not like. Osman, like his predecessors, was faced with the task of fighting corruption, which had by now become endemic. The whole country was reeking of corruption; that of the presidential shop-lifters had opened the way down the line for public officials to freelance, some in order to make an unearned income, many others to make ends meet. The indomitable Dr Idris had by now enlarged his area of operations to include oil and sugar. With the increase in public debt it was decided to shop around for sugar, preference being given to suppliers who produced facilities for payment. 1978, we recall, was the year of self-sufficiency in sugar, according to the aborted development plan. Dr Idris produced a well known Yemeni trader by the name of Shahir Abdel Haq. Shahir is a very successful trader who knows very well which side his bread is buttered. He stuck to Idris, abandoning his former representatives, Abul Ela Trading. Several sugar deals were concluded with Shahir, the price often inflated way above the London market price. This was always justified by the claim that high risks were involved in financing the 'insolvent' Sudan. It is very costly to be poor, they said. The argument made sense, if it were not for the fact that priority has always been given to repayments to Shahir and always through the good offices of the palace.

The country's insolvency also affected the importation of crude oil. Saudi Arabia, which could have ensured constant supplies to the Sudan had the proposed jointly owned refinery gone through, was now extending help intermittently to the Sudan, financing purchase of crude from Petromin. On one of those occasions the Saudis made available to the Sudan the crude oil it needed for a few months, to be lifted from Ras Tanura. Dr Idris pulled one of his well-known tricks. The Saudis wanted the lifting to be done by a carrier named by them, Baba Naft. Idris claimed that the company was insolvent and the Saudis wanted to help it. The said company belonged to Mazin Faroun, a leading, successful Saudi businessman. Idris, in order to make his story plausible, claimed that Saudi reticence in allowing the lifting of the crude was due to this; in other words, take it or leave it. Finance Minister Osman got in touch with his Saudi counterpart, Aba al Khail, to enquire about this 'insistence' on a certain carrier, particularly as there was a delay in the lifting. Osman added that if the Saudis wanted to extend a helping hand to an insolvent Saudi carrier then the difference in cost ($12,000,000 over offers made by other carriers) should be borne by the Saudis. The Saudi Finance Minister told Osman in a few words that the Saudis could not care less who carried the crude;

there were no strings attached to the deal. The delays in lifting were due to the fact that the Saudis were waiting for some returns from the Bank of Sudan as to how their previous budget support for the Sudan was used. That was the measure of Saudi trust in our institutions, not without reason. The Saudi monetary authorities by now were demanding evidence as to how monies they made available to the Sudan were used. Before their very eyes the unsuspecting Osman was now giving yet another reason for their doubt as to how the Sudan managed the monies they made available to it. Osman conveyed all this to Nimeiri, warning him of the seriousness of the matter and the untenability of the situation should the affair be divulged to the press and Parliament (the hear-all, see-all institution). Nimeiri pretended he understood and that he was in agreement.

In fact, Osman was not alone, for Abdel Fatah Salih, a director of the Sudan Petroleum Corporation, was also vociferous in his attack on the deal. During a meeting arranged at Idris' office, attended by the ubiquitous Doctor and certain Saudi gentlemen, an envelope containing $10,000 changed hands. The men had underestimated Abdel Fatah's integrity for he went with the envelope straight to Security. Abdel Fatah's recalcitrance cost him his job. The Minister of Energy who gave his wholehearted support to the deal, could not tolerate having such a 'troublesome' officer in his Department. With Osman out of the way, on a trip outside the country, the agreement was signed with the company. Sudan was to pay more for shipping its oil across the Red Sea than it had paid for its shipping from Iran! The 'lifters,' moreover, made sure that supply of crude oil exceeded the storage capacity of the Port Sudan refinery, allowing them to sell the excess crude on the spot market. The story found its way into the press in Kuwait. Not a word in Khartoum. Osman, rather than go ahead with his stabilization programme, was busy warding off encroachments, as Mansour and Beheiry had done before him.

For Shahir Abdel Haq it was a simple step from sugar to oil. We said above that the Saudis had, at certain times, made credit available for Sudan to purchase Saudi crude; these intermittent aids proved insufficient to meet the country's needs. The gap was bridged by purchases from the oil market through intermediaries promising finance, the leader among whom was Shahir. Shahir, the trader, had neither refineries nor tankers. His *modus operandi* was quite diabolical. He monitored the traffic of oil tankers mainly from Aden and the Mediterranean, and, aware of the country's thirst for oil, he would go to the authorities claiming that he had a tanker waiting near Port Sudan and ready to unload. He would insist on immediate payment or being granted a cotton contract, and the authorities would succumb. Cotton is the main foreign currency earner in the Sudan and as a result of these unconscionable transactions the country's cotton produce has been mortgaged for years to come. Shahir, having obtained the money or the cotton, would buy the oil that did not belong to him in the first place, and deliver to Sudan at many dollars above the spot-market price. Shahir, like Adnan, made millions in the Sudan but was not prepared to invest a penny in its economy. His investment went elsewhere, mostly north into Egypt, whose economy was more viable.

Another soldier of fortune active in this period, was Mohammed Abd Rabbo, a Sudanese of Yemeni origin (there seems to be an affinity between Idris and the Yemen). Abd Rabbo, a round man with an ample belly, has an ampler lust for wealth, a real money-grubber. He also has the knack. He started his career as a junior official in Shell Company in Port Sudan. Later on he left his job to run a small flour mill in the town. He was very low-key in all respects, a very modest man with a lot to be modest about, till he met Idris who introduced him to the Koreans.

Abd Rabbo the miller now moved up to bigger things, industrialization on a large scale. He applied for an approved enterprise licence for a tyre factory. The application was rejected by the technical committee under Musa Belal; the reasons given were that the industry was totally dependent on imported labour and raw materials. Badr el Din Suleiman, who followed Belal, persisted in his predecessor's position, adding that the industry was neither strategic nor timely. Both of them must have thought not only of the regulation of industry, but also of their former colleague Clement M'boro, sentenced to prison by Nimeiri's revolutionary courts for doing precisely this.

Enter Idris and the Koreans and the licence was given by Presidential order. A finance facility of £S80,000,000 was made available by Unity Bank. The Koreans would provide the machinery, guaranteed by Unity Bank; no Korean capital investment. None the less they were to have a 40 per cent equity in the project. The President, even before the factory started producing, issued a ban on the importation of all types of tyre in order to protect Abd

Rabbo's enterprise. This was unprecedented. Industry would have to produce first, and on the basis of a market study as to its ability to satisfy market needs, prices etc., protective measures would be taken. This applied even to industries entirely dependent on local raw materials and labour, e.g. textiles. The ban continued even after it was realized that the factory, once in operation, was not able to produce tyres for heavy-duty trucks and vehicles, including agricultural machinery. All these were immobilized by the President in order to mobilize Abd Rabbo's business. Many people in both government and business circles were flabbergasted. The Koreans must be a sleeping partner for somebody of moment. Abd Rabbo is too insignificant a person for all these measures to be taken in his favour, a doubt confirmed by what followed.

In 1979 the issue of the tyre factory came before the National Assembly. It was raised by the Mayor of Omdurman and a representative of businessmen and entrepreneurs in the Assembly, Ali Abersi, a bold defender of causes, often lost ones. He was later joined by Eissa Kabashi, the representative of the Red Sea constituency (where the factory is situated). Ali was equipped with facts and figures on the factory's productive capacity and its inability to meet local demands. Supporting reports from end-users in transportation and agriculture were at hand. The Assembly appointed a commission of investigation led by Ahmed Mohammed Yassin. Its report was damning. The then Minister of Industry, Izz el Din Hamid, was called before the Assembly for questioning. His revelations on the company capital structure and the way the licence was issued were of no help to Abd Rabbo either. The Minister was soon dismissed for 'indiscretion'; he divulged to the Assembly more than he should have done. Nimeiri assumed the portfolio of Industry, claiming that this would be a part of a campaign he would personally undertake in all Ministries to ensure their proper functioning. Industry was the only Ministry that received that privilege, the President relinquishing it shortly afterwards to a new Minister.

In the course of this debate the whole Assembly was speaking with one voice, except for two members: the President's cousin, Mubarak Sinada, and his niece, Soraya Osman. The President rapidly called the Speaker, Rashid el Tahir, and told him that the debate should be stopped. The Speaker argued that the matter was beyond him, for there was already a commission of investigation. At that point the President made up his mind as to the next step, the dissolution of the Assembly. The third Assembly was dissolved on 4 February 1980. Soon thereafter all the records of the debate disappeared from the Assembly, and so did the records of the Ministry of Industry, thanks to the stint of the President in that Ministry to 'ensure its proper functioning'.

More privileges were to be heaped on Abd Rabbo. By 1979 Badr el Din Suleiman assumed the portfolio of Finance, replacing Osman Hashim Abdel Salam. One of his first decisions was the liberalization of the foreign currency market, removing all exchange controls. He also established a parallel currency market, the official one offering a lower rate for the dollar. The official market was to be used for financing the purchase of production inputs and basic consumables, e.g. medicine, fertilizers etc. All other imports were to be financed through the parallel rate. The decision was a concealed devaluation of the Sudanese pound and the measure was meant to curb the importation of unnecessary items. Nearly all the transfers for private investors were made on the parallel rate, causing much hardship to many. Abd Rabbo, however, sought and got through presidential intervention what the Saudi and Kuwaiti investors failed to get, the official rate of transfer. Some of those Arab investors had placed hundreds of millions of the cash that had flowed into the country, all in projects run and managed by Sudanese. Arab solidarity apart, enlightened self-interest alone should have counselled preferential treatment, if any, to Arab investors. It is only through such treatment that the flow of Arab cash into the Sudan can be uninterrupted. Unlike the Koreans, Arab investors were in the main working through institutions, not intermediaries. In Nimeiri's Sudan that is hardly the way to succeed in business.

Only four years had elapsed after the dissolution of Parliament when the ample-bellied Yemeni was in a new wrangle. With more and more heavy-duty vehicles immobilized the Minister of Commerce, Ahmed Salim, decided to issue licences for the importation of tyres not locally manufactured, i.e. by Abd Rabbo. An announcement was made in the media giving a list of the different types, sizes and weights of the tyres eligible for importation. Many applications were made and deposits paid. The President, who could not tolerate Parliament (his eye that sees and ear that listens) would certainly not countenance the 'stupidity' of a Minister who failed to read all the signals sent by the President. So Nimeiri declared that he would supervise personally the Minister of

Commerce (not again). So the President moved into Commerce, with all the usual alarums and excursions, to oversee personally the functioning of the Ministry. A few days later he dismissed the Minister (who was away on duty), appointed a new Minister and passed two important decisions, one cancelling the authorization for the importation of tyres; the other, to which we shall come later, concerned cigarettes. In all probability Abd Rabbo and his protector were afraid that issuing import licences for tyres might open the floodgates for importation of tyres produced locally. So they might as well keep the sluice gate shut. It was not the promotion of Sudan's dwindling exports or ensuring the supply of basic needs (food, agricultural inputs, medicine) that were of concern to the President, who sought to apply his weight and prestige to the Ministry of Commerce; only Abd Rabbo, even at the cost of immobilizing agricultural machinery. Earlier we said the Koreans were thought to be a sleeping partner for someone big!

Abd Rabbo, however, went from strength to strength, increasing the range of his activity. By 1980 he decided to enlarge his milling activities so he applied for permission to increase the output of his flour mill from 240 tons to 500 tons per day; the Minister of Industry, Beshir Abbadi, refused to grant permission, arguing that the market was saturated. New mills were under construction in Atbara (run by Ahmed Abdel Wahab), in Rufa'a (run by the local authority), in New Halfa (run by the Farmers' Association and Co-operative Society). That was in addition to many privately owned mills in Khartoum North, which were in the process of increasing their output. Dr Idris got in touch with the Minister, asking for the reasons behind his refusal to grant permission, as if these were not good enough reasons, whereupon Abbadi returned a note of all the reasons listed above. Nimeiri's reaction was hilarious. He issued the authorization under his own signature and dismissed the disobedient Minister.

Born in the Purple

Having reached this point unscathed and unopposed in any manner, Nimeiri sought to combine corruption with nepotism. He was able, in the course of the years, to get away with too many infractions of moral and legal rules, aided by a wide conspiracy of silence. The few voices murmuring objections were always scotched. The President's monopoly of the media made it easy for him to engage in king-size corruption while pettifogging the issue only to mystify. As for his nepotism, the Sudan was lucky to be spared an extended Nimeiri family. His only living brother Mustafa made up for that. Mustafa Nimeiri, a sixth-former, started his career as a store-keeper in Sudan Mercantile, Wad Medani, where his father used to work as a janitor.

Nimeiri, however, was very proud of his origin, often vaunting it in his speeches. We had all liked him for that. At long last it was one of the real people, the sons of the toiling masses, who had made it to the top. Mustafa was soon to be recruited in one of the major sugar schemes (Geneid) as a junior store-keeper (1963). He was later transferred to Khartoum, at his own request, to undertake, in a junior capacity, the co-ordination of transport activities for the enterprise: a transport officer. Mustafa was needed there to attend to some family affairs in Omdurman. He remained in his junior post for a few years after his brother, Gaafer, assumed the presidency. But more important things were awaiting him.

Nimeiri's grandfather, Wad Nimeiri, who had lived in a village named after him, near Dongola (Northern Sudan), where he inherited a large mud-brick house situated on a commanding plateau. The villa belonged to the Turkish governor of the region (during the Ottoman occupation of the Sudan in the last century) and he had served as a guard to the governor. He was known for his ruthlessness with the locals.

In latter days the President, becoming more and more vainglorious, decided to resurrect his ancestral home in Wad Nimeiri. The man was now being called the ruler of Wad Nimeiri, the mud house the palace of the ruler. All are important trappings for a man born in the purple. The family (read Nimeiri) decided to establish a co-operative society engaged in the welfare of the village. 'I am setting an example for every able Sudanese to help raise the standard of his kith and kin in the rural Sudan,' said the President. But the 'co-operative' set to raise the standard of Wad Nimeiri soon meandered into other areas, from transportation between Omdurman and Dongola, which was plausible, to metropolitan transport in the capital. The 'co-operative'/corporation was granted the representation of Magirus Deutz, among other things.

The unbending former Minister of Public Works, Mustafa Osman, now reinstated as Minister of Transport, advised against

191

the use of these buses in the town. Armed with a report from his engineering adviser, Ali Amir Taha, an honest and incorruptible technocrat, the Minister ruled that the buses might be good as inter-city buses but not as town buses, for their use in Khartoum streets poses many risks. The Minister was overruled by the President. He described the upright Minister as a dunce. Nine months later 80 per cent of the buses were off the road, not fit for use. The Omdurman–Dongola buses too had no better luck. Mustafa Nimeiri, however, had no difficulty in disposing of them. They were sold to the Army, with the help of the Supreme Commander of the Armed Forces, His Excellency the Brother. So from the grandfather Mustafa has inherited his entrepreneurship while Nimeiri got his cynicism and ruthlessness; the two traits of character seemingly have had a lasting effect on the family genes. With the emergence of Mustafa Nimeiri on the business scene people were no longer talking about satellite evil. Accusations against Nimeiri himself were now gaining common currency.

Chapter Six

Half-way through Madness:
Emaciation of the Institutions
1980–1983

It is terrifying to see how easily, in certain people, all dignity collapses. Yet
when you think of it, this is quite normal since they only maintain their
dignity by constantly striving against their own nature

Albert Camus, *Notebooks*

By 1979 Nimeiri's options were narrowing. He spurned compromise, so a genuine national reconciliation has never materialized.
He was cynically oblivious of the economic signals, so the
economic crisis deepened. Meanwhile the SSU, driven by the President himself into irrelevant battles with the newcomers, was completely sapped of its vitality. In the end it was deposited in a
terminal ward suffering from a deadly political sclerosis. The SSU
was able neither to inspire, nor to educate and mobilize. Whatever
apparent support there was was more synthetic than real, e.g. contrived mass rallies to be addressed by the President. The SSU was
also pitifully helpless in checking all the moral and political deviations of the President and his cronies in the Palace. The constant
sacking of politicians who disagreed with the President, or dissen-
ted from his policies, had made a mockery of the claim that the SSU
would be the intellectual powerhouse of the regime. Accordingly,
the hegemonic single party that was to guide, educate and mobilize
had, by 1979, become politically timid, intellectually fallow and
morally suspect.

As far as Nimeiri was concerned the SSU had outlived much of
its usefulness. Under the pretext of wanting to put an end to the
divisiveness of party politics Nimeiri endorsed the creation of a
one-party system, outlawing all party activities. The SSU helped
contain his enemies: the politicians of the *ancien régime* and

the Communists after the July coup. Sadiq el Mahdi and Hassan al Turabi (i.e. everybody who was willing to be integrated into the system) were also contained and banished to the SSU, the Siberia of Sudanese politics. The latter was later given a taste of authority but, as we shall see, it was never meant to be real authority.

Under the slogan of *Hakimiyyat al Tanzim* (supremacy of the party) the President, in February 1975, had launched a crusade on his Ministers and the executive. SSU people were his window-dressers, personal squabbles were given the appearance of ideo-logical disputes, and the sacking of ministers and reshuffles were depicted as policy-oriented and corrective measures. During all this period the language was socialism, only to be replaced later with a more emotive and powerful one, Islam. Nimeiri has always been as socialist as he wanted and as non-socialist as he could afford. And so were all the ayatollahs of socialism in the SSU.

The SSU, however, could still be of some use to Nimeiri, for an outward commitment to it and to the one-party system was a good way of stopping others from forming their own parties and it was too valuable a scapegoat. With the economy in the state it was in, Nimeiri had a desperate need for scapegoats. He therefore opted not to dissolve it but to trim it.

The Inquisition

On 7 August 1979 Nimeiri launched a bitter and lengthy attack on the SSU. He told a joint meeting of the Politburo, the government and the general secretariat that ten years of experience, in his opinion, should have been enough for the SSU to assume its role as a 'leader of national action' (point 1). He also said that the SSU was intended to be a training-ground for a new leadership, an alterna-tive leadership to what he called the 'historic leadership' (of which only he was now left, point 2). The new emerging leadership was, of course, meant to be an alternative leadership to all the historic leaders save himself.

Nimeiri went on to say that if he had shunned, after the events of July 1976 and of September 1975, the principle of concentration of power in the hands of one person, it was because he still believed in the role of the institutions (point 3). September 1975, we recall, was the month when the constitution was amended to give the President additional power to make orders, having the force of law, in order to maintain republican institutions and uphold the achievements of the May revolution. The President who shuns personal power and respects the institutions has used that very added authority, given to him under article 82 of the constitution, in order to maintain the achievement of the revolution by undoing the Addis Ababa agreement, the one and only abiding achievement of the revolution. He also used it to confiscate a modest house in Khartoum North allegedly used as a brothel. It had never dawned on the institutional President that such actions could have been taken at the lowest level of authority by the People's Local Government Council of the area. The two incidents reveal how presidential authority was abused and demeaned. Nimeiri became more and more bent on personalizing power even in trivia. None the less he was never out of countenance when he raised point 3.

The watchful President went on to say that he had been observing and monitoring and that he had opted to 'stay out' because he wanted to give the 'deviant' elements the chance to go back on their errors (point 5). Nimeiri said the same thing about his Ministers in the requiem of 1975. He then went on to explain the reasons for distancing himself from the SSU; he wanted to give the 'base' the chance to lead (point 7) because he believed 'that [his] national role is limited and transitory' (point 8). However, the 'distant' President who wanted the base to lead was very much around, involved in all trifles within the SSU, ranging from the appointment of junior staff to the authorization of leaves of absence, as we have seen. Nimeiri concluded by posing a few questions by way of criticism.

'How do we explain the failure of the SSU as the political organ to combat the causes of the people's sufferings, either by helping to organize distribution or curbing consumption, uncovering the network of hoarders, co-operating with the special organs in exposing the centres of hoarding and the means by which goods are being smuggled out of the country?'

That was his first question. The President's economics was a strange thing indeed: the problem was one of distribution of goods, hoarding and smuggling. Inflation, trade deficits, the parity of the Sudanese currency, high-level corruption and dwindling production etc. meant nothing to him. In question 11 Nimeiri demanded

195

to know (not really, because he did not wait for answers to his questions) how the SSU would explain the phenomenon of strikes which were spreading, and spreading despite the fact that the revolution had done more than it should for the workers, giving them in one year $153,000,000. If Nimeiri had ever waited for an answer someone could certainly have referred him to the different memoranda presented to him by his economic advisers on the relationship between inflation, the cost of living and wages. Once again the President's selective memory had chosen to obviate some unpleasant memories – the admonishing of his economic advisers Beheiry and Nimir, his statement that he was not frightened by those figures, the memory of all the advisers constantly fighting and constantly losing battles with him.

The inquisitional President went on questioning. Question 14 was very interesting; what sort of effort had the organs made in order to turn national reconciliation into a reality? . . . Why didn't they endeavour to strengthen it so as to stop it from becoming a mere temporary pact and a struggle between the old cadre and the newcomers? Nimeiri's selective memory must have once again played tricks on him. From him there were constant accusations against the SSU elements (wearing the national reconciliation hat) and against newcomers (wearing the SSU hat), playing one against the other. Equally, he has frustrated all efforts for democratization and power-sharing, and reneged on undertakings, particularly the publicly announced ones with el Hindi in London.

The President went on with his hectoring speech till he came to the deepest cut of all, question 30. By that question Nimeiri wanted to know why the SSU had not been explaining our course, problems and indeed achievements to the people (i.e. why had it not been busy diverting people's attention away from the state of the economy and what he called 'people's sufferings'). One of the achievements he enumerated was the presidency of the OAU. That the chairmanship of the OAU summit should be considered as an achievement was indeed funny. African presidents are chosen in rotation, depending on their ability to host the summit in their countries, for the course of the year in which they have hosted the conference. That 'honour' was once bestowed on General Amin Dada. Nimeiri saw himself in that year, not as the current president of the OAU, but as the President of Africa. The real achievement would have been gained if the President in question had used his office and prestige to further African causes. Nimeiri's record, in this regard, not only shamed him, it shamed the Sudan, a country with an unblemished African record. See chapter 9.

Nimeiri put more questions to his audience, adding that he could still think of even more. He hinted at what was to come when he said: 'If the cause of this malfunctioning is the shape of the party, its name or structure or form and organization . . . then there is no difficulty at all in reviewing all this; of course, after offering the alternatives to the popular base to choose from' (*Al Ayam*, 7 August 1979). It is remarkable that the aspects capable of reform that Nimeiri had chosen to enumerate were the very issues raised by Sadiq el Mahdi. While using the stick on the SSU, Nimeiri was extending the carrot to Sadiq. As for the reforms and alternatives to be 'presented to the popular base to choose from', Nimeiri did not wait. He took the decisions personally on behalf of the people. So review it he did, and drastically so, but offer alternatives to the popular base he did not.

On 13 August 1979 Nimeiri dismissed Abul Gasim Ibrahim as Secretary-General of the SSU. With Ibrahim's dismissal, the SSU was left at Nimeiri's behest, doing whatever he wanted. Ibrahim was the last ex-member of the RCC who had the political weight to challenge Nimeiri and to oppose his measures. Ibrahim did not lie low, as we shall see. He continued fighting as a loner, abandoned by his former colleagues, whom he had also abandoned before.

On 14 August Sudan had a new heir presumptive. Abdel Magid Hamid Khalil became the first Vice-President. General Abdel Magid was soon to be promoted to Lieutenant-General like Nimeiri and also made secretary-general of the SSU, replacing Abul Gasim. To all intents and purposes he was the heir presumptive prepared by Nimeiri to succeed him, according to his 1977 declaration. Nimeiri, however, with his chestful of medals would not tolerate seeing a commissioned officer ranking with him, not in the same country. So he decided to promote himself to Field-Marshal. Nimeiri, we thought, belonged to a different league of leaders. President Boumedienne, for example, who led the Algerian Army (ALN) in seven years of combat, continued to lead that Army till he died as a Colonel. It was the Bokassas and the Amins of the world who became Field-Marshals. When Nimeiri proudly broke the news to the Politburo there were smiles, congratulations, glee all around, only to be broken by Bona Malwal. Bona, the six-footer plus, reached to the sky when he said to the President: 'I do not know whether this promotion is called for and it certainly would do no honour to the President or the country if Nimeiri is to be equated with Bokassa, for example.'

On the same day that Nimeiri appointed Khalil, he spoke of his imminent re-organization of the SSU and asked workers to purge their ranks of Communists. The Communists were, therefore, to go to hell, and never come back. He described the Communists as those who do not say the Muslim Shahadah, 'I believe that there is no God but Allah and Mohammed is his prophet.' Nimeiri's definition included also Christians and animists, many of whom were working with him and under him. This shows the extent to which he was prepared to go in using religion as a political tool. The Communists, however, were not alone at the receiving end of his venom; there were the reactionaries, the foreign agents and the envious ones etc. Nimeiri, unabashedly, was blaming the whole world for the country's ills.

Talk ... Talk ... Talk

The long promised change in the fabric of the SSU came on 19 August. From all the points made in my memorandum of 1977 Nimeiri took only the ones calling for a reduction in the size of the Politburo (reducing its membership from twenty-seven to seventeen) and the reduction of the Secretariat to three administrations. The rationale of that memorandum (and Nimeiri's declared intention) was to turn the SSU into a more effective and responsive policy-maker. His reasons, however, were quite simple; to convince people that something was being done, that he had diagnosed the disease and found the remedy. This is how the change was described in the headlines of *Al Ayam* of 14 August. 'Measures to alleviate the people's suffering. . . . Review in the leaderships of the political and executive organs soon.' So everything was turned on its head overnight, but only in form. That was good enough for the newcomers (the carrot) and for the gossipy circles of Khartoum, subject-matter for frivolous debate and gloating for a few weeks. The vitriolic speech on the SSU which he delivered on 7 August before a joint meeting of the Politburo, the government and the general secretariat was one of a series of what he termed confrontation encounters. Rather than dialogue, Nimeiri intended the forum to be a battleground; he envisaged a scenario with the participants trading accusations and counter-accusations, with him playing his favourite role of umpire. Nimeiri concluded his encounters with an ostentatious motto, a saying of Omar Ibn al Khatab, the second Caliph: 'There is no good in us if we don't voice it, and there is no good in me if I do not give ear to it.' Omar was sincerely referring to counselling, advice and criticism of the ruler.

Next on his agenda for confrontation was the leadership of local government. Moves like that are very portentous; those who predicted a major change in the shape of local government were not wrong. There were lots of complaints about the malfunctioning of the system. There were also many cases of corruption. The system did not function properly because of its infrastructural inadequacies that were supposed to be compensated through self-help and popular mobilization. The man who sat at the top of the SSU and arrogated all powers to himself should be the first to explain and account rather than question and blame. As for corruption, we know by now that revolutionary purists were not all pure. Corruption at the top induced corruption all the way down the line. To Nimeiri, however, what was important was not the answer; it was the question. So in his meeting with the local government leadership Nimeiri expressed his commitments to the principles of local government and decentralization, emphasizing the principle of rule by the people (the local government that was not fit to be entrusted with closing a brothel). Nimeiri raised twenty-five questions by way of criticism of the performance of the organs of local government.

As he was fighting a war on two fronts, the SSU and local government, Nimeiri sought a truce with the executive. The government was lauded for its performance in general but asked to purge its ranks of the 'few bad elements' (it was not Dr Idris he had in mind). This was the same government that was blamed in 1975 for every sin. Had government Ministers been as keen on slogans as the SSU people, they would have raised the slogan of *hakimiyyat al hukuma* (the supremacy of government) to describe the new *modus vivendi*. This, of course, was more in the nature of a reprieve and a truce than a change of heart. Besides, neither of the two organs was supreme, only Nimeiri the omnipotent. In his meeting with the executive on 23 August Nimeiri addressed the economic problems, repeating some of the very issues raised by his dismissed Ministers Beheiry and Khatim (he had now espoused the position paper presented by Osman Hashim Abdel Salam, which in fact replicated the views of his predecessors). Unfortunately Osman was a few days late and a few dollars short. But in spite of all the economic problems he raised, Nimeiri still pretended in his speech that the Sudanese were grazing in lush pastures.

Public speeches were becoming more and more Nimeiri's tool for handling problems, a tendency encouraged by his penny-a-liner speech-writer Mahgoub (his only way to survive was exercising authority without responsibility). In effect, when Nimeiri appointed him as Information Minister, a few years later, he managed to have the decision reversed within a week, the shortest-lived ministerial appointment. To Nimeiri public speeches were very convenient; no debate and no questions but always scape-goats. Accusing Ministers and aides became the staple of Nimeiri's speeches, more and more evasive and incoherent. The circularity of the argument in those speeches was often meant to dazzle and obfuscate rather than illuminate. Even the economy was not saved from these verbal exercises. Figures were never used, page numbers excepted. It was all self-serving fabrication and distortion of facts. People beset by problems hardly took those speeches seriously. Boredom was the general reaction. For the many who had to undergo the agony of reading them and surviving it, e.g. Ministers, foreign missions, researchers, Nimeiri's long speeches had to be read vertically in order to skip the verbose embellishments and the platitudes trotted out. What was alarming about the whole exercise was what it had revealed of Nimeiri's character and mentality, the utter disrespect for people's intelligence, presupposing that his audience was completely incapable of relating cause and effect.

Reflection, Introspection and Debate

In that fateful August I was already in Washington, having left the Sudanese political scene in October 1978. I had quit the stage as an active actor, in dismay but never with a spirit of resignation. Some people might choose to live uprooted. I am not made of that timber. I have always been deeply involved in my country's politics in a manner that would not allow me to abdicate my national responsibility as a citizen. My stint at the Smithsonian was a period of reflection and introspection, but whatever I was reflecting on and recording was not for the present.

When the President, however, challenged people, posing many questions that were left without answers, I chose to pick up the gauntlet. I knew all along that he was bluffing, but decided to call his bluff. President Nimeiri was calling his restructuring of the SSU a new political era. Every Cabinet reshuffle is baptized a *marhala*, i.e. an era. There are on the average two eras a year. To me all the allegations made in his blistering attack on the SSU and the executive, both of which he heads, were beyond fact and reason. I was also incensed by the complete silence of those who were normally vociferous within the SSU. Were they brainless, cowardly or accepting ignominiously the indictment? That is a matter of judgment. The few who answered skimmed the surface, never pointing to the central core of the malignancy.

In February of 1980 I went on to publish about twenty articles in *Al Ayam*, one of the two SSU organs. Nimeiri was briefed about them and he grudgingly accepted their publication, knowing that the alternative was worse: publication abroad of more damaging material. He had still to swallow my 'disloyalty' which was reflected in an interview with *Al Hawadith* in January 1979, in which I criticized deified leadership. The articles dealt with the SSU, the constitution, the economic situation, the Army, corruption, outlining where we had gone wrong in all those areas. Among other things the articles dealt with the President's hampering of the democratic process, the frustration of the rules of the game, the emasculation of Parliament and the constant government reshuffles which led to administrative chaos. On national reconciliation the articles pointed out that, in view of the political crisis the country was undergoing, the process should include everybody, not excepting the Communists. The Army was also dealt with, its role and its place within the political scene, maintaining that the Army should never be used as a tool of terror for that would turn out to be a double-edged sword. I chose as a title Nimeiri's quotation from Caliph Omar.

What stunned me most was not Nimeiri's reaction, which I expected all the way, but the sense of indignation of some and the puzzlement of others. The former, the defenders of the faith, saw the articles as a stab in the back which would only comfort the opposition, as if I had not said in those articles that the nation is above party and leader. The latter did not hide their astonishment at the fact that the articles were written at all; how dare one write this? Explanations galore came. The articles were commissioned by

President Nimeiri and this was what the new era was all about. The more imaginative were categorical that the whole thing was hatched in Washington (as indeed it was) and I had been chosen as the marketing expert to sell it to the Sudan. Such monstrous imaginings were even expressed by some elements of the opposition. This was indeed a sad commentary on our times, for it simply went to show how castrated people had become. In a sense there was a universal feeling of resignation. Nimeiri was invincible and nobody could challenge him. What people had failed to realize was that Nimeiri was as strong as the others were weak. On the other hand, Nimeiri could do nothing with intellectual challenges other than level insults, and no man dies from insults. Sure enough he tried a bit of that treatment in his *Face the Nation* programme referring to the articles, and more of it in the articles he had dictated, which were written by his speech-writer. Needless to say, when people start calling you names, you should assume that you are hurting them badly and they can do nothing about it. Violence is, of course, a last resort, but no Army can kill an idea, particularly one whose time has come.

The reaction to those articles was indeed revealing. It came from three sources:

a. The culpably naive who still believed in a paradise that was long lost. Honest as they may have been they had no business being in politics. The regime's shortcomings were before them and regimes as we said, are not to be judged by their ability to remain in power, rather by what they do with power once they have conquered it and are comfortably established. The May regime and President Nimeiri should be judged by their record and not their longevity, the record of both achievement and failure.

b. The sycophants of the court who were set in locomotion by the man who holds their robes from behind, President Nimeiri. I generally lose no sleep over the reaction of these hapless souls, nor did their needling ever rattle me.

c. The make-believers, bending over backwards to justify the unjustifiable.

My trouble was precisely with this last category, in which there were a few men I still continued to respect. They knew, as I did, that in politics, while compromise on points of detail was permissible, politicians should never allow their philosophical gyrations to be out of focus, i.e. no compromise on matters of principle. The focus of the May revolution was the creation of a purposeful, widely based, incorruptible and democratic system of government. No *apologia* for the regime could erase the record of deviation and betrayal. By 1979 the revolution was just a shadow of its old self; all ideals, values and institutions were trampled upon and, more than anybody else, by the guardian of the constitution and the protector of the achievements of the May Revolution, Nimeiri.

None of what I diagnosed and prescribed was new to many of those friends within. I have always been on record, more than anybody else in the contemporary political scene, and the record was there for those who cared to look at records. My views on the constitution were explained on the *Face the Nation* programme, those on corruption had caused me to leave the Foreign Ministry twice within six years, those on the economic predicament were voiced in the Council of Ministers and resulted in the relinquishing of my portfolio, and those on democratization of the SSU were the subject of an elaborate document presented to the Politburo and dismissed by that body in two hours. Evidently I had chosen not to settle for descriptive writing; my treatise was rather prescriptive. Historians describe; politicians and political analysts, on the other hand, predict and prescribe. Prescriptions may be bitter, but that was our case.

In one of those articles I recalled that a few years before May I had written a series of articles which were far from being complimentary to the regime of the day. I never felt that time that I had to justify my writing nor was I constrained to do so. If I had ever felt such constraints today, in the system that I have helped build, then there should be no running away from the conclusion that something was, indeed, very rotten in the state of Denmark.

Challenging the Hero

Nimeiri, as we said, was telling his Ministers about the lush pastures in which we were all grazing. Some of them knew better, but all of the Sudan realized that the truth of the matter was different. People were seeing in front of their own eyes the collapse of services and amenities, they were absorbing the impact of inflation, they were suffering from chronic shortages of necessities etc. As a result of all that, they were engaged in continuous industrial action with a litany of demands for increased wages. August 1979 was a summer of discontent, and worse summers were to come. If the speech on lush pastures did not convince them, something else would or would at least divert their attention. Nimeiri, the magician, would never run short of ideas. He always had something up his sleeve, a few more cards to play.

Following the summer of discontent when doctors, railwaymen and Gezira farmers came out in a rash of strikes, Nimeiri decided to convoke the National Congress of the SSU and seek a new mandate as President of the SSU. That was uncalled for. Nimeiri was elected President in January 1977 and his term of office was to run to 1983. The whole thing was a smoke-screen. Nimeiri was addressing his challengers in the SSU and beyond. He wanted to say that he had gone to the people and they had confirmed his mandate, i.e. his right to do with the Sudan what he pleased. At the front of his mind were his decisions of August 1979: Nimeiri, in his own style, wanted to prove the point he had made then about the historic leadership (no leadership in perpetuity). Addressing the Armed Forces during the confrontation encounters he said, 'I have taken this decision in fulfilment of a promise I made that no one is above vetting and no one is immune from it' (*Al Ayam*, 26 October 1979).

Nimeiri's re-election was not a smooth one; Abul Gasim Ibrahim was not going to leave the political arena in the unceremonious way a few others did. He decided to run against the hero of May. So after lying low for a few months he suddenly announced in December his candidacy for presidency of the SSU, which is synonymous with the presidency of the republic. Nimeiri was not equal to the challenge. He summoned the assistant secretary-general of the SSU, Yahia Abdel Magid, and told him that he was stepping down; he was not seeking re-election. By that move Nimeiri hoped Yahia and others would go out and mobilize the street behind the leader, pulling one of the old tricks, after which Nimeiri would emerge saying, 'I accept because it is the will of the masses.'

Yahia did nothing of the sort. A technocrat through and through, he was not steeped in under-the-table politics. He took Nimeiri at his word and informed the Chief Justice, seeking his advice as to the constitutional measures to be taken. Nimeiri, his bluff called, had to eat his words and withdraw his resignation, a resignation that was tendered in the privacy of his office anyway.

Although Abul Gasim did no overt electioneering, when returns for delegations to the National Congress began to be counted, it transpired that his supporters had collected thirty-eight out of the forty seats in Khartoum Province, the seat of Nimeiri's power. Cries of vote-rigging were raised (a very strange thing, for one is used to hearing such charges from opposition groups and not the ruling party). Nimeiri asked the Khartoum Commissioner, Mahdi Mustafa al Hadi, to declare the elections in the capital null and void. This was the very Nimeiri who declared in August 1979 that he wanted the popular base to exercise its will. In due course the 2,350 delegates filled the Friendship Hall and, more than willingly, re-elected Nimeiri for another term.

Shoving Responsibility to the Regions

Nimeiri's re-election was not the only card, for there was also the card of regionalization to be played. Regionalization was not an end in itself. Nimeiri would be the last person to relinquish authority. There is no dearth of evidence to prove that. He is hardly a believer in the maxim that governments rule best by ruling least. But regionalization is a ploy that helps defuse many a problem and keeps people busy for a time.

The SSU Congress met in February 1980, endorsed Nimeiri's regionalization plan and then re-elected him as SSU President. Regionalization had been in the air for quite some time. As we mentioned earlier the governor of Kordofan Province (western Sudan) Mahmoud Hasseib, raised the question of regionalization during the meeting of the preceding SSU Congress in 1977, only to be heckled and silenced by Nimeiri arguing that regionalization was not on the agenda.

Late in 1979 Nimeiri took over the subject of regionalization himself, asking Dr Zaki Mustafa, the former Attorney-General, who now practises law in Jeddah, to come up with a plan to complete the regionalization of the North, which Zaki did. Nimeiri did not want to involve the institutions within the country, so the card up his sleeve could not be uncovered. Zaki, however, made it clear to the President that before any precipitate steps could be taken, three things needed to be done.

1. Resources should be made available for setting up the requisite infrastructure.
2. Personnel should be trained in the new system of government.
3. The proposals should be widely and openly discussed by the people who are going to apply them and those to whom they are going to be applied. (He suggested a period of eighteen months of consultation.)

To Nimeiri neither the legal niceties nor the economic, managerial and political considerations mattered much. He was not interested in regionalization *per se*; his reasons for introducing it, against all level-headed judgment, were three-fold.

1. Placating the regions, especially western Sudan (memories of the events of September 1975 stayed fresh in his mind, in addition to the riotous demonstrations in Kordofan Province in 1979).
2. Diminishing the power of the national Parliament (Nimeiri once threatened that he might have to abolish the People's Assembly and in its stead introduce a body that meets periodically, drawn from all regional assemblies), as well as the central government, i.e. the Ministers (Nimeiri hates to see anybody exercising authority next to him).
3. Shifting the responsibility for the desperate state of services away from Khartoum, i.e. from him and into the regions. Whenever things go wrong (they already have done), there will always be a ready answer: 'I have given you authority and you are simply incapable of coping with it.'

More Parliaments, Ministers and councils in the regions will also increase the area of patronage and make more aspirants happy. Autocrats, inclined though they are to rid themselves of institutions, are usually shrewd enough to surround themselves by certain quasi-institutions which act as shields between them and the people they govern.

When Nimeiri undertook a visit to famine-stricken Darfur in order to explain the Zakat law and the populace, he denied knowledge of the famine (he was not told) and shifted the responsibility onto the regional government who had failed on two counts: to inform the President of the disaster and to take the necessary measures. News of the severe famine, in fact, was all over the world. One is surprised to learn that news of the famine should escape the President who claims he is aware of all the seditious gossiping that takes place in London.

Regionalization is but a natural off-shoot of our policies of decentralization and Southern autonomy, both enshrined in the constitution. No one quarrelled with that. But in matters of government things should be done in style. Southern autonomy could not have become a reality had it not been for the tremendous effort spent on mobilizing resources, from both within and without, to prepare the necessary infrastructure for the system. Without it there would have been frustration, or worse still, accusations of betrayal. Inadequate regional governments, therefore, can hardly cope with the new responsibilities shovelled onto them, let alone play the other important role of stimulating production. They need the tools. This is much more so in the absence of mobilization and motivation. These issues were not on Nimeiri's agenda. His concern, apart from widening the domain of patronage, was basically to take the responsibility for the collapse of services off his back. Another concern was to destroy central government's authority, i.e. the authority of the Ministers around him. Nimeiri never wasted an opportunity to tell his Ministers that the days of empire-builders were numbered. There should only be one empire and one emperor.

By 1980 services and amenities had, to all intents and purposes, collapsed. Black-outs and electricity cuts had become the rule rather than the exception. The water people drank was often muddy and sometimes infested with bacteria. Streets were torn up and sewage was leaking into a smelly atmosphere that was hardly in register with the posters all around hailing the 'great leap forward'. Sick people were lying on the floors of hospital wards sharing the fate of roaming cats, as if Nimeiri's health advisers had never read Florence Nightingale: 'Hospitals if they are to do anything must not spread disease.' Nimeiri, a master of passionate perfidy, often appeared in public rallies saddened with what he saw but blaming it all on Sudanese reactionary forces, Ethiopia, Libya, the Soviet Union and the ever-ready Communist Party. Nimeiri, the omnipotent President with all powers in his hand, also never wasted an

occasion to put part of the blame for those inadequacies on his subordinates, all his own choice. Not in one single instance did he have
the courage to assume responsibility for failure, though he never
wasted a chance to receive all the accolades for the achievements of
those very subordinates. And with all this pitiful collapse of basic
services and amenities, the one obvious question nagging everybody, which Nimeiri never cared to ask himself, was that, when
governments fail to fulfil such basic functions, generally entrusted
to town clerks, the people's query will no longer be how could such
governments stay in power for so long, but rather why they should
be in power at all?

Rather than facing the challenge, if not the embarrassment, of
this question, Nimeiri decided to shift to the inadequate regions not
only the responsibility for the emerging new problems of development and services but also the onerous legacy of past ills resulting
from mismanagement and economic chaos. Khartoum, the
national capital, was to be given its local authority to attend to the
down-trodden services: roads, hospitals, education and community
health etc. What about the tools of management, one asks? The
answer: elaborate laws with sweeping powers and long lists of
political promotions. For example, the new Commissioner of
Khartoum was promoted to Vice-President status, five Ministers
were appointed with all the retinue that followed. What else does
the capital need for a face-lift?

As for the central government which Nimeiri strove to destroy,
one would have expected to see it reduced, trimmed and stripped
to the bone. None of that happened. In effect its numbers
increased, under-secretaries were elevated to State Ministers,
State Ministers elevated to full ministerial rank and twelve new
presidential advisers were appointed with ministerial rank or above
(1983). All was patronage, political bribery and attempts to keep
the boys happy. The boys were those who had the dubious distinction of serving the President loyally for years, mainly in the palace.
Dr Hassan Turabi, the most senior among these advisers and the
only one of them with an identifiable power-base, summed it up
well in his interview with Jean Gueyras of *Le Monde* on 14 October
1983. He told the French journalist that 'the advisers of the President receive rather than give advice.' Turabi went on to say that the
President had weakened all state institutions, that there was a wide
gap between the government and the people and that one should
never exclude the possibility of a Jerry Rawlings or a Sergeant Doe

in Khartoum.

So Ministers were not to exercise authority and advisers were not to advise but none the less there should be more of them. President Nimeiri's contradictory action is more cynical than irrational. He was out to please everybody (or rather make-believe that he did); one adviser from the Ansar, another from the Khatmiya, a third from the Muslim Brothers, a fourth from the SSU people, and the family (Nimeiri's) should also not be forgotten in the assignment of the boon. Whether any of the lucky recipients really represented what he was presumed to represent was a different matter. Nimeiri believed it, so why the fuss?

The Cabinet too (the organ that needed trimming) was enlarged after regionalization. Nimeiri was no longer man-hunting and scouting for talent as he used to do up to 1977. Ministers, by now, were picked as fancy took him and kept in office as far as whim dictated. Government became trivialized with his latter-day appointments. He was putting his faith more and more in upstarts and effete civil servants; the former never answered back and the latter were disciplined, obedient and ran on rails, so that once out of them they became muddled and confused. They attended to the business of the department they knew. (Who cared about the constitutions, the charter, the strategies and the situation in the South?) Nimeiri, however, was always shrewd enough to have a few firm hands around, particularly in the economy and security. Their role is to put out fires he kindled. He constantly imperils and they constantly strive to salvage, without success in many instances. From his advisers Nimeiri sought no counsel but justification, from his aides not just loyalty but submission and from all not merely deference but holding him in awe.

Nimeiri had far outdone his predecessors, including al Azhari, whom he had so often criticized for reshuffling governments and dismissing Ministers. By 1978 the Ministry of Defence had witnessed eleven ministerial changes, the Ministry of Foreign Affairs fourteen changes, the Ministry of Finance and National Economy fifteen changes, the Ministry of Transport eight changes, the Ministry of Industry nine changes and that of Internal Affairs ten changes. In a few cases the same Ministers had remained in office during all these changes. Such discontinuities and abrupt changes militated against the orderly functioning of these essential ministries. Nimeiri knew that reshuffles caused instability and were detrimental to good government, so constant shaking of the executive demonstrated his lack of concern for good government and his preoccupation with the perpetuation of his rule through silencing opponents and critics among his advisers.

Shoot Anybody!

With the economic situation worsening all the time a committee of the two top officials of the regime, General Khalil and General Omar el Tayeb (Head of Security), and Sadiq el Mahdi and two of his aides was formed in March 1980 to review the situation and come up with solutions. Sadiq thought that Nimeiri meant business by his so-called new era, his commitment to national unity and his call for the restructuring of the SSU. The era turned out to be bleak and bloody. The committee agreed unanimously upon a programme of radical reform but Nimeiri had already found the solution; he pressed ahead with his regionalization programme. (The committee was only meant to talk and keep the frivolous circles of Khartoum talking till he had decided on his next step.) Northern Sudan was divided into five regions, Darfur, Kordofan, Central, Northern and Eastern. The original plan envisaged three, Northern (including the Red Sea), Central and Western, combining both Kordofan and Darfur. That arrangement made more sense in so far as economic integration was concerned. However, the Red Sea members fought hard against the proposal and got their way; they wanted a separate region. Darfur, which has more claim to autonomy (Darfur was only integrated into modern Sudan in 1918), did not want to be outdone by the Red Sea. The committee on regionalization headed by Abel Alier met with the Darfur representative and recommended a separate region for that province. The recommendation was to be endorsed by the Congress. Nimeiri, knowing that Darfur was one of his problem areas, asked Abel not to make such a recommendation, but rather to suggest that the matter should be referred to the President for his 'kind' consideration. (The SSU Congress is the supreme political authority of the land from which the President draws his legitimacy.) Those constitutional refinements meant nothing to Nimeiri; he wanted to curry favour with Darfur. On the closing day of the Congress Nimeiri declared that he had been 'observing and monitoring' the debate. He had learned of the wish of the people of

Darfur and HE had decided to accede to it. There was lots of applause and shouts of 'long live Nimeiri.'

Elections for both the national and regional assemblies were held in April. Nimeiri was only buying time. With his options becoming increasingly limited he was more and more looking for solutions to the problems of the day; tomorrow would take care of itself. Since 1979 Nimeiri had been living only in the present tense. The political disturbances that took place during the rest of 1980 and 1981 showed the emptiness of his solutions and the myopic nature of his politics. Facts were obvious to everybody who wanted to see, except for the wilfully obtuse President.

Those two years saw the emergence on a large scale of dissenting movements in Kordofan and Darfur (Western Sudan) and among students. The Muslim Brothers, it seemed, had failed to deliver their side of the bargain. (Nimeiri's deal with Dr Turabi was simply 'You stay in power if you can contain the Universities.') Also in 1981, the Lawyers' Association held a symposium in which they criticized the regime for its disregard for the constitution (the parts which had not been amended). There were also demands and attacks from the judiciary (200 judges meeting on 13 May 1980) with 80 per cent of the judges tendering their resignations; the major clash between Nimeiri and the judiciary was yet to come in August 1983.

The most important and effective disruption of public services which took place in the summer of 1980 was the railway strike. Railway workers form the largest and most influential union in the country. This union was responsible for the making and unmaking of governments in the past. Its political leverage stems from the dependence of the economy on railways for the transportation of goods and fuel. The railway union in Sudan is characterized by a strong feeling of solidarity between its members. When the railwaymen went out on strike everything came to a halt. Nimeiri was enraged. He decided to abolish the defiant union and arrest its leadership. He ordered that all the trade unionists should be dismissed (45,000) and the government quarters they occupy all over the country be vacated within twenty-four hours. He also amended labour laws, making strikes a treasonable act punishable by death. The railway workers, who were fighting their battles alone with no support from other unions, went back to work, with a sense of disappointment rather than defeat.

Once again Nimeiri was convinced of his invincibility. Addressing the nation he urged people to make sacrifices and eat, if need be *baleela*, i.e. boiled grain, a cheap popular dish. Leaders who make demands for excessive sacrifices of their followers must at least make modest ones of themselves. There are certain things that can only be taught by an example to be followed and emulated, and sacrifice is one of them. The Nimeiri of the 'eighties, in spite of all the religiosity and the calls for sacrifice, was still gallivanting around the world, going places and enjoying the good things of life. Closer to home the austere President calling for sacrifice was actually enlarging his own life style. At the same time as he had expelled railway workers from government quarters, he also ordered the expulsion of six officers from houses they occupied around his official residence at the Army HQ and the demolition of these houses to make room for a garden. (Compare this with his previous condemnation of the lavishness and wastefulness of the *ancien régime*.) Nimeiri's claustrophobia, his making room around his house, has its parallel in the political sphere, his demolition of the various political organizations and institutions. To the house and the claustrophobic President we shall come later.

But it was not only sacrifice that Nimeiri wanted from people; he also wanted their complete subjugation. In that same speech made at Obeid, during the inauguration of the Regional Assembly, he made one of his most outrageous statements in years. Addressing the nation and particularly the railwaymen he said: 'Beware, I am empowered by the constitution [it was article 82 he had in mind] to take any measures I deem necessary for the protection of the victories of the May revolution.' Pointing to one of his armed guards, he went on to say, 'According to the constitution, I can order this guard to shoot anybody and he would have to obey me.' (My God, have we already reached this point?) It was remarks like this that made many people think that Nimeiri was by then already assuming the mien of a demented leader. Even General Amin was careful enough to cover up his brutality.

In a sense people were not guessing. Since 1978 Nimeiri had been suffering from an undiagnosed malady. Several times he freaked out, going into temporary *dementia*. Often he collapsed, coming a purler, and had to be supported by aides. In 1979 he was sent to the Walter Reed Hospital in Washington and subjected to an intensive examination. He was put under treatment to control the disease, a clot in one of the arteries obstructing the free flow of blood to his brain. In 1980 he went back to Washington to be operated on; the clot was removed, but he had to continue with several medications. Less than a year after his operation Nimeiri addressed the Army generals in the course of their annual meeting in Khartoum and declared that his state of health would not allow him to continue in office. He added that the medicine he was taking sometimes affected his mental faculties and judgment. He urged the officers to reflect on the question of succession and to look for an alternative President, since he did not intend to stay beyond August 1982. There were a few tears from the faint hearted as well as calls from a few sycophants of the type, 'What can we do without you?' The rest of the officers were aghast at the surprise announcement.

Nimeiri's message to the officers was suspect. As a constitutional President he knew very well the rules of succession according to the constitution. He also knew that the only organ empowered by the constitution to decide on a successor was the SSU. That was, however, Nimeiri's tortuous way of telling the soldiers that they were the only force he could rely upon (the experiences of September 1975 and July 1976 proved it). The Army was now being used as a countervailing force against the SSU. In fact, Nimeiri gave several signals in the executive, telling his Ministers that if things continued to go the way they were, he would militarize the government. Nimeiri, however, had underestimated the Army, as we shall see.

The Year of the Hungry, the Angry and the 'Cowards'

Towards the end of 1981 the country's economic situation was so bad that Finance Minister Badr el Din Suleiman had to prescribe another dose of bitter medicine. The axe was brought down on services and subsidies on some important commodities: sugar and fuel (the usual IMF stuff). The country was in the throes of a serious economic crisis and whatever price was needed to satisfy the IMF would have to be paid. This sparked off a widespread movement of protests and demonstrations (mainly by students) which were brutally suppressed. Several demonstrators and some innocent bystanders were killed. The alarming thing about the demonstrations was that they had covered the whole country; they were almost synchronized. The summer of discontent was followed by a winter of rage. A gripping sense of crisis permeated the whole country. Nimeiri's rhetoric, never meant to communicate but to reconstruct reality, was not good enough to contain the uprising. It filled neither the empty bellies of the hungry nor the emptier vaults of the Bank of Sudan. Nimeiri was to turn yet again to the north-west for an outlet. The agitators were described as Libyan agents and the agitation as instigated by Gaddafi. There were also food shortages, a high inflation rate, dwindling production and demands for more wages. Nimeiri did not bother to trace the troubles to these factors, nor to the bitter IMF medicine, in spite of the public attacks by some SSU elements on those policies. People were meant to accept all manner of shortcomings in daily life and remain grateful to God for keeping their benevolent President alive. What incensed Nimeiri more than anything in these demonstrations, was the tendency of the protestors to attack him and members of his family personally, particularly his brother Mustafa. (Boys chanted 'Ismat Nimeiri' on the streets, comparing Nimeiri's brother to Sadat's Ismat, whose trial for corruption was taking place at that time in Cairo.) There was also other vulgar abuse, some not fit to print.

On 18 January 1982, the President called for a meeting to assess the situation. Instead of initiating a debate with and between policy-framing and executive organs of the state, i.e. SSU Central Committee, national government and Parliament, giving them *carte blanche* to implement such measures as they deemed necess-ary, he decided to hold a jamboree. This meeting was composed of everybody who was anybody: there were the SSU people, the Regional and National Assemblies, Ministers, civil servants, trade unionists, Army officers, business men and notables. Nimeiri knew well that nothing could emerge out of this meeting, but he hoped that somehow this confrontation would help defuse the situation.

The President delivered a speech in which he outlined the state of the nation as he saw it. He then withdrew, allowing the delegates to debate, criticize and recommend, i.e. to say things they would not have said in his presence out of fear but mostly out of deference to the person of the leader and fountain of patronage. Khalil, the first Vice-President was in the Chair. Before he withdrew, Nimeiri made an off-the-cuff statement on a decision taken a few weeks earlier by the Mayor and Council of Omdurman not to renew licences for liquor stores in the town. It was not a prohibition decision, rather an attempt to discourage people from drinking by curtailing its availability in the city. The Council is empowered by its constituent orders to exercise such an authority. Nimeiri, in a sharply hostile statement, admonished the Mayor and Council. The President (the believer in devolution of authority) claimed that the Council had gone beyond its powers. He added that drinking could never be prohibited by law. He also urged local government to attend better to the problems facing the community, e.g. community health, education etc. rather than engage in fictitious battles. Nimeiri cautioned that licensees were already envisaging legal action against the Omdurman Council for breach of contract, a matter that might lead to heavy compensation being paid.

Only eighteen months later it was Nimeiri himself who was leading a 'fictitious battle', imposing prohibition all over the country, supervising personally the destruction of liquor, including what was till inside crated containers held in the duty-free zone of Port Sudan. (They could have been returned to their suppliers.) The destruction of that crated liquor has resulted in claims for compensation to the tune of $5,000,000 to be paid by Sudan. For those who cannot see the rationality of all that, we refer to the multi-layered personality of Nimeiri. For one thing, Nimeiri always wanted to be number one, so if there was to be a prohibition it should be Nimeiri who should proclaim it. For another, Nimeiri was then appeasing the vociferous townees. Many of them were condemning the Council's decision; his reaction against the Council would please them. The occasion needed a scapegoat and the Omdurman Council was as good as any. Some new fodder for gossip was also needed and the President–Muslim Brother nexus was also as good as any. 'You know the President is now turning against the Muslim Brothers,' would be a good story to make the rounds in the Khartoum circles for weeks, with all added embellishments. At the same time, prohibition was also a trump card to be used against the same vociferous townees themselves, when their circles of gossip in clubs and social gatherings needed to be broken. That did not take long to happen.

Nimeiri watched the debate on a closed-circuit TV. A few members, including some Army officers, swallowed the bait, hook and all, and spoke critically of Nimeiri's concentration of power. Others talked about corruption in high places. The President, who is beyond reproach, grew restive as the debate grew more critical. He stormed back into the conference, shouting at the rebels, 'You are cowards, you would not have dared say what you have said had

I been present.' He attacked them all but did not wait for a reply. Instead he rushed out saying, 'I am resigning. . . . Find another President.' Nimeiri is generally sensitive to any slight, real or imagined, though he never minded treading on other people's sensitivities without qualms. In this particular case, however, one assumes that Nimeiri should have known his men better. All remained silent as if they were made of cardboard. None stood up on tiptoe to say that the President was wrong. Worse still, some of the politicians assembled in that jamboree (Politburo and Central Committee), rather than say enough is enough, called the President's bluff and summoned the appropriate officials of the SSU to take the next step, i.e. decide that the constitutional process for succession be engaged. They chose another demeaning route, adding insult to injury.

In fact Nimeiri's abuse of the political, administrative, academic and military leadership of the country was an invitation to some of those sycophants to burn more incense on his altar, which they did. Led by Rashid el Tahir, a group of Ministers and members of the Politburo followed him like a flock of startled birds, trying to persuade the President, who had no intention of abdicating anyway, to stay. They were cheering each other up. Nimeiri was angry but not to the extent of abdication (he never will go of his own volition). As for the startled birds, they surely knew well that, for them, it was either staying with Nimeiri or sinking back into their holes. Those delegates who turned their wireless sets on that evening expecting to hear the news of the President's resignation (the only honourable course for an honourable man) were disappointed.

On 21 January the final communiqué of the conference spoke of the open, frank and constructive discussions and of the 'democratic' atmosphere in which it was all conducted. It also spoke of the President as the epitome of the people and the symbol of its unity. Nimeiri, for his part, praised the delegates for their work and spoke of conferences as an opportunity for democratic discussions (never mind the 'you are cowards' stuff), which put the interest of the nation and the people above everything else and where national action in general was discussed, focusing on the programme of economic rejuvenation (*Al Sahafa*, 22 January 1982). Nimeiri may have emerged as a titan, but he was a titan among midgets, the hero of toy town, for it was all child's play.

The Army ... who needs one?

With the civilian organs of the state, government, Parliament and SSU unable (and unwilling) to stand up to the President, it was left to the Army to take up resistance against the Commander-in-Chief a few days later. Nimeiri, as we have seen, had already intimated to the officers in one of their regular meetings with him the effect that the drugs he was taking were having on his mental capacity. Thanks to them, by his own admission, he was not fit to govern; his attitude in the aforementioned jamboree confirmed it. The commanders of the armed forces flexed their muscles at a meeting with the President, and spared him nothing. They were critical of the regime's mismanagement of the economy, they complained about the activities of Dr Idris and Nimeiri's brother Mustafa and his overgrown Wad Nimeiri Corporation. Nimeiri decided to bide his time, dispatching some of his trusted friends to assess the situation, pinpoint areas of danger and play officers against each other. He also tried to play off his two top aides (General Khalil and General Tayeb) against one another; both were long-time buddies.

Surprisingly, none of the officers challenged Nimeiri's presidency. The few voices that called for his forcible removal were scoffed at by General Khalil, who said that they had to act within the constitution. Khalil could have assumed power at will, had he been minded to do so. But he, a soldier's soldier, was concerned with his oaths of allegiance (these things mean nothing to Nimeiri) rather than the power game that was going on. Khalil, whom Nimeiri admired as a soldier, said a bit too much, particularly when he committed a few sacrileges, e.g. challenging the corruption of the palace cabal and reiterating the misgivings expressed by many officers about the role and behaviour of Nimeiri's private doctor Mustafa Kamil (an officer in the Medical Corps and also the President's brother-in-law). Khalil was the Aristeides of Nimeiri's Athens, and like him he would have to be ostracized for his constant exhortations to morality; an irritant reminder to the corrupt. He was admired by many as the Mr Clean of the regime, but Nimeiri has no good word for anybody with a good public image. So Khalil had to go. Nimeiri, who was supposed to abdicate in August, would stay very much on the scene for many years to come. In effect he never meant to abdicate in the first place. He was lying through his teeth yet again, for on that very same day (22 August 1982) Nimeiri stated to SUNA that he would remain in his position in order to protect the achievements of the revolution and the unity of the people.

Khalil did not go alone. With him twenty-two senior officers, some of them the best in the Army, were routed out. Some of these officers had been groomed by Nimeiri himself to occupy higher places in the Army, others had just finished their staff training outside the Sudan, emerging with distinction. The officers were removed but not disproved. But the ease with which they were dispatched (because of Khalil's loyalty and respect for the law rather than through Nimeiri's strength) made the President feel that he was unassailable. From now on he would play the Almighty.

Nimeiri took over the Ministry of Defence and the command of the armed forces, while the post of Chief of Staff remained vacant. A soldier himself, Nimeiri should have known that no modern Army can function without co-ordination. Perhaps that was as well since it was turning into another source of opposition. Nimeiri heaped insults and scorn, in that meeting, on the Chief of Staff, General Izz el Din Ali Malik, who conveyed the officers' message on corruption. 'I thought that your knowledge of public affairs was better than your proficiency in military affairs,' Nimeiri told the General he himself promoted and appointed as Chief of Staff. The President was completely destitute of charity. (The vindictive bully in him was emerging.)

Nimeiri also sought to demolish the Army's self-image, telling the officers in the meeting that the Army did not amount to much, not as much as it thought of itself. It constituted only a fifth of the nation. The statement says a lot about Nimeiri's mental capacity and his way of thinking. Firstly, his statement was a misinterpretation of the SSU's dictum that the People's Armed Forces were one of the five popular forces in the Sudan and, secondly, the Army is a tool in the service of the whole nation and not an interested class or faction of it.

The Army was to suffer severely from these measures, not least from the absence of twenty-two of its senior generals and the abolition of the post of Chief of Staff. This became apparent when it was tested in the South and during the alleged Libyan air attack, to which we shall turn later. Nimeiri, the soldier, was blinded by what he conceived as an Army challenge (though the challenge was to corruption and mismanagement rather than to Nimeiri's authority) and decided to destroy the Army. This was the very Army he was, a few months earlier, threatening to use to militarize the government. It was also the very Army whose unconditional support he strove to gain during the presidential elections. (Nimeiri declared in his electoral manifesto that he would only accept the mandate if a clear plurality emerged with the proviso that the support of the Army should be 100 per cent.)

It could not have escaped Nimeiri's mind that, in any modern Army, co-ordination between line commands (down to the platoon level) and the general staff was essential for its efficient use. The Chief of Staff and his general staff are the brains of the army, planning and supervising the execution of plans; the line command is its body. A regular interchange between staff and line commands was always undertaken in the Sudanese Army to ensure cross-fertilization of talent. Nimeiri, the Sudanese commissioned officer, must have had occasion to learn about all this in his military college and to see it practised during his thirty years in the Army. On the other hand, Nimeiri, the staff officer, must have had occasion, during his training at Fort Leavenworth, to read a bit of military history. In the course of these readings he must have come across the US National Security Act of 26 July 1947, making the Chief of Staff the principal military adviser to the Commander-in-Chief on all the activities of the military establishment and the conduct of war.

This is much more necessary when the Commander-in-Chief is neither available nor capable of undertaking his day-to-day command functions. President Nimeiri, after the removal of General Khalil, appointed himself Commander-in-Chief, but he was hardly seen by the Army after that, and understandably so. Nimeiri, by now, had become Sudan's chief diplomat, security officer, economist, author, information officer and, of late, preacher, judge and executioner. The Fort Leavenworth officer may also have had time to look into some of the basic readings on military history to which staff officers are referred. The reports of the Secretary of War, one supposes, are among those readings. Elihu Root's has a place of distinction among those reports; it is the Bible of Army organization. (Lord Haldane called it the last word concerning the organization and place of an Army in a democracy.) Root wrote:

> When an officer is appointed to the position of Commanding
> General of the Army he naturally expects to command
> himself. . . . The title of Chief of Staff, on the other hand

219

denotes a duty to advise, inform and assist a superior officer
who has command, and to represent him, acting in his name
and by his authority in carrying out his policies and securing
the execution of his commands (*Report of the Secretary of War
1903*).

Obsessed with the need for inter-service co-ordination, and wary of
the lack of it, the US Army went a step further, creating the post of
chairman for the Joint Chiefs of Staff, a post to which President
Roosevelt appointed Admiral D. Leahy as the first chairman. In
fact, even this arrangement was thought not to have gone far
enough to ensure co-ordination, for in 1982 the Armed Services
Committee of the US Congress recommended, after hearing the
retiring chairman of the JCS, General David Jones, that the system
should be revamped and the chairman be included in the National
Security Council.

In fact, the order abolishing this important co-ordinating office
was taken by neither Nimeiri the officer of the Sudan Defence
Force nor Nimeiri the staff officer trained in one of the top staff
colleges; it was Nimeiri's vindictive policy that was in action.
After the 1982 confrontation the other Nimeiri was bent on cutting
down the Army to size, i.e. incapacitating it and seeking to corrupt
its officers. The Army, according to article 199 of the constitution,
is to guard and secure the country, preserve the safety of its territory, participate in development and protect the constitution.
From 1982 on the Army, according to Nimeiri, was only to be kept
as a tool of terror with enough fire-power to intimidate and
overawe. Its main reason in life would be to defend and protect the
President (or rather his whims and excesses) and frighten his
opponents. To that end the Army needed neither modernization
nor good management. Like the SSU, the Cabinet and regional
and local governments, it was to be turned into another domain of
patronage.

No sooner had Nimeiri cashiered the twenty-two officers than he
engaged in wholesale promotion, filling old posts and creating new
ones. Field-Marshal Nimeiri created five new posts for lieutenants-
general, including one bestowed on the Commander of the Music
Corps, not for his achievements in war but for his 'heroic' accomplishment in composing an anthem glorifying Nimeiri. Sudan had
no lieutenant-general when the May revolution started and none
right up to 1974. There was only one such post during the regime of

the parties and also under Abboud. One may recall here that the creation of that post during the regime of the parties came after a tough struggle between the Prime Minister Abdalla Khalil, and the Under-Secretary of Finance, Hamza Mirghani, supported by his Minister, Ibrahim Ahmed Mirghani maintaining that the Sudanese Army, given its size and hierarchy, did not justify such a post. Hamza Mirghani never relented and the compromise he and his Minister accepted was that their decision be overruled by the Council of Ministers. Neither all this historical record nor managerial refinements meant anything to Nimeiri, not even the balance between soldiers and officers, higher ranks to lower ranks, combatant to non-combatant personnel etc. Not even concepts of hierarchy structure, almost ritualistic in armies, were his concern. It was all selling and buying, never minding the financial implications that his decision entailed. Probably some of the most serious of these decisions were taken on the same day that Nimeiri was reciting to the nation some aspects of his economic stabilization programme, e.g. reducing government expenditure. In what Sadiq el Mahdi described as the trial of the regime by the Army (in an article in *Sharkal Awsat*) Parliament, Ministers and the SSU played no supporting role whatsoever. Instead of backing the rebellious Army officers they chose to wait for the outcome of this confrontation to sing songs of praise for the victor.

The poor souls were too pleased to see someone else on the receiving end of Nimeiri's coups and blows. Nimeiri the bully, having destroyed the Army, which Nimeiri the lofty dreamer was proud of and striving to rebuild with his team of competent professional officers, soon metamorphosed into a third Nimeiri, the superstitious. The third man went back home and ordered two sheep killed at the gate of his Army residence, one black and one white. The conjurers had so ordered. In Nimeiri's reign of mediocrity there was no difficulty in finding black sheep.

Enrichessez-vous!

If it was corruption and misappropriation of state funds the officers were complaining about, they should be given their share of the spoils. Nimeiri set up a Military Economic Corporation and entrusted high-ranking Army officers with running it. He made sure he put at its head one of his buddies, Zubeir Rajab, a former railway

221

official. In the Army which was by now free for all, Rajab, the rail-wayman, was made a General, his alias General Z. R. el Tom.

The establishment of the Military Economic Corporation was, first and foremost, Nimeiri's tool to corrupt the Army; as he had destroyed it professionally, it should now be morally destroyed. A wily manoeuvre was needed to justify the act, so it was presented as an attempt to make the Army both productive and self-sufficient. One would have expected something in the nature of an Army co-operative engaged in supplying the Army with its locally produced day-to-day needs, but Nimeiri had something else in mind. The Army was to be entrusted with the running of civilian economic concerns. To justify his decision, Nimeiri declared that the military were competent and efficient managers and that their managerial skills should be harnessed. The Field-Marshal was referring to the same Army whose top brass were accused of inefficiency. This accusation was not only restricted to public statements in the media, but repeated by Nimeiri in his inspection tours of Army units. It was particularly addressed to the soldiers and NCOs. They were Nimeiri's main audience and he needed to enlist their support against their officers. They were, he said, 'abandoned by the officers who never cared for their social or professional needs'. Nimeiri told the rank and file that he identified with them and that for them a new dawn had come as a result of the creation of the Military Economic Corporation: plenty of food, free schooling for their children up to university level, Army hospitals, housing. The millennium was around the corner.

Instead of being given the ailing sector of the economy to rejuve-nate the new military managers were given the most profitable companies, all trading corporations. Trade has quicker returns and larger commissions. Trade, of course, was hardly the economic sector that needed the application of new managerial skills by the military. The Sudanese private sector had been doing it for decades, and doing it well. The new skills were needed elsewhere, in industry and agriculture, where the battle of production was to be fought and won by the 'General' managers and their Commander-in-Chief.

It may be recalled that the public corporations inherited many different fortunes after the sweeping nationalizations of 1970 had gone through. Following the re-organization initiated by Mamoun Beheiry in 1977, on the basis of a World Bank report, and carried further by his successors, many of these corporations were incorporated under the Companies Act as limited liability companies. They were to perform as independent entities away from bureaucratic constraints. The system worked and the companies, after years in the red, registered some profits. The two leading companies (Khartoum and Kordofan) were the first to be handed over to the military. The third (Coptrade) was to follow. That company was originally a co-operative association serving all co-operatives in the Sudan. In the course of the re-organization of public corporations it was decided, in view of the success of the experiment, that the co-operative association should also be incorporated as a limited liability company, with the proviso that part of its profits should go to support the co-operative movement in the Sudan.

As if all that was not enough, the military corporation soon started encroaching upon the domain of the private sector, e.g. the export of melon seeds to Egypt, traditionally an activity of that sector. The military corporation was soon to extend its tentacles beyond the Sudan border, establishing overseas trade offices. By a providential coincidence this happened at the same time that Nimeiri decided, for reasons of economy, to close down embassies in twenty-two countries, including some trade missions. This proliferation of activity was only necessary to provide room for the discontented, the dangerous and the inquisitive among the officers.

Nimeiri was bent on pursuing this policy and was ready to go to any limits in its defence, as he proved. For example, the military corporation came under heavy attack from the Paris Consultative Group, as we shall see. It also came under even heavier attack from the present administration in the USA. The attack was two-pronged: first, the feeling that the organization smacked of corruption and second, its encroachment on the private sector did not endear it to the powerful protagonists of free enterprise within Washington ruling circles. The USA almost decided to stop shipments of wheat when they were told that the clearance of those shipments would be entrusted to the corporation (Coptrade). Surprisingly, Coptrade had traditionally carried out this function, but by now it had come under the cloak of the discredited military corporation. That much was brought to the attention of President Nimeiri by his Ministers. It was also subtly explained to him by the US Ambassador. Subtlety, however, was wasted on Nimeiri. He decided to go to President Reagan.

The President, who gave in to the USA on many more important issues, decided to fight this one out. Nimeiri wrote to President Reagan late in 1983, complaining that some of 'his aides', i.e. Reagan's, were frustrating Sudan's efforts to deploy the Army in the service of development by putting the economic corporation of the Army in an unfavourable light. He then went on to talk about the wheat wrangle. Reagan's answer was cryptic. He expressed his delight in learning that the Army was engaged in development, but as for the issue raised by Nimeiri on wheat deliveries it had better be left to the competent quarters in both countries. It is remarkable to note that the President's concern, at a time when bread-lines were lengthening by the day in Khartoum, was not with ensuring that wheat supplies should be shipped and unloaded by hook or by crook. Rather, he was striving to have it done only by crooks, i.e. for his cronies to have their share, not of the cake this time, but of a whole wheat cargo.

This incident demonstrates the extent to which Nimeiri was prepared to go in order to make his point or please his cronies. Furthermore, it reveals the depth to which government and diplomacy had sunk. Nimeiri must have been expecting President Reagan to exercise his presidential powers against his own institutions, not knowing that Article II of the US constitution has only four sections on executive power, none of which resembles the amended articles 82 and 83 of the Sudan constitution.

President Nimeiri, in his response to attacks against signs of larcenous wealth, often claimed that material wealth came with development, notwithstanding the fact that it was Nimeiri's own institution (the Central Committee of the SSU, March 1975) that had cautioned against the emergence of pockets of illicit wealth, middlemen, commission agents and the rest of the parasitic toads. It is precisely this class, devoid of entrepreneurship or professional and managerial abilities, that has been encouraged and nourished by the President. The military economic corporation was simply a link in a chain, so that with corruption now extended to the armed forces the circle was complete. The President may not have heard of the French historian François Guizot, the leader of the constitutional monarchists under Louis-Philippe, but without knowing of him he had undoubtedly followed his footsteps. Guizot's call to the French was 'enrichessez-vous'. So is Nimeiri's to the military and all those desirous of joining the company.

Where is my Commission?

The officers' complaints about the corruption of Nimeiri's brother Mustafa went unheeded. Far from restricting his activities to Wad Nimeiri and keeping a low profile, Mustafa remained at large. In 1980 he visited West Germany to claim his commission on the several Magirus deals. Mustafa was accompanied by his lawyer, since he sensed trouble looming, created by the former marketing expert of Magirus in Khartoum, Mr Muller. 'I want my commission, all my commission,' shouted Nimeiri's brother in his hotel corridor. (Who cares for a bunch of Germans around?)

Mustafa in fact wanted the Sudan Embassy to help him in getting the German authorities to arrest a German citizen in his own country. Muller, who had incurred the wrath of the President's brother, was dismissed by the company and returned to Germany, in spite of the fact that he was in disagreement with Mustafa on his mode of operation which, he thought, was detrimental to the company's interests. The company, which knew Sudan better, was not ready to antagonize Nimeiri's brother. Mercedes Benz recruited Muller because he had knowledge of the Khartoum scene. Mustafa, enlisting the support of his mighty and 'righteous' brother, got the state security organization to arrest and then expel the German from the country as a 'security risk'. So, on the instructions of Nimeiri, Muller was thrown out of the Sudan. Some revelations in the German press (der Spiegel) on Nimeiri's foreign accounts were believed to have emanated from Muller. Mustafa, afraid that the man might still muddy the waters for him with his old employers, wanted to have him coerced and intimidated in his own country. 'He is a security risk,' Mustafa told the Sudan Embassy officials, possibly adding that he was a Communist or a Gaddafi agent. At some pains, the officials told him that things were different in West Germany. The sixth-former had to go all the way to Bonn to learn about that.

The commission that Mustafa was after related to several deals. One of these deals stood on its own. A few months before his trip to Germany the Army ordered large quantities of spare parts for the Magirus trucks, many of which were now in disuse. Mustafa alerted his principals who soon worked out their pro-forma invoices which reflected costs, insurance and freight, without forgetting the other additives. At the same time Sudan's military attaché in Bonn was busy doing his own shopping, for not all the parts were produced by the truck producers. On comparing the two lists of prices flagrant discrepancies emerged; the prices on some items were inflated by over 30 per cent. The military attaché would not tolerate the underhand deal, so he relayed the story to Khartoum. But the Khartoum that had overruled the Minister of Finance on loans, the Minister of Commerce on trade licences, the Minister of Transportation on the roadworthiness of vehicles had no difficulty in putting the young officer in his place. Buy through Magirus was the order and sure enough that order went directly to the suppliers. Somebody wants his commission.

Corruption inside the regime continued unabated despite the various anti-corruption crusades that Nimeiri launched. Nimeiri was ostensibly taking up the issue of corruption (during the third SSU General Congress), promising to fight and eliminate it when the British Parliament became concerned with an arms scandal involving a member of his Cabinet. *The Observer* (20 February 1983) revealed that Argentina received French Exocet missiles despite the French embargo. Apparently the Sudanese Minister in question had issued an end-user certificate which enabled arms dealers working for the Argentine government to buy the Exocets. The Minister, *The Observer* revealed, received 200,000 dollars for the certificate.

The sale was a matter of investigation by both the British and French securities and following *The Observer* story the issue was brought before the British Parliament by Mr Tam Dalyell, as we said, at the time when Nimeiri was promising to be even more vigilant and to monitor even more closely. Nothing of this appeared in the Sudanese press or was taken up by the vigilant President or his Security. A similar newspaper report (this time *The New York Times*) involving a senior Egyptian government official (Deputy Prime Minister Ahmed Sultan) led to an investigation by the Egyptian authorities and a trial in which Sultan was exonerated. But from Egypt Nimeiri only wants security, not examples of good government to be emulated.

The Suicide of the SSU

With the army demoralized, frustrated and almost destroyed Nimeiri now turned to the SSU. The destruction of the SSU, we

argued, started in 1977 with the introduction of members of the opposition into its ranks. The dismissal of Abul Gasim Ibrahim and
Nimeiri's tirades in August 1979 represented another stage of this
process. On 25 January, immediately after his coups against the
army, Nimeiri dissolved the Politburo and the Central Committee
(both elected) and the General Secretariat. The President issued a
decree stating:

> The President of the SSU, after consulting article 15 of the
> basic rules of the SSU and in order to enlarge [!!] the area of
> participation in the building of the Sudan decided (1) to renew
> his commitment to the principle of one political organ which is
> based on the coalition of the popular working forces and which
> encapsulates the Sudanese people and (2) to dissolve the
> Central Committee, the Politburo, the office of secretary-
> general and the General Secretariat of the SSU and form a
> popular committee to develop the activities of the SSU on all
> levels and to review the charter, programme and rules in order
> to ensure the positive participation of the Sudanese people.

This left him as President, in charge of all the activities of the SSU
up to January 1983, when the Congress would be convoked to
review the organization, goals and aims of the SSU.

Whenever Nimeiri wanted nothing concrete to emerge from a
conference he organized a jamboree where every shade of the political spectrum was included and where nothing but generalities
were discussed. Whenever he wanted discord to prevail, allowing
him to sway the conference his way, he invoked slogans such as
national forces, democracy and national dialogue. This last
jamboree was called the Popular Committee on the Development
of the SSU.

The motley committee held sixteen sessions between 30 January
and 21 March, supposedly in an attempt to find remedies for the
SSU's ailments, e.g. unpopularity, lack of popular participation in
its activities, lack of responsiveness and lack of democracy. In the
course of the discussions and deliberations of the Popular Committee some biting attacks and criticisms of the SSU were made.
There were a few good recommendations for democratizing the
SSU and opening up its ranks put forward. The final communiqué
reflected none of that, for the recommendations were in consonance with Nimeiri's wishes. So much was admitted by the

committee itself when it said that it had 'discussed matters related to the goals, tasks, organs, membership, leadership and finance of the SSU, and the bases and principles of its organization' and that 'it has been guided by the President's opening speech ... and aspirations of the national forces.'

The recommendation paid special attention to political organs on the regional level and decided to abolish the regional secretariats except for the Khartoum secretariat. The final communiqué went on to describe the composition of the reduced National Congress; to be included were any 'additional number of delegates chosen by the President of the SSU from the regions and Khartoum in order to ensure the required parity in representation.' Thus Nimeiri could stack the National Congress with his supporters. The Central Committee was also to have its appointed members; 10 per cent of its membership was to be fixed by the President, according to the communiqué. 50 per cent of the 150-strong membership was to be chosen directly by the Congress, with 40 per cent chosen by the electoral colleges.

On the question of the abolition of the Politburo, the communiqué said

> The Committee is of the opinion that there is an overlap
> between the present functions of the Politburo and the
> General Secretariat. It is also of the opinion that the General
> Secretariat, by virtue of its composition, is more capable of
> running the day-to-day activities of the SSU and accordingly
> recommends the abolition of the Politburo and the transfer of
> its functions to the General Secretariat.

In other words, in the opinion of the committee, the Politburo was no longer a policy-making organ but an executive secretariat, so it might as well be abolished. The secretary-general too was to be appointed by the President of the SSU. This was hardly the SSU Nimeiri preached in 1972, the progressive democratization of which commenced in 1974 and reached its zenith in 1977. Nor was this the logical response to the cries of the street for more participation and devolution of authority, which were echoed in the very conference Nimeiri himself organized to put forward viable alternatives.

To this jamboree Nimeiri invited a few of the old politicians in the regime of the parties. They were there in their personal capacity. Some of them must have infuriated Nimeiri. The meeting, however, was fortunate enough not to have to endure the humiliation of accusations of cowardice; nevertheless there were a few biting remarks. Nimeiri would not miss an occasion to offend, for it made up for a strange innate sense of insecurity. One of these biting remarks in particular deserved an answer. Addressing his unnamed critics (he must have been watching them through closed-circuit TV) Nimeiri shouted, 'Some of you were talking about democracy. What democracy were you talking about? Is it the democracy of "to whom it may concern, greetings"?' Nimeiri dared his audience to answer. Without demur, he got away with it. Nimeiri, in fact, was referring to his predecessor Ismael el Azhari, who was, in his own fashion, extremely authoritarian. In dealing with his party colleagues, el Azhari used to handle 'trouble-makers' swiftly and without much ado; he always pulled out one of his blue papers (he kept sheaves of them) and wrote a short note of dismissal to be publicly circulated under the rubric 'to whom it may concern, greetings.' That was el Azhari's measure of scorn. He had, at least, a sense of humour and was never offensive.

Nimeiri was evidently ill-placed to make the remark he made about his predecessor. Many of those who received the sack from el Azhari, often unjustifiably, were the following day reacting to it in public, voting against him in Parliament, attacking him in the press, staging demonstrations against him in the streets, and some-times forming another party. But that was not all; more import-antly, it was those very excesses of el Azhari that produced Nimeiri. That obvious truth never dawned on the inquisitorial Pres-ident, nor did anybody care to draw his attention to it. Megaloma-niacs live under a hypnotic spell that could only be broken by constantly banging them on the head with the realities in whose faces they are flying.

So the 'popular' committee that had met for sixteen sessions to develop the SSU and enlarge democracy within it ended by circum-scribing it further, concentrating more power in the hands of the President. Nine months later the recommendations were put before the General Congress of the SSU (February 1983) and were unanimously adopted. The SSU had committed suicide. There were no regrets. By its very action and inaction it had lost both support and honour.

Chapter Seven

After me the Deluge

Nothing is ended with honour
which does not conclude better than it began.

Samuel Johnson

Foibles and Excesses

1983 was a watershed in Sudanese politics. In May (that blessed
month) Nimeiri renewed the mandate that was to be his last (as he
publicly declared in his speech after he was elected for a second
term in 1977 and as he told Yahia Abdel Magid and others in 1980
and the Army officers in the summer of 1981). In fact in January
1982 he declared that he was staying at the helm indefinitely and
dismissed his heir apparent Abdel Magid Khalil. In 1983 there
were three palace coups, against the SSU, the Addis Ababa agreement and the judiciary, the first before the elections, the second
and third after it (a very even distribution of tasks). Also, in
September, there was the introduction of Shari'a law.

The avalanche of coups carried by Nimeiri against himself, were
not only the excesses of a megalomaniac, they were also the foibles
of a ruler feeling more and more insecure. Nimeiri's actions, all this
time, were in fact guided by his fears and insecurity and dictated by
his instinct to survive. His policies were irrational and discordant,
and every one of them became its own frame of reference. His political vision, increasingly one-dimensional and myopic, meant that
he could not see connections between the different measures or the
implications and consequences of those measures.

Starting from the common-sense point, Nimeiri had no alternative but to go, but common-sense is not so common with megalo-maniacs. They behave as if they are ensconced forever. And by 1983 Nimeiri had too many skeletons in his cupboard and had allowed too many moral breaches and legal infractions to feel comfortable enough to go at will. With his innate mistrust in others (brought about by his own constant betrayal of friends and foes alike), Nimeiri would never trust any guarantees for his safety and the safety of his cronies and family. In fact, many of these played a very important role in discouraging him from abdicating and cultivated his fears as to what might happen if he did. Nimeiri, therefore, thought that he might as well stay and go on doing his thing. For over a decade he was using power adroitly to intimidate, cajole, coerce, corrupt and suppress, actually misusing rather than using power. Purposeful politics presupposes a constructive use of power.

We have also had occasion to see how Nimeiri had allowed several opportunities for redressing the situation to slip; institutionalization (August 1976), national reconciliation (1978–9), confrontation with the army and development of the SSU with a view to expanding the frontiers of democracy and curbing corruption (1982). Statesmen transform challenges into opportunities. Nimeiri, in a vengeful spirit, transmuted opportunity into a personal challenge. Typically, he reacted by destroying his own institutions, the Army and the SSU, thus burning all his bridges. From then on it became only a question of time.

1982 witnessed the end of the military discipline with which armies respond almost instinctively to calls of duty. The Army became demoralized, ill equipped and frustrated. (That was the way Nimeiri wanted it.) The SSU, on the other hand, became more isolated, unpopular and irrelevant, an expensive political monstrosity. It became so isolated that the HQ of the SSU, the party of the masses, became a fortress guarded by sentries armed to the teeth and studded with security agents all over. (It was Nimeiri they were protecting.) Mass parties only succeed when they relate to people as fish to water, in the words of Mao Tse-tung. Not even at the height of struggle against the British was the Sudan Club (the SSU HQ had been a club for senior British officials) so well guarded. The National SSU Congress, which used to meet in tents up to the mid-'seventies, was meeting now under heavy guard. Members (not visitors) were frisked by metal detectors during the whole duration of the Congress. Nimeiri could not see in all that where his political itinerary has led him. It was Nimeiri who introduced and refined the art of personal communication between leader and led and narrowed the gap between ruler and ruled in his early years, as we have seen.

Government was also destroyed and Ministers kept away from the centre of things. Not much was to be expected from the inadequate regional governments except the satisfaction of the aspirations of elitist elements (governors, Ministers, assembly members and senior civil servants). That is not to say that there are not still many politicians and administrators in the regional governments who are trying to make the best of an inadequate system. The Cabinet, first emaciated through regionalization, became increasingly a forum where Nimeiri delivered speeches. From Nimeiri's new breed of Ministers nobody expected much. The cronies were busy making money, the apolitical technocrats were more concerned and restricted to their own departments and the political careerists were crouching at Nimeiri's feet. All were gripped by an almost reverential awe; fear by now was ingrained in the marrow of the bones of many. The few firm hands (the fire brigade) knew only too well what was expected from them and stuck to their fire extinguishers. They also knew too well that, to Nimeiri, they were only as important as the man next door. Corruption and mismanagement? Who dared to talk about that? The centre of the malignancy lies in the danger zone ... so the less said the better. Mismanagement, therefore, became a rule and corruption became collective by the very act of collective obliviousness to it. With this quality of governance the regime was shorn of both a collective conscience and collective wisdom.

In this political landscape Nimeiri went on alone, using his Presidential prerogatives (articles 82 and 83 of the constitution) which became wider and greyer. Government was, therefore, immobilized. It is almost axiomatic in management that concentration of power is impotence. On the other hand, Lord Acton's dictum that absolute power corrupts absolutely was redundant in the case of Nimeiri. He was already corrupted before his absolutism. Nimeiri, therefore, had no other way but to resort to his old ploy, shock tactics, i.e. to confuse people with unpredictable decisions and keep them guessing. There was more of that the more the situation deteriorated.

Nimeiri has a flair for political gambling though, with all his debauchery, he was never known to be a gambler. None the less, like one, the more exciting the wager became the higher his stakes went. Nimeiri had always minimized risks in his encounters, not because of his daring but because there has always been somebody to get him out of it, Omar el Hag Musa and different alibis during his early involvements in coup attempts, his RCC colleagues and the Army in September 1975 and July 1976, the 'fire brigade' within the economic and security sectors, the SSU people who absorbed the shocks on his behalf etc. From all these shocks Nimeiri came out unscathed and never bothered to assume responsibility for the mistakes or to be grateful to the saviours.

To make up for his isolation at home President Nimeiri increasingly depended on the outside world, mainly Egypt and the USA. Since 1978 Nimeiri had made an annual pilgrimage to Washington. His trip in the watershed year was like the others except that Nimeiri had occasion in the course of it to see how the US President relates to his aides. Nimeiri had met at length with Reagan. They talked a good deal and he agreed with him on everything: Libya, Ethiopia, the Cubans in Africa, the Soviet Union and possibly Antarctica. But Reagan had another preoccupation then, the tragedy of the marines in Lebanon. The Secretary of Defence was being taken to task by Congress and the press was unkindly making mincemeat of him. It was too much for one man, particularly when he should not be the only person to bear the brunt. So in the course of a press briefing at the White House, where Presidential aides were putting the case of the administration President Reagan unexpectedly emerged at the press briefing, though he was not scheduled to. He came to give the last word: 'If there is to be blame, it properly rests here in this office and with this President. And I accept responsibility for the good as well as the bad.' Forget about the Arctic and the Antarctic; the Sudan could have been much better off if Nimeiri had learned from his friend Ronnie (Sadat, Nimeiri's latter-day mentor, used to talk of his friend Jimmy) something about the grace and sense of responsibility that comes with the Presidency.

This is the background against which all of Nimeiri's actions, particularly in 1983, are to be viewed. Nimeiri's different layers of character were catching up with him, the vindictive one fighting with the dreamer, the bully giving way to the weak-kneed one and the superstitious one dominating the scene. In the reign of irrationality this is not surprising. From now on many of the President's decisions could hardly be dignified by rational analysis.

Coup against the South

Nimeiri's most serious coup in the watershed year was his coup against the South, the demolition of the Addis Ababa agreement. For the man who claims to be the apostle of regionalization in the whole country, destroying the one and only working regional government in the country did not make sense. The system was working despite the charges of corruption and inefficiency, not all without justification. The President, evidently, is not a believer in Lord Salisbury's cautionary advice: 'If it works, leave it alone.' Nimeiri, in 1972, gave the impression of having, more than all his predecessors, realized the nature of the Southern problem, the cultural uniqueness of the region. If he did, then with all this insight he fell short of accepting its logical consequences; autonomy has its own dynamics. But in fact Nimeiri had never been genuinely committed to the principles of the Addis Ababa agreement. For the architects of the agreement the settlement was the corner-stone of national unity; for Nimeiri it had a completely different significance. Autonomy was a price he was prepared to pay to the Southerners in return for their support against his enemies in the North. As the Southerners sought to exercise their semi-independence and assert their autonomy Nimeiri's role was reduced to that of formally passing decrees appointing and dismissing Ministers on the advice of the Regional President and Parliament. In the instances when Nimeiri refused to abide by their recommendations the Southerners stood firmly against him. He could not tolerate this defiance because it came from a power centre which was outside his sphere of influence and it might encourage the institutions of the North to follow suit and play their constitutional role.

In his assault on the Addis Ababa agreement Nimeiri set out to exploit the divisions and conflicts inside the ranks of the Southerners. Southern politics had been dominated by one tribe (the Dinka) which outnumbered the other tribes. The Equatorians, unhappy about their subordinate share of power, asked Nimeiri to effect a political division of the Southern Region into three regions, enabling them to hold the helm in a small entity. This, needless to say, was opposed by the majority of the Southerners. The Addis

Ababa agreement, though silent on the issue of redivision, provided for means of settling disputes.

To ensure the sanctity of the agreement article 8 of the constitution provides that the Southern Provinces Regional Self-government Act 1972 (the Addis Ababa agreement) 'shall not be amended except in accordance with the provisions thereof'. Dividing the region into sub-regions entailing the abrogation of the Southern Government and Assembly (symbols of an autonomous South) amounts to an amendment of the agreement and the Act. Article 4 of the Act provides that 'The provinces of Bahr el Ghazal, Equatoria and Upper Nile as defined in article 3 (iii) shall constitute an autonomous region within the Democratic Republic of the Sudan and shall be known as the Southern Region.' The Act, therefore, speaks of an integrated region. Demolishing that region should be construed as a breach of the agreement unless the decision is taken in the manner prescribed by the law. The Act demands that amendment to the agreement can only be effected through a set procedure, i.e. first carried by a three-quarter majority of the national Parliament and then approved through a plebiscite by a two-thirds majority in the Southern Region. Nimeiri was not only aware of the Act and the constitutional provision; in fact he cautioned his own Ministers in 1978 not to tamper with the Addis agreement. Trouble arose then between the Southern Region province of Bahr el Ghazel and the Northern Region province of Kordofan, as to whether a border community belonged to North or South. The issue which was blown up into a North/South conflict was only defused when Nimeiri referred the contestants to the agreement, which provides that province boundary problems should be settled by referendum. In effect article 3 (iii) of the Act, referred to above, provides that the 'Southern Provinces of the Sudan means the provinces of Bahr el Ghazal, Equatoria and Upper Nile in accordance with their boundaries as they stood on 1 January 1956 and any other areas that were culturally and geographically a part of the Southern complex as may be determined by referendum'.

It was neither because of lack of political insight nor precedents that Nimeiri had sharpened his knives and decided to charge for the kill; he was motivated by sheer vindictiveness and petulance, harsh though this may sound. In January 1980, following a conflict between the Regional President, Joseph Lagu (Equatoria) and the Speaker of the Regional Assembly, Clement M'boro, on the issue of redivision, Nimeiri decided to dissolve both the Southern Cabinet and Assembly. He had no constitutional authority to do so. In both cases he was acting outside the law and the constitution, but he justified his act by his desire to act as an umpire and choose an independent interim government headed by an Army officer, to ascertain the wishes of the people and prepare for a referendum.

General Gasim Allah Abdalla Rasas was selected for that purpose. What Nimeiri sought was simply a reprieve; he was not interested in a referendum. Nimeiri was testing the waters; he wanted to know how the Southerners would react to his encroachment on the constitution and the agreements. On 23 February 1981 Nimeiri showed his real colours; he was for redivision. His declaration to that effect was made at a meeting of the Central Committee of the SSU and it was clear that he wanted to go along with it. There was no reaction in sight to his dissolution of the Regional Assembly, in spite of the opposition of the Speaker, Clement M'boro. The Southerners, he thought, like their brethren in the North, had accepted his constitutional encroachments.

But Clement is a tough nut to crack. Like Nimeiri he too was making his calculations and planning the next step. He was only waiting to see if the President's interim government was going to deliver the goods, i.e. solve the problem of redivision in accordance with the letter and spirit of the constitution and the Act, i.e. by holding a referendum. The defiance was to follow. On 5 October 1981 Clement established a Council for the Unity of South Sudan (Clement is not a Dinka; he comes from a minor tribe). The Council was presided over by Clement himself with Samuel Aru Bol (Dinka) as deputy chairman and Joseph Oduhu (Equatoria) as secretary-general. It was composed of twenty-one Southern leaders. On 22 December 1981 the Council sent a memorandum to Nimeiri complaining about his failure to pay heed to the Southern opposition to division, as expressed by the Southern Parliament and Southern members of the SSU and the National Assembly.

'It should be Your Excellency's point of pride,' the daring Southerners told Nimeiri, 'to see these bodies [Southern Regional and Nationai Assemblies] doing their job in a bold and regular manner. Yet the fate of these two Assemblies has been their dissolution.' The memorandum reminded His Excellency that 'a Round Table Conference was held in 1965.' Northern delegates insisted on multiple regions for the South. Southern delegates rejected this proposal. Northern delegates also insisted on the selection of Southern leaders of the regions by a Northern President. Southern delegates insisted that Southerners must elect their own leader. Because of these two points of disagreement it was not possible to achieve peace. The memorandum reminded His Excellency that peace was only achieved when the North conceded on these counts. It also urged him to observe neutrality in his dealings with Southerners, i.e. not to side with the Commissioner of Eastern Equatoria in 'his open campaign and high-handedness in the cause of division'. They impressed upon the President not to extend the time table of six months for the interim government. Nimeiri ordered the arrest of all twenty-one members of the Council.

Nimeiri's meddling with the Addis Ababa agreement, his treatment of Southern leaders and his high-handed action galvanized the South against him. The Southern leaders found themselves spearheading a movement which cut across tribal boundaries. It was not a Dinka movement, for its chairman came from a minor tribe and its secretary-general was an Equatorian from the province allegedly clamouring for separation. Nimeiri decided to go to the South and see for himself, under heavy guard this time. It was no longer the carefree President of 1972, milling with the multitude of Southerners, chatting, cracking jokes and dancing with them. There was an air of tension all over the place, only to be broken by a rowdy demonstration against the President in Rumbeik. Its organizers were the pupils of the town's only secondary school.

Nimeiri should have been accustomed by now to putting up with schoolboy demonstrations. There were a lot of them in Khartoum. It was these young souls who had exposed the nakedness of the emperor and led Nimeiri to disavow his own government (1982). Sadly they were alone; their elders were either sottishly watching or busy looking for bread. In the reign of Nimeiri (the new dawn that rose) men and women of the North have learnt to live by bread alone. In the South the matter was different; their elders were too much at the helm or so they hoped. Nimeiri was visibly enraged. He shouted back at the demonstrators and ordered them arrested. He also took two decisions right there and then: to close the school indefinitely and put the boys on trial. Petulance apart, Nimeiri's decisions were wrong on two counts: (1) decisions such as the closure and opening of schools fell within the purview of the Minister of Education, not requiring presidential action, and (2) according to the Addis Ababa agreement matters of education are a purely Southern concern and, therefore, under the jurisdiction of the President of the Southern Region and his Minister of Education.

There is always a chance, unluckily for Nimeiri, to compare his actions with those of his predecessors and aides. One cannot help recalling, in this particular instance, the attitude of Nimeiri's top aide, first Vice-President General Khalil, at the University of Khartoum less than two years before the Rumbeik incident. Nimeiri was to have attended the occasion, as the patron of the university, but decided at the last minute, knowing about the impending hostile reception, not to make a showing. He contrived a trip to Port Sudan for the day. Nimeiri surely knew well, by then, that he was the man whom all the Sudanese most loved to hate, but Field-Marshal Walter Mitty did not want to believe that there were still some people around the Sudan who were ready to express this hate to his face, so he might as well not go and face them. Khalil was to face the music. Khalil did it with dignity. The boys shouted everything down, sparing nobody. The General, undeterred, continued with the ceremony, his address, his visit to the campus, and then left. Back in his office he was even more dignified, instructing Security to consider the matter closed.

After Rumbeik the petulant President decided to carry his vindictiveness further, to divide the South and destroy the Regional Government. He hurriedly called a press conference at the palace on 5 June 1983 to announce his new measures in the South. Nimeiri went ahead with the division and three regions were created, based on the three provinces comprising the region. The Southern Assembly and Government, the two symbols of Southern unity and autonomy, were abolished. In announcing the division of the South, Nimeiri said that the decree would take effect for a transitional period of eighteen months, after which matters would be handed back to the Southern people. In his press conference Nimeiri denied that the decree contravened the Addis Ababa agreement, saying that the Addis Ababa agreement was part of the law of the land and that the law was governed by the constitution, which was protected and preserved by the President of the Republic! Whatever one may figure out of this tautology, Nimeiri's real self came out in the open when he was cross-examined by the journalists.

The journalists could not take it, and they persisted with questions on the Addis Ababa agreement, the procedure for amending it and its constitutional guarantees. One of these questioners was the correspondent of Radio Juba. The President, losing his temper, came out with a sadly ludicrous answer: 'The Addis Ababa agreement is myself and Joseph Lagu and we want it that way.' And before people woke up from the shock of that remark Nimeiri went on: 'I am 300 per cent the constitution. I do not know of any plebiscite because I am mandated by the people as President.' One may say, however, that Nimeiri, was, in a sense, asserting a literal truth; his action proved it and the inaction of others confirmed it. As to the Southern Government and Assembly Nimeiri's answer was amazing. Fuming with anger and scratching for words the President shouted, 'I am not going to dismiss anybody. . . . How can I? Even this man whom I appointed as Speaker . . . what is his name . . . [pause] . . . Izz el Din I cannot dismiss.' It was all incoherent, pathetic and too deep for tears. The man he referred to, who became a non-person, was Izz el Din el Sayed, the Speaker of the National Parliament and elected by the Parliament. Nimeiri did not appoint him, for he was nominated by the Parliamentary Party of the SSU and elected by the Assembly. He was the man before whom Nimeiri gave an oath of allegiance. All went to show the disdain with which Nimeiri treated people.

To the President the whole issue was now reduced to the level of Regional Ministers and parliamentarians continuing to draw their salaries during the lifetime of the elected Assembly. All was confused in his mind, political functions and pecuniary gain, the powers of the President and the coeval power of the people to say yes or no in a plebiscite, decisions of the Parliamentary Party and his own personal role as chairman heading a meeting and ensuring its good functioning. People were watching another piece of evidence of the truth of the adage: whom the gods would destroy, they first make mad. For those who watched this surrealistic spectacle on TV it was the film of the day. All were watching the President blowing his top and making a fool of himself; few can have had their eyes riveted to the banner behind the President, on which was emblazoned the following words: self-reliance, self-respect and self-restraint. These are the archetypal mottoes of the SSU, 1983 model. Nimeiri, undoubtedly, more than anybody else, was in need of the latter two.

Nimeiri went ahead with the division of the South, buying his way by creating three assemblies and three governments with shoals of ministers and under-secretaries. There were, of course, three regional governors in addition. It was all patronage, without looking at the bill. But money would have to be found; the President would not break his promise, even if the government had to break into a bank. They did, so to speak. It was the Bank of Sudan, in the fashion of another Field-Marshal, el Hadj Field-Marshal Dr Amin Dada. Amin's Uganda was reported to have been, like Nimeiri's Sudan, in similar dire straits. The Governor of Uganda's Central Bank decided to draw his President's attention to the tragic situation by conveying to him that money was no longer available to government, which had gone way above the permissible borrowing ceiling. Amin was inflamed; he took the Governor by the scruff of the neck to the Bank and asked him to open the vaults. Evidently the vaults were not literally empty. 'How dare you?' shouted Amin to his chief banker, palsied with fear. Indeed how dare they? With some field-marshals it is all a world of make-believe.

Unfortunately for Nimeiri things did not work his way in the South: seventeen years of war were not in vain. The master calculator, who thought that having subdued the North he would now get away with this one too, had a shock. He needed a shattering crisis and he got one. Instead of a committee of Southern elders striving to instil some sanity into the President's mind (not a very easy task after 1982) Nimeiri found himself facing a military insurrection led by younger elements, many of whom had been trained in the ranks of the Sudanese Armed Forces. Their claim was no longer secession or autonomy, but rather to rid the whole Sudan of Nimeiri. The problem is not in the South, it is in Khartoum, said their declarations. Nimeiri, oblivious to all these facts, typically blamed the whole thing on his neighbours to the north and the east (Libya and Ethiopia). The two villains may have committed many sins but certainly the dissolution of the Regional Assembly, the sacking of the Regional Government and the division of the South were not among them. Politics being what they are, the two countries did not hesitate to use the situation for their own ends, and the Southern crisis was given to them on a silver platter by Nimeiri. Ironically, Nimeiri, faced with the bloody situation he himself created, reached out to Clement M'boro in his self-exile in Nairobi to come and help him with the mess. This is the very man he had refused to listen to two years before and instead deposited in jail. By 1984 the picture in the South had completely changed, thanks to Nimeiri. The elders were no longer at the helm, and the young were talking with bullets.

No Justice . . . Nothing Happens!!

Nimeiri's second palace coup was the coup against the judiciary. It came in the summer of 1983. Resentful of the judiciary's defiance in 1981 and the popular support it had received he announced the retirement of some fifty judges as corrupt. He also accused the judiciary, as a whole, of inefficiency. Furthermore, he declared that more measures would be announced later. Included in the list of retired judges, naturally enough, were the members of the committee which organized resistance in 1981.

The Sudan constitution stipulates that 'judges shall be independent in the performance of their judicial duties, subject only to the rule of the law, and shall be responsible to the President of the Republic for their proper performance in accordance with the law' (article 187). In other words judges, in the performance of their duty, are not to be subjected to any constraints save the constant moral imperative of the rule of law. The constitution also empowers the President to remove judges 'in the manner prescribed by the constitution and the law' (article 188). The removal of judges, therefore, is not to be dictated by whim but essentially only for conduct unbefitting their profession and only in the manner prescribed by the constitution. The constitution provides in article 191 for the establishment of a 'Supreme Council of the Judiciary' whose function is, *inter alia*, to advise the President on the appointment, removal, promotion, transfer and discipline of judges. So the procedure for removing judges is not left to be catered for in the law, as in the case of government officers and officials, but made subject to the manner prescribed by the constitution. The words 'in the manner prescribed by the Constitution' were added advisedly. In effect it is only in the case of the judiciary and the Auditor-General (article 206) that removal of officials is subjected to procedures or limitations reflected in the constitution itself and not left to be determined by the law.

These are fine distinctions of the law for which Nimeiri had no time. By now he had become above the law. He was 300 per cent of the constitution and did not mind saying so. So, article 191 or no article 191 the judges had to go. A few of those who were retired do not deserve the shedding of a tear, but others were among the finest, with long years of experience and excellent training and unblemished reputation. The judges, however, would not let Nimeiri have it all his own way. The judiciary were united behind their colleagues, they demanded the nullification of Nimeiri's measures and threatened to resign. In the interim they came out on strike. Nimeiri did not pay any heed; he sought to replace the Sudanese with Egyptian judges (this shows the importance Nimeiri attached to his institutions and how much he knows of Sudan laws).

The judges went out on strike for three months, resulting in the total breakdown in the administration of justice. Nimeiri was not moved. In a public statement he declared that despite the strike for three months nothing had happened, nothing had happened to his person, that is, which is what mattered, for the battle was between his person and the judiciary. The remark was also revealing in another sense. Any head of state, in his right senses, would have considered the collapse of the legal system as a constitutional collapse. To Nimeiri, as long as he was in power, not physically challenged, without the impact of crisis leading to street confrontations, then nothing was happening. Only eighteen months before Nimeiri had decided to review the whole political system because a few thousand school-children took to the streets. With his instinct for survival he would never allow such a situation to deteriorate to the point of getting out the soldiers with their guns to face the boys, and not because of his kind heart. Nimeiri knew only too well, with the experience of October 1964 still fresh in his memory, that in such a situation the order of the commanding officers might suddenly change to: 'About turn and shoot in the other direction.' These situations have their own dynamics. As for the causes of an action involving millions of pounds, that was left unsettled, and the thousands of detainees awaiting trial who were rotting in prison because of the judges' strike, all amounted to 'nothing'.

The situation, however, soon became untenable. The Lawyers' Association joined hands with the judges and started organizing political debates that meandered from the judges' dispute into the whole crisis of government. University professors and students joined the league. All these were ominous signs. So, by a *tour de force*, Nimeiri managed to give the dispute a new colour. Instead of a dispute about principles of interference and independence, he made it into one about pay, privileges and selection procedures. So on 12 August he passed a decree abolishing certain posts, reviewing the procedures for selecting judges and, above all, offering judges more money and benefits. The procedural changes allowed Nimeiri to dress bribes up as a revolution in the judicial system, as it was described in the press (*Al Sahafa*, 12 August 1983). He also reinstated some of the judges unjustly victimized.

The increases were beyond anything that the judges had dreamed of, inducing in their tail a chain reaction which led to another crisis (with the doctors this time) to which we shall come later. Nimeiri, deviously, sought to clothe his backing-down in ideological garb, the change of the legal system. The introduction of Shari'a law was a good way of interrupting the judges' strike; the reasons behind the introduction of Shari'a law, however, are multifarious and complex.

The Fall of the Giant

It is evident from all the discordant decisions taken by Nimeiri throughout his reign and particularly in the watershed year that the President never paid attention to the implications of his own decisions, nor did he care to. Sudan's crisis, a political one, deepened further, but the most jarring shock of these policies was the one on the economy. For not only were all the measures Nimeiri had taken disruptive for the country's development plans but they were also dysfunctional for its newly introduced economic stabilization programme.

Perhaps the only fact that Nimeiri knows about Sudan is that it is the largest country in Africa. The President loves to call the Sudan (increasingly his personal estate) the Giant. 'The May revolution,' he said, 'came to pick up the Giant from his fall' (President's speech, 11 November 1972). The Giant was to fall again, thanks to the obstacles the Hero of May and his cabal put in its way. We have had occasion to go through the development plans that were meant to pick up the Giant from his fall.

We have already mentioned that some of those plans were, initially, misbegotten. This failure was one of planning, e.g. textile industry. However, three main factors have also contributed, to a large extent, to the failure of Sudan's development endeavours. Those are consumerism, mismanagement and corruption. The debt crisis was a result rather than a cause.

In the early 'seventies, the current account of Sudan's balance of payments was approximately in balance. Government savings (the difference between current revenue and expenditure) were equivalent to about 2 per cent of the GDP, gross national savings were equivalent to over 11 per cent of GDP and the inflation rate and debt service were low. The economy was virtually stagnant. The mid-'seventies witnessed a great extension of public sector economic activity and the launching of an ambitious development programme. This energetic development drive was not without its reasons. As I told *Sudanow* in March 1980, one 'cannot develop an enormous country like Sudan in any other way than by large-scale development projects.' In fact public investment in the mid-'seventies did stimulate rapid growth for several years.

The tendency towards consumer-led demand was, generally speaking, the result of two factors, first, the abortion of plan targets, particularly self-sufficiency in food, and second, the regime's encouragement of the emergence of an ever-lengthening parasitic class. To add to the confusion, while this was going on the cheer-leaders were still preaching the totems of socialism and frustrating the efforts of the few firm hands who were labouring hard to save the country and the economy. The adverse import/export trends resulted in an increase of borrowing, especially external, and a distortion of the economy. Gross budgetary imbalances led to increased deficit financing by the central bank. The consequences of all this were soaring inflation rates and debt service obligations.

Mismanagement is another topic which I dwelt upon in the interview with *Sudanow*. According to the Paris Report of the World Bank Consultative Group, 1984,

> inadequate provision was made for the maintenance of existing export-oriented public irrigation schemes, and project selection and implementation problems in the increasingly over-extended public sector prevented the new investments from generating anticipated returns in a timely fashion. . . . The external debts began to fall due before the physical assets could be brought into full production . . . which in turn led to production problems in agriculture, under-utilization of infrastructural and manufacturing capacity, an erosion of the revenue base, and a decline in overall economic activity.

By the middle of 1983 Sudan, which was to have become the bread-basket of the Arab world, was in dire straits. The Sudanese economy was lumbered with a huge external debt which it could not repay. Since it started defaulting on payments, the arrears due have soared; in April 1983 they stood at 1.74 billion US dollars. As of 30 June 1981 Sudan's foreign debt totalled over 7 billion US dollars, and latest figures put it at 8 or 9 billion US dollars. The annual rate of change of real GDP fell in 1982–3 by more than 2 per cent, this after a rise of 6 per cent in 1980–1 and 7 per cent in 1981–2. Although exports increased by 48 per cent in 1982–3 and imports fell by 8 per cent there was a trade deficit of 1,179.2 million US dollars as Sudan's imports totalled 1,742.5 million US dollars. Petroleum imports alone account for 26 per cent of the 1981–2 import bill (494.8 million US dollars) and for 25 per cent of the 1982–3 import bill (439.6 million US dollars).

Table 7.1 *Projected Dept Service. (Interest and repayments. Total external obligations of public sector) US $m*

1982	619.2	*1984*	1145.8
1983	1178.2	*1985*	1086.8

Source: IMF

Table 7.2 *Sudan – foreign debt as of 30 June 1982 (US$ millions)*

MULTILATERAL		1235
BILATERAL		
Paris Club	583	
Other industrial countries	158	2508
Saudi Arabia	1011	
Kuwait	756	
Other countries		909
COMMERCIAL BANKS		972
RESCHEDULED DEBT		
Paris Club	560	
Commercial banks	973	1541
Others	8	
TOTAL		7015

Sudan is still importing sugar; its imports in 1982–3 stood at 52.5 million US dollars. The figure is an improvement on the 1981–2 figure of 153.3 million US dollars and the 1980–1 figure of 183.6 million US dollars. This was due to an output increase in Kenana, which rose from 102,000 tonnes during the first nine months of

1982–3. There is, however, little cause for congratulation since Kenana's output is still short of its capacity of 330,000 tonnes, which was meant to satisfy export demands. Furthermore, output from Sudan's other sugar factories at Geneid, New Halfa, Sennar and Assalaya fell from 100,000 tonnes in 1980–1 to about 98,000 tonnes in 1982–3. The four factories have a designed production capacity of 360,000 tonnes. The sugar industry, with a designed production capacity of 690,000 tonnes is producing about 314,000 (i.e. at 45 per cent of its capacity). When in 1980 (during the third General Congress of the SSU), al Tayyib Harun (an eminent tribal leader from western Sudan) took issue with mismanagement in general, giving the example of Malut, he was silenced by the President. The Malut project was conceived as part of an economic programme aimed at developing and rejuvenating the South. Amongst other such projects are the sugar factory in Mangala and a cement factory in Kapoata (Equatoria). Sadly the progress made in the agricultural part of the Malut project was not matched in the industrial one. Although some of the Belgian-made machinery reached the site, a large part of it was left standing in Port Sudan and Kosti. Production of the rest of the machinery was stopped by the Belgians because Sudan defaulted in payment. In fact, it was Sudan's inability to meet its financial obligations in the above project that led to the creation of the Club of Paris to look into Sudan's finances. Delays in the execution of the Kenana project and production bottlenecks arising from inadequate management and maintenance of plants and factory equipment and shortages of fuel have meant that when Sudan should have been a major exporter of sugar it was importing it. Had the plants been operating at the envisaged full capacity sugar exports would have provided Sudan with 250 million US dollars.

With cement it is the same story. Thanks to the interference of Adnan Khashoggi, plans for a Red Sea cement factory were shelved. The combined annual capacity of the two plants at Atbara (Maspio Cement Corporation) and Rabak (Nile Cement Corporation) is 320,000 tonnes (this is expected to rise to 550,000 tonnes with the completion of the expansion of the Atbara plants). The Red Sea cement factory which never came into existence would have doubled the production capacity resulting in input savings. Even with a production capacity of 320,000 only 182,900 tonnes are being produced annually. Transportation and fuel problems, deteriorating crushing equipment, and a shortage of proper bags(!)

caused output to decline by 18 per cent to 150,000 tonnes in 1980–1. Though output picked up in 1981–2 and 1982–3, it is still far below capacity. Industry in general has a worse output to capacity ratio, e.g. textile industry (ranging between 20–30 per cent).

Here, we the planners are largely to blame. Our decision to have the weaving done at different locations proved to be short-sighted. The rationale behind the decision was that weaving should not be concentrated in Gezira (Hag Abdalla) where the spinning is done; it should be done at different locations up and down the country thus distributing the benefits of this industry. Weaving sheds were to be set up in Port Sudan, Nuba mountains (Kadugli), Southern Sudan (Mangala) and in the North (Shandi). The location of these plants presented us with all sorts of difficulties, mainly in transporting material for constructing the factories and the transportation of yarns.

Mismanagement, shortages of electricity and petroleum products and transportation bottlenecks compounded the problem. A 72,000 spindle factory in Port Sudan remained idle for three years due to power shortages. According to the Paris figures the manufacturing production of some industries witnessed a precipitous decline in the period 1977–83. For example, textiles fell from 132.6 million metres in 1977–9 to 63.2 million in 1980–1, shoes from 13.6 million pairs to 8.8 million in the same period.

The saddest story is that of cotton production, which in 1973–4 stood at 1.24 million bales with a yield per acre second only to Egypt's. In 1980–1 the production had plummeted to 544,000 bales and the yield per acre to just a quarter of Egypt's. Even with the recovery in both 1981–2 and 1982–3 on the basis of a World Bank financed plan, cotton production reached only 540,000 million tonnes in the latter year, i.e. still equivalent to only just over three-quarters of the level reached a decade earlier.

As for transportation, in 1970–1 Sudan Railways carried 2.8 million net tonnes/kilometres of freight while in 1980–1 the volume dwindled to only 1.5 million net tonnes/kilometres. The railway system, which needed to be overhauled, is in a state of virtual collapse. On 17 April 1983 the general manager of Sudan Railways told *Al Ayam* that 60 per cent of the engines had been immobilized. He attributed this to shortages of fuel and hard currency to buy spare parts for the rolling stock, engines, cars and tankers. He also spoke of corrosion of the rails, which led to a decrease in the tonne mileage and in the income of the corporation. The Railways made a loss of up to 40 million Sudanese pounds a year.

As an example of the President's utter cynicism, barely a few months later the same Sudan Railways staged a show at Khartoum for the President of the Republic. The reason for this jubilation was that a few immobilized engines had been made operational again. So the fact that 60 per cent of the engines remained out of order and that no programme was devised for track renewal to ensure the efficient running of the few operational engines was temporarily forgotten and Sudan Railays welcomed the Leader. For a few minutes the eyes of the nation (including the watchful eyes of the President) turned and gazed at the few engines that were working. It was not the efficient running of Sudan Railways he was after; it was the show. And there was no lack of apple-polishers to organize one.

According to the figures released by the Bank of Sudan to the Paris meeting Sudan's import bill in 1977–8 stood at more than 1.3 billion US dollars and rose to 1.885 billion US dollars by 1981–2. There was a decrease of 0.142 billion US dollars between 1981–2 and 1982–3, nearly half of which was due to a decrease in imports. During the meeting of the Club of Paris in December 1983 the 'extremely high real interest rates paid by the Central Bank of Sudan on its short term borrowing as, for example, the short term loans to finance petroleum imports' were singled out as one of the external factors behind the 'disappointing growth and balance of payments outcome of 1982–3'. (Remember the palace cabal and the Yemeni connection.) According to the Paris figures Sudan was paying annually nearly 100 million US dollars in excess of the spot-market price for fuel. A large part of that money has gone into commissions and kickbacks. It is particularly for this reason that the Paris meeting urged the Sudan to buy its fuel through a system of competitive bidding involving established suppliers rather than brokers. In fact corrupt dealings in oil not only cost the Sudan the badly needed cash paid in commissions and kickbacks, it also meant losing friends who would have been the first to come to its aid, e.g. Saudi Arabia and Kuwait. We have seen in earlier chapters examples of shady dealings with the Saudis on crude oil and refining. As for Kuwait, Sudan imported from that country (APG), in the course of the early 'eighties, three cargoes of combined refined products of 20,000 tons each. One was a government-to-government deal at 8 million dollars, the other two were through brokers, at 12 million dollars and over 10 million dollars each. The Kuwait government is still awaiting repayment while the other two deals are already settled. So it was not only the badly needed millions of dollars that the Sudan lost, it was the goodwill of friends too.

President Nimeiri often blames Sudan economic ills on the international economic situation, while glossing over self-inflicted lacerations. No one denied the effects of the international situation on the economy, least of all his economic advisers. The Club of Paris also singled out the drought of 1981–2 and the adverse international economic situation. But while not all of Sudan's problems were of its own making, many were. The adverse effect these shortcomings had on the economy were on a par with droughts and recessions.

Another problem of Sudan's own making which the Club dwelt upon was the Military Economic Corporation, which is but another manifestation of corruption. The report expressed alarm at the prospect of the corporation extending 'its operations into transport, industry, banking and housing'. The corporation was meant, according to Nimeiri, to satisfy the needs of the Army. A few years later it had become an economic giant (though with feet of clay) wandering aimlessly into every area of the economy, for it is not only competing with other projects in the public investment programme, it is often deviating from and acting contrary to this programme.

Since Sudan is a one-man show it is important to give the reader a glimpse of this man's economics, of the peculiar science of Nimeiri-metrics. On his return from the US where he underwent a medical examination he made a stop-over in London. Talking to Asharq al Awsat on 20 February 1983 he said, 'Thank God my health is good, my visit to America was only for the purpose of general and routine check-ups; these examinations have put our mind at ease that everything is normal.' (Words mean different things to different people.) The President who felt strong and thought everything was normal went back to the Sudan to fight three battles, with the economy, the Southerners and the judiciary. When asked about the economy and whether the internal problems of the Sudan – inflation, housing, electricity and water shortages etc. – could be solved, the President said: 'These problems, we all know, are all over the world. . . . They are not problems of poverty or weakness . . . but problems of international inflation! . . . For example, our presence in England gave us the opportunity to witness some of its present-day problems. How the exchange value of the sterling falls and how prices rise [an interesting concept]. . . . Under God we confront these problems by development and hard work.' To Nimeiri the economy is a strange *mélange* of dreams, wishful thinking, slogans and concocted figures. So when Nimeiri was asked about Sudan's foreign debts he denied that they amounted to 7 billion dollars or even 4 billion; the figure, he said, was more like 700 million. (Both the Bank of Sudan and Morgan Grenfell must have been engaged in science fiction.) It seems, however, that Nimeiri and his government Ministers get their figures from different sources.

On another occasion when asked about the 7-billion-dollar Foreign debt, Nimeiri told the editor of the Saudi newspaper *Ukaz* (13 May 1984) 'Seven billion dollars is the size of Sudan's debts, as you say . . . but the question is what this figure means; seven billion dollars is insignificant when compared to the losses of one Arab market advertised a few months ago [an uncalled-for remark on the collapse of al Manakh in Kuwait]. Despite all this, Sudan's debts did not go into consumption; its value has multiplied. [The debts] are the thousands of kilometres of road, the largest sugar factory in the world, new cultivable land equivalent to four times the amount that used to be cultivated, five new universities, hundreds of schools.' Sudanese officialdom, however, read the figures differently. One of these officials put it this way: 'Out of the 7.2 billion US dollars which is now being put down as our total burden, no more than 2 billion went into development projects. If most of that debt had gone into development we would have been in a much better economic position.' This is what Yousri Mohammed Gabir, Deputy Under-Secretary for foreign loans and technical assistant in the Ministry of Finance and Economic Planning told *Sudanow* on 6 June 1984. He is supposedly the man who keeps the count and *Sudanow* is the official organ of Nimeiri's Ministry of Information.

In fact the ratio of development expenditure to total government expenditure never exceeded the 25 per cent mark (24.5 per cent in 1982–3) and was as low as 20.4 per cent in 1978–9. Current expenditure continues to be the major source of expenditure (65.6 per cent in 1982–3). Although there has been a gradual decrease in current expenditure (as a proportion of total expenditure) during the 1978–9 to 1981–2 period, a few facts are worth noting. Referring to Table 7.3, also made available to the Paris meeting by the Sudan government, we note that defence and security account for 21 per cent of current expenditure while that on education and health and economic services a mere 13.2 per cent. In fact expenditure on defence and security (Nimeiri's) has increased from 13.4 per cent to 21.0 per cent during that period. The increase attains a more sinister tone when one remembers that Sudan had been relieved of various military commitments. (Sudan, up to 1977, maintained a military force in Sinai.) The solution of the Southern Sudan problem is another case in point; we told the world then that Sudan cannot make war and progress at the same time. More money, real money, therefore, is now being spent on keeping Nimeiri in power or paying for his blunders, e.g. the war in the South.

The direct consequence of the economic collapse was the total collapse of services. Fuel shortages affected industry and motorists alike. Visitors to Sudan in 1983 could witness queues of hundreds of cars and taxis waiting for hours on end. Power cuts have become the order of the day and sometimes last for several days. The telephone system does not work and Sudan Airways had earned itself the appellation Insha'allah Airways' ('God-willing Airways') because of the unpredictability of its flights.

Cars, electric power, telephones and airplanes are 'luxuries' people in the last century managed without. For the Sudanese, however, who were resigned to the fact that the Hero of May was bent on taking the country, in more than one way, back into the last century (and perhaps earlier), this was not the end of the matter. Water (somehow vital for human beings) is not potable. The Minister of Energy made a statement in the summer of 1983 in which he said that in view of recent floods there was 70 per cent sedimentation but none the less the water was still hygienic. This was rejected by the Minister of Health, who said the water was infested with bacteria. The Minister responsible for water supply had a right to explain away the failure of his department; he did not have, however, to insult people's intelligence, for freshmen in the biology department of any college would know that a human being is 84 per cent liquid, so 70 per cent sedimentation would hardly be a flowing stream, possibly a wall.

At the same time the annual increase in the cost of living continued on the ascendant, reaching 37.7 per cent per annum in 1982–3 for the higher salaried employees. The rapid increase in 1982–3 was largely the result of increased cost of food, beverages and tobacco which together account for 60 per cent of the weight of the index. The recorded increases in prices are the result of continuing excess demand pressure, currency depreciation, and increase in

Table 7.3 *Sudan – The Structure of Central Government Expenditure,*
1978/79–1982/83

	1978/79	1979/80	1980/81	1981/82	Estimated Actual 1982/83
	(As percent of total expenditure)				
Current	70.3	69.5	66.8	65.6	65.6
Development	20.4	23.8	23.0	20.6	24.5
Equity	9.3	6.6	3.9	2.1	1.7
Other operations (net)	...	...	6.3	11.7	8.3
Total	100.0	100.0	100.0	100.0	100.0
	(As percent of current expenditure)				
Defence and security	13.4	16.6	15.6	21.0	...
Education and health	7.9	8.0	7.8	8.5	...
Economic services	5.2	5.1	4.3	4.7	...
Transfer to local governments	23.2	32.4	31.2	30.4	26.5
Debt service	5.6	7.4	8.1	8.1	17.6
General administration and unallocable	44.6	30.4	32.9	27.3	...
Total	100.0	100.0	100.0	100.0	100.0
	(As percent of development expenditure)				
Agriculture and irrigation	33.7	21.1	20.6	19.5	...
Industry, mining electricity, and water	20.4	17.1	11.0	29.0	...
Transport and communication	15.9	15.2	13.6	14.5	...
Other	30.0	46.5	54.8	37.1	...
Total	100.0	100.0	100.0	100.0	100.0

Source: Government of Sudan as presented to the Paris Meeting.

controlled prices following the decision to eliminate budgetary subsidies for essential consumption goods.

So the Giant was beaten back to the ground by the very man who laboured hard to give him a lift. Sufficient reasons have been given as to how the hopes of the 'seventies were dashed. It is no wonder, therefore, that insofar as debts are concerned, the arithmetic of the 'seventies has evolved into the calculus of the 'eighties. What is left of development plans today is only the shadow. The economy could still have been saved if Nimeiri had listened to the urgings of his advisers since 1978. All that they were after was for him to tame his wanton urges and control his ruinous whims. When he listened to them, he only did so for as long as it would have taken them to sign a letter of intent with the IMF or unload an oil tanker in Port Sudan to take off the heat from the 'combustible' crowds besieging the Khartoum petrol stations. Concern, of course, was always with the city crowds, not the forlorn plantation schemes or the desolate and immobilized industries. The town folk demonstrate and make riots; trees and machines do not. That, in turn, compounds the tragedy.

The economy could also have been saved had Nimeiri told his cronies if not as early as 1974–5 when the onslaught began, at least by the mid or late 'seventies when the stabilization programme was initiated, to stop milking the ailing cow. Myriads attempted unsuccessfully to ward off the cronies, only to be disowned by Nimeiri. Nimeiri would not listen because, to him, corruption was neither an anomaly nor an aberration; it is policy. He has refined it to an art form. Nimeiri, unsurprisingly, still denounces corruption more and more vehemently without choking at the word, though the audience often pauses for breath. But to him, corruption, like beauty, is in the eye of the beholder. The comparison stops there.

Policies like this eventually land their perpetrators in a cul-de-sac. It is then that the desperado within them emerges, to make it hell for anybody who casts a covetous eye on the Presidency. If that means destroying all institutions, root and branch, so let it be. In the watershed year Nimeiri's motto became: after me the deluge. From now on it is the vindictive bully who is in charge. Since the mid-'seventies Nimeiri has ridden roughshod over all his institutions, political, legislative and executive. He did the same with his economic advisers, both Sudanese and expatriate. However, in his economic exploits and blunders he rode for a fall. By 1984 he and everybody else felt the sting; the sting always lies in the tail.

Chapter Eight

The Year of Divine Visitation: 1984

Men never do evil so completely and cheerfully as when they do it from religious conviction.

Pascal, *Pensées*

Islam: a Tool of Politics

In a sudden but not surprising move in September 1983, Nimeiri issued a new penal code for the country, which included the five canonical Islamic punishments. He announced that he would work towards the full Islamicization of the country, its laws, institutions and political system. Although the abrupt introduction of the new penal code at that juncture served to interrupt the three-month-old judicial strike, the judicial strike itself cannot account for this move of Nimeiri's.

Various explanations have been put forward for Nimeiri's introduction of Shari'a. Some saw it as an attempt by Nimeiri to appease the Saudis, whose friendship and financial backing was so desperately needed. Nothing is further from the truth. Saudi officialdom had learnt to live with all types of government in the Sudan, including Nimeiri's socialist state. They never proselytized in the Sudan, nor had they been known to exert pressure on other states to adopt their system. They also have enough extremism on their eastern flank to contend with. Another theory, a psychological one this time, sees Islamicization emanating from internal conflicts in Nimeiri's psyche; his physical and mental debility, his feeling of guilt for the many public and personal sins he has committed and his desire to atone and rescue his soul from ruin. Religion is a source of comfort and solace to people tormented from within.

Any theory that ignores the political motives behind Nimeiri's introduction of Shari'a law misses the point. Nimeiri was seeking neither religious certainty (the way he used religion to intimidate and humiliate opponents showed it) nor atonement. If he had, he would have spent the rest of his life tortured by his conscience rather than continuing the torture of others. A cursory examination of Nimeiri's statements and actions before the introduction of Shari'a reveals his awareness and appreciation of the power of religion as a political tool. During the meeting of the National Congress of the SSU in 1980 he said in a press conference, obliquely addressing the Muslim Brothers, who were brandishing the weapon of Islamicization, 'We do not want any Khomeinism in the Sudan.' Later he went on to side with Iraq against Iran in the Gulf War (after several tirades against the Ba'ath Party) confirming his anti-Khomeini stance. In effect he was not driven into the Gulf War by his sympathy for Iraq; he was exaggerating to make a point to Sudanese pro-Khomeinis. On the other hand, when the leader of the Muslim Brotherhood, Attorney-General Hassan al Turabi, launched a process of legal Islamicization, Nimeiri came out strongly against excesses, cautioning that Islamic laws that were contrary to the constitution were not acceptable for Sudan, as the country was not only for Muslims. Nimeiri's aversion to excesses in religion was also seen in his violent reaction against the decision by the Omdurman local council declaring the city dry. He quashed the decision and accused the council of religious overbearing. He told them that customs and *mores* could not be changed overnight through legislation. Nimeiri is, evidently, no religious fanatic and his introduction of Shari'a law is not an act of religious fanaticism. A religious fanatic is a person blinded by his faith; he does not weigh the consequences of his actions. The religious outlook is essentially unconsequentialist.

Nimeiri proved to be very Machiavellian in his approach to Islam and the application of Shari'a laws Consequently Nimeiri's Islamicism should hardly be an insoluble mystery. The political considerations which were at the back of Nimeiri's mind when he introduced Shari'a law can be divided into two categories: short- and long-term. The short-term considerations had to do with the judges' strike which lasted from June to September 1983 and the doctors' strike early in 1984. There was also Sadiq el Mahdi's publication in Saudi Arabia of a book on Islam. The judges' strike influenced the timing of his imposition of Shari'a law and the doctors' strike led to the declaration of a state of emergency.

By allowing el Mahdi to publish his work on Saudi soil the Saudis, Nimeiri thought, were endorsing his programme and recognizing his future role in Sudanese politics. If that is what the Saudis wanted, he (Nimeiri) should be the one to deliver the goods. On the other hand, Nimeiri's ghost-written book *The Islamic Way: Why?* should be the last word on the faith, at least within the bounds of Sudan. Not that those who had the stamina to wade through it were more informed at the end about Islam.

Nimeiri knows that Islam is a potent tool. He has seen his erst-while adversaries still profiting from it in spite of a fifteen-year labour by the May revolution to strip them of authority and weaken their power base. People, particularly in rural Sudan, are still clustering around el Mirghani and el Mahdi (leaders of the Khatmiya and Ansar sects respectively). He was more irritated with the latter who was ready to use openly whatever was left of his power base to challenge Nimeiri politically under the guise of religion. So if the only power el Mahdi had was the Imamate, then Nimeiri would metamorphose into an Imam, the one and only Imam of the Sudan. Those who know the way Nimeiri's mind works could certainly have seen more than meets the eye in his statement to Sadiq el Mahdi in Liverpool: 'If you are the Imam of the Ansar, I am the leader of all the Sudan.'

Faced with this challenge Nimeiri wanted to take the wind out of Sadiq's sails. A few months before the declaration of his Islamic code another incident took place that made Nimeiri furious with Sadiq, the Id prayer celebrating the end of Ramadan at Aba Island, the stronghold of the Ansar. What enraged him even more was that all his wiles to destroy Sadiq's grip on his followers by supporting and promoting Sadiq's uncle, Ahmed el Mahdi, as an alternative leader did not meet with success. Sadiq's Id prayer was more of a political demonstration, attended by an estimated crowd of several hundred thousands. In his sermon the Ansar leader dealt with several political issues and was critical of many aspects of Nimeiri's governance. The prayers were videotaped for Nimeiri to see. It was considerations such as these that loomed before Nimeiri's eyes when he precipitated his decisions.

It is no wonder, therefore, that Sadiq was quick to rise to his feet when Nimeiri adopted his Islamicization measures. In a sermon

during the celebration of the Adha Id he denounced Nimeiri's Islamicism. He told the worshippers that justice is a pillar of the
Islamic faith, citing the saying of the Muslim scholar Ibn Taymiy-
yah: 'God will give victory to a just nation even if it is non-Muslim.'
He also dwelt on the principle of consultation (*shura*) citing the
second Caliph who said: 'If any of you detects a deviation, let him
correct it,' whereupon the people retorted, 'If we detect a deviation
in your action, we shall rectify it with our swords.' Omar thanked
God. El Mahdi maintained that political exploitation of the Shari'a
was doing a disservice to the cause of Islam. He also accused
Nimeiri of opportunism and of applying Islamic punishments to
protect his regime. He added that Islamic punishments should be
applied only within an Islamic social order which fights crime by
spiritual, moral, social and economic means. The application of
Islamic punishments, he said, should have been preceded by an
Islamic education and the prevalence of justice.

In addition to the short-term considerations that loomed before
Nimeiri's eyes and precipitated his decisions there were some long-
term considerations:

1. Taking the wind out of the sails of all the Sudanese Islamic
   movements (the Muslim Brothers, Mirghani and Sadiq el
   Mahdi). He knew that Islam was gaining momentum inside
   and outside the Sudan.
2. Skirting the haunting internal problems and turning people's
   attention from government mismanagement, reflected in the
   total collapse of services, unemployment, soaring inflation
   etc. The Sudanese were being asked to exercise self-discipline
   and accept their lot in this world; they were to think of the life
   to come and store up treasures in heaven. The role of the
   leader is no longer to rule and deliver the promised goods, but
   to impregnate people with faith through the drone of oratory,
   this time from pulpits.
3. Turning people's attention away from government
   corruption, mainly palace corruption. People should no
   longer talk about Nimeiri's cronies but about friends,
   relatives and neighbours of theirs who have been accused of
   and tried for alcoholism, adultery and other heinous acts.
   These trials are broadcast daily as major news items to give a
   new staple for gossip, keeping busy many of the Khartoum
   tattlers with their known gluttonous appetite for idle talk.

Islamicization, therefore, would not only take the wind out of the opposition sails but also divert the people. Allegations and accusations of corruption inside the palace would be countered by accusations of drunkenness, womanizing etc. against the plaintiffs. In this purification campaign Nimeiri was unabashedly selective, amputating the hands of petty thieves while Presidential shop-lifters were at large, and slandering the smaller fry for attempted adultery (a crime of Nimeiri's invention and unknown to Islam) while the senior womanizing rascals stood piously behind the Imam. By making the Shari'a as it was interpreted by Nimeiri and his vicars the law of the land, most of the Sudanese became godless criminals. The whole nation was portrayed as fellow-travellers in sin. Nimeiri, in fact, was seeking to anaesthetize the people's con-science: in the very act of entrenching religion by applying religious codes he was destroying religious moral imperatives.

It was not coincidental that Nimeiri launched his new era of Isla-micization by pouring millions of gallons of alcohol into the Nile for, to his mind, drinking alcohol is the greatest vice and refraining from it is the essence of Islam. It is easy to see why this should be so if one remembers that Nimeiri wanted a weapon with which to in-timidate people and keep them at bay. Drinking is a relatively light offence punishable by flogging. Adultery, on the other hand, is punishable (if proven) by death; because of the seriousness of this crime the Shari'a dictates that four valid witnesses be produced for indictment, all four attesting to having seen at the same time the very act of penetration. That was why Nimeiri's courts invented the charge called attempted adultery. In the case of drinking alcohol, though Shari'a also imposes certain rules of evidence, the offence is easier to detect and establish. Nimeiri could pick and choose from among his opponents and the hapless creatures would be publicly flogged and humiliated. Humiliation is an end in itself. In one such incident, when a regional Minister (Darfur) told Nimeiri some-thing not to his liking, the Minister was accused of being drunk. The allegation was denied by the accused and the doctor that examined him confirmed that the Minister was sober. Nimeiri, in a peevish retort, insisted that his own private doctor should ascertain the alcohol level in the Minister's blood and his verdict was, needless to say, that he was drunk.

Another important factor in Nimeiri's Islamicization is that the regime needed a new window-dresser, a new ideology and a set of slogans. Nimeiri's regime had, in fact, dropped all pretence of being socialist except at very selected moments. Nimeiri could pose as the Hero of May and capitalize on the Sudanese people's antipathy to the excesses of the early years of the revolution, as well as the achievements of the years of promise, until the memories of that era faded away and only the stark realities of the present regime remained. In fact, for those old enough to compare the two eras of the May regime, the revolution of May, to their minds, is more of a revolution of dismay. Nimeiri was well aware of this and had long ago substituted the revolutionary greeting with which he used to start his speeches by misquoted Qur'anic verses. The peacockish Field-Marshal's uniform he used to don was often discarded in favour of the flowing *gallabiyah* (national dress) and the turban, the soldier metamorphosed into an Imam. The military uniform was not abandoned, for it was to resurface whenever people had to be reminded of the power buttressing the kingdom of Allah, i.e. the Army, for example, when declaring the state of emergency.

Witchcraft and Death Obsessions

To emphasize the political and opportunistic overtones of Nimeiri's move is not to deny the personal and psychological elements. Throughout this book we have endeavoured to bring out these two dimensions of Nimeiri's personality, i.e. the calculating/deliberating one (evident in his using Islam to attack Imam al Hadi and the Communists) and the superstitious one (evident, for instance, in his fear of the power of certain sages and his preoccupation with witchcraft and the casting of spells on his enemies). On the psychological level, Nimeiri's reasons for introducing his so-called Islamic measures are complex. Nimeiri's spirituality, as we have seen, is a hotchpotch of Islam, superstition and witchcraft. An appreciation of the multi-dimensional nature of his character is essential for understanding whatever genuine commitment he might have had to Islam. Nimeiri made believe that he was chosen to lead his people, for the failure of the two July and September coups were acts of divine deliverance. He also believes that he is divinely guided (an essential attribute of the Mahdi or the Imam), for his arriving one hour early in July 1976 was such an act of divine guidance. One is not surprised to note that, of late, all Nimeiri's public utterances on Islam oscillate between the irrational and the superstitious, albeit always interspersed with verses from the Qur'an, misread, misunderstood and misconstrued.

Nimeiri's ignorance of Islam is matched only by his ignorance of economic management, indeed management of any kind (shown in his derision of reports of the governor of the Central Bank, his statements to the press on Sudan's debts etc.). Completely blinded by his overblown ego, he has failed to detect that, in religion, he was treading on dangerous ground. This is much more so when it comes to the interpretation of Qur'anic verses and tenets of Shari'a. These are sciences that are mastered after long initiation, learning and practice. On the other hand, because of this intellectual limitation, Nimeiri's vision of Islam was shaped more by superstitious notions alien to true religion and often emanating from animistic vestiges. Nimeiri could not see these intellectual refinements. The tragedy was compounded when he surrounded himself with religious obscurantists (who do not pose a challenge to his authority). An example of this form of misguided religiosity is to be gleaned from Nimeiri's belief in the magical power of some sages who are endowed with supernatural powers to affect the lives of others. This belief of his is rather akin to that of the Azande tribes of Southern Sudan. These latter believe that every mishap is due to the active malevolence of a certain witch. They seek, therefore, to protect themselves against witches by detecting and eliminating them. Several other tribes in both North and South believe in such witchcraft. We have seen in earlier chapters how Dr Idris and others were to exploit this aspect of Nimeiri's spirituality by recruiting witches and witch-doctors alike. Nimeiri's belief in magical powers is a legacy of the pre-Islamic era which is totally unacceptable to orthodox Muslims.

The second psychological reason is Nimeiri's insecurity and his fear of death, generated, or rather enhanced, by his illness. Nimeiri's obsessive fear of death has always haunted him. A year before his visit to the USA he asked the National Security officers to raid Sudan Airways and arrest a number of officials, including air hostesses. The charge was a plot to poison the President during one of his travels. Among those suspended was the managing director of Sudan Airways, a highly competent and respected person. Security tried to persuade the President that the whole story was improbable (possibly an invention of the palace cabal to keep the master on his toes). A few weeks later, after Security revealed that the whole thing was imaginary, Nimeiri decided, in an act of vindictiveness, to dissolve Sudan Airways as a corporation and offer it for sale. The decision was a spiteful response, not a well considered policy decision. For this reason many months elapsed with no action taken as to the future of the airline.

None the less, Nimeiri's illness intensified his fear of death. The history of the illness, we recall, goes back to the late 'seventies, when symptoms of drowsiness and physical infirmity first appeared. In 1979 he undertook a trip to the USA, where his illness was diagnosed as vascular. He underwent an operation the following year. A clot of blood was removed from an artery in his neck which had affected the flow of blood into his brain. Ever since then death loomed in the distance and at times it stared him in the face. Before he boarded his plane to the USA in 1983 (where he was to undergo another operation) he spent a few hours with the Army commanders discussing funeral arrangements. He had been told by his American doctors that it might be necessary to perform a second operation which he might not survive. Instead of calling the constitutional officials to talk about his succession he called the top three Army officers, not to discuss security problems and how an orderly transition of power could be effected, but how the nation should mourn and honour its greatest son. He had in fact built a new mosque (al-Nilein) at a cost of several million Sudanese pounds; it was there, he told the commanders, that he should be buried. The mosque would become his mausoleum. He who seeks splendour even after his death cannot really be the ascetic religious leader he claims to be. All the discredited Sudanese leaders – el Azhari, Abdalla Khalil, Abboud – lived an austere life and died a simple death, and are eternally resting in the deserts of Sudan.

Nimeiri: God's Messenger

Nimeiri's introduction of Islamic laws in September 1983 was not, therefore, the result of a sudden conversion or change of heart. His proclivity to use religion for political ends pre-dates September 1983 and so does his hotch-potch of spirituality. He launched this new era of religious puritanism with ceremony. Millions of litres of alcohol were poured into the Nile as the country was declared dry. (Why he did not sell it back to the infidels, I do not know.) Readers will remember that the May revolution inaugurated its regime of 'revolutionary purity' with the trial and imprisonment of ministers of the *ancien régime*. Nimeiri's religious revolution was inaugurated with an opposite measure; thousands of prisoners (some hardened criminals) were released. On the 'historic day' of 30 September Nimeiri ordered the release of thirteen thousand prisoners. Thousands of them assembled in the court of the Kober Prison to listen to the Leader cum Imam tell them that he had forgiven them as Joseph forgave his brothers and as the Prophet Mohammed forgave the people of Mecca who persecuted him.

'Today,' he said, 'history witnesses the forgiving nature of Islam and the greatness of its Shari'a and witnesses Khartoum pouring alcohol in the streets, an action in Islamic history unprecedented since the time when the compatriots of the Prophet poured it in the streets of Medina. You entered prison when alcohol drinking was permitted and came out with drinking forbidden and with flogging as the punishment for drinking.' Nimeiri's decision to release prisoners was taken without consulting his police and prison authorities. Their hair must have curled to see so many hardened prisoners set at large. The most astounding part of his statement, however, was the comparison of his Islamicization declaration with the Prophet Mohammed's victorious entry into Mecca and his magnanimous act of forgiving the infidels. It never dawned on God's new messenger that Sudan's infidels had been led for over a decade by the very man who was now conquering them and converting them to the faith.

Nimeiri now increasingly equated himself with the Prophet, referring often to his mission. His references to this mission give one reason to believe that, deep in his psyche, he is starting to make believe that he is God's messenger to save the Sudan. His speeches are now invariably started by verses from the Qur'an. In one such speech he quoted two verses, one referring to male believers giving the Prophet the *bay'aa* 'under the tree' and the other instructing the Prophet to accept the *bay'aa* of certain female believers. The fact that the speech was made to a congregation of men and women who had given Nimeiri the *bay'aa* suggests that for him the two acts (giving the *bay'aa* to the Prophet and giving it to Nimeiri) were comparable. He went on in that speech to describe his mission as 'establishing the religion (Islam) amongst your ranks' which was the mission of the Prophet Mohammed. He asked God to help him in executing what he was asked to do which shows that he believes that his so-called mission was placed upon his shoulders by God (quotes from *Al Sahafa*, 25 May 1984).

In his speech declaring the state of emergency Nimeiri made an even more striking remark. Speaking about the enemies of his Islamicization and how they spread rumours claiming that Nimeiri is ill (that is, Nimeiri is dying) he quoted the Qur'anic verse 'Mohammed is but a Messenger; of a surety, all Messengers before him have passed away. If then he die or be slain, will you turn back on your heels? He who turns back on his heels shall not harm Allah a whit. Allah will certainly reward the grateful' (*Qur'an*: 3:145).

Nimeiri went on to say, unaware of the uncanny and uncanonical comparison, 'Who worries still about Mohammed's death, who knows how and when one will die? Death will find us, God willing, assured and believing in him.' So not only were the people of the Sudan equated with the infidels of Mecca; their new-born Imam, by his own insinuations, is now to be equated with the Prophet.

Muslim Brothers versus Old Guards

The Muslim Brothers, for their part, decided to ride the wave and sing Nimeiri's gospel. He welcomed their support, which gave a measure of legitimacy to his Islamicism; theirs was a marriage of convenience. They, in turn, looked to Nimeiri to do the dirty work for them (such as the subjugation of the infidel South and holding the Communists at bay). Their aim is to inherit the earth after him or, probably, in spite of him, by staging a palace coup, putting an end to Nimeiri's excesses in the application of Shari'a and thus emerging as the saviours of Sudan and Islam. For that they were prepared to give him their insincere support. A battle in fact ensued between the Muslim Brothers and the old guard of the revolution, each group trying to sway Nimeiri their way. The old guard stood for Sudanese nationhood and identity, for the unity of the Sudan and for the supremacy of the SSU and the constitution. The Brothers wanted Islam to replace Sudanese nationhood, even at the cost of alienating the Southerners by insisting on the application of the Islamic legal system to Muslims and non-Muslims alike. They also wanted to do away with the socialist political

The Year of Divine Visitation

system, while continuing to pay lip-service to the one-party system.

On the eve of Independence Day Nimeiri delivered a speech in which he voiced the thinking of the old guard (particularly of Badr el Din Suleiman, who wrote the historic speech). The main theme was the assertion of Sudanese nationhood. He started his speech by paying tribute to the national heroes, including Southerners, members of the *ancien régime* (such as el Azhari and Mahgoub) and some of his traditionalist opponents, i.e. leaders of religious sects. He greeted and acknowledged all those 'who have contributed and donated, those who have striven and given, those who have proved that allegiance is to the Sudan, firstly, secondly, thirdly and last. Loyalty and belonging to the Sudan is above all other loyalty and belonging.' He also greeted the May revolution which has 'established institutions and given primacy to its constitution and whose strong, firm and eternal nature [the institutions and constitution] will outlast and survive all individuals, and whose political organ, the great SSU, stands above legislative and executive organs, abides by the constitution and derives its authority from it.' He said that the proof of Sudan being governed by institutions was illustrated by the fact that its President had been absent from the country for six weeks.

'The Islamic way in the Sudan,' Nimeiri reassured the non-Muslims, 'is not the door to civil strife and shall not be, for Islam is the religion of coexistence between the different beliefs and is the religion of friendship between the believers [Muslims, Jews and Christians]. The Islamic way in the Sudan has never been and shall never be but a means of uniting, bringing together and spreading love between all its sons, between those who believe in it [Islam] and those who subscribe to other heavenly religions [Christians and Jews] and noble beliefs [animists].'

Nimeiri asserted that everybody is united in a united fatherland where rights and duties are equal. 'The Islamic way in Sudan is the brotherhood of people and unity in the fatherland and there is no compulsion in religion and no compulsion through religion, there is no divisiveness in religion and by religion.' The Islamic way in the Sudan, he reiterated, 'is not the enemy of Sudanese nationhood and shall never be. It is not the enemy of national unity and shall never be. It is not the domination of the minority by the majority and shall never be. It is not irreconcilable with or in opposition to the constitution, the political organ of the national and regional institutions, and shall never be.'

The Islamic way in the Sudan, furthermore, will not be at the expense of the May revolution and nor shall it be at the expense of the one-party system, according to Nimeiri. 'The Islamic way in the Sudan does not constitute a rebellion against the May revolution nor its recognition of the special characteristics of the different regions.' This Islam, he continued, 'is not rigid but moves with time and circumstances for *ijtihad* (the evolution of juris-prudence through legal reasoning) is allowed' (*Al Sahafa*, 1 November 1983).

Those whose hopes were raised by this speech were to be bitterly disappointed. In the following months Nimeiri went on to do the exact opposite of what he had promised. He proceeded with a far-reaching programme of Islamicization to be applied to Muslims and non-Muslims alike. On the other hand, his proposed amend-ments to the constitution, as we shall see later, were precisely aimed at the abolition of the constitution and institutions he promised to safeguard. The Southerners, who were assured of con-tinued citizenship on an equal basis with the Northerners were to have their autonomous status withdrawn and were to be subjected to Islamic laws. His first flagrant action which belied his Indepen-dence Day promises was his declaration of a state of emergency and the imposition of martial law late in April, after months of civil disturbances, strikes, riots and demonstrations.

The Doctors and the Lowest Depths of Hell

The first to go on strike were university professors, followed by judges and doctors. The latter threatened that if they did not receive a pay rise they would resign. Nimeiri, who was at the time on a visit to Italy, instructed his Finance Minister to reject their demand (the Minister was himself against it because he feared it would unleash a chain reaction). Both the First Vice-President, General Tayeb, and the Minister of Health, Dr Ali Fadl, supported the doctors' demands, for both security and professional consider-ations, but, unlike the Minister of Finance, neither of them viewed the problem in its global context, i.e. the effect of meeting the doctors' demands on other wage-earners.

The doctors resigned *en masse* and Nimeiri issued an ultimatum. If they failed to return to work in seventy-two hours he threatened to have them prosecuted for high treason. Instructions went out to the Security agency and the governments of the regions to arrest doctors who failed to respond to the ultimatum. He warned the people, meaning the doctors, that if they persisted in their defiance he would take measures which would harm the country's interests. People were left guessing. Nimeiri's decision was taken in spite of advice from politicians and security officers not to escalate the crisis.

The doctors rejected the ultimatum and, on Nimeiri's orders, the doctors' union was dissolved, seventeen so-called ring-leaders, including the doctors' executive, were arrested and several meetings were held by the SSU which Nimeiri addressed, confirming his unbending position. He accused all Sudanese doctors of being Libya's puppets. With the passing of the time limit Nimeiri found himself in a tight spot, for the engineers and the accountants threatened to join the doctors.

Nimeiri, now fearful that this might turn out to be a repeat of the events of October 1964 which brought an end to the Abboud dictatorship, decided yet again to eat his words and lie his way out. He ordered the release of the arrested doctors and received their committee in the palace, not to admonish them this time but to woo them. He told the astounded doctors, who all read and heard his ultimatum, that he had never issued an ultimatum or an order for their arrest; he had just found out about their strike from Tripoli Radio. He also told them that they were free to resume their trade union activities and that all their demands would be met. 'Liars and hypocrites' the Qur'an says 'will be in the lowest depths of the fire [hell]: no helper will be found for them' (Sura 4:154).

Nimeiri, the Islamic leader, was stooping to conquer even at the cost of going to the lowest depths of hell, for a few days later he did what he had threatened to do, taking measures which would harm the nation's interest. He declared a state of emergency and imposed martial law. Not even after the July coups of 1971 and 1976 did the regime feel it necessary to take such a measure. This alone reflects the fragility of Nimeiri's regime of 1984.

Protecting the Faith by Martial Law

In his statement declaring martial law on 30 April, Nimeiri

announced that 'in order to protect the faith and the fatherland from schemes of schemers and the mischief of Satan, and in order to protect the gains of the believing people and fulfil my national duties and constitutional responsibilities, I have issued Presidential Decree number 258 (1984) announcing the imposition of martial law throughout the country; this, in pursuance of the aims of the revolution.' The aims of the revolution are seemingly endless, for they are now to protect the fatherland from the mischief of Satan. 'At the time when work has become a religious duty,' Nimeiri continued, 'Satan and his aides were active, leading to a series of strikes which went against the simplest of religious tenets.' The strikes were furthermore fomented by foreign agents who were frightened by the saying: 'There is no god but Allah.' The strikers were also apostates who turned their backs on their religion.

Nimeiri started his apocalyptic speech with a Qur'anic warning: 'O Ye who believe, whoso from among you turns back from his religion let him remember that in his stead Allah will soon bring a people whom he will love and who love him ... They will strive hard in the course of Allah and will not take to heart the reproaches of fault-finders.' The strikers were likened to those who stayed behind and refused to fight with the Prophet Mohammed, 'averse to striving in the cause of Allah'. Nimeiri repeated the Qur'anic warning, 'Remind them: the fire of hell is far fiercer in heat: did they but understand. So let them rejoice less at the supposed success of their stratagem and weep more at the contemplation of the punishment of their duplicity awaiting them.'

Nimeiri's cataclysmic warnings were all politically inspired. The doctors' strike, like that of the judges before it, was an act of manly defiance; if allowed to go unchecked it might turn into insurrection. Nimeiri, despite the constant references to the Qur'an in his speech, was indeed taking a leaf from Hitler's *Mein Kampf*: the bigger the lie the more people will believe it. His aim was simply to intimidate the disputatious professionals and drown trade-union controversies in a mire of mystification. Typically, the President never paused to ponder the implications of his martial law decisions. For example, the implications for the economy are daunting; the daily allowances for maintaining the forces in a state of full alert alone cost the exchequer nearly half a million Sudanese pounds daily.

Nimeiri went on, in his speech of 30 April, to deal with the South. As to the Southerners, those who were fighting with John

Garang, they were also enemies of God and development (development was now given a metaphysical dimension). They waged their war 'under a "red banner" a Communist-Leninist-Marxist banner' against religion 'be it Christian or Muslim, so as to put an end to the worship of God in this country, from which Satan had been expelled.'

The Muslim Brothers gave Nimeiri all their support. Hassan al Turabi defended the emergency laws, claiming that the emergency courts which were instituted were the nearest thing to Islamic courts!! The state of emergency, he said, is a well known concept. According to his *ijtihad* it was akin to the case of ablutions. Muslims are normally required to wash and clean themselves with water before praying. If water is not available or obtainable they can use sand or stone to cleanse themselves. This is the sort of *ijtihad* (legal reasoning) that Nimeiri had in mind and did not hesitate to apply himself, to the consternation of many learned Muslims.

One example of this peculiar brand of *ijtihad* was offered by the President in his speech celebrating the fifteenth anniversary of the May revolution. Nimeiri rightly said that Islam gives people the benefit of the doubt and ensures the inviolability of residence and person. Islam he said, 'condemns people with proof and is a religion of discretion in which the shortcomings of people are not publicized, a religion in which the way to mercy and forgiveness is unobstructed and in which privacy is inviolable because of the dictum "enter houses only through the doors and enter only after obtaining permission of the owners".' This, Nimeiri said, is the Islamic way, and all this is the righteous Islam. Suddenly Nimeiri assumed his bullying character and stepped into an area which is more familiar to him: scurrilous and profane threats. 'Islam has its state of emergency,' he said, 'and when society is seen to have become corrupted and to have deviated strongly . . . we declare a state of emergency . . . we enter houses . . . we search . . . we search people everywhere . . . he who drinks behind doors . . . he who commits adultery . . . the houses of prostitution . . . every house we shall enter and search. . . . Islam has ordered us to take such measures as well, for despite it being the religion I have mentioned . . . we are now in the phase of correcting and amending . . . we shall arrest drinking drivers . . . [without Shari'a he could have done that under the Sudan penal code] and the bribing driver . . . Although Islam is the religion of forgiveness, the religion of brotherliness and the religion of honour and integrity,' he was going to 'continue to flog people publicly and to publish names in papers ... because the Muslim hates to hear his name.... We shall continue to publish ... to flog ... continue to amputate hands ... until we establish a righteous Islamic community' (*Al Sahafa*, 25 May 1984). The message was, therefore, clear. People have to be overawed and subdued; if imprisonment was not enough of a deterent then slandering and muck-raking would do the trick, i.e. silence the vociferous townees.

An Imam with a Foul Mouth

For Nimeiri to justify his profane aims in the name of religion he had to resort to a lot of logic-chopping. Listening to some of Nimeiri's speeches one gets the impression that he was talking about Sodom and Gomorrah rather than present-day Sudan. In one speech in the town of Wad Medani he said he was aware of what was taking place under bridges; whatever had befallen Wad Medani people was a just punishment for promiscuous people. The town where Nimeiri was born and raised had become a sink of iniquity. In another speech in Kassala (eastern Sudan) Nimeiri told his audience that they had only themselves to blame for what had befallen their town (a flood); they had sinned against Allah and his Shari'a. The problem was not one of managerial failure, i.e. the lack of precautions by preparing dykes and embankments in time, but divine punishment. Kassala had sinned its soul to perdition.

Nimeiri has overreached himself in his attempts to slander people, sometimes out of vindictiveness and sometimes to denigrate the whole nation, only to prove that it is not the fawning parasites around him who alone are corrupt. But all the time he absolves himself from responsibility for the lamentable state of the nation, for which the regime alone is to blame. Surprisingly Nimeiri is still proud to rule for life over all these people condemned for every sin that makes the gorge rise. His speeches become more and more *risqué*, often daringly close to heresy, when he compares himself to the Prophet Mohammed. His information officers were now encumbered with an added burden, paraphrasing the President's speeches for the sake of decency. To the gossip-mongers the speeches became an evening recreation, to the majority of Sudanese they were the sort of utterances they would make sure their children did not listen to. That indeed speaks volumes of the man who was set up to be the symbol of national conscience and value.

In the end the President not only succeeded in uniting the Sudanese people against him in indignation; sadly, he also made them question the role of Islam in politics. The Islam which the people of Sudan knew and lived under was a religion of tolerance, forgiveness and respect for life and property. The Imams people knew and prayed behind were not foul-mouthed, nor could they have soiled their lips with the utterances of Kassala and Wad Medani. For Islam the 1984 measures were counter-productive. They did not galvanize the pious Muslims behind Nimeiri; on the contrary, Sudanese Muslims believe that these decisions defiled Islam.

Speedy Justice: a Sham

Nimeiri was very proud of his misguided application of Islam and the achievements of his new emergency courts. By the middle of June 1984, 871 people had been tried under martial law. This was a source of pride to the President Imam whose *jihad* consisted of re-crimination against the Sudanese people. When asked by the London Arabic weekly *Al Tadamon* whether he had any qualms with respect to the justice of these courts Nimeiri replied, 'I have no qualms with respect to their justice, and I believe that this is the best type of justice in Sudan's history, because of the speed with which matters are settled and the speed with which sentences are executed' (*Al Tadamon*, 26 May 1984). Quick indeed, for people were found guilty, given arbitrary sentences and denied the right to appeal. More than half of his victims were indicted on alcohol-related offences. Out of the 871 who appeared before the courts only 134 were vindicated; 341 were found guilty of dealing in alcohol, 74 of drunkenness and 19 of drunkenness and disturbing the peace. This explains the initial emphasis on alcohol and the ceremony with which he declared Sudan a dry country.

Nimeiri, not content with the daily broadcast of the sentences of his emergency courts in radio and TV prime time, also urged the press to announce to the world the statistics of crime and punishment. A prominent place is reserved in the daily press for these trials. For example, the headlines of the Khartoum daily *Al Sahafa* (9 June 1984) were not about Nimeiri's achievements in improving the economy or solving the problem of food shortages. There were other important preoccupations. The headlines read 'Emergency courts in one month only, 333 years of imprisonment, fines totalling £S557,141, and 19351 lashes'. The lofty dreamer has nothing to be proud of other than flogging and hand amputations. Nimeiri also issued orders to his Ministers to attend the amputations of hands and legs. The leader of the Muslim Brothers, Dr Turabi, fainted while watching one of these gruesome scenes. His three-year stint in Paris had not been wasted, after all (Turabi got his PhD from the University of Paris). According to well-informed sources the number of persons subjected to this harsh punishment by Nimeiri's courts in only three months were more than all those who suffered the same fate in the whole reign of King Abdel Aziz al Saud, the founder of Saudi Arabia.

Assault on the Constitution

In June Nimeiri decided to demolish the last pillar of the early period of the May regime, the constitution, which had in fact become a dead letter. This attack took the form of proposals by the President to amend the constitution to make it 'more Islamic'. In Nimeiri's new version of the constitution Islam was made to appear not the religion about *adl* (justice) and *shura* (consultation) but about the imamate (the office which combines both temporal and spiritual powers). Nimeiri did not entrust the task of his so-called Islamicization to the Muslim Brothers but to two upstarts whom he could keep under control, unlike the Brothers who had their own powerful constituency. To entrust the process of the new legislation to the Muslim Brothers or to the Ulema (religious scholars) would have been to create a power centre outside his sphere of influence. It was not doctrinal veracity and legal excellence he was after; it was the justification of his earthly designs using the word of Allah. To him, Islam is a tool of worldly power and authority. The Muslim state is to be buttressed by the Army and security agencies and guarded in the heavens by the Awacs. Nimeiri heretically

271

thought that by engaging the name of the Lord in his constitutional endeavour he could give sanctity to his own words. Nimeiri and his two fledgling lawyers sought to amend no fewer than 123 out of the 225 articles of the constitution. We shall attempt to show how the amendments constitute a repeal of the constitution, in letter and spirit, underlining the constitutional loopholes and inconsistencies of this supposedly more Islamic constitution.

The first few articles of the constitution deal with the identity of the Sudan and the Sudanese people and define the roles of religion. The amended article 1 reads 'The Democratic Republic of the Sudan is a unitary, and sovereign Islamic Republic and is part of the Arab, African and Islamic entities.' The amended article 1 also makes Islamic law (Shari'a) the only source of legislation while Sudan's current constitution provides in article 9 that Shari'a and custom are both major sources of legislation. On the other hand article 16 of the present constitution provides that the state 'shall endeavour to express the values of Islam, Christianity and show respect for the "noble aspects of spiritual beliefs"'; the latter refers to the large non-Muslim and non-Christian population of Sudan. The proposed amendment of this article not only requires the state to express Islamic values in 'legislation, institutions and in its activities' but deletes the reference to the 'noble aspects of spiritual beliefs'. It also deletes sub-article 16 (d) which requires the State to 'treat followers of religions and noble spiritual beliefs without discrimination as to the rights and freedoms guaranteed to them by this constitution.' None the less article 14, which states that Sudanese society is established . . . on the principles of freedom, equality and justice, is retained.

The Southerners, who had achieved autonomy after seventeen years of struggle, were robbed of that prize. Article 8 emphasizes the special nature of the law relating to Southern autonomy and declares that 'within the unitary Sudan, there shall be an organic law, . . . which shall not be amended except in accordance with the provisions thereof.' Reference to the Southern Provinces Regional Self Government Act 1972 was to be dropped in the amendments and, consequently, the reference to its inviolability. In addition the constitutional chapter on decentralization (see chapter 7) introduces three new regions in Southern Sudan, destroying its unitary character. The regions, according to article 181 (a) (amended) are: Equatoria, Upper Nile and Bahr el Ghazal. It is recalled here that President Nimeiri has claimed that his decision to divide the South was a temporary measure to be reviewed within eighteen months. The final decision, he said, rests with the people in accordance with the constitution. Nimeiri is now reneging on his own commitments, for the division is to be made permanent.

We now come to the interesting part defining the role, powers and duties of the President. The President of the Republic who was, according to article 80, 'the head of state and chosen by a plebiscite' was to become 'the leader of the faithful (*Qa'id al Mu'minin*) and the shepherd of the Sudanese nation' as well as the head of state. He is to act according to a legally constituted *bay'aa* (oath of allegiance and contract). The amendment to article 84 makes the President into a President for life. The President should not take an oath to serve and 'to protect the Presidential socialist revolutionary system which was brought about by the May revolution' as stipulated in the present article 85; his oath is now 'an oath of loyalty to God'. The President is not to have deputies, for Nimeiri hates that idea. They are to be called assistants and are required to swear an oath of obedience to the President.

The proposed amendments do not abolish the now defunct institution called the People's Assembly; Nimeiri's lawyers were devious people and knew that no Assembly would ratify such amendments. Much as they loved their leader and Imam, the Assembly was unlikely to sacrifice itself on his altar. The Assembly was instead subsumed into a greater entity, the supposedly Islamic Majlis al Shurah (consultative council). All of the powers, duties and prerogatives of the Assembly were to be transferred to this new Majlis. Ministers and Prime Ministers were accordingly not responsible to the Assembly as stipulated in article 91 but to the Majlis. It is now the Majlis which ratifies treaties (article 105) and declares a state of emergency (amendment to article 111), not the Assembly.

The composition of this all-encompassing body, the Majlis, is dealt with in a new article replacing the deleted article 114. The Majlis al Shurah is composed of the President of the Republic (President), the First Secretary of the Central Leadership of the SSU as deputy and the following members: members of the Executive Bureau of the Central Leadership of the SSU, speakers and members of the People's Assemblies (national and regional) and members of the President's council (government). Members of this Majlis furthermore have to, according to a new article 117, swear an oath of obedience to the President.

273

To place responsibility for this constitutional muddle on Nimeiri's legal fledglings alone would not be fitting, for it takes a Nimeiri to produce such a jigsaw puzzle of constitutional conundrums. Nimeiri provided the ingredients, they did the cooking. In the end, as we shall see, all of them were stewing in their own juice. The proposed amendments not only reflect the inexperience of the legal draftsmen, but also the cynicism of the big chief and his disrespect for tradition, institutions and the principles of good governance. According to the present constitutional set-up there are, textually, different levels of responsibility and checks and balances. For example the President is to swear an oath before the People's Assembly (Parliament) being the officially elected representatives of the people. Nimeiri in his amendments wanted the Assembly to be reduced to a minor body working under him and owing allegiance to him. On the other hand, the SSU represented by its Central Leadership, is entrusted within the present scheme of things with formulating policies and monitoring the implementation of those policies by the executive. Nimeiri's amendments now lump the SSU together with the executive where the roles are indivisible and unidentifiable. The government (Cabinet), a decision-making body, is to be, perforce, a restricted action-oriented body, now that it is incorporated in an amorphous body known as the Majlis al Shurah. That government is an intellectual process, a managerial operation and a deliberately structured institution, did not figure in Nimeiri's mind when he dictated his new constitution. What he wanted was to assume absolute power and to be given absolute immunity. He is almost intimating infallibility.

The amendment to article 113 on succession establishes a new type of succession. No plebiscite is needed for the election of a new President, for the incumbent President, i.e. Nimeiri, nominates his successor in a sealed writ. When the President's office is declared vacant the writ or will is to be opened before the Majlis and the latter 'has to swear an oath of allegiance (*bay'aa*) to the nominee.' Nimeiri, having ruled the country for life, could now continue ruling it from his grave.

The Southerners, needless to say, were infuriated by the proposed amendments. Joseph Lagu and Abel Alier addressed a very critical letter to the President. They told Nimeiri he was unmaking the Addis Ababa agreement, the corner-stone of national unity and the *sine qua non* of stability and peace. The Assembly, they reminded him, cannot turn itself into a constituent

Assembly to pass the proposed amendments; it was not elected to repeal the constitution and make a new one. What Nimeiri called amendments to the constitution were in fact a repeal. They also reminded him that if he had carried the day in the South it was only because of his ability to see the true nature of the Southern problem.

Amending the Amendments

Nimeiri, undeterred, went ahead and put the proposed amendments before his pliable Assembly, which he thought would not dare defy the Leader and Imam. In an interview with the Saudi daily *Ukaz*, in Saudi Arabia when he was performing the *umra* last July, he declared that the new constitution would come into effect at the end of Ramadan. To him it was a *fait accompli*, but a surprise was awaiting him. He had underrated the Assembly's Southern members and a few SSU figures as well. The Southern members stood as one bloc against the amendments. Abul Gasim Ibrahim, the former RCC member, came out of his political hibernation to address the Assembly and plead with the members to reject the amendments for the sake of the May revolution. Hassan al Turabi, on the other hand, defended the amendments, saying it was the best possible Islamic constitution under the circumstances, the absolute immunity of the Imam notwithstanding. Nimeiri was to be given what the four caliphs of the Prophet Mohammed never got or indeed claimed, absolute immunity.

The Southern members put up a concerted fight against the amendments and prevailed upon their Assembly colleagues not to commit political suicide and turn Sudan into a *de jure* personal estate for Nimeiri. The President was thus forced to back down and make amendments to the amendments; he wanted to make the changes more palatable. And here we see Nimeiri the politician at his best, for if his proposed amendments were indeed Islam then he should have stood his ground and fought for it on principle. Nimeiri's brand of Islam, after all, is supposedly immutable and does not permit give and take.

Al Turabi was after political expediency no less than his Imam, and was directly involved in the drafting of the amendment to the amendments, giving *political* advice on what would be accepted to

275

the Assembly. This argument on the immutability of Shari'a was flung by Nimeiri and the Muslim Brothers in the face of the critics of the Islamic penal laws introduced in 1983. Consequently, the basic law (the constitution) should be as immutable, if not much more so. Those who are set to resurrect God's kingdom on earth should, in principle, have no concern with power brokerage. The doctors' strike, we were told, was ungodly and inspired by Satan; God alone knows who could have inspired power bargaining in the name of Allah.

To placate the Southerners Nimeiri reinstated the 1972 Act into article 8, and to placate SSU members he went back on his original proposal to drop the reference to the SSU as the sole political organization in the Democratic Republic of the Sudan. He also had to make concessions on his Imamate. According to the new amendments the President would be chosen by a plebiscite but would then be given the *bay'aa* (oath of allegiance). The President is not an Imam for life but an Imam for six years (a novel concept in itself) who can be elected for any number of terms. This Imam for six years does not appoint his successor. When the presidency-imamate becomes vacant 'the Leader of the People's Assembly shall assume the office temporarily and shall be followed by the President of the Supreme Court. The interim President shall convene the Majlis to select a new President who will be approved by a plebiscite and a *bay'aa*.'

Notwithstanding the drollness of such an office as an Imam for six years, the new amendments contain no real concessions. For example, we referred earlier to the composition of the Majlis; now in the new amendments the membership of the Majlis is increased to include more appointed members, with the result that the appointed members will outnumber the elected members of the Assembly. By appointing the right people the President Imam will ensure his re-election and the election of the person he nominates after his death.

What should have emerged from our discussions of the amendments and their amendments is that Nimeiri, to prevent the Muslim Brothers and the Ulema being given credit for his Islamicization measures, was ready to go to the extent of entrusting this serious task to legal upstarts who would not question his authority and would dutifully carry out his will. On the other hand, to surprise the people with the shock tactics of his new legislation, he did not hesitate to ignore all his advisers and institutions, Cabinet, Attorney-General, SSU, Southern leadership etc.

Theatre of the Absurd

As to the two legal upstarts who sprang from obscurity, theirs is a story bordering on the absurd. The two young men graduated in the early 'seventies and had had most undistinguished careers before they met the Hero of May who was thinking of becoming an Imam. One of them was the son of the religious leader of a very minor Sufi sect called Abu Qurun, i.e. the man with horns. Nimeiri met Nayal Abd el Gadir Abu Qurun at a remembrance service, a mystical ceremony in which rhapsodies and verses of the Qu'ran are chanted to the accompaniment of drums. The scene includes frenzied dances, incantations and the like. Nimeiri was apparently very much taken by the ecstatic experience and took an instant liking to the eccentric figure of the young participant Abu Qurun; his braided hair, black turban, eyelids darkened with kohl (no sign of effeminacy as many dervishes use it) and above all the almost noxious fragrance imparted by the attar he always wears, all adding to an aura of mysticism that captivates ignorant and vulgar minds.

Nayal was soon to be appointed by Nimeiri to a palace job with the nebulous title of judicial assistant; the court of St Nimeiri was now turned into a magistracy. Judicial assistants have no place in the executive hierarchy, but Nimeiri contrived the title in order to appoint the junior judicial official which Nayal was. In fact, Nayal had to be advised by the Chief Justice to abandon his eccentric attire which did not befit the dignity of his office. He was also warned not to turn his court into a clinic for he often volunteered to cure lawyers and other parties appearing before him. His pharmacopoeia included, among other things, vinegar and honey and unguents.

Nayal later introduced his friend Awad el Jeed Mohammed Ahmed to Nimeiri as a legal wizard. Jeed, who was to become Nimeiri's *alter ego* (there have been loads of them in the course of Nimeiri's fifteen years in office), had a no more distinguished legal career than his soulmate, Nayal. He started as a legal assistant in the early 'seventies with Attorney-General Zaki Mustafa, and, a few years thereafter, he established a modest office as an advocate dealing with insignificant cases. What attracted his soulmate and eventually Nimeiri to him were other capabilities with which other qualified lawyers were not endowed, including an ability to transcend ordinary human knowledge. Nimeiri, the believer, accepted uncritically the story about Jeed's abilities. In fact, early in 1984 when one of the doubting souls in the SSU quizzed the President obliquely about his new aides, Nimeiri reprimanded the questioner, adding that in his fifteen years in office he had never had aides as competent as Nayal and Jeed. Nimeiri was not without reason, for both he and Jeed were living in a world different from that known to the rest of us mortals.

Talking to the Beirut weekly *Al Sayyad* (13–19 June 1984) Jeed said, 'My brother the Leader Imam was waiting in the shade of the tree of certainty. When he saw us, he approached us and gave us the embrace of a scholar [Nimeiri, the scholar!], the embrace of a leader for his soldiers. He shook our hands warmly and went towards the light, never turning nor looking backwards as Lot did when God had given him the instruction "No one shall look back," and as Ali [the Fourth Caliph and the Prophet's cousin] marched on Khaybar [one of the Prophet's battles] having been told by the Prophet, "March and do not look backwards".'

Elaborating on his relationship with his brother, the Leader Imam, el Jeed said, 'From the beginning, and before drafting a single law, the Leader took an oath of allegiance from us and we took a promise that our relationship with him should be that of an Imam and his flock; he agreed and we agreed. We then gave the Leader an absolute *bay'aa*. The *bay'aa* is a pact before God; to betray him (Nimeiri) is to betray God.' We can see now why Nimeiri had reason, and why the daring questioner of the SSU was completely off the mark. The Imam and his flock were beyond what has remotest contact with human experience. The SSU, politics and government are about real life; Nimeiri was marching on Khaybar. In that Nimeiri we meet the superstitious man who is mesmerized by the young Mephistopheles of Abu Qurun.

What el Jeed did not tell *Al Sayyad*, however, was Nimeiri's warning to them. Nimeiri was reported to have told the two young lawyers in 1983 that they had to observe strict secrecy and not discuss the new laws with anybody. (Nimeiri's shock tactics, for he wanted to surprise people.) Not anybody, he said, including the man next door. The man next door was Hassan Turabi, the constitutional lawyer, the former professor who had taught the two legal greenhorns, the Islamic scholar and until recently, Nimeiri's legal adviser. And it is statements like this warning that show the multiplicity of facets in Nimeiri's personality, so that it is not the superstitious Nimeiri that we see, but rather the duplicitous calculator.

The disciple, however, was not as pure as his words seem to suggest, for they were all sanctimonious. The upstart lawyer's practice generally consisted of petty cases. His *cause célèbre* involved defending a member of Parliament called Gaafer Isheigir who was also chairman of a local government council in Khartoum. Isheigir was accused of receiving bribes to allot parcels of land to undeserving persons. He was prosecuted under the State Security Act. El Jeed was his lawyer and, in his defence, he maintained that the law under which his client was prosecuted was unconstitutional. This very same unconstitutional law was integrated by el Jeed himself into the so-called Islamic Penal Code which he drafted in 1983. It had never dawned on him to caution his brother Imam, as he advised him on flogging and the amputation of hands, that Islam has its own concepts of state security too. The disciple knew better for, if he ever dared to raise the issue, he would have been rebuffed by a different Nimeiri (another facet of the personality), not his brother Imam this time but the down-to-earth politician who wants to survive in office by all means, legal and extra-legal, not excepting Shari'a.

Abu Qurun kept playing second fiddle to el Jeed who had, almost heretically, established telephathic communication with the Prophet Mohammad. El Jeed told Nimeiri when they first met that the Prophet had appeared to him in a dream and told him that Nimeiri was destined to save the Islamic nation. The two obscurantist young lawyers report to Nimeiri's house frequently, often carrying such messages. On entering Nimeiri's offices they are reported to make a point of turning their faces left and right, greeting the invisible souls of the angels. Nimeiri joins in the salutations. One can read in all this nothing but expressions of insular parochial delusions, blissful ignorance and a complete lack of the faculty of reason. Islam, we maintain, is a religion of learning; it has no place for false illusions resistant to reason.

Nimeiri's Bay'aa and Shura: a Heresy

According to learned Islamic norms some of Nimeiri's new

institutions border on heresy. The *bay'aa* and its conditions, for example, are heretical in the extreme. Orthodox Islam does not recognize an absolute *bay'aa* because infallibility and immunity (*ismah*) are unique to the Prophet. All the successor caliphs of the Prophet were not immune. We have cited, in this context, the story of Omar's followers who swore to fight him by the sword if he deviated. The method of succession which was put forward in the first amendments and by which Nimeiri appointed his successor in a will (*wasiyya*) is also totally unacceptable to Sunni jurisprudence, to which all the traditional sects of Sudan subscribe, including the Muslim Brothers.

Every Friday a *mubay'aa* (swearing allegiance) was held in a different part of the Sudan. The Leader Iman took the prayers and delivered a sermon in which he attacked his opponents (and therefore opponents of God), heaping abuse on them. These tirades were termed consultative meetings (consultation for Nimeiri is a one-way process). After prayer the notables rushed to the Leader to give him their *bay'aa*. Many of them took it jokingly. Imams, as we said, are not foul-mouthed and they do not indulge in acts of hatred and vengeance, certainly not from pulpits in mosques. To Nimeiri, however, abuse is now sanctified; the secular fibs of the 'seventies have become the canonized lies of the 'eighties.

Nimeiri gave these sermons the appellation of meetings of *shura* and *wassiya*, i.e. consultation. In Islam, even an inconsequential person can advise and correct the Imam. Islamic history of the early caliphate is replete with stories in this regard; the one often cited is the dialogue between Omar, the Second Caliph, and in-significant lady who queried the veracity of his judgment on a certain issue. Omar conceded, adding, 'The lady was right ... Omar was wrong.' Omar's words have become a classic dictum in jurisprudence.

As for an Imam who would have flogged people, entered houses and arrested people, irrespective of what Islam says, *shura* too has a different interpretation. In one of his *shura* meetings in a Khartoum mosque last August a businessman from Omdurman asked to speak to the President. Descending from the pulpit, the President refused to discuss matters publicly and asked the man, Salah al Din al Misbah al Mahdi, to report to his office, for the President dreads challenges in public. Salah al Din refused, insisting on discussing matters publicly, because this was his Islamic right and also because Nimeiri himself has chosen mosques as a forum for *shura*. He went on to attack the *shura* and the *bay'aa* as they were interpreted by Nimeiri. The man was not allowed to complete his statement; he was arrested and brought before the emergency courts. He was found guilty of 'disturbing the public peace, inciting hatred against the state and obstructing the Islamicization of the Sudan'. The merchant, in his late forties, was sentenced to five years in prison (later commuted to two years) and publicly flogged with eighty lashes. Describing the exercise by a Muslim of his right to debate in public with the Imam matters pertaining to religion as 'obstructing the Islamicization of the Sudan' says it all. Misbah called the bluff and Nimeiri, his vicars and the so-called Islamic courts are now exposed for what they are. In fact, just as the President was unable to conceive or countenance the implications of his own decisions in politics, e.g. Southern Sudan, constitutional limitations etc., he, also fell short of rising to the demands intrinsic to *shura* (consultation) and *wassiya* (counsel). As to his judges, the so-called Islamic judges, they were no less inadequate.

Thomas Fuller, a few centuries ago, forewarned against polluted justice. 'He who buyeth the magistracy, must sell justice.' What Khartoum courts witnessed last August was not the high-minded justice of Caliph Omar, who was proud to be at fault and corrected by a common woman, but rather the injustice of reigns of terror. The *bay'aa* as an institution is a contract between the people and their Imam. On the part of the Imam, the promise is to uphold the rule of Islamic law and to act and rule on and by consultation. The people promise obedience as long as the Imam acts within the law. As to whether the people can, or indeed should, depose an unjust ruler, Muslim jurists differ. For the contract of *bay'aa* to be binding on the people, however, their consent is necessary; a *bay'aa* given under duress or coercion is not valid.

Historically, it has not been necessary for all Muslims to give their *bay'aa*. Several scholars accepted the appointment of an Imam by a limited number of those who are eligible to 'bind and dissolve' (*Ahl al-aqd wa al-hal*), i.e. an electoral college. The problem is to determine who these electors are (*Ahl al-aqd*) in any one society at any one time. This problem has never been resolved and it is not difficult to see why.

The first *bay'aa* in Islamic history was that given to the Prophet. It was analogous to the act of Islam itself (submission to the will of God), in that it was the acceptance of the prophethood and authority of Mohammed. His immediate successors were chosen in Medina by the prominent companions of the Prophet and the leaders of influential clans, a leadership which could be ascertained without difficulty because of the still very tribal structure of Arab society.

This well defined electoral college, so to speak, which existed during the early Caliphate, came to an end with the death of the companions and the expansion of the Islamic state, a process which disturbed and gradually obliterated the tribal order. Furthermore, the *modus vivendi* which existed between the new Islamic elite and the clan leaders collapsed during the caliphate of the third Caliph Uthman, resulting in the first civil war in the Islamic state. Since the establishment of the Umayyad dynasty the Muslim state or states have been ruled by monarchical dynasties and military rulers, save for the caliphate of Omar ibn Abdel Aziz. The *bay'aa* was simply a means of legitimizing the *status quo*.

The institution of the *bay'aa* should, therefore, be viewed within its historical perspective. The main sources of Islam in the Qu'ran and Suna (the prophet's words and deeds), neither defined nor established procedures for the nomination of the Leader Imam. In a modern state, like Sudan, the historical *bay'aa* institution becomes irrelevant. New methods were devised for ascertaining the will of the people, e.g. the ballot box, and there is nothing un-Islamic about having recourse to it. If Nimeiri and the Muslim Brothers were to establish their brand of Muslim state, based on these classical, historical concepts uncritically copied, then their amendments (and the amendments to the amendments) to the present constitution should have gone a step further and deleted constitutional references to non-discrimination on the basis of religion and sex.

We said earlier that classical, historical interpretations by the *fugaha* (Islamic jurists) restrict the imamate to male Muslims. The implications of this to Southern non-Muslims and women in both North and South need to be underscored. It would be the height of hypocrisy to claim that one has established a Muslim state of this nature while one continues to pay lip service to principles of non-discrimination on the basis of religion and sex. This is precisely what the authors of the constitution had cautioned against when provisions like article 16 were introduced. For that reason nowhere in the permanent constitution was religion or sex made a condition for the assumption of office. On the other hand, if there was any deliberate discrimination within the May political institution, it was only discrimination in favour of the historically underprivileged, e.g. the provision in the local government laws that 25 per cent of the membership of local government councils should be women. Nimeiri, however, wants to have it both ways, claiming the immutability of historical institutions and interpretations of Qu'ran when it suits him and adopting or rather paying lip-service to modern concepts when political expediency dictates, even if it goes contrary to his so-called immutable laws.

Be that as it may, the *bay'aa* Nimeiri is receiving is not valid, on three grounds at least:

1. In the absence of an electoral college the people must choose their Imam by a public vote.
2. Whoever is giving the *bay'aa* must give it with his free will, i.e. not under duress.
3. The election of an Imam should be a real choice: the community should be allowed to elect any male member who has reached the age prescribed by the Shari'a. The Sudanese have no such choice.

Realities and the Tree of Certainty

In earlier chapters we have seen examples of Nimeiri's tortuous journeys in politics, diplomacy and the economy. His journey in religion was no less tortuous, from the superstitious man taking delight in every forbidden fruit and relating to religion only through amulets and the blessings of sages, to the political opportunist exploiting religion as a weapon to galvanize pious citizens and intimidate opponents and eventually to act as God's regent on earth. By the end of this journey Nimeiri had convinced himself that he was Sudan's greatest leader, and made so bold as to suggest that he was also God's messenger to deliver Sudan. It is all a make-believe world of fantasy.

None the less the stark realities remain, ugly, hallucinating and hitting people in the face, Nimeiri and others. Nimeiri may have seen things waiting in 'the shade of the tree of certainty', but, obviously, not the certainty of the problems endured by the Sudan that were casting their heavy shadow on the country: a raging war in the

South and an economy in tatters. Neither Nimeiri nor his competent nor half-competent aides did much about either. The first of these problems, the guerrilla war in the south, is escalating by the day. Since his declarations on redivision Nimeiri has had at least six meetings of the Central Leadership of the SSU, all to listen to Nimeiri's speeches and then disperse. In none of those meetings was the question of the South debated. And if Nimeiri could afford to marginalize the highest political institution in the country in dealing with an issue like this, he would do the same to the Cabinet, diplomacy etc. As for the Army 'theirs not to reason why', they are 'but to do or die'. The responsibility for the mess rests squarely on his own shoulders.

The war was triggered by Nimeiri's division of the South, an act which rejuvenated the Anya Nya movement under the leadership of twenty trained senior officers. The bulk of this new movement known as Anya Nya II is a Southern army unit which had mutinied at Bor in May 1983, when between one and two thousand Southern soldiers deserted the Army and took to the bush. A sizable number of ex-Anya Nya members decided to desert the Army and join the new movement because of Nimeiri's decision to disperse Southern-composed Army units. That decision constituted yet another breath of the Addis Ababa agreement which stipulated that out of the 12,000 troops to be stationed in the South, 6,000 must be ex-Anya Nya guerrillas. The integration of the ex-Anya Nya into the national Army was not an easy task. In the mid-'seventies, a few years after Addis Ababa, a number of former Anya Nya men mutinied at Akobo (Upper Nile) refusing transfer to the North. When their commander, a Southern Dinka, Colonel Abel Chol, tried to prevail on them they shot him dead and fled to the bush. Instances like this were not uncommon, given the nature of disciplining and integrating a rebel force into a regular Army. Southern men were, more often than not, controlled by Southern officers serving in the national Army, like Colonel Chol. They were ready to die for the cause of integration.

The picture in the 'eighties has drastically changed. It is now both the men and their officers who are deserting. Chief among those officers who deserted was Colonel John Garang, who leads the Sudan People's Liberation Army (SPLA). The SPLA has, apparently, succeeded in integrating within its ranks, through persuasion or coercion, all Southern elements that had deserted the Army (including Anya Nya II). Rebellion is now spreading throughout the South, fuelled by Nimeiri's Islamicization programme and his insistence on its application in the North and South alike. Shari'a, in fact, is not applied in the South, not because of Nimeiri's special dispensation for Southern non-Muslims but in spite of his orders and edicts. Southern law-enforcing agencies simply refused to apply the law and there was nothing Nimeiri could do about it short of declaring a *jihad* and subduing the infidels. Nimeiri did not realize, however, that this is the first time in the history of post-independent Sudan when national laws are being defied with impunity, by any region in the country. Even in the height of the civil war in the 'sixties national laws were not challenged; only the politics of Khartoum were.

Nimeiri took advantage of the rift which existed between the Dinka leadership and the leaders of the smaller tribes, especially General Lagu, who came out strongly in favour of the division of the Southern region, hoping to get a better deal for himself inside Equatoria. We have dwelt on Nimeiri's reasons for dividing the South and destroying its institutions. He was not championing the cause of the smaller tribes in the face of Dinka domination; he was simply dividing to misrule. In any event, whatever differences existed between the Southern leadership were soon put on a back burner by those leaders following Nimeiri's Islamicization programme. Nimeiri has united the South (as much as this notoriously divided region can be united) in opposition to his policies and his regime. Witness the Southern response to Nimeiri's proposed amendments which was signed jointly by Abel Alier and Joseph Lagu.

A number of prominent Southern political leaders, including Bona Marwal, who had served as Minister of Information and National Guidance, have been detained (Bona was later released and lives in self-exile in the USA). A number have fled into Ethiopia, such as Joseph Oduho, and Nairobi, such as Clement M'boro. These men are not Dinka, for they belong to minor tribes. The former comes from Equatoria, the province allegedly championing division. All this belies the assumption that the problem can be reduced simply to one of tribal jealousies. In March of 1984 a delegation of the Sudan's armed opposition movement arrived in London to campaign for European support for their cause. The delegation was led by Joseph Oduho. The Southern rebels work under the umbrella of a Southern all-embracing organization, the Sudan People's Liberation Movement (SPLM). The military wing, the

Sudan People's Liberation Army (SPLA) is led, as we said earlier, by Colonel John Garang, a Dinka. Garang served in the Sudanese armed forces and lectured on a part-time basis in the University of Khartoum's Faculty of Agriculture. While in the Army, he earned a PhD in rural economy from Iowa State University. He was accused by Nimeiri of being a Communist, an accusation obviously intended for American consumption. The Americans, who have personality profiles on everybody and everything that moves within their country, certainly knew better about Garang's leanings, for there is very little on him that they would learn from Nimeiri's framed reports.

The new element in the Southern rebel movement is its national identification. 'Secession is not what we are working for,' said Oduho. 'We are appealing to all the opponents of Nimeiri to join us in our campaign for a progressive Sudan and to sweep away his ideas of Islamicization ... It is absurd for anybody to imagine that the Shari'a laws could be imposed on the 30 per cent or so of Sudanese who are not Muslims.' (*Third World Reports*: Colin Legum 23 March 1984). Apart from campaigning in Europe, the SPLM is currently engaged in explaining its cause to African governments and to the OAU.

So we are back to square one, in fact worse. The Southerners are lobbying Western and African governments to help them against the government in Khartoum, as they did before 1972, only this time they can present their case as one of religious domination. The weapon of religious and cultural domination was used in the past by some southerners and Christian groups in the West. It was more imagined than real. Save for certain small Islamist groups, political parties in the North never viewed the Southern question as one of religion, nor did they seek to impose Islam forcibly on the South. Their inadequacy was political and intellectual; condescending paternalism and an inability to see the issue as one of cultural distinctiveness. Unity of the Sudan can only be preserved within a concept of unity in diversity. It is, therefore, ironic that credence to what has always been a doubtful allegation, presenting the North-South conflict as a religious issue, is now given by the actions of the very man in whose reign peace was restored to the South.

Ironies, however, do not cease to accumulate. Another one is that Colonel Gaddafi, who had opposed the Addis Ababa agreement and tried to prevail upon Nimeiri to abandon it, is now standing on the Southerners' side. Both Ethiopia and Libya were presented with a golden opportunity with the conflagration in the South, an opportunity for which they have long been waiting. If Nimeiri is harbouring Libyan opposition and calling on the world to kill Gaddafi, then Gaddifi will not hesitate to pay Nimeiri in kind where it hurts most. So would Mengistu who is threatened by the ever-present Eritrean insurgents. His message to Nimeiri is, 'I am bleeding, so you might do so as well.'

Of late, Nimeiri has been in touch with the World Council of Churches in an attempt to secure their support in solving the Southern Sudan problem. He also got in touch with President Moi of Kenya. The two met in Khartoum early in 1984, for Nimeiri wanted him to play the role Emperor Haile Selassie had played in 1972. A few months after Moi's visit Nimeiri dashed any hope of reconciliation by declaring a state of emergency and pressing ahead with his Islamicization programme. Moi came out with a statement in the Kenya press (in the third week of May) in which he expressed Kenya's concern at the new measures. So the mediator is now himself in trouble, if anything because of the impending influx into his country of hordes of refugees from Southern Sudan.

By alienating the South, Nimeiri has dealt yet another blow to the country's bid to recover economically. All the oil discoveries so far made in the country lie in the South and the West, the most important being in the former. Chevron estimates that the wells in Bentiu district in the Upper Nile Province will yield five billion barrels. Explorations by a French company (CPF–Total) near the Bor area also showed promising results. The foreign companies, however, can only proceed reluctantly because of the war that has been rekindled by Nimeiri. In fact the rebirth of Anya Nya coincided with the actual start of the oil operations. Until tranquillity returns to the South, Sudan is not likely to benefit from its newly-found oil. Oil discoveries had played their part in Nimeiri's wishful thinking. With the failure of economic development plans, largely due to his misdirection of the economy, he was more and more pinning hopes on oil discoveries to help him deliver the goals he promised in the 'seventies. This is one reason why he decided that none of his economic Ministers should have anything to do with oil. Not surprisingly, therefore, he bungled this one too.

Another casualty of Nimeiri's new Islamicization measures is the economy. This problem too stares the nation in the face, though the President and his vicars cannot see it. Their vision must be dimmed by the shade of the tree of certainty. Flogging, the amputation of hands etc. in the end affect a small minority, but the impact of economic decisions is much more far-reaching. The economic ailments of the Sudan, as we have seen, have been well diagnosed and the medicine prescribed. It was universally admitted that the economy needed more firm hands and less amateurism. There was, moreover, an awareness of the importance of co-ordination and streamlining of the economic decision-making process, more responsibility in dealing with money and a better sense of priorities. Since the application of Shari'a laws, however, the economy has become a non-issue for Nimeiri. People, rulers and ruled alike, have been kept busy with the lurid details of the emergency courts and the soporific sermons of the Imam. The press, radio, TV and government delegations abroad were involved in propagating, explaining and defending the so-called Islamicization, Nimeiri's new metaphysical preoccupation. Nevertheless, as the state of the economy went from bad to worse Nimeiri introduced a law on *zakat* (a religious tithe) abolishing some fifteen taxes without consulting his economic Ministers. A special bureau for *zakat* was established, responsible to Nimeiri personally. The tax laws abolished were the tools with which the Economic and Finance Ministers control, manage and direct the economy. But neither Nimeiri nor his two young lawyers were aware of the implication of the repeal of all these taxes on the country's economic policy or finance. And once again, for the sake of surprising all the nation with his decisions, Nimeiri chose to keep all his economic advisers in the dark, even at the cost of destroying the whole economy. Nimeiri appointed another nonentity as Minister for *Zakat*, responsible to him. The new minister, Babiker Abdalla Ibrahim, was introduced to him by the chief of military intelligence, General al Sir Mohammed Ahmed. The man is alleged to be endowed with supernatural powers. As to his knowledge of the economy, that was reflected in his declaration, readily reproduced by the President himself, that the *zakat* will yield to the treasury 600 million Sudanese pounds on grains alone. The Sudanese exchequer was told that very soon they would have more financial resources than they would be able to disburse. These were the econometrics of the supernatural. Sudan's whole foreign earnings from the proceeds of sale of its grain are about that amount. (The *zakat* levied represents 2½ per cent of the capital, i.e. the grain in question.)

The wizard was soon put to the test. He failed to deliver the goods and the Finance Minister was left with no source of revenue for the fiscal year 1984–5 in view of the abolition of all taxes save custom duties. Nimeiri could not face that situation. He dismissed the rogue, suspended the *zakat* laws, allegedly for one year, after having travelled personally across the country to explain the *zakat* and educate regional governments on its application. His Minister of Finance was asked to produce a budget according to the normal, unIslamic procedures. Needless to say Nimeiri had to reinstate all the tax laws he had abolished; the clumsy decision-making process that led to this upheaval was a non-issue. Neither did Nimeiri care to reflect on that, nor did the institutions dare question him. Among these institutions is the People's Assembly, which had bovinely endorsed his *zakat* law and hailed it as an achievement. Without chagrin they also endorsed the reinstatement of the old laws. The fiscal year was also changed from 1 July to 1 Muharram (the beginning of the *hijra* year) without a realization that in Sudan the fiscal year was related to production cycles; it is not a religious matter.

Islamicization was soon to affect Sudan's banking system. Nimeiri ordered all national banks, including the Central Bank, to abstain from receiving interest, for *riba* (usury) is prohibited by Islam. His banking advisers cautioned him against any precipitous action in this regard. There was need for more in-depth studies, they told him. As to the Islamicization of the Central Bank, Nimeiri was reminded that even the Saudi Arabia Monetary Authority (SAMA) had not felt able to take such a radical step. They knew that they were part of an international network and, unless and until they liberated themselves from that linkage, they would have to play by the rules of the game. Nimeiri received both the Minister of State for Finance, Dr Abdel Rahman Abdel Wahab, and the Deputy Governor of the Bank of Sudan, Mahdi al Faki, who pleaded with him the case of the bankers. One point brought to Nimeiri's attention was that all national banks would collapse if these measures were hastily taken. Nimeiri was unimpressed. Instead he read them a thirty-page document on what Islam says about *riba*; it was a sermon. Nimeiri was obviously concerned with the theological, rather than the statistical aspect of economics, and in theology you do not work on pluses and minuses. This is hardly the way banks function.

Nimeiri refused to listen to his advisers but the pious Imam was soon to waive God's laws when applying them became too costly.

289

His Ministers informed him that the Club of Paris would withdraw its support if Sudan did not pay its service debts. Dr Chester Crocker, the US Assistant Secretary for Africa, also visited Nimeiri to explain, among other things, the concern of US banks about Nimeiri's decisions on banking. The Imam, who would not listen to the *wassiya* (counsel) of his own advisers, gave way and instructed his Ministers to go along with the wishes of impious governments and organizations and ignore the laws he had passed on *riba*. Shari'a can wait until Sudan becomes solvent again. This was the pragmatist (or rather the opportunist) in Nimeiri.

In his latest bouts of intimidation, Nimeiri asked the Auditor-General to supply him with a list of names of all firms and persons who obtained facilities from national banks; these were to be his new scapegoats. He accused them (in a Friday sermon) of sabotaging the country's economy and usurping government funds, despite the fact that the facilities obtained by them had been negotiated with the banks in the ordinary course of business. People had begun to be bored with the daily news of flogging, for attempts by the media to ram it down their surfeited throats were counterproductive. New carrion was therefore needed for the gossip wolves. Nimeiri was deliberately ignoring such refinements as how banks work and money works, or the fiduciary relationship that exists between banks and their customers. Bankers who knew their business well were dumbfounded and advised the President about the damage that banks would suffer if they were to divulge banking secrets, but the whims of the Imam were now to be constructed as divinely inspired commands. The books were thus opened to the pious Imam and, rather than looking into the deals of Abd Rabbo (the tyre-factory man) or the Wad Nimeiri corporation, Nimeiri cast his eyes on those whom he wanted to intimidate and slander. Friday prayers, considered by the Muslims as an occasion of forgiveness, were used by Nimeiri for this end.

On one occasion the victim was a banker who drew the President's attention to a basic fact about banking: clients are not usurpers of government money, they provide securities and there are means to deal with them when they default in payment. The banker Abdel Rahman al Seeni, a former general manager of Unity Bank, made his views known to Nimeiri through the Governor of the Central Bank. The President's response was a smear and a slander of the banker in a Friday sermon. He was accused of obstructing Shari'a. In fact, the President, who is overseeing how the Sudan is handling an eight billion dollar debt, with nearly five sessions on rescheduling within the last three years, needed no advice from Seeni or others on bank loans and debt rescheduling.

His second victim was an old friend of his, a journalist turned businessman, Abdel Karim al Mahdi. Al Mahdi challenged a bank on the basis of Nimeiri's new laws, refusing to pay interest. His name was included in Nimeiri's list of infamy. Nimeiri was enraged, for the laws of Allah are to be applied at Nimeiri's pleasure. Al Mahdi, the defiant, was taken to prison and told: you either pay the principal and interest or you will rot in prison. Needless to say, al Mahdi bought his way to liberty by transgressing Allah's laws.

Our Lives' Sweetness

In this blessed era of asceticism one would expect the pious Imam who is shepherding the believers into the kingdom of God to shun the good things in life, the life of the earthly. We have earlier referred to Nimeiri's craving for splendour after death, and his claustrophobia that led him to tear down six large villas occupied by senior Army officers, to make way for a large garden in his official residence in the Army barracks. Now the President, who has also turned into an Imam, decided to venture outside the barracks. He acquired a plot of land (105 *faddans*, about a hundred acres) in Wad Madani (Abasiya). The plot is registered under the name of 'citizen Gaafer Mohammed Nimeiri'. Various government departments were engaged in building and equipping the Imam's small Versailles (designed to house 300 persons).

For any other Sudanese President, indeed for Nimeiri himself, there is nothing wrong, under normal circumstances, in owning a house and developing a small parcel of land. But circumstances are not normal, and neither is Nimeiri a normal President, with his claims to the imamate, pretences of austerity, exhortations of people to resist the temptations of this life and think only of the life hereafter. With these habits in mind there are many conclusions to be drawn from this story. The refurbishing and extension of his Army residence, for example, is a restatement of the sad fact that he no longer sees a time limit to his role, despite the pledge he made after his election for a second term in 1977. He is now seeing himself as both immovable and imperishable.

Sudanese Presidents do not live in Army barracks. In fact plans for building a permanent residence for the President were, for a long time, on the drawing-board. Nimeiri's case is exceptional. As an Army officer, leader of the revolution and several times Commander-in-Chief, he opted to be near his men. No other President will want this though, if Nimeiri believes at all that he will have a successor. Nimeiri virtually said before his re-election in 1983 that he is staying until the 'aims and goals of the revolution' are achieved. Come 1984 and Nimeiri not only turned himself into a President for life but also into an Imam. His avowed mission in life now is no longer to fulfil 'the aims and goals of the revolution' which brought him into power, but rather to stay until the laws of God prevail and the corrupt and licentious Sudanese mend their ways.

His entrenchment inside the barracks with his larger garden and the tunnel underneath has another aspect to it; it reveals that he is well aware of his unpopularity. He is no longer the carefree Nimeiri of the early 'seventies. Instead of setting out to cure the causes of this unpopularity, however, he chose to protect himself against its militaristic manifestations, i.e. attempted coups. Finally, the building of the Versailles belies his sermons on austerity and the transient nature of this life. Like the rest of humanity he too is as worldly as ever, in fact more worldly than ever. His illness has increased his attachment to this life and made him more determined to get the most out of it. 'O, our lives' sweetness.'

Megalomania is the highest expression of vanity. The imamate is only a culmination of a process. For a long time Nimeiri has ceased to describe himself as one of the people, as he did in the early years of his rule. He stands over and above the rest of the Sudanese people. In 1983, for example, he ordered a clause to be entered in the SSU Congress rules of procedure requiring members to stand up when he entered the hall. The Congress is supposedly the highest political authority in the land and Nimeiri chairs its meeting as a head among equals. Nonetheless, members deferentially often gave him standing ovations. This act of deference need not be an order, but by now all is confused in Nimeiri's mind.

His person also became beyond criticism or reproach, according to the amendments to the constitution which he wanted made. As we have mentioned earlier he sought such an amendment in

September 1975 but was dissuaded from it. Parallel with this was an inflation of the status and standing of his family and clan. In the *Face the Nation* programme of April 1976, in answer to a question put to him by an unnamed questioner, wondering whether Nimeiri owned various houses and whether that was the reason for his silence on the big increases in rent, he said, 'I would like firstly to say to the sender of this letter that I, thank God, do not own any houses in Khartoum. ALL that I own are two houses which we, myself and my brother, have inherited from my father and they are humble in the extreme. One is in Medani, Hilat Derdig, and the other in Wad Nubawi in Omdurman. . . . One is inhabited by my brother.' His brother has come a long way since then, as we have seen.

Phantoms and Bulldozers

After his declaration of martial law a very revealing incident took place which also involved members of his family. Being driven through the seat of his caliphate, Khartoum, Nimeiri was enraged by the unruly nature of the kiosks which lined the streets of the capital. (These were owned by widows, invalids and disabled people.) He ordered their removal. Consultations were made between the local government officers and the Commissioner of Khartoum on how to go about executing the wishes of the Imam. But consultation is time-wasting and militates against quick execution of orders in the era of speedy justice. Passing through the same streets Nimeiri was enraged when he saw people still impudently practising their petty trades. This time he got the Army to demolish the kiosks. As the Army worked their bulldozers indiscriminately and mercilessly through the kiosks they felled a national monument and a shrine. This was a public fountain built by Nimeiri's family in memory of his deceased uncle; the idea is that passers-by stop at the fountain, quench their thirst and say 'God rest his soul.' The practice is common in Sudan and other Muslim countries. There was an immediate outcry, not however on behalf of the kiosk owners nor by the general public whose thirst will no longer be quenched by the fountain, but by the Nimeiri clan who resented the destruction of a family shrine by a member of the family. Nimeiri got his Minister of Information to issue a statement

293

denying that he had anything to do with the whole affair, yet another lie. The official statement said that 'somebody' had exploited the President's name and issued the directive to demolish the kiosks. Nimeiri did not have to be reminded that, if the story was true, Sudan must be a no-system one-man government where army bulldozers, local government officers and governors would be mobilized by phantoms. Everybody knew that the President, to save himself from shame, was lying in his teeth. Needless to say it was the family shame rather than the plight of the invalids that has troubled his conscience.

Smoke Silk Cut

No chapter is complete without a section on corruption. This time the by now ubiquitous Military Economic Corporation was involved. The Corporation allegedly went into a deal with Gallaher, the company producing Silk Cut, buying large stocks of this make of cigarettes. In order to capture the Sudanese market they had to dislodge the biggest dealer, the National Tobacco Company (25 per cent owned by the government). Dealing in cigarettes is very rewarding and the Corporation needs the cash. This is the very corporation which was criticized by the Paris World Bank consultative group for spreading its tentacles where it should not.

Nimeiri, in an attempt to drive the National Tobacco Company out of the market, notwithstanding the 25 per cent government ownership, imposed a ban on the importation of cigarettes with more than 15 per cent tar (the level of tar in Silk Cut) thinking that Benson and Hedges (the company's main sales item) would exceed this limit. The ban was justified on medical grounds. But if medical reasons prompted the caring President to limit the tar the Sudanese inhaled from foreign cigarettes, he should likewise have looked into locally produced cigarettes which have a much higher tar level. He did not care about the local tar, only the imported variety.

Benson and Hedges, it turned out, has less than 15 per cent tar and Nimeiri was forced to come up with a new pretext. The National Tobacco Company was accused of having bought Benson and Hedges at seventeen dollars per thousand cigarettes and claimed twenty-two dollars per thousand, thus pocketing five dollars per thousand, in addition to their normal profit (Silk Cut was offered at seventeen dollars per thousand). No attempts were made to substantiate this serious accusation. National Tobacco explained to Nimeiri's Minister of Commerce that Benson and Hedges has less than 15 per cent tar and that they were ready to import the cigarette at seventeen dollars per thousand, not because that was its real price but because they had bought a large stock and would rather make a loss of five dollars than lose the market. They also explained that the five additional dollars were justified by the fact that the cigarettes were air-freighted to ensure freshness and that the foreign currency needed to pay for the commodity was bought from the parallel market, i.e. at a higher rate of exchange. The Ministry of Trade, in the face of all those revelations, could not but issue an import licence.

Nimeiri was enraged. He dismissed the Under-Secretary who issued the licence and withdrew the licence. He went on the air telling the Sudanese that all Benson and Hedges found in the country would be presumed contraband. A few weeks later, when one of his Ministers took out a packet of Benson and Hedges during a visit to the President, the President leapt from his seat, destroyed the packet and sent the Minister out. The story, like many other Nimeiri fables, is hilarious. The President cannot help personalizing everything. Smoking a brand of cigarettes which he ordered banned, allegedly for health reasons, became a personal defiance.

This is the President who in a *Face the Nation* speech (April 1976) congratulated the Assembly's supervisory committee, saying, 'I was delighted by the resolutions which the Assembly passed . . . which aimed at extirpating the causes of deviation by the roots; be it in relation to the means by which the Ministry of Trade issued import licences or the Department of Mechanical Transport issues licences of roadworthiness.' The Assembly was then debating the issue of alleged irregularities in both the Ministry of Commerce and the Mechanical Transport Department concerning the importation of Romanian trucks by the local import–export company Basit. Of his transgression of the regulations relating to mechanical transport licences we have already seen an example in the Magirus deals. As to trade licence violations by the very President who was hailing the Assembly for its vigilance, they ranged from the importation of tyres to that of cigarettes.

Chapter Nine

Diplomacy: Clichés and Indiscretion

... there was no deity that he would not dethrone, no principle that he would not abjure, no direction change, friend abandon, enemy embrace. He struck no attitude of which, in his real self, he was not the antithesis. He was constant only in his inconstancy. The politics changed, and out of recognition; only the person, his rhetoric, his very words – intemperate, demagogic, alternatively abusive and obsequious remained opportunistically, mendaciously the same.

David Hurst and Irene Benson, *Sadat*

A Tumultuous Diplomatic Itinerary

With all the pride and prejudice of megalomaniacs, President Nimeiri never brought himself around to differ politely or tolerate disagreement with his aides and advisers. Disagreement with him was often construed as disobedience, the parting of the ways, subversion if not insurrection. That is why all Nimeiri's send-offs for his Ministers had always been accompanied by boisterous, sometimes ribald, unimaginative abuse. Leaders, if only for the sake of decorum, never allow their anger, even justifiable anger, to dim their better judgment. This, in a sense, reflects President Nimeiri's lack of self-confidence, and understandably so. Nimeiri's oversized ego has always been constrained by his intellectual inadequacies. Those among his aides who made up for the inadequacies were also a constant reminder of his shortcomings; the more self-assured they were, the more he was frightened of them and consequently quarrelsome. President Nimeiri has indeed given the opportunity to many educated Sudanese to serve their country under him. He rightly expected them to be grateful to him for that opportunity. They owe him a lot and they know it. What Nimeiri does not know, however, is that he too owes them more than he can repay. Simple truths like this hardly dawn on him. We have come across a few of his scurrilous attacks against his aides, aides who disagreed with him, including the ones against those who have catapulted him to power, i.e. members of the RCC. In these attacks, Nimeiri almost intimates that rather than engaging talent, he was actually extending favour to his nominees. Consequently he views differing with him only as an act of ingratitude. In disagreeing with his aides, however, he often inadvertently goes to the extent of demolishing the achievements of his own regime, including those he was publicly lauding.

One such attack that is of relevance to this chapter is his statement to *Al Sayyad* about his Foreign Minister (13 October 1977). Referring to the Minister, indeed to the achievements of his own government, Nimeiri said that he (the Minister) had views which were not in harmony with those of the people. 'I have given him two opportunities and he has failed. The foreign policy that I want is the policy of development and not . . . of cocktail parties. I am confident that al Rashid el Tahir will execute the foreign policy I dictate to the letter.' The reader who is puzzled that Nimeiri should disown his Foreign Minister for not abiding by the will of the people and go on to say that he was appointing someone who would execute 'his foreign policy to the word' should be reminded that, for Nimeiri, *le peuple c'est moi*. The two chances Nimeiri referred to were given in August 1971 and February 1977. Both came at a critical juncture in the life of the May regime. The first was after the abortive Communist coup of July 1971 and the second in the wake of the opposition insurrection of July 1976.

My immediate main task on coming to the Ministry of Foreign Affairs (MOFA) in 1971 was to formulate a credible and balanced foreign policy that would lend respectability and seriousness of purpose to the regime. The medium- and long-term aims and functions of the MOFA were set out by Presidential Decree number 4 (12 October 1971) and expounded by Presidential Decree number 3 (8 May 1973) which replaced the October 1971 decree. That decree described the MOFA as the official link between Sudan and the international community, entrusted with pleading its causes, defending its interests and reflecting its political, economic and cultural vision within international and regional gatherings and organizations. Among the specific tasks set for MOFA were development of political, economic and cultural co-operation between Sudan and other nations on the basis of mutual respect for sovereignty, recognition and respect for international law and agreements, avoiding friction between nations and the severing of relationships, active participation in the support of the struggle against colonialism and racism (particularly giving impetus to the Arab and African liberation struggle) and the protection of human rights.

To include the furthering of national interests, the decree provides that diplomacy is also to be mobilized in the cause of development and national unity.

The foreign policy of the Sudan during the last fifteen years has gone through many a tumult, often compounded by President Nimeiri's erratic way of dealing with the world. Vindictiveness and petulance, as we have seen, have prompted many of President Nimeiri's domestic policy decisions. In foreign policy extremism and virulence, more often than not, were major influences on his approach to diplomacy. The extremism is more than revealed in Nimeiri's diplomatic itinerary, from the man who declared in 1969 that he would turn Sudan into the Cuba of Africa to the one who virtually transformed the Sudan, a traditionally non-aligned country, into the banana state of the region. For since 1978 Sudan (i.e. Nimeiri) has contracted that disease, well known in the Caribbean, by the name of US clientelitis. Sudan foreign policy, because of its tumultuous nature and its ramifications, cannot be encapsulated in one chapter; it merits an independent work. Consequently we shall limit ourselves in this chapter to the two discredited periods to which President Nimeiri referred. We shall also delve, at the end, into Nimeiri's brand of diplomacy of latter years, the 'diplomacy of development' as he dictated it and wanted it carried out to the letter, particularly in the post-1978 period. We shall also deal with the implications of this policy for, and its relation to, the purposes and objectives of Sudanese foreign policy as they were defined by the competent political organizations and embodied in the laws promulgated by Nimeiri himself. In order not to encumber the reader with details of Sudan's manifold relations we shall limit ourselves to the country's relations with the super-powers, some of its neighbours, the role of diplomacy in nation-building and development and Sudan's commitment to Arab, African and non-aligned causes.

For years President Nimeiri and the consecutive congresses of the SSU were praising what they called Sudan's diplomatic achievements in the early and late mid-'seventies. One should assume that, when President Nimeiri, in his own words, disowns whatever was accomplished in those years of so-called 'cocktail diplomacy', he would have either been deliberately oblivious of those diplomatic endeavours or genuinely ignorant of their import. It is for this reason that we are compelled to recount the details of certain incidents, not to belabour the reader with unnecessary anecdotage but to stress and corroborate.

Sudan and the Soviets

We have dwelt in Chapter 1 on the way Nimeiri set out to woo the Communists and enlist their support against his traditionalist enemies. This, inevitably, had an impact on foreign policy, for in the first year or so of its life the May regime looked eastwards. Pro-Sovietism in that era was diluted only by Nasserism. Presidential speeches were stridently anti-American, the jargon blatantly communistic and the news reporting very markedly 'demi-Tass'. The mitigating influence of Nasserism was reflected in a few incidents, for example, Sudan's decision to sever relations with Romania when that country decided to resume relations with Israel. Romania was the first East European country to do that after the 1967 Arab-Israeli war. In fact Egypt's reaction against Romania was less radical, limited to withdrawing her ambassador from Bucharest. Babiker Awad Allah, who had a great influence on Sudan's decision, considered the matter as one of principle in view of Sudan's declared position that its relations with other countries should be determined by those countries' attitudes towards the Palestinian cause.

In November 1969 Nimeiri visited the Soviet Union. The Soviets promised to buy more Sudanese cotton (the country's main cash crop) and to supply capital goods as part of a programme aimed at strengthening economic and political relations between the two countries. In effect the main Soviet economic aid in this period was limited to the utilization of the undisbursed balance of the aid offered by the USSR to Abboud's regime in 1961. That aid was partly used by Abboud's government in industrialization, i.e. milk, fruit and vegetable canning. As for the May regime, the undisbursed balance of Soviet aid was used for the construction of a university hospital and a veterinary research centre. Apart from this and on-going cultural co-operation agreements the most important Soviet aid was in the military field, e.g. military

299

hardware and training.

The recognition of East Germany was another move designed to emphasize the 'progressive' nature of the regime. A cultural agreement was signed between Sudan and East Germany on 15 June 1970 which involved an exchange of visits between educationalists, writers, sports teams, exhibitions and folklore troupes. The decision on East Germany, at that time, was momentous, for it could have been construed as a choice between the two Germanies (East and West) for that was the era of the so-called Hallstein doctrine in the FGR; West Germany would sever diplomatic relations (where such relations existed) with any country that established relations with East Germany. Sudan's relations with West Germany had been severed since 1967 (before Nimeiri) in the wake of the 1967 Arab-Israeli war. The doctrine lapsed after Egon Bahr's *Ostpolitik* and the reconciliation between the two Germanies. East Germany repaid the Sudan generously, again not in development assistance but mainly in revamping its security apparatus.

Relations with the West necessarily worsened. The USA was accused in July 1969 of supporting a coup attempt against the regime and a number of the US diplomatic teams who were 'directly involved' in the alleged attempt were expelled on 15 July. The USA denied the charge.

As for the other Western country closely linked to Sudan, the UK, the nationalization in May 1970 of banks and commercial firms (the majority British) ushered in a period of uneasy relationship between the two countries. The measures were designed to impress more than anything else, and they did impress the Chinese, as their Vice-President Hsieu Mien made clear in his speech at a banquet given in honour of a delegation from the Sudanese government in June 1970. The two parties expressed their conviction that friendly relations and co-operation between the two countries would develop further. This was followed by a visit by Nimeiri in August. Chairman Mao Tse-tung congratulated him, together with Rubaya Ali of South Yemen, on their victories against imperialism.

The July coup and the war of words that ensued between Sudan and Communist countries changed everything. The Soviets bitterly attacked Nimeiri's anti-Communist campaign and the execution of Communist leaders. On 25 July the Soviets sent a letter to Nimeiri asking him to refrain from passing harsh sentences. Nimeiri was undeterred and both the secretary-general of the Communist Party, Mahgoub, and the veteran labour leader, Shafie Ahmed al Sheikh, were executed. The latter's execution caused an outcry in the Eastern bloc countries on account of his long-standing involvement in the international labour movement. On 24 July Nimeiri had warned the Soviet Union that, if it went on with its media campaign, relations between the two countries would be seriously damaged; meanwhile, he suspended the activities of Soviet military advisers. He also accused the Soviets and Eastern Europeans of exaggerating the stature of the CP inside Sudan. The media battle continued and at the beginning of August Sudan recalled its ambassadors from the Soviet Union and Bulgaria; the ambassadors of the two countries were expelled the following day from Sudan.

I took charge of the MOFA on 4 July. The Communist campaign was at its zenith; harsh, sustained and well orchestrated. Sudan was inundated with protests from all over the globe, Eastern Europe, Western Europe, Asia etc. Conspicuous by their absence in that venomous campaign were the Chinese and the Romanians (with whom Sudan had severed relations). It was, therefore, obvious to us who the *chef d'orchestre* of the campaign was. As a result the MOFA issued a statement calling for restraint and adding that we would not sit idly by if the hostile campaign continued. We were careful, however, to emphasize that there would be no major changes in our policy towards the Soviet Union as a result of the July coup. It was also made clear that we did not intend to break relations with anyone but, if we were compelled, we would do so. There was nothing to be gained from breaking relations, for it is naive to think that the closing down of embassies would put an end to intervention and harassment. The Soviet Union exists and this is a fact of life we have to live with. Although Sudan's attitude to and relationship with the West was in need of revision, we tried to guard against a swing (by reaction) to the West, something which might well have happened, given the anti-Soviet feeling. Diplomacy would become a zero sum game; you quarrel with old friends and make up with old enemies.

Both countries maintained their diplomatic relations for a short while without ambassadors. Less than two years later we decided to normalize relations. I discussed the matter with the veteran Soviet diplomat Jacob Malik. Malik, with whom I had cultivated excellent working relations, was for years his country's ambassador at the UN. Malik understood the message and organized, at his residence, a meeting with Soviet Foreign Minister Gromyko. I was accompanied by the Sudan ambassador to the United Nations, Rahmat Allah Abdalla, and the ambassador designate, Mustafa Medani. Gromyko's reception was correct but his cold impassivity was ominous. The meeting was so frosty that I thought I should break the ice by making an almost banal statement telling Gromyko that bygones were bygones and we wanted to normalize relations on the basis of mutual respect and benefit. Evidently there was nothing earth-shaking in my 'ice-breaker'.

Gromyko's response was terse: 'It is not the Soviet Union that is to blame for the bad relations. If you want to normalize it, go ahead. The Soviet Union can do without the Sudan; it is you who need us.'

That was stunning, in a particularly surly manner of speaking. I could have walked out, but in the trade of diplomacy people should learn how to subdue personal prejudices and much more so personal impulses and reactions particularly when supreme national interests are at stake.

Unflaggingly I persevered: 'No, Mr Minister, we certainly need you but you cannot tell us that the Soviet Union, with its avowed global strategies, can afford to do without the largest country in Africa which has, by its sheer geographic presence, an impact on eight neighbours.'

Gromyko retorted with still another fit of the sulks: 'Maybe you are happier with your new friends, the imperialists.'

Being angry and showing it is one thing but casting aspersions is a different matter. If only for the sake of self-respect and national honour, accusations like this could not be left unanswered. So still unruffled (by now it was all put on, a false front in the best tradition of diplomacy), I answered: 'I presume we are not here to make value judgements on the policies of each other. However, since you have raised the question may I say that words mean different things to different people. What you, Mr Minister, call imperialism is not necessarily what the Chinese describe as imperialism.' Mustafa Medani nodded to me, for he thought I was about to go too far. Far from it; we wanted to accomplish a mission and in diplomacy you can do that only by keeping cool while taking the bull by the horns. I went on to tell Gromyko that, if he was referring to the resumption of our relations with the USA, then that decision was determined both by our own vision of non-alignment as well as considerations of national interest. We were not more imperialist for receiving American grain than the Soviet Union was. Nonetheless, I continued, we still need American technology and know-how as much as we need that of the Soviet Union and China. In conclusion, I told the Soviet Minister that Ambassador Malik would tell him that the Sudan's record of voting on international issues was, more often than not, alongside that of the Soviets, not because we were aligned with or obliged to them but because the USSR has sided, on all these issues, with us.

In diplomacy least said, soonest mended. Malik, the veteran diplomat, knew when to intervene. Jocularly, he stepped in to say, 'Now that you have got it off your chests, I take it that we are soon going to have an exchange of ambassadors provided you promise that you are not going to accuse our ambassador to Khartoum of being a Communist subversive.' A few weeks later there was an exchange of ambassadors. We sent to Moscow our most senior diplomat, Fakhr el Din Mohammed. In those days of rabid anti-communism in the Sudan we needed both a firm hand and a man who was not paranoid about Communists.

In spite of Gromyko's attitude one had some doubts as to the Soviet evaluation of the July events. One is inclined to believe that their action had largely been prompted by a sense of solidarity with the beleaguered CP. This view is confirmed by the fact that only two years after the July 1971 events the secretary of the Czechoslovak Communist Party, Belag, in a very tortuous way began questioning the wisdom of the July adventure. Be things as they may, by that year (1973) relations were back to normal with all the Socialist countries of Eastern Europe with the revival of all cultural and economic co-operation programmes: Czechoslovakia (21 May 1973), East Germany (7 June 1973) and USSR military protocols (December 1973).

By the same token we were also careful that what others presumed to be an anti-Soviet stance (there was none as far as Sudanese diplomacy was concerned) should never be exploited by these others for their own ends. For example, in the second discredited era (1977–8) when a senior Sudanese security officer, Abul Rahman al Rashid, was approached by a Soviet diplomat with a view to recruiting him to undertake intelligence work, MOFA cautioned against making too much of the incident. The matter was to be handled in a responsible manner with the minimum fuss. Espionage and counter-espionage are one of the ugly faces of diplomatic life, and governments, while taking all necessary precautions to protect their national interests, should learn how to live with it. We had no interest in embarrassing the Soviets; catching their diplomat red-handed should have been enough embarrassment. Our immediate reaction, therefore, was to summon the Soviet ambassador, relate the facts to him, declare the accused diplomat *persona non grata* and tell him that it was not our intention to make a publicity event out of the incident. If others wanted to gloat over Soviet discomfiture, it should certainly not be at our expense. The message was clear; while we were not seeking to humiliate the Soviets, none the less, we could not countenance activities injurious to our national security.

President Nimeiri thought that our response should have been more forceful. The incident, possibly, deserved a *Face the Nation* speech, an occasion to lash the Soviets with his sharp tongue. Fortunately, the chairman of the National Security Council, General Baghir, agreed with our line of action. Later, when two of our diplomats were expelled from Moscow in retaliation, Nimeiri was almost gloating: 'I told you so.' He felt that we had made him miss an opportunity to abuse and humiliate the Soviets. Baghir, on the other hand, was embarrassed; he thought the Soviets were ungrateful and their action was unjustified. Again MOFA was not excited; such retaliations were normal in diplomatic life and particularly with the Soviets. They, like others, have their hotheads too. The Soviets would not countenance the expulsion of a Soviet diplomat by a small country. To MOFA the action signified nothing more than that, and the answer to it should be simple, naming two new diplomats to replace those expelled. That was soon done and a positive response came from Moscow within a week. In the end, it was only by this spirit of restraint that we were able to maintain a correct working relation with the USSR, eventually culminating in contacts between the two countries at the political organization level for the first time since July 1971. This was reflected in the participation of the Soviet Communist Party at the SSU Congress in 1977 for the first and only time after July 1971.

Sudan and the United States

After the signing of the Addis Ababa agreement, Nimeiri made an unsolicited declaration at Wau (Southern Sudan) in which he expressed his intention to resume full diplomatic ties with the USA

(Sudanese relations with the USA were severed following the 1967 Arab-Israel war). Nimeiri had already received our report on the contributions made by the US voluntary organizations to the rehabilitation of Southern Sudan, in spite of the absence of formal diplomatic relations. His action was thus not politically motivated, rather an expression of gratitude. In fact a few months earlier Sudan had received an eminent US diplomat, George Bush, the present US Vice-President. Bush, who was at the time the US ambassador to the United Nations, was participating in the first meeting of the UN Security Council to be held outside New York. The meeting was to discuss African issues on African soil, in Addis Ababa. Sudan was then chairing the Council. Bush, in spite of the absence of diplomatic relations between the two countries, accepted an invitation to visit Khartoum and acquaint himself with our efforts towards solving the Southern problem. We were then in the process of organizing a conference on the rehabilitation of Southern Sudan refugees. His role in sensitizing both US governmental and non-governmental agencies to Sudan's efforts to restore peace is undeniable.

The President's declaration at Wau spurred the Americans, who were extremely isolated inside the Arab world after the 1967 severance of diplomatic relations with a number of Arab countries, to take up the initiative. The Secretary of State, William Rogers, who was visiting Ankara at the time, telexed us, offering to come down to Khartoum for a joint declaration on the resumption of relations. For the offer we were thankful, but we answered by advising him that the visit would be untimely. We impressed on him that a final decision had not yet been reached on the matter. Our response to Rogers was prompted by reasons of political expediency, not principle; we were persuaded by the arguments in favour of resumption. Knowing that the Khartoum political scene was populated by all types of political animals claiming to represent the conscience of the nation, the spirit of the revolution etc., it would have been foolhardy to go along with a decision like that without preparing the ground. So in order to ascertain people's feelings about the decision we asked Security to conduct a thorough investigation to find out what the reaction of the man on the street would be to the resumption of diplomatic ties with the USA. Instructions were also sent to all our ambassadors abroad, particularly in the Arab world, to report on reactions in their respective stations.

Based on all those findings a report was prepared for a joint meeting of the government and the Politburo. We expressly asked for an open discussion and an open vote, so that nobody should claim that the decision was taken behind their backs. All facts were there to help a sensible decision-maker to arrive at a rational decision, rather than one based on pet phrases and fuzzy slogans. The facts included guide-lines for our foreign policy formulation as they were expressed in the National Charter, i.e. diplomacy in the service of national interest, non-alignment, co-operation with countries of differing social and economic systems on the basis of mutual benefit, regional and continental obligations etc. It took the meeting two hours to discuss the matter, after which the votes were counted twenty for to five against. Those against thought that we should be capitalizing on the new momentum in Sudan–US relations. Sudanese diplomacy was vigorously engaged in exploring all avenues of co-operation between the two countries. Foremost in our concerns was the influence the US could exert in getting the World Bank to commit itself to our major agricultural endeavour – then, the Rahad project. We were also interested in the revival of the World Bank Consultative Group on the Sudan which had been held in abeyance since 1967. The first meeting of the committee, after the resumption of relations, took place one year later. We managed, however, to see to it that the committee reflected the new configuration of Sudan's variegated diplomatic relations. So in addition to the West European countries, the USA and Japan, who made the core of the committee, we also invited Kuwait, the UAE, Romania and Yugoslavia.

The Rahad agreement with the IDA was signed in 1973. US aid to other projects was to follow through Ex-Im Bank, the Overseas Private Investment Corporation (OPIC) and American private banks, e.g. a Sudan satellite station, Sudan Airways (Boeing), Sudan railways (locomotives), Port Sudan weaving, agricultural research, commodity aid under PL480 and the first agreement with major US oil companies on petroleum exploration. George Bush again played an important role, not only in apprising exploration companies about the potential of the Sudan but also in making available to us vital new information discovered by remote sensing and relating to the hitherto untapped important resources in the South and South-west. In the past all efforts in oil exploration had been concentrated on the Red Sea area.

Although one had always called for a good working relationship with the USA and worked towards it, one never envisaged a sell-out or a compromise of our principles or an abdication of other friendships. This much was made clear in 1973 to Joseph Sisco, then the Under-Secretary of State, in the course of a dinner organized by the US Secretary of State in honour of African Foreign Ministers. Sisco sitting next to me turned to me saying 'If I am sitting next to you, it is not a coincidence.' He explained that he wanted to express his country's anger at our 'deplorable' action in releasing the Palestinians who had murdered the American ambassador in Khartoum. The Americans were obviously enraged by that action particularly as the new US ambassador had been kept completely in the dark till the Palestinians had already left the country for Egypt, accompanied by MOFA Under-Secretary Fadl Obeid. The Palestinians were put on trial and convicted but handed over the same day to the Egyptian authorities and PLO representatives in Cairo.

At a personal level, I told Sisco, I was as sorry as many Americans were for the death of the ambassador, Cleo Noel, who was a friend. However, we like any other country worked within a certain political framework and were constrained by certain commitments. The Americans should realize that no Arab country had ever condemned a Palestinian to death and we were not going to be the first. In the same vein, no Arab country had ever put them on trial and convicted them. We did, in spite of the many pressures we were subjected to, including those from trusted friends like President Boumedienne of Algeria. If we insisted on doing that it was because we were incensed by the act. More than that, we were asked to do what no other country has done, save Israel. Reference was made to Holland and Austria, where Palestinians were arrested for holding hostages and killing people but were none the less simply deported.

Sisco, in his rhapsodic voice reminiscent of captivating Arab orators, answered back, 'But my friend, none of those you mentioned was an American ambassador.' At this point I thought it was not Sisco but Kissinger speaking. It was Dr Kissinger who wanted to teach people lessons, the hallmark of his policy being that America is mighty and its might should not only be used but be seen to be used, even if it meant going to the brink. He was a refined version of John Foster Dulles. That was the sense in which I understood Sisco's words.

As always, there was another face to the question. 'Mr Sisco,' I said, 'Your remark is well taken note of but, if I ever repeat this argument to a Dutchman or an Austrian, don't you think that their immediate reaction will be: "God, those Americans are racists."' I hope that Sisco got my message too. Relations between the two countries continued to be icy, in spite of the efforts of many of Sudan's friends within the administration and Congress until the downfall of Nixon and his Metternich.

Thereafter relations warmed up, especially after Nimeiri's goodwill mission to the USA in which he visited several states. Sudan's new ambassador to Washington, Dr Francis Deng, who knew the American scene well, did a worthy job in promoting his country's cause, not only in Washington circles, but also in the business, academic and communications worlds. Sudan–US relations were also in the ascendancy during the Carter administration, with co-operation going far beyond the bilateral level, e.g. consultations over southern African problems and those of the Horn of Africa. To that end Ambassador Andrew Young undertook two visits to Sudan. But at no point during all this period under the different administrations was the improvement of our relations with the USA contingent on espousing American causes in international forums. On the contrary Sudan was on record in the UN against American policies in Vietnam, Cambodia etc. Also our stance in support of third world causes was not limited to immediate regional engagements, i.e. Africa and the Arab world; it extended much farther, e.g. support of Prince Sihanouk in Cambodia and support for Panama in its conflict with the USA at the Security Council in the early 'seventies, when Sudan was a member of the Council.

Sudan and Egypt

Good neighbourly relations was to be the basic tenet in links with our neighbours, irrespective of differing economic and social orders, for in the end it takes different people to make a world. Of those neighbours Egypt stands on its own, in view of the special nature of a relationship which is governed by impelling geographic, cultural and historical considerations. The Egypt–Sudan nexus has always been a significant factor in domestic Sudanese politics, often exploited, taken out of context, misconstrued or misunderstood. The relationship was never articulated meaningfully in a manner that takes into account both the interests of and realities in both countries. On the other hand, direct Egyptian involvement in Sudanese affairs during the regime of the parties had only helped to increase these misconceptions and misapprehensions, even within the pro-Egypt parties, e.g. the conflict between Ismael el Azhari and the integrationists within his party when the former opted for the declaration of independence (el Azhari for years was the standard-bearer of unity with Egypt). Our role, therefore, was to formulate a policy that isolated subjective prejudices from objective realities. The realities were clear in our minds; neither of the two countries can live without the other.

Like all of Nimeiri's political and diplomatic itineraries, his course with Egypt was also full of twists and turns. His sinuous path had gone from calls for complete unification, including Libya (following his visit to Tripoli with President Nasser on 25 December 1970 on their way back from the Arab summit in Algiers), to a spiteful war of words between the two countries in the early days of President Sadat and eventually to the espousal of Sadat's policies in the late mid-'seventies. Egypt, however, has always stood by the May revolution since its inception; her support was unconditional during the Nasser era and unflinching during the 1971 Communist coup. Egypt also stood with Sudan in the ensuing quarrel with the Soviet Union, officially announcing on 2 August 1971 that 'The permanent position of the United Arab Republic is complete support for the glorious revolution of 25 May and the rejection of any form of interference in the domestic affairs of the brotherly Sudan' (*African Diary*, 1971, p. 5629).

The summer and autumn of 1972 witnessed a gradual deterioration in the relationship with Egypt, culminating in the recall of Sudanese military units stationed in Sinai. The Egyptians were ostensibly incensed by the resumption of diplomatic relations with the USA, but there were other reasons for their unhappiness. Chief among these reasons were:

1. Sudan's decision to close the Egyptian trading company el Nasr.
2. Sudan's request that the role of the Khartoum branch of the University of Cairo be reviewed; emphasis was inappropriately placed on the humanities when the Sudan was short of engineers, mathematicians and scientists.

3. A letter which I had sent to the Egyptian government recalling a certain provision in the 1959 Nile Waters Agreement, which had remained dormant for over a decade.

According to that agreement, Sudan would release 1.5 milliard cubic metres of its share of the Nile waters to be used by Egypt and to be recovered when Sudan's agricultural development needs it. The agreement also provided for joint endeavours to develop additional water resources to be used by both countries.

There was a bitter attack in the Egyptian press, particularly against the Foreign Minister, who was portrayed as the villain of the piece. More fuel was added to the fire by some Sudanese elements, whose vision of the relationship between the two countries was warped by the prejudices and misconceptions of the past. Regrettably these elements were equally unable to extricate themselves from their emotional engagements, even when the implications of those engagements went contrary to policies they were espousing and advocating. For example, one point of interrogation on the Foreign Minister's 'misdeeds' was how he dared to raise the Nile water issue. Not even the discredited regime of the parties did that. The question, surprisingly, was raised by the very people who were singing night and day the 'bread-basket' melody, as if water was not an important ingredient of any agricultural development endeavour.

For one to succeed in diplomacy, however, one should not allow oneself to be carried away by subjective reactions, even to the egocentric or misguided prejudices of others. This is much more so when the question relates to vital national interests. One may give vent to one's feelings by such reactions, but achieving desired ends is a different matter altogether. With this spirit of restraint an energetic effort was made to contain the crisis, culminating in the Foreign Minister's visit to Egypt in June 1972 and the return visit to Sudan by Egypt's Foreign Minister, Dr Mourad Ghalib. Ghalib, a seasoned diplomat who knows the ways of the world, played a considerable role on the Egyptian side in defusing the crisis. Sudan's ambassador to Cairo, Mohammed Mirghani, was equally up to the situation.

With President Sadat the matter was different. Ghalib arranged a meeting with Sadat at Alexandria. He was apparently reluctant to receive me had it not been for Ghalib's persistence. Sadat, the jovial and expansive President, was not himself when I met him.

His greeting was polite but chillingly reserved. I could see that he was inflamed. There were the normal diplomatic courtesies, banal and hypocritical, as they usually are. Then the man could hide it no more; the words came cascading out: 'If you don't want my university', referring to Cairo University in Khartoum, 'I can do with the saving of a million pounds.' That was the opening shot. I told him that the last thing we wanted to do was to close a university. Besides, we were all nourished in one way or another by the Egyptian cultural media: authors, press, cinema etc. It was not his university that we did not want; all we were asking for was what he himself was labouring hard to achieve in Egypt. I particularly referred to the reports of the Hatim Committees (a series of scientific committees headed by Abdel Gadir Hatim, an assistant to the President, who was entrusted with reviewing the performance of the state apparatus in Egypt). On education, these reports called for the reviews of the system in a way that would put more accent on science and technology and make education more responsive to developmental needs. We were happy, Sadat was told, to have more Egyptian schools and universities going in line with our development efforts, i.e. producing more engineers, agronomists, mathematicians etc.

Sadat, still angry, asked 'And what about el Nasr, has that also got to do with your development needs?' The answer again was sure enough it has, for the matter was to do with the reorganization of our trade, particularly in strategic export commodities, i.e. foreign currency earners. That was not all. Sadat was also reminded that he himself, in his attacks on what he used to call the 'power centres', had accused the el Nasr company of being part of an intelligence network. To that Sadat said nothing. After a brief fiddling with his pipe and a deep sigh, he said tersely: 'Mourad [referring to his Foreign Minister] told me that you are discussing all these outstanding issues, so go ahead discussing; Egypt does not want anything from anybody.' I thought that was not good enough for a conclusion; the man must have been smouldering with anger.

Sadat, a good actor, did not normally wear his heart on his sleeve. Not this time though. In a sense that was a blessing in disguise; knowing the man's real feelings one can wipe the slate clean. So while thanking Sadat I went on to say that there were two things that I wanted to make clear to His Excellency. First, the last impression I would want him to have of me was that I was out to ruin Egyptian-Sudanese relations. I knew very well what such an action would mean in terms of cost to both countries. I reminded Sadat that the first decision I had taken, in the fall of 1971 when I went to the UN General Assembly, was the removal of Sudan's complaint against Egypt on the north-eastern borders issue. The complaint had been lodged in the 'fifties and had remained an active item on the agenda of the Security Council since then. Successive Sudanese regimes, with some very friendly to Egypt, never cared to remove it, maybe out of ignorance but mainly due to inadvertence. If I did, it was because I thought that the continuation of this complaint on the Security Council agenda was a diplomatic eyesore.

Secondly, I implored Sadat to see that it would be in the interest of both countries if Egypt would use official channels for ascertaining the thinking and desires of the Sudanese. That would be more conducive to a better relationship between the two countries. Intrusions by private persons in Sudan, the self-appointed protectors of Egypt's interests, more often than not confounded decision-makers in both countries. To that Sadat made a surprising remark to the effect that Egypt considered all the people of Sudan as friends but, if I was referring to the hundred or so persons who were on Egypt's payroll, those were people who were only receiving pensions to maintain them. That too Egypt would cancel, making some savings for her treasury. The comment was out of place for I had no specific person in mind, nor did I care a farthing as to who was receiving what from Egypt. It was the institutionalization of the relationship between the two countries that I was after.

Ghalib's effort to comfort me on our way back to Cairo revealed the degree of his embarrassment. He did not have to, I told him. We need, both of us, to concentrate on our business. None the less I appreciated Ghalib's feelings because I knew how untenable was the position of Foreign Ministers serving erratic Presidents. I told Ghalib that we had a senior and trusted ambassador in Cairo, Mohammed Mirghani, who should be our main conduit. Ghalib reciprocated by sending to Khartoum an honest and viable envoy, Saad Fatatry. Fatatry did not endear himself to the self-appointed emissaries, for he worked through the institutions and did a commendable job.

The resumption of diplomatic relations with the USA came a few weeks later (July 1972). Sadat could not take that one and considered it a stab in the back. He admonished his Foreign Minister

Ghalib, who claimed that he had established excellent working relations with us while decisions as important as this one were not even relayed to Egypt before their announcement. Sadat was unfair to his Minister because in fact we had both laid the ground for excellent co-operation between the two countries. Ghalib, a diplomat unencumbered by the paternalistic attitude of the politicians of the party era in Egypt nor the Big Brother high-handedness of some of the diplomats of the Nasser era, could unmistakably appreciate what we were up to.

Ghalib conveyed Sadat's displeasure to me at Georgetown, Guyana, during the non-aligned ministerial council. Sadat thought that we should have consulted with him before resuming relations with the USA. He thought that the implications of our decision would go far beyond Egypt, upsetting a general balance in the region. To that accusation I told Ghalib that the decision was taken in a meeting that had lasted for two hours, a good part of which was spent on the impact of the decision on Egypt and the Arabs. So that factor was well considered in the balance of judgment. As to consultation with Egypt, we believed that the process of consultation was a two-way road. Almost exactly when our decision on resuming relations with the USA was being taken President Sadat had decided to expel all Soviet advisers from Egypt. We were not informed either. That decision, I said, certainly had a greater impact on the overall Arab situation than our decision on the USA. After all, the USA had functioning embassies in the majority of Arab capitals, including Tripoli (Libya was in a union with Egypt then). Ghalib smiled slyly. His dismissal by Sadat one month later explained that smile. Ghalib was against Sadat's decision on the expulsion of the Soviets which, in the humiliating manner it was done, gave comfort to their adversaries without any palpable consideration in return.

Nevertheless the momentum created by our agreement with Ghalib continued. Meetings between delegations, particularly at the party level (SSU), succeeded one another both in Cairo and Khartoum. One of these delegations was led by Sayed Marei, a close aide to President Sadat and for a long time the grey eminence in his palace. Marei had occasion to visit different parts of the country and see for himself how the regime was not as disturbed as some elements in the Egyptian press and other agencies sought to portray it. Technical missions also commuted between the capitals, exploring areas of functional co-operation and reviewing problem areas in education, trade, irrigation etc. The groundwork was being laid for the integration of the two countries in a realistic and rational manner, i.e. progressive functional co-operation. Our aim was economic integration and the creation of a permanent mechanism for bilateral co-operation. The world is going towards wider unities, we thought, and it only stands to reason that countries with a common heritage and permanent mutual interests should be the first to follow this inevitable trend.

To encompass all these functional endeavours a skeletal structure was needed. Ideas of unity, union, unification, had never been articulated or incorporated into the body politic of either system, for they had remained slogans. For this reason unimaginative politicians could see no framework for the *Anschluss* other than classic formalistic superstructures imposed from above and always with no relation to realities. Experience showed this, for they have all crumbled. Sadly enough the satisfaction of personal ego, of noble and ignoble minds, was often equated with the given truth. On the other hand, what we were offering was not a panacea; it was all trial and error, though one is inclined to believe that policies related to real life, with all its apprehensions, prejudices and above all, interests, had more reason to succeed.

As in the Ghalib era Sudan was fortunate to have at the helm in Egypt in 1974 a man of great charity of mind, insight and humility in the person of Prime Minister Abdel Aziz Hedjazi. We were equally fortunate in having a great friend of Sudan in the person of Deputy Prime Minister Abdel Aziz Kamil, who never looked at the country through intelligence reports and personality profiles. Sudan and the Sudanese people were a subject in which he was both intellectually and emotionally involved as a human geographer. Discussions for the finalization of the new format for co-operation took place on 12 February 1974 in the outskirts of Alexandria at an Egyptian military post. The joint communiqué used the nebulous term 'somewhere in the Western desert' to describe the venue of the meeting. President Nimeiri met Sadat and they exchanged generalities and congratulated themselves on the high level of co-operation between the two countries. A committee was formed to work out a joint declaration, which we suggested should be more in the nature of a plan of work. There was Prime Minister Hedjazi, Foreign Minister Ismael Fahmi and Under-Secretary Usama al Baz from the Egyptian side and Omar el Hag Musa, Minister of Information, Ibrahim Moneim Mansour,

Minister of Finance and myself from the Sudanese side. On that evening the plan was finalized. The final communiqué stressed that the programme and philosophy of political action and economic integration between Sudan and Egypt was an expression of the desire of both countries to deploy human and non-human resources in each country for the joint benefit of both countries. The two Presidents decided to strengthen ties between the two countries at all levels, political, economic, cultural and military, by establishing institutions which would ensure continuous co-operation. The programme called on the two countries to do the following:

1. Hold meetings between the two Presidents periodically (at least once a year) in order to discuss matters, exchange views and review the situation.
2. Form a ministerial committee to include the Ministers of Foreign Affairs, Economy, Irrigation, Transport, Agriculture, Information, Education and a wakfs (religious affairs) to meet periodically in the two capitals, report to the two Presidents every six months and form specialized committees.
3. Form a political committee to include three members from the general secretariat of the political organization in each of the two countries to meet quarterly.

In the joint communiqué which accompanied the declaration of the programme, the two parties agreed to take the following steps:

1. Form a joint technical committee charged with the task of planning the execution of specific projects in the field of agriculture and animal resources.
2. Work towards the formation of a company to organize river navigation between the two countries and the development of fisheries.
3. Complete the feasibility studies on the Jongeli Canal and the Upper Nile projects.
4. Remove the various obstacles standing in the way of increased trade between the two countries and the movement of people and the exchange of goods.
5. Implement the special agreement in the field of

315

telecommunications, trade, cultural and artistic exchanges and
to strengthen the spiritual and religious values of the two
countries by increasing the number of Egyptian cultural
missions in the Sudan.

There could have been no better forum for me to articulate our
line of thinking on the basis of co-operation between Egypt and
Sudan than the Sudanese ambassadors' global conference. In an
address to that conference (January 1974) the following points
were made relating to Egypt–Sudanese relations.

You will all agree that it does no credit to either country that
irrigation and water storage projects long agreed upon are not
finalized and executed. Nor does it say much for either country
that food supplies should be one of Egypt's major quests while
vast stretches of virgin soil are untapped in our bounteous
land. It is distressing to reflect that those of us who have taken
a traditionally anti-Egyptian attitude have been no less at fault
than those who have tried to exploit Egyptian support to
resolve petty personal squabbles. Any system that fails to
appreciate, exploit and expand areas of mutual co-operation
cannot be beneficial to either country. It goes without saying
that a Sudanese who fails to review these areas of common
endeavour within the context of Sudanese interest is not
worthy of representing his country. Nor is an Egyptian who is
not mindful of his country's best interest worthy of
representing it. I may also add that should either fail to
appreciate the interest of the other, he would simply be
suffering from political immaturity.

Intense diplomatic activity was generated between Cairo and
Khartoum, exchanges of visits and contacts between the political
organizations, consultations among technicians ironing out differences on problems of trade and irrigation. All augured well and
ushered in an era of vast and genuine co-operation. Six months
after the joint declaration and accord the high-level joint ministerial committee envisaged in that accord met in Alexandria to
approve different projects that were the real stuff of integration:
road links between Egypt and Sudan (from the Egyptian shores of
the Red Sea to Port Sudan), improvement of telecommunications
(linking the Cairo–Aswan microwave network with that of Sudan

at Atbara), rationalization of education with specific propositions of converting some of the Egyptian secondary schools in the Sudan into trade and technical institutions, a new framework for commerce and trade etc. The two most important things that were approved at that meeting were the projects relating to irrigation and agriculture.

In fact, when the question of the water loan was raised we never anticipated that Egypt would provide the Sudan with water it did not have. Nor did we envisage withholding water from Egypt, notwithstanding the disastrous effect that would have had on her means of livelihood, for it would have been the height of irresponsibility even with an enemy country. We were also aware that the 1.5 milliard cubic metres loaned to Egypt had by now become almost an acquired right, legal niceties aside. On the other hand, we were aware of the fact that the 1959 agreement provided a way out of this dilemma and Egypt's officialdom would have to come round and agree to Sudan's thesis in this regard. What we had in mind were articles 1 and 2 of part 3 of the 1959 Nile Waters Agreement. That part of the agreement provides that, in case of new agricultural extensions requiring additional waters, either party may undertake works in the Upper Nile reaches to retrieve some of the water lost through evaporation in the Sudd region (Southern Sudan), i.e. the marshes of Bahr al Jabal, Bahr al Ghazal, Bahr al Zaraf and Sobat. And while the party in need is to initiate the process, the other party shall assume half the cost involved and be entitled to one-half of the net proceeds of the water retrieved. Sudan, at the technical level, i.e. Irrigation Ministries, had already indicated its desire to apply part 3 of the Agreement and asked for an Egyptian commitment, only to be faced with reluctance on the part of the Egyptian bureaucracy, particularly as Egypt was not in immediate need of increasing her share of the Nile waters. Our letter on the water loan therefore was simply meant to bring out a simple home truth.

In the high-level ministerial meeting at Alexandria the same bureaucracy did not relent in pursuing its negative position, putting all sorts of impediments in the way of an immediate agreement. By way of delaying tactics they proposed that more technical studies and financial analysis were needed, including the re-evaluation of Sudan's real needs. Dr Hedjazi, a man who could tell the wood from the trees, was sharp in his reaction to his own Minister of Irrigation. 'Let us start from the basic premise. We want Sudan to be a bread-basket for us and the Arab world. How can they do that

317

without water?' he asked the Minister of Irrigation.

Kamil, the Egyptian Deputy Prime Minister, picked up the ball, adding, 'I simply do not understand references to more studies. I have been teaching my students both in Cairo and Khartoum about the Upper Nile projects on the basis of studies that go back to 1924. Let us forget about the story of more studies and go right to business.' Both, unlike some of the so-called unionists of Khartoum, knew how to relate cause and effect. If Sudan is to develop and intensify its agriculture for its own benefit and the benefit of others, somehow water must become an issue.

So the Jongeli project was born in that meeting. That was the best birthday present given to our Minister of Irrigation, who was almost in tears. For years the Nile waters question had been shelved by the regimes of the parties, all of them: the unionists, separatists, progressives, conservatives etc., and for no reason other than built-in prejudices. Furthermore, since 1972, efforts to deal with the issue had been frustrated by the limitations of an Egyptian bureaucracy that could not see the wood for the trees. The Jongeli Canal, 300 kilometres long, would provide four milliard cubic metres of water annually to be shared by both countries. From now on it made sense to talk of Sudan as the bread-basket of the Middle East and the bastion for Egypt's plans for food security. The vast stretches of land to be developed needed several essentials, of which water was one.

This functional approach characterized the relationship for a few years to come. It also paved the way for meaningful co-ordination and consultation at both the technical and political levels. As we shall see later, since 1979 all this has been pushed to the back seat to give way to questions of defence and security, the major preoccupation of President Nimeiri rather than of Egypt.

Sudan and Libya

There is a tendency in Western political circles to appropriate all the blame for our quarrelsome and hostile relationship with Libya to Gaddafi, his incessant interference in the affairs of other countries and his harbouring of and assistance to opposition leaders. Nimeiri's incessant accusations of Gaddafi lend credence to this belief. None the less there are two facts that are overlooked by political observers: on the personal level Nimeiri's antipathy to Gaddafi equals, if not exceeds, the latter's hatred of Nimeiri and Gaddafi is not always to blame for the misfortunes of Sudan though he has never hesitated to exploit one if it came his way. So while some uprisings like the one of July 1976 were perpetrated with Libyan aid, others like the one of July 1971 or the current Southern Sudan insurrection and the several strikes by professionals were entirely Sudanese affairs. We have seen for example that the September 1975 coup was staged by some of the very elements that had moved to save Nimeiri and the regime in the summer of 1971. We have also seen that the root cause of the raging current civil war in Southern Sudan was Nimeiri's high-handed action in dealing with the division of the South, in spite of all the limitations imposed on the national government and the guarantees of autonomy provided by the Addis Ababa agreement and the constitution.

The abortive 1976 attempt to overthrow the Sudan government and Libya's implication in it increased Nimeiri's hatred and paranoia. The national reconciliation provided an occasion for patching up the relationship between the two neighbours. In this connection a very vigorous effort was undertaken by the First Vice-President, Abul Gasim Ibrahim, General Omar el Tayeb (Head of Security) and Sadiq el Mahdi who was entrusted with that mission by Nimeiri following the Port Sudan meeting. Later, when his friend and ally Sadat was assassinated and his feeling of insecurity increased, Nimeiri went overboard, launching a world-wide crusade against Gaddafi. This personal animosity between the two leaders played a cardinal role, not only in poisoning the atmosphere between Libya and Sudan but also in frustrating all efforts to achieve a *modus vivendi* between the two countries. Quiet diplomacy was always thwarted by eccentric tirades coming from one end or the other.

The first major clash took place in September 1972, when the Sudan forced five Libyan planes carrying military equipment to Uganda to land in Khartoum. Sudan believed that the role of African states was not to exacerbate the situation in that region, but rather to defuse it. There were some ominous skirmishes between Uganda and Tanzania. Gaddafi was irate and memories of his action in forcing down the BA plane carrying the leaders of the July 1971 coup against Nimeiri were fresh in his mind. His reaction was a short telex to Nimeiri saying: 'God forgive you.' He never forgave him himself. From then onwards it was a fight to death

319

between the two.

A tense, albeit correct relationship continued, and there was no war of words or verbal exchanges at the official level. In effect the efforts of the successive ambassadors of both countries were mainly directed towards maintaining bridges. Sudan was incensed at the hostile position taken by Libya towards the solution of the Southern Sudan conflict. Libya made a big hullabaloo about the mediation of church groups in the Southern affair. Efforts were mainly directed towards the restoration of relations to a normal and civilized if not confiding level. Our aim was to live and let live.

One such effort to improve relations, or at least arrest degeneration, was made during the meeting of the Arab League Council of Ministers in Cairo to discuss the issue of Arab aid to Africa. To that meeting I was reporting on behalf of the OAU ministerial committee of six, responsible for following up the implementation of the OAU summit resolution of Afro-Arab co-operation. Attention was drawn to the fact that two Arab states had not yet made their position clear as to the nature and size of their aid. No names were mentioned. Libya was one of the two countries, but I had neither time nor desire to exploit the situation for ulterior motives. I was there in an African capacity seeking to accomplish an African mission. It would have been both clumsy and counter-productive to use the occasion to embarrass a country simply because one was at odds with it on other issues.

The Libyans were appreciative; their head of delegation, Abdel Atti al Obeidi, conveyed that much. Obeidi thought that the occasion was propitious for discussion of our bilateral relations, adding that he would personally wish to see that the cloud hovering over those relations was soon dissipated. To those open arms I reciprocated by an invitation to him to visit Khartoum. A week later Obeidi arrived, fully authorized by Gaddafi to mend fences and restore propriety to the relations between Sudan and its neighbour.

As expected, Obeidi raised the question of Libya's representation in Khartoum, for though the Libyan embassy was carrying on its business normally in our capital city, that embassy had remained without a head of mission for months. The name of the new ambassador was lying on the President's desk awaiting agreement. Nimeiri was not in a hurry, in spite of several reminders to the President's office from the Protocol Department of MOFA.

Obeidi met the President the same day he arrived. The meeting soon warmed up and Nimeiri dominated it by anecdotal asides on his good old days with Gaddafi. There was much cracking of jokes and roaring laughter. The Libyan guest soon raised the question of the ambassador, only to be told that the President knew nothing of the matter. He would, however, soon give his instructions to MOFA. Obeidi extended an invitation to Nimeiri, on behalf of Gaddafi, which the former accepted. He went to Tripoli in November 1974, thus placing the seal of presidential approval on a new era of co-operation with Libya.

Nimeiri's disclaimer of any knowledge about the nomination of the Libyan ambassador was an insignificant incident in itself. In situations like this presidential aides were expected to act as shock absorbers and save their President all manner of diplomatic embarrassment. That was the way I took it then. With the benefit of hindsight, however, the issue could be viewed in a completely different light, particularly as the remark was uncalled for. All that the Libyans wanted to hear from the President was his agreement to the accreditation of their ambassador designate. With hindsight Nimeiri's reaction was in line with similar ones, not isolated, but part of a string of similar fibs. Whenever Nimeiri found himself in an embarrassing situation, including the ones he himself had created, his first response would be to absolve himself from personal responsibility by putting the blame elsewhere. On the other hand, whenever he felt that praise was to accrue to someone, he made sure that he was the one to receive the accolades. In this respect the restoration of good neighbourly relations between Sudan and Libya would be symbolized by the return of the ambassador, and sure enough the morning press saw to it that notice was served on the whole world that the President had kindly agreed to the nomination of Libya's ambassador designate, thus ushering in a new era in the relationship between the two sisterly countries. All these were symptoms of insecurity, for no adequate chief should be jealous of his own aides or gratuitously seek to undermine his own institutions.

Another reason why that insignificant incident is worth recalling is the opportunity it offers to compare Nimeiri's attitude to that of some of the personalities who had had the misfortune to work under his leadership. One such personality was First Vice-President Khalil, who was approached by the Soviet Ambassador after my removal from MOFA for the second time. The Ambassador called on Khalil to tell him that now, with the pro-American man out of the way, the two countries should try to patch up their differences. The ambassador was referring to the cessation of the services of ninety military experts on 12 May 1977, purely for reasons of military security. There were no political or ideological considerations behind the decision, which was taken at a time of great tension on the eastern borders. Military security thought that the presence of Soviet military experts on the other side of the border made the presence of their comrades in our midst too close for comfort. Khalil gave the ambassador a piece of his mind, adding that decisions such as that could not be determined by whim or simply be the work of any one person. They were matters of policy arrived at by institutions. He also added that the decision was conveyed to MOFA as the competent department simply to transmit it to the Soviets. Khalil had too great a sense of proper regard for his own institutions to allow them to be depreciated or slandered.

Relations between Sudan and Libya were yet to deteriorate to the point of severing diplomatic relations, which happened after the July 1976 events. The regime's anger was indeed justified. But, as in the case of the Soviets in July 1971, certain realities could not be erased from the map, e.g. the existence of other countries whether we liked it or not. This is much more true of neighbouring countries. In the case of Libya there was also a new dimension to our relationship: the presence of a large number of Sudanese living in that country, particularly after the oil boom. Sudanese diplomacy could not afford to be oblivious of such particulars.

So again in the second discredited period of 'cocktail diplomacy' (1977–8), we were to take another initiative to restore relations between the two countries. A meeting to this end was organized in Cairo, once again in the course of the Arab League Ministerial Council. Sheikh Sabah al Ahmed, the Foreign Minister of Kuwait, was the mediator and on the other side was Libya's Foreign Minister, Dr Ali Triki. Kuwait was looking after Sudanese interests in Tripoli. The dialogue was direct and frank with few ifs and buts. We both agreed that neighbours should learn to live together with due respect to national sovereignty and differing social and economic systems. At the regional level, Arab and African, while our aims were similar, ways and means to achieve those aims could be different. It was precisely because of inability to draw the line of demarcation in these issues that hopes for permanent good neighbourliness were often derailed. I told Dr Triki that, given the depth of the wounds of the 1976 events, our approach to normalization would have to be progressive, starting with the resumption of flights between Khartoum and Tripoli. In the end time and mutual comprehension would alleviate the grief caused by those events.

I was removed two weeks later from MOFA. Sheikh Sabah, mistakenly, related my removal to the Cairo meeting. 'I have a feeling of guilt; were you removed from MOFA because of your Libyan initiative? In Egypt they say walls have ears,' he told me. Nothing was further from the truth, there were other, more subversive things going on in Khartoum to justify my removal from government. One need not go through them here, for chapter 5 told them all.

Sudan and Ethiopia

The third neighbour with whom our relations followed a zigzag course during the May era was Ethiopia. In latter years the twists and turns were sharper and more erratic, Nimeiri often zigging when he should have zagged. Ethiopia, of Sudan's eight neighbours, is the country with whom we have the longest common borders (2,200 kilometres), with common tribes and interlocked interests all along those borders. The two countries are also fed by a number of rivers and streams, of which the Nile is only the main one. All these streams originate in Ethiopia. Given this physical and human contiguity, hundreds of thousands of people abandoning their homeland through political persecution, real or imagined, found refuge in the other country, Eritreans from Ethiopia and Southerners from Sudan.

That was the context in which we viewed our relations with Ethiopia; ideology, systems of government, rulers were all marginal. To us, the only objective reality policy-makers had to contend with was people and geography; both are there to stay. Such realities would undoubtedly look awry if policy-makers indulged in viewing them through ideological lenses, and an aberration if viewed through the distorting prism of personal prejudice. Our policy, therefore, was to start from a basic premise: we and the Ethiopians have to live together on the basis of live and let live. Not so many people in the early years of the May revolution viewed things that way, invariably because of ideological predilections.

The revolutionaries of the day would not have any truck with the imperial government of Ethiopia. The 1972 decrees defining the functions of MOFA stipulated that Sudan's relations with other countries were to be based on 'the principle of mutual respect for sovereignty'. To us in MOFA that was the guiding light in our actions and transactions with Ethiopia.

So in the course of 1971 and 1972 a vigorous campaign was launched to repair bridges and restore confidence. Our priorities were clear, addressing ourselves from the outset to areas of conflict, e.g. refugees, border encroachments and common waterways. There was no desire on our part to play the old game of clever negotiators who were often too clever by half. Things were to be called by their proper names without distortion of facts, for the Ethiopians knew what was happening in the Sudan as much as we also knew what was happening on their side of the borders. It was only with such a spirit of frankness that we were able to enlist each other's help in the solution of chronic bilateral problems going right to the root causes of some of them, i.e. Southern Sudan, Eritrea and the Nile waters. This open and frank approach enabled us not only to dispel the mistrust that had clouded our relations with Ethiopia, but also to usher in a golden era for those relations. Undoubtedly our job was faciliated at the functional level, to a large measure, by the reciprocal comprehension of our Ethiopian counterpart, the Foreign Minister, Dr Menassie Haile. He had both the perceptiveness and intellectual honesty to see Ethio-Sudanese relations beyond the biases of ideology and prejudice. For those who knew the Ethiopian political landscape he, too, was fighting a rearguard battle in Ethiopia.

In this atmosphere, and only because of it, Sudan was able to engage Ethiopia's support in the solution of Southern Sudan problems, paving the way for a role for the Sudan in the Eritrean cause (the three-point plan of 1975 for the cessation of hostilities leading to eventual negotiations, to which reference was made in chapter five). One of the most important diplomatic feats in 1972 was the conclusion of a definitive agreement on the Ethio-Sudanese borders. The problem, we recall, had been with us for over seventy-five years and there were at least a dozen communiqués between the two governments, asserting the opposed positions of the two parties. The boundary problem was made more complex by the intricate boundary treaties concluded in the last century by the European powers who controlled the area.

Came 25 July 1972 and this major thorny problem that had muddled relations between us was at long last laid to rest, only a little under five months after the conclusion of the Addis agreement.

In the course of the July 1972 border negotiations other important agreements were reached, e.g. plans to improve the road link between Sudan and Ethiopia (Metema-Gelabat), transit trade, improvement of telecommunications with a view to establishing microwave links from Sennar (south-eastern Sudan) with Ethiopia, utilization by Sudan of Ethiopian ports (Mossawa) to help ease the pressure at Port Sudan etc. However, one of the most important agreements reached was the one relating to joint technical discussions on common waters. Ethiopia had not yet got over the fact that it had been completely discounted at the 1959 negotiations between Egypt and Sudan over the Nile waters. Their anger was more in the nature of national pride bruised in being taken for granted.

The agreement itself did not discount the rights of other riparians; on the contrary, it provided that whenever claims over the Nile waters were formulated by a third-party state both Egypt and Sudan should define a common position in response to that claim (article 5 of the Nile Waters Agreement). Our strategy was to carry co-operation further by enlarging the Egypt–Sudan bilateral mechanism on the Nile to include other riparian states. We thought such an approach would be the only way to bring to an end all claims and counter-claims, eventually laying the ground for global management of the Nile by all riparians. This in essence is what African unity is all about. None the less, aware of the constraints of article 5 of the Nile Waters Agreement, which presupposes a joint Egyptian–Sudanese position before we can engage in negotiations with a third-party state on the regime of the Nile, both governments agreed on development programmes for common rivers other than the Nile, i.e. Baraka and Gash. On 10 February 1974 both parties drew up a plan for a joint project to be financed by the UNDP, on the basis of a joint request by the two governments, with a view to undertaking hydrometrological studies of the two rivers. The studies were to concentrate on developing the water resources of the river systems and the control and management of those resources. Concurrently both parties also agreed that a joint request be presented to the government of Finland to help in the physical implementation of the boundary agreement, e.g. identifying boundary areas and affixing marks along the 2,200-kilometre border. Finland had intimated to us, in the course of a goodwill visit to that country a few months earlier, that as a small country they wished to concentrate their technical assistance to Africa only on East Africa.

All these agreements remained the basis of co-operation between both countries for a few years after the overthrow of Haile Selassie's government. The 1972 agreement with Ethiopia was also the corner-stone of a trilateral agreement that brought Kenya in with her two neighbours. With Ethiopian help Sudan strove to achieve a boundary settlement with Kenya, where differences still existed regarding the south-eastern triangle.

Things were to deteriorate in the mid and late 'seventies following the heightening of the struggle against Ethiopia's new regime by both Eritreans and elements of the *ancien régime*. Sudan was accused by Ethiopia of giving comfort to these elements. Ethiopia, on the other hand, extended facilities to Sudan opposition elements, mainly Sharif el Hindi, who was beaming his war of words against the Sudan from Ethiopian soil. After the unsuccessful 1976 bid for power by the opposition and the 1977 reconciliation that ensued between Nimeiri and Sadiq el Mahdi the tension eased, while a few time-bombs remained undefused. A commendable effort was made by the Security Chief, General el Tayeb, and the Sudanese Ambassador to Addis Ababa, Mirghani Suleiman, and later on by the Minister of Defence, General Khalil, to reduce areas of conflict and place problems within their right context. Defence and security departments in the Sudan were the ones which had to carry the brunt of the conflict. Their concern was, therefore, justified. Meanwhile, the President went on personalizing the conflict. In addition to Gaddafi the 'madman' he has now added to his catalogue of presidential insults Mengistu the 'pirate'. The role of his immediate aides and advisers was, therefore, made difficult if not impossible. Presidents are normally expected to stay behind the scenes, calm and serene, healing wounds and playing the arbiter. In the Sudan the roles were reversed, making it hard for rational decision-making and much harder for the conduct of diplomacy. The Ethiopian head of state, chairman Mengistu, with all his excesses, tried to avoid personalizing the conflict. Indeed, he served notice on the Soviets that he meant business as far as the restoration of good neighbourly relations with Sudan was concerned.

Diplomacy and National Unity

So much for Sudan and its neighbours. Diplomacy, as far as including national interests was concerned, was to attend to some specific functions, e.g. national unity and development. As regards the former, our strategy from the outset was to concentrate on the Southern Sudan problem; its solution would be the corner-stone of unity. In one sense the improvement of relations with both our eastern and southern neighbours was an essential condition for the solution of that problem. The civil war in the Sudan was the embodiment of age-old fears and misconceptions, mainly created and fanned by colonialism but also perpetuated by the myopic and condescending attitudes of a large section of Northern politicians. The reality of a new African solidarity that transcends race, religion and nation had never dawned on some of these politicians. Among them the so-called 'Arabists' were in a more pitiful position than the others. Entrapped in their old parochial conceptions of Arabism and Africanism they hardly learned anything from the teachings of the apostle of modern Arabism, Nasser. It was, in fact, Nasser who, for the first time in Egyptian political history, brought the whole weight of Egypt behind African liberation, development and unity causes. Africa since Nasser was no longer a disposable quantum; it was to be viewed as a force and an ally. To us the solution of the Southern Sudan problem was not only the beginning of national cohesion nor the end of chauvinism and bigotry; it was a great contribution to African unity. Sudan, with all its different races, religions, languages, and other cultural attributes, is the microcosm of the continent.

Africans viewed the Addis agreement in that way, and this view came from both African political extremes. The veteran liberation leader Amilcar Cabaral (Guinea Bissau) told the African summit at Rabat (1973) that Sudan's peace achievement was the greatest contribution made to the cause of African liberation. Speaking on behalf of all African liberation movements, Cabaral declared to the summit that the Sudan was not called upon, for the time being, to extend a helping hand to the liberation movements; all its resources should henceforth be concentrated on consolidating unity. 'Africa needs a strong united Sudan,' he said. He also urged African countries to extend all possible help to Sudan to make a success of its newly won unity. Cabaral's noble thought and generosity never made Sudan abdicate its responsibility towards African liberation, for shortly after the Rabat summit Sudan received another eminent liberation leader, Augustino Neto (Angola) to finalize with him negotiations on the training of certain elements of the Angolan freedom fighters.

Similarly, President Senghor of Senegal saw the North-South accord as a giant step towards African unity. Addressing President Nimeiri at the same Rabat summit he said, 'I am not congratulating you on behalf of my country, nor on behalf of West African countries, but as an African historian who believes that African unity could not be achieved before the unity of its parts is achieved. Your name will be recorded in history as a hero among other heroes of Africa.' Sadly, Nimeiri's choice will make his name recorded for other ignominious acts (like the unmaking of the Addis Ababa agreement). Nimeiri could not die like a hero (the incidents of 1971, 1975 and 1976 showed it), but he could have lived like a hero had he had a better sense of history and purpose.

It was not only African unity that was to be enhanced by the restoration of peace to Sudan. Sudan's new image and its newly won African alliances enabled it also to play a more effective role in energizing African support for the Palestinian cause. Nimeiri's visit after the Addis agreement to countries like Gabon and the Ivory Coast (the first by an Arab president to those countries), helped a great deal to expose them to the realities of the Arab-Israeli conflict, changing their attitudes towards Arab causes and eventually leading to the severance by those countries of diplomatic relations with Israel in 1973. The Palestinian issue itself was included for the first time ever as an agenda item in the OAU meeting in 1972–3. The opposition to its inclusion had always come from those very countries claiming that the problem was an extra-African one and, therefore, should have no place in the agenda of the organization.

The Addis Ababa accord was not a result of a midsummer night's dream. It was a saga that requires a book of its own. However, in the preparatory work for the agreement as well as its implementation MOFA played a sizable role. At the outset, there was the expounding of our point of view to African and Western powers and organizations who were extending a helping hand to Southern fighters. Our aim was not only to convey Sudan's new vision of the problem but also to secure their support, co-operation and mediation. Without that support peace could not have been so easily achieved. Efforts were by no means restricted to the period immediately preceding the signing of the agreement, for there was also the active enlisting of financial aid for the resettlement of refugees and later on for the rejuvenation of the South.

To this end a conference for the repatriation of refugees was convoked in Khartoum a few months before the conclusion of the agreement. Prince Sadruddin Aga Khan, the UN High Commissioner for Refugees stood steadfastly behind us, with both the weight of his office and his personal prestige and wide network of contacts. Two other unknown soldiers in the refugee rehabilitation conference were Prince Henrik of Denmark who gave, by his personal presence, an impetus to the meeting and ensured a large Scandinavian contribution to the endeavour, and the other was Paul Marc Henry, president of the OECD Development Centre and a household name within the UN and international aid circles. Henry carried his effort further after the conclusion of the Addis Ababa agreement as chief co-ordinator of all UN aid for the rehabilitation of the South. The Addis agreement added to the momentum of the refugee conference. All the pledges made at that conference were the nucleus for the special fund established in 1973 to finance the repatriation and rehabilitation of refugees after the agreement. To that fund contributions, both in cash and kind, were made by Arab, African, Eastern and Western governments and international governmental and non-governmental organizations. Some of these governments and organizations established permanent aid offices in Juba (Southern Sudan), e.g. Kuwait and the Lutheran Federation.

Diplomacy and Development

Nimeiri maintained that the diplomacy he was seeking was that of development. Indeed it should have been. We shall come later in the chapter to Nimeiri's brand of diplomacy, the one he dictated and wanted carried out to the letter, and how it was related to development.

The term 'diplomacy for development' goes back to the Presidential Decree of 1972. The concerns of Sudanese diplomacy in the past were mainly limited to defending and safeguarding internal national interests, e.g. national security, self-preservation etc. But in a world of global interdependence these classical concepts of diplomacy are becoming increasingly outmoded. They are being replaced by a more sophisticated concept of an equitable balance of interests, whether one calls it *détente* and coexistence among the big powers or interdependence among the big, medium-sized and small states.

Between 15 and 20 January 1974 we organized an international symposium on diplomacy and development. Our hope was to engage international talent to help draw up a conceptual framework for development diplomacy, as well as to exchange views on how diplomatic tools can be refined to achieve desired ends. The meeting's agenda included issues like diplomacy and international co-operation, multilateral and bilateral aid as tools of development, diplomacy as an instrument of economic integration, development and new trends in the law of nations etc. The meeting was not a jamboree. The participants ranged from high-powered diplomats, e.g. the president of the UN General Assembly, Edvard Hambro (Norway) and Lord Caradon (UK) to leading development experts like Abdel Moniem Kayssouni (Egypt), Abdel Latif al Hamad (Kuwait) and Richard Gardiner, executive secretary of the UN Economic Commission for Africa (ECA). Government aid agencies were also represented at a very high level, e.g. Professor Karl Heinz Sohn, Minister of State of Technical Cooperation (GDR), Paul Marc Henry, chairman, OECD Centre, R. K. Anderson, director of the Norwegian Agency for Development etc. There were a number of parliamentarians, leading journalists and academics too. The symposium was not only an intellectual forum where minds interacted and young diplomats were exposed to the knowledge and experience of old hands in the trade, it was also an occasion for Sudanese professionals in finance, banking and trade to establish contacts or renew old ones with decision-makers in order to settle outstanding issues, engage in new commitments, or give first-hand information on plans, problems and achievements.

But diplomacy for development was not only an intellectual and public relations affair, it was also action at different levels, e.g. bilateral co-operation, regional integration and the international campaign to achieve a new order for global economic relations. We have alluded earlier to examples of the use of diplomacy to achieve developmental ends through bilateral mechanisms, e.g. the Jongeli Canal and joint food, security and agricultural projects with Egypt, assistance through governmental and non-governmental agencies for the rehabilitation of Southern refugees etc. We also had occasion to see samples of co-operation with the USA after the resumption of diplomatic relations, and with West Germany, which by 1976 had become Sudan's largest development aid partner in the West. The first economic and technical co-operation agreements between Sudan, Italy and France were also concluded in this period, setting the scene for co-operation in major development projects, e.g. France in the Jongeli project and Italy in road and bridge construction. Similar agreements were reached with other European countries, leading to the involvement of these countries in several development efforts, e.g. Austria in the electrification of pumps in many of Sudan's major agricultural estates, Denmark in agricultural development in Southern Sudan, Norway in the construction of roads joining Sudan and Kenya etc. As for Sudan's traditional development partner, the United Kingdom, the settlement of the dispute over the nationalization of British firms in Sudan, as we mentioned earlier, had opened the way for several joint endeavours in development, e.g. higher and general education, the construction, textile and sugar industries.

These bilateral endeavours have cut across ideological boundaries. For example, following the normalization of relations with the USSR and the socialist countries of Eastern Europe the first action undertaken with those countries was the revival of economic co-operation programmes: the cultural programme with Hungary (26 September 1973), protocols with Czechoslovakia (May 1973), East Germany (7 June 1973), the Soviet Union (May 1973). Co-operation with Hungary, in particular, assumed another dimension. Following the revival of the protocols for bilateral co-operation with the country and the successful deals with Sudan Railways for the provision of carriages, Hungary offered to engage on a tripartite basis with an Arab country in agricultural development in Sudan. The Hungarian Deputy Minister of Agriculture visited Sudan in December 1974 for that purpose. Kuwait was willing to join as a party in this trilateral endeavour, but nothing materialized on this score in view of the twist relations with Eastern Europe had taken in the late 'seventies. As to other socialist countries who had chosen to stand aloof from the July 1971 events, i.e. China, Romania and Yugoslavia, the period witnessed several economic co-operation agreements, e.g. with Romania on river transportation and construction (Parliament House), with China on the textile industry (Hassaheissa), the fish industry (Nuba lake) and rice plantations in Aweil (Southern Sudan), and with Yugoslavia on the revamping of Sudan's merchant marine.

Sudan, Saudi Arabia and the Gulf

The most significant evolution in our bilateral relations insofar as development was concerned was that relating to Saudi Arabia and the Gulf countries. The latter part of 1971 witnessed the end of the futile exchange of insults with our big neighbour across the Red Sea, which was the hallmark of the earlier phase of the May revolution. From the end of 1971 our strained relationship was replaced by serious constructive discussions and various joint ventures. Following the exchange of visits at ministerial level, President Nimeiri made his first official trip to Saudi Arabia between 30 April and 4 May 1972. That visit helped remove the clouds of doubt that had overshadowed the relationship between the countries for a couple of years, hampering joint endeavours and bringing to a grinding halt on-going ones. In the course of that visit and the ministerial missions that preceded it to help restore relations to a dignified level our aim was modest: resuming joint endeavours and improving communication channels. Confidence had to be restored before we could aspire to bigger things. Insofar as the improvement of communications was concerned both countries agreed to strengthen telephone communications through an underwater cable across the Red Sea. Relations soon warmed up and continued in the ascendant with the Saudis moving energetically into the Sudan development scene. A few projects, as we have seen, were aborted. In fact the institutionalized relationship between the two countries was marred only by the incessant interference of middlemen.

One very important agreement in this period, if only for its symbolism, was the conclusion on 16 May 1974 of the agreement to explore and exploit jointly the mineral resources of the Red Sea. Saudi Arabia, in the course of the UN debate on the laws of the sea, announced that the limits of its territorial waters extended to 200 nautical miles. This claim would have impinged on Sudan's rights and our view was expressed to the Saudi Foreign Minister, Sakkaf. In view of the excellent relations that obtained between the two countries, both of us agreed that differences should be composed through quiet diplomacy and a creative approach. There was a need to look for an imaginative framework for co-operation in the Red Sea in a way that would safeguard the interests of both countries without impinging on their primordial sovereign rights. The matter was entrusted to our Attorney-General, Dr Zaki Mustafa, who was handling the law of the sea negotiations at the UN on the Sudan side, and Dr Zaki Yamani on the Saudi side. Yamani is also a lawyer in his own right. The new arrangement worked out by the two lawyers involved the establishment of a joint authority charged with supervising the exploration and eventual exploitation of the mineral riches of the bed of the sea. The jointly owned area was defined as the point where the depth of the sea reached 1,000 metres on both sides (the greatest depth of the Red Sea is established at 7,254 feet). The continental shelf and territorial waters beyond this point should be deemed to be under the sovereignty of the littoral state on either side. The Red Sea Authority was created soon afterwards, financed by Saudi Arabia.

The economic gains which our improved relationship with the West, Saudi Arabia and the Gulf Arab countries allowed were enormous. The new, more balanced and conciliatory approach in foreign policy paved the way for tripartite co-operation, i.e. Arab money and European finance and technology brought together to harness Sudan's natural wealth.

The ayatollahs of socialism who viewed the improvement of relations with the West as a sell-out were not all too pleased with the *rapprochement* with the so-called conservative Arab states either. For them, to be progressive was to align yourself with one bloc and contrive enmity with the other. On the Arab level, to be revolutionary is to befriend the so-called progressive countries and keep at arm's length from the kingdoms and sheikhdoms. We were not deterred, for the price to be paid in terms of development for this foolhardy approach was too great. The priorities of any rational policy in the developing world are development, development and development. No such development can be achieved without large inputs of external resources. This in turn can be attained only through well planned political and diplomatic dialogue to secure support for development from both bilateral and multilateral sources, encouraging foreign investment, promoting trade, improving and streamlining bilateral, regional and multilateral aid mechanisms. In a world of regional integration and global interdependence all countries must learn to live with each other on the basis of mutual respect.

In this connection, i.e. regional co-operation and global inter-dependence, Sudanese diplomacy was engaged on two fronts: harnessing regional resources through established regional mecha-nisms and labouring hard with the countries of the third world to help restore an equitable balance to international economic re-lations. At the regional level of improved relations with Saudi Arabia and the enhancement of co-operation with Kuwait (which was engaged in several development endeavours with Sudan at both the public and private levels), we were up for bigger things. Development, in a country as large as Sudan, would have to be, if anything, on a large scale. We referred in Chapter 2 to several projects financed by Kuwait which were either addressed to improving infrastructure, like the satellite station and the pipeline, or preparing the ground for future investment, e.g. master plans for transportation, grain storage etc. However, the major project concluded during this period was the creation of the Arab Auth-ority for Agricultural Development (AAAD).

The story of the AAAD goes back to discussions that took place with the Foreign Ministers of Kuwait and Saudi Arabia (Sabah el Ahmed and Omar Sakkaf) at the Arab Summit in Algiers in September 1972, with a view to organizing a conference for Arab governments to pledge finances for Sudan's ambitious agricultural programme. Bilateral aid was already secured or in the process of being secured for a few individual projects, e.g. Rahad, Kenana etc. Other major projects both in rain-fed and irrigated areas were on the drawing-board, e.g. animal production in Western Sudan, grains in Eastern and Southern and South-Eastern Sudan, new irri-gation schemes from untapped resources like the Atbara river, including the Setit dam etc.

Following the New York discussions letters were sent out to the Foreign Ministers of Saudi Arabia, Kuwait, Bahrain, Qatar and the UAE. A similar letter was also addressed to Sayed Marei, assistant to President Sadat. Answers to all these letters were soon received, all in the affirmative except for that of Kuwait. Kuwait communicated instead the views expressed by that country's Minister of Finance, Abdel Rahman al Attigi, an ardent friend of Sudan and an old hand in the world of finance and investment. He advised a different approach; rather than calling a pledging con-ference one of the Arab development funds should be entrusted with the preparation of a master plan for agricultural development in the Sudan, based on both national plans and relevant regional studies. The plan should be ready within a limited period of time. On the basis of that plan and the analysis of its financial implications Arab countries should be invited to commit themselves to a permanent agricultural fund. The fund should not be limited to government contributions, but should also be empowered to attract both Arab and non-Arab investors.

On 19 January 1974 Attigi's proposition and our agreement to it were conveyed to the five governments. On the same day the State Minister for Commerce, Hassan Beleil, who was on a mission to Kuwait, was telexed by MOFA to follow up the proposal with Kuwait's Finance Minister. In the course of 1974 the study was completed and the AAAD was born. It was not an easy birth, since a few countries were of the idea that the agricultural development programme should not be limited to Sudan. Others were against having the seat of the fund in Khartoum. It was a tough battle for Sudanese diplomacy. Fortunately we were not alone in that battle; all those who sponsored the idea insisted on concentrating efforts on Sudan, given its size and potential for agricultural development. Being the major contributors to the new fund, they carried the day.

To give meaning to our claim on South-South and tripartite cooperation we decided to use our ambitious agricultural development programme as a test case. To that end we called for a high-powered meeting in Khartoum. The world was then engrossed in yet another crisis; in 1973 it was energy, in 1974 it was food. A world conference under the auspices of the UN (FAO) was organized in Rome in November 1974. Its final report said that the problem of famine which had haunted man through history 'had now taken an unprecedented scale and urgency and could only be dealt with by concerted worldwide action'. The conference set as an objective the removal of hunger and malnutrition within a decade. The conference also reaffirmed that high priority should be given to policies and programmes for increasing food production in developing countries so as to achieve a minimum agricultural growth rate of 4 per cent per annum.

The theme of the Khartoum meeting was what should be done after Rome. In addition to Sudanese Ministers and experts involved in development, agriculture, irrigation etc., the meeting was attended by representatives of FAO (Sartaj Aziz), the World Food Programme (Francisco Aquino) and the United Nations (Richard Gardiner). The regional organizations also participated, sending William E. Mboumoua (secretary-general of the OAU), Kamal Ramzi Stino (Arab Agricultural Development Organization) and Abdel al Sakkban (Council of Arab Economic Unity). To give meaning to the concept of South-South co-operation representatives of three third world countries leading in agricultural development were also present: Jagjivan Ram, India's Minister of Agriculture, Osman Badran, the Egyptian Minister of Agriculture and Malik Khanda, special assistant to the Prime Minister of Pakistan on agriculture. Among the development aid agencies the meeting had occasion to listen to the views of the Kuwait Development Fund, the EEC, the Norwegian Agency for Development etc. Attending too were representatives of private financial and business entities like ENI (Italy), Chase Manhattan and the Agrobusiness Council (USA) and Sogreah (France). Sudan's master plan for agriculture, which was presented both by the country's Minister of State for Agriculture (Dr Hussein Idris) and one of the chief Arab experts who helped articulate the plan (Dr Khalid Tahsin Ali), was the centre of discussion by this eminent group. Sudan in its striving to develop its own resources sought to be outward-looking, for indeed this is the essence of global interdependence.

As regards the international economic situation, Sudan strove with countries of the third world towards the creation of a new scheme of global economic relations. Our aim was to achieve positive mutual co-operation within a context of equality and sovereignty. The reconstruction of international economic relations is not only limited to North/South relations, it goes beyond that to South-South co-operation, a review of international economic accords like Bretton Woods and the restructuring of international economic institutions. In all these areas Sudan was in the forefront with other countries at the regional, continental and international levels, e.g. Sudan's role with Arab countries in expounding ideas for securing sensible trade policies following the energy crisis of 1973 (Copenhagen summit and West European visits), Sudan's participation with Africa in creating permanent structures for Afro-Arab co-operation (the efforts of the Committee of Seven to ensure energy aid to Africa and the creation of the Arab Bank for African Development based in Khartoum) and at the international level Sudan's active participation in the Lomé negotiations and those relating to the restructuring of the UN system to make it more responsive to the challenges of a new international economic order.

The Watershed

The years 1975 and 1983 are described as watershed years in Sudan's internal politics. In 1975 Nimeiri dealt his first major blow to the institution builders: the coup proved to be the first of a series of palace coups against the executive arm of the state and signified the triumph of the palace cabal and the beginning of the end of Nimeiri's constitutional Presidency. 1983, on the other hand, witnessed the destruction of the institutions in three palace coups, against the SSU, the South and the judiciary, following that against the Army in 1982. The watershed year in foreign policy was undoubtedly 1978.

Controlling Presidential Excesses

In the period before 1978, Nimeiri operated to a lesser or greater extent within the limits and along the lines prescribed by MOFA, having recourse to his Ministers and his diplomatic corps for guidance and information. Apart from the control exercised by Foreign Ministers with varying degrees of efficiency and forcefulness, there were several other reasons for this disciplined activity. First and foremost there was the need to pay lip-service to the causes which he outwardly espoused in an effort to contain the opposition, i.e. el Mahdi and el Hindi. This had a mitigating effect on his relationship with Sadat's Egypt, Libya and the Soviet Union in that it acted as a check on his tendency to express unconditional support for Sadat and blind hatred for Gaddafi. As for the Soviet Union, it meant the maintaining of a certain semblance of non-alignment. The other restraining and mitigating factor was the role played by certain SSU elements in tempering and diluting his extremism towards the Soviet Union, chief among whom was Badr el Din Suleiman. There was also the role played by Defence Minister Abd el Magid Khalil and Head of Security Omar el Tayeb as far as his relationships with Ethiopia and Libya were concerned. They were the ones who knew about what was happening on the ground, so to speak, and who appreciated the need to defuse crises diplomatically.

In the first ten years of his rule Nimeiri had ample opportunities to be exposed to the outside world. One would have expected that this experience would have broadened his horizons and instilled in him an appreciation of international diplomacy, as well as an awareness of limitations for himself and his country. However, megalomania and an oversized ego led Nimeiri to believe that he had mastered the art of foreign policy and that he could go it alone, replicating internationally what he was doing internally. There was no lack of toadies around to confirm Nimeiri's image of himself.

Since he had completely marginalized his institutions and discarded his advisers (both Ministers and diplomats) Nimeiri depended more and more on his palace cabal, the speech-writers and others who were as myopic as their master. With the extension of their activities into foreign policy Sudan entered the period of megaphone diplomacy, that is, diplomacy through the media. Last but not least there was also the influence of the soldiers of fortune like Adnan Khashoggi; not that Mr Khashoggi had been idle in this respect in the past. We have dwelt in a chapter almost entirely devoted to him on how, wishing to pose with the Pope and wanting to endear himself to King Faisal, he came up with a scheme to solve the Jerusalem problem and also how he constantly bombarded Sudanese embassies in order to secure VIP treatment from some of them (London and Beirut), against all protocol conventions.

One might mention here another of Khashoggi's forays into the sphere of international diplomacy which took place before the watershed year of 1978. This was in June 1977, when he wanted to use Sudan's political weight to get a friend of his out of trouble. During Nimeiri's official visit to China in 1977 I was informed by the Sudanese ambassador, Mubarak Rahama, on my arrival in Peking, that Adnan was desperately trying to get in touch with Nimeiri in time. He wanted him to insert a denunciation of the coup in the Seychelles, which had taken place the day before, as Soviet inspired. I asked him to convey the message personally to the President. Nimeiri unquestioningly asked me to do what Khashoggi asked of him. I told him what I knew and thought of the Seychelles coup, that the conflict between Mancham, the overthrown President, and René, the new President, was one between two war-lords. René, the coup perpetrator, may have been supported by Tanzania but certainly the Soviets had nothing to do with the matter. Nimeiri was not impressed, retorting, 'How did you know?' as if it was not the job of the Foreign Minister to monitor African affairs. I decided to come out with it saying that the story of Soviet involvement would only have come from Khashoggi. He asked why with annoyance. I told him of Khashoggi's friendship with the ex-President (a known frequenter of Parisian pleasure circles) and how the former was casting a covetous eye on the island known as the Garden of Eden. It has tremendous opportunities for investment, particularly in the tourist industry. Sure enough no reference to the Seychelles was made in Nimeiri's banquet speech.

By a providential coincidence, a couple of years later my suspicions about Khashoggi's relationship with Mancham were confirmed when Khashoggi's name was mentioned in the UN commission of inquiry report on the Seychelles coup attempt against René in 1981 as the one who procured arms for the coupmakers. Although the London-based Seychelles exiles who were interviewed by the UN commission said they did not think Khashoggi was directly involved, some of the mercenaries implicated in the Seychelles said that the arms they used had been obtained by the leader of the coup attempt, Colonel 'Mad' Mike Hoare, through Khashoggi (quoted in *The Weekly Review*, 15 June 1984). Khashoggi, it seems, was determined to retain a foothold in the island, a mooring-place for his pleasure boat and his holiday resort at Beau Vallon on the island of Mahé, which René had confiscated. Khashoggi's involvement in the 1981 coup attempt against René was brought up by the Kenyan assistant commissioner of police, Jeremiah Odene Odede, in his report to the Njonjo commission of inquiry which was investigating the licensing of arms imports to Kenya. Besides drawing the commission's attention to Khashoggi's involvement in the Seychelles coup, Odede dwelt on how Khashoggi was 'introduced by high-ranking government officials as a "VIP" who should be given assistance by the firearms bureau and customs department to acquire firearms licences and import guns into the country [Kenya]' (ibid.).

Revolutionary Sudan identified itself, for the first year or so, with the so-called progressive states. Like all progressive regimes, Sudan sought to underline this by lending recognition to progressive states. Thus East Germany was recognized in 1969 and so was North Korea; not South Korea, however. Wishing to break its political isolation, the South Koreans went around the third world making financial promises in return for recognition. It was another occasion for Khashoggi to meddle in Sudan's foreign policy, for he had connections with Chairman Kim's Dawoo group. Khashoggi secured an audience for the Koreans with Nimeiri. They pressed for recognition. Since Sudan's revolutionary and pre-revolutionary regimes had always maintained that the problem of the Koreas could only be solved through unification, our response in MOFA was lukewarm. The records of the special political committee of the UN General Assembly reflect this position taken by consecutive Sudanese governments. I maintained that this policy should be kept to. I also insisted that contact with the Koreans should not be made at any level higher than that of Under-Secretary for Economic Co-operation and the Head of the Asia Division in MOFA.

To me the objection was not one of principle; after all we had recognized North Korea and were dealing with it. That, however, was a political and sovereign act. The same could have applied to the South, for South Korea is a country that had made giant strides in development and there were lots of things that we could do with them. For the time being we could co-operate with South Korea without going into fully fledged diplomatic relations, e.g. working through trade centres. Recognition should come in the fullness of time, and not be rammed down our throats by others, particularly soldiers of fortune who wanted to use the Sudan for their own ends. Khashoggi and Chairman Kim promised Nimeiri the moon as a price for recognition: hundreds of millions for road construction, agriculture, industry. He believed them. Invitations were extended by the Seoul government to several Ministers, including myself. My response was that while technical Ministers could visit Seoul to discuss specific projects, the Foreign Minister should not go there before recognition. Nimeiri insisted and I persisted. He acquiesced only to wait for my departure to the UN for the General Assembly meeting.

No sooner had I left for New York than he instructed the State Minister for Foreign Affairs, Dr Francis Deng, to undertake the trip. Dr Deng called me in New York and I advised him to tell the President that my argument still stood and that the visit was untimely. The US Congress and administration (President Carter) were then launching a vehement attack on the Seoul regime for abuse of human rights and corruption. These were the friends and overlords of the Seoul government. Two days later it was all over the wires, the visit of the Sudanese Foreign Minister to Seoul.

Nimeiri forced Deng to undertake the mission. As for the hundreds of millions for development, we have already seen a glimpse of them in a hotel and a celebrated tyre factory. Not that South Korea could not have done more, but those who were pressing for recognition were merely concerned with securing quick returns for themselves. South Korea's contribution to the development of Sudan should not, none the less, be deprecated, for they made another important contribution to the people of Sudan by ensuring the safety and security of their beloved leader. Dawoo was responsible for the installation of the palace electronic surveillance devices, supervised by Dr Idris, as well as the construction of Nimeiri's official residence in the Army barracks with its bunkers.

Another good example of the role played by MOFA in curbing the adventurism of the Nimeiri clique was during an attempt to involve Sudan militarily in a war in the tip of the Arabian peninsula. In 1974, following an agreement between the Shah's Iran and Iraq on the Shat al-Arab waterway (the Algiers agreement), the Shah decided to pull out his troops that had been fighting alongside Sultan Qabus' against the Dhufar rebels. The Sultan, wanting to fill the vacuum created by the Iranian withdrawal, used a Libyan, 'Omar Yahya' as a go-between between himself and Nimeiri. Yahya was one of the elements introduced to Nimeiri through the good offices of Dr Idris. The Libyan managed to secure a foothold inside the Khartoum palace by making his private plane available to take the President to West and North Africa in 1974. I knew nothing of the contacts between Nimeiri and Yahya until I caught wind of the news of the presence of the Omani Foreign Minister, Qais Zawawi, and the Defence Minister, Fahar ben Timour, in Khartoum. I immediately got in touch with my Omani counterpart, whereupon I learnt that he had come to Sudan with proposals from Sultan Qabus and that he had asked about me but had been told that I was out of the country.

I phoned Nimeiri, and, incredible as it may sound, he played possum. He thought, he told me, that Dr Idris would have informed me. The Omanis, he explained, wanted us to send an expeditionary force to fight in Dhufar. I told Nimeiri that we ought to consider the political implications of such an action and its likely consequences, particularly in view of the fact that the Arab League had formed a special committee to look into the matter and try to reach a negotiated settlement. The secretary-general of the League, Mahmoud Riyad, was entrusted with that mission. I insisted that Nimeiri should not meet the Omani Ministers until we had formulated a policy at MOFA and until the matter was amply discussed with the Army. Nimeiri has a tendency to take everybody for granted, including the Army. He agreed to the proposition and I immediately contacted the Chief of Staff, General Bashir Mohammed Ali. General Ali and myself met in my office. I expressed our point of view, which was simply that Sudan had never sent such an expeditionary force before and that, on the contrary, our military involvement has always been as a peace-keeping force; such was our role during the Congo crisis, the squabble between Qasem's Iraq and Kuwait in the 'sixties and later in Lebanon. Sending an expeditionary force would constitute a breach with our past tradition of not taking sides in military disputes. General Ali agreed.

I telephoned Nimeiri and told him about our decision, whereupon he said to my surprise, unashamedly, 'But these people have come for this purpose and are ready to give us a grant of $3,000,000.' I told Nimeiri that he could tell our Omani friends that the matter had been referred to the appropriate departments and that we were ready meanwhile to continue consultations with them. Nimeiri met the Omanis and received a cheque for $3,000,000 from Sultan Qabus. The cheque was handed over to the Minister of Finance, Ibrahim Mansour, whom I prevailed on the President to invite to the meeting; not easily though. Nimeiri, before handing over the cheque to his Minister of Finance, made the foolish remark, 'but the cheque is drawn in the name of the President.' To that Mansour answered, 'Everything in the government of Sudan is under the President including our Central Bank.'

The two Omani ministers understood our predicament. Both are seasoned and level-headed men. They insisted, however, that in view of the urgency of the matter we should immediately proceed with them for further consultation in Muscat. General Ali, Jamal Ahmed, then adviser to the Foreign Minister, and I flew with the two Ministers to Oman. There we made it clear to our Omani interlocutors that our active participation in the fighting was out of the question, that all we could do was to offer military and technical assistance and training for their personnel, as we were doing elsewhere in the Gulf. In Arab disputes we were ready to take part only as a peace-keeping force within the context of the Arab League, we maintained.

Running Amok

As Nimeiri emancipated himself and got rid of the yoke of institutions, bureaucrats and officials, the palace cronies were given
free reign. There was no one to hold them back. The doors of
foreign affairs were also open to newcomers, to more soldiers of
fortune. Nimeiri was, from then on, running amok, and foreign
policy became free for all.

It was not only the palace cabal who worked in Khashoggi's PR
department but also Nimeiri himself, who undertook a visit to
Spain in the watershed year. The purpose of that goodwill mission
was in effect to introduce Khashoggi to Spanish dignitaries. Khashoggi, wanting to make inroads into Spain's industry, was chosen
to carry a letter from Nimeiri to the Spanish King and entrusted
with the preparations for the President's visit, a task which our
embassy staff in Madrid were deemed incompetent to carry out by
themselves. Later, in order to strengthen the Khashoggi–Spanish
connection Nimeiri prevailed upon the Army to buy Spanish arms
through Khashoggi. The deal was negotiated by Khashoggi's
envoy, Abdel Rahman al Asir, who met the President on his sick-
bed. The President was then indisposed and all his appointments
were cancelled, including the ones with his own Ministers. As to
the Army, which had a list of its own, its officers were told what
their real needs were; Khashoggi had already determined them.
The incident took place after the air raid on Omdurman. One
would have thought that the Army needs then would have been
something in the nature of air defence and early warning systems.
And indeed, that was what the Army had asked for. Nimeiri
wanted them to buy Spanish personnel carriers and river transport
barges.

Adnan Khashoggi is larger than life itself. He aims high and
goes for the big fish; when he used Nimeiri, he asked him to meet
popes and kings. Sad as it may sound, one cannot help admiring the
Saudi wheeler-dealer for his ability to employ heads of state as his
PR men. Others, however, lesser men than Khashoggi, managed
to use Nimeiri for their own petty purposes and less grandiose
schemes, such as obtaining an entry visa, as did Ahmed Yahya al
Shorafa, a young Yemeni. This young man had just graduated

from the Khartoum medical school and was introduced to Nimeiri by God knows who. The Yemeni claimed he had good connections with the Canadians and that he wanted to help the Sudan. He offered to carry a letter from Nimeiri to Trudeau. Nimeiri was never short of words so he wrote a letter to Trudeau which the Yemeni dutifully carried, and that was that. Trudeau received the letter and the Yemeni did his business.

On his way back he stopped in London and got in touch with the Sudanese embassy, claiming to be the President's adviser and asking them to arrange for him to meet the Minister of Overseas Development. His credentials were a copy of Nimeiri's letter to Trudeau. The diplomats must have said to themselves, if he could meet heads of government, why couldn't he meet the lesser souls? The meeting was arranged, unfortunately for the Yemeni, with Neil Marten. Marten was just back from Khartoum where he attended a conference on refugees. The two met. The Yemeni started to talk in platitudes about the Sudan, repeating the often heard statistic: Sudan is the largest country in Africa, it has many million acres of arable land etc. and is, he concluded, a perfect place for investment. Marten cut him short and told him what he knew about the Sudan and what the UK was doing there. The British were the last people to be educated about Sudan by Mr Shorafa. Marten then said sarcastically, 'Why don't you put your Yemeni hat on and let us discuss aid to Yemen?' For those who know the Sudan well, like Marten, this could hardly be the country they knew. Stories like this not only show the abyss to which Sudanese diplomacy had plunged, but also the disgrace the President brought on a country that deserves and is capable of better. The many lacerated souls among his diplomats, young and old, were left with nothing but a sense of loss and self-depreciation.

Egypt: Back to Sloganism

Having taken foreign policy into his own hands Nimeiri became more and more of a liability to his friends and a source of embarrassment to the Sudanese. In the first part of this chapter we spoke, for instance, of what we have achieved with the Egyptians on the basis of the principle of economic complementarity, which nearly became an alternative to the empty slogans of unity between Egypt and Sudan which had never been articulated. The functional concept of unity, which was mainly geared towards economic integration and co-ordination in other areas, had become of late more and more in the nature of a defence and security pact. The centre of gravity shifted from the economy to security as Nimeiri's insecurity increased; more visits to the Sudan by Defence Ministers and Ministers responsible for security, than Ministers of Agriculture, Irrigation and Planning. The fact that for Nimeiri unity is synonymous with mutual defence arrangements is borne out by his speeches on integration with Egypt, whose purpose was to serve notice to the Ethiopians and the Libyans by rattling the Egyptian sabre. In the process Nimeiri has often embarrassed Egypt, for example, by his references to an Egyptian-Sudanese military role in Chad, to which Egypt always reacted by asserting that its actions in that country would only be guided by the resolutions of the OAU.

This period also witnessed a return to sloganism, to political niceties and rigmarole. Thus we had the creation of a common Parliament (the Nile Valley Parliament) with no powers whatsoever (not that our National Assembly had any) and a series of visits and photographic sessions with Sadat and later Mubarak. The personalization of the relationship was the very thing we tried to guard against by creating the various institutions and committees. The functional working relationship was simply replaced by an exchange of flatulent statements which were designed to impress and deter.

The creation of the common parliament was portrayed as a step taken in order to accelerate the process of integration, but the Egyptians, who knew better, would not swallow the bait. The parliament had only the one, inaugural meeting and all other scheduled meetings were cancelled, in spite of Nimeiri's incessant promptings. With Nimeiri's erratic foreign exploits and his misguided religiosity Egypt could not afford to give Nimeiri and his vicars an opportunity to use that forum for advocating policies pernicious not only to Egypt's foreign relations but also to the very cohesion of Egypt itself. Egypt is a country which is maintained by careful religious balances.

Another step taken with this end of complete integration in view was the instruction to Sudanese and Egyptian embassies and delegations abroad to co-ordinate with each other on matters and issues affecting the two countries. On important issues, embassies were

345

told, there should be total agreement. This again was lip-service to unity, for, as we shall show later, no such co-ordination ever took place on major issues, simply because Nimeiri's (not Sudan's) priorities were elsewhere. There was a divergence of views on the condemnation of South Africa on apartheid, the issue of Grenada and Sudan's involvement in Libya's case against the USA in the Gulf of Sirte incident.

The best example of such a lack of co-ordination, at the highest level between Egypt and the Sudan, was Nimeiri's failure to attend the meeting of the non-aligned movement in New Delhi. Egypt dispatched its Minister of State, Boutros Ghali, to impress on Nimeiri the importance of his participation at the non-aligned summit. Egypt, with some countries striving hard to isolate her in all international forums, needed her friends to be around at New Delhi. Nimeiri opted not to go to India for health reasons, although, while the meeting was in session, he flew over India to South Korea. There were no business deals in India.

In the first part of this chapter we alluded to Sudan's effort with her sister nations in the third world to achieve a new international economic order through North–South dialogue, as well as the enhancement of South–South co-operation. Nimeiri has been paying lip-service to this idea as late as 1983, making various statements about South–South co-operation, particularly during the Socialist Inter-African congress in Khartoum. He also made this theme the basis of his trip to South Korea. South–South co-operation, however, is not a two-country affair, it is both a political engagement and a common endeavour by the third world countries within the framework of relevant international institutions, such as the non-aligned summit and UNCTAD.

Nimeiri deliberately missed the Delhi meeting of the non-aligned countries, in spite of his being advised that among the themes to be discussed there would be the formulation of policy options for the non-aligned countries in UNCTAD IV. The third world needed to formulate a new strategy after the débâcle of Cancun. The advice came both from those with whom policy was to be co-ordinated (Egypt) as well as his diplomats, who took his statements on international economic issues seriously.

As for UNCTAD Nimeiri decided that Sudan should not be represented at ministerial level at the UNCTAD meeting in Belgrade. Sudan could not afford it, he told his entreating Ministers. The country was in dire financial straits. But a few months later the country that was so hard up was able to pay for Nimeiri's holiday visit to Italy and France, accompanied by no fewer than 120 persons, fifteen of whom were of ministerial rank. He begrudged Belgrade one Minister. To underscore the importance of the UNCTAD meetings, Indira Gandhi (representing the non-aligned movement), Husni Mubarak (his ally) and Nyerere, as well as other heads of state, were there addressing the meeting. Nimeiri was accompanied to Seoul by several aides, including the head of the Military Economic Corporation. There were deals to be concluded. Coordinating with and extending a helping hand to Mubarak at New Delhi and formulating a new strategy for the South at Belgrade were not endeavours that pay; they deserve only lip-service and SSU pronouncements.

Ethiopia: Presidential Quarrels

Our relationship with Ethiopia underwent the same pernicious process of personalization. Nimeiri had always been prone to attacking Mengistu, calling him the pirate and calling Ethiopia Abyssinia in the period of diktat diplomacy. The departments of Defence, Security and Foreign Affairs worked hard averting crises and mending fences that Nimeiri smashed. One such attempt took place in Gabon in 1977. There was a harsh exchange between the two Presidents during the OAU summit meeting at Libreville. Mengistu initiated the debate by a vehement attack on Sudan, accusing it of meddling in Ethiopian affairs. The Ethiopian head of state was inflamed by Nimeiri's personalized attacks. In fairness to him, Nimeiri had accepted our advice not to say a word about Ethiopian–Sudanese relations in his address that preceded Mengistu's. His prepared speech was drastically changed accordingly. We were already engaged in an attempt to mend fences through the good offices of the then Liberian Foreign Minister, Cecil Dennis, and we could not afford any hiccups. To that address by Mengistu we answered in kind. No sooner had the meeting ended than both Ministers, in the presence of their Liberian counterpart, met to continue the debate about arresting further deterioration in the relationship, for the relationship had to be maintained despite the quarrels of Presidents. As a follow-up to our meeting the two Presidents met in Freetown, Sierra Leone, less than a year later. I had left the Ministry by then to go to the SSU.

Khalil, the Minister of Defence, and el Tayeb, Head of Security, continued afterwards to exercise a restraining influence on Nimeiri and to work for conciliation until Nimeiri's coup against the South, the rekindling of the Southern war and the influx of Southern refugees into Ethiopia. That presented the Ethiopian regime with a golden opportunity. Nimeiri had promised to raise an army from the ranks of the Ethiopian refugees in Sudan and topple the 'Communist puppets'; now they were threatening to do the same. Mengistu, to be fair to him too, was genuinely interested in establishing a good working relationship with Nimeiri after Libreville and Freetown. Witness, for instance, the remarks he made during his visit in 1982 to the Soviet Union. During the banquet that was held in honour of the Ethiopian delegation, the Soviet leader did not mention Sudan in his speech. Mengistu, however, took up the subject and interposed a statement to the effect that Ethiopia had excellent relations with the Sudan and that the relationship was one between two peoples who outlive governments. Mengistu was well aware of the antipathy between the Soviets and Nimeiri and was keen to impress upon them that he did not want this antipathy to affect adversely his relationship with Sudan. He was also serving notice on the Marxist diehards at home who were not overjoyed by the Nimeiri–Mengistu *rapprochement*.

Kill Gaddafi

As we said above, national reconciliation and the need to pay lip-service to it was one moderating factor in Nimeiri's relations with some countries, especially Libya. He had undertaken in his meeting with Sadiq in the summer of 1977 to work for a better relationship with Gaddafi and charged Sadiq with the task of opening negotiations with the Libyan leader. Again there was a role to be played by Omar el Tayeb in calming the situation. After a brief calm spell on the Nimeiri–Gaddafi front in the wake of all those missions scurrying to Tripoli, Nimeiri launched his personal crusade against the 'Communist puppet' Gaddafi, more bitter and more damaging than ever.

In April 1981 Nimeiri called for a worldwide crusade against Gaddafi. He said he was at war with Colonel Gaddafi and added,

'I think all the world should try to get rid of him.' The West, he claimed, 'was not doing enough because it needed Libyan oil. . . . We have to do something together to get this man out of the government by any kind of war, by taking him out, killing him. . . . Nonetheless,' he maintained, 'we do not want to become the Cubans of the United States.' What he wanted was US financing for improving rudimentary Sudanese facilities to deter Soviet threats against Sudan. Such facilities, he added, could be made available to other friendly forces. Nimeiri reiterated his interest in a US training mission in Sudan, especially in military intelligence. And, playing on the Reagan administration's paranoia about Communism, he noted how the Soviet KGB had helped Gaddafi operate in Africa (quoted from the *International Herald-Tribune*, 2 April 1981).

1983 witnessed another round of the anti-Gaddafi tirade. Nimeiri instructed his UN ambassador to take part in the Security Council debate on the Gulf of Sirte incident, in which American planes shot down two Libyan fighters. Libya took its case against the USA to the Security Council. The debate was mainly between the two contenders. Libya was supported by the Soviets and several Western European members of the Council chose not to engage in the debate. Sudan, which was not a member of the Security Council, chose to. Nimeiri, in spite of the urgings of his diplomats, insisted that the Sudan, a non-member, should participate in the debate and side with the USA. On the other hand, Egypt, with whom co-ordination on diplomatic matters was made an article of faith, did not participate in that debate, and nor did many of the Americans' friends in Africa, Asia and Latin America.

The assassination of Nimeiri's friend Sadat increased his paranoia and insecurity; his instinctive reaction was to intensify his attack on Gaddafi. During Sadat's funeral news reached Cairo that the Libyan ambassador to the UN had been stopped from going to Washington to address a conference. Mahgoub, the pressman cum diplomatic adviser, misunderstood the news and told Nimeiri that the Libyan ambassador was arrested. Nimeiri got in touch with the First Vice-President in Khartoum, asking him to call the US ambassador and file a request for the extradition of the ambassador to be tried in Sudan as a war criminal. The Vice-President did not know how to handle this one. It was a pot-pourri of ignorance, naivety and irresponsibility. No Libyan ambassador was in fact arrested in Washington; the US authorities only advised the head of the Libyan delegation to the UN that he was unwanted in Washington, where he was meant to address a gathering of Libyan students. According to the UN HQ agreement, the USA can restrict the movements of UN diplomats to New York only. But even if there had been such an arrest there are norms and procedures in the law of nations that govern extradition. Any junior secretary in Sudan's embassy in Cairo could have advised the President on that. But Nimeiri, by now, would not have recourse to advice; he knew it all. The story is both astonishing and lamentable, revealing the intellectual penury and professional inadequacy of those surrounding the President. It also shows, if more evidence is needed, the level of Nimeiri's unjustifiable disdain for his own institutions.

In a series of twenty-seven interviews after the funeral of Sadat, Nimeiri made his most belligerent statements yet. He told the Beirut daily *Al Nahar*, 'It is possible defence could be best ensured by attack. I mean carrying the battle into Libya. It is not impossible to find me staging an operation inside Tripoli. We do not shun death; we search for it' (as he did during the July 1976 rebellion!).

Nimeiri also claimed, after his talks with US Secretary of State Haig, who was attending Sadat's funeral, that he had been assured by the Secretary of State that the United States is not going to allow such an attack as the Libyan intervention in Chad to happen again, and so they were going to stand fast with the Sudan and Egypt. He also said that he was training agents to infiltrate into Libya in an effort to subvert the regime of Gaddafi. 'I have every right to send them,' he said, 'It is a kind of active defence, as you call it in the army. They think they are the only ones who do hell-raising, but we can do it also' (*The Washington Post*, 13 October 1981). Nimeiri also claimed that Sudan would take part in operation 'Bright Star' and establish joint military exercises the following month, including practice for the air-lift of Egyptian troops to Sudan in US transport planes. Haig, however, in announcing the expansion of the exercises the day before, said that Egypt, the United States and Oman would participate. He did not mention Sudan. Nimeiri wanted, willy-nilly, to catch up with the Joneses. His exaggeration of US commitment to help him and punish his enemies, which was meant to deter them, put Haig in an embarrassing position. Some senators cautioned against a new Vietnam in Africa. Haig was made to put things in their proper perspective. Nimeiri has by now become a liability to his friends.

Striking Right, Left and Centre

The above cases of provocation were not the exception but sadly the norm. Because of his isolation, his lack of sophistication in the art of diplomacy and the absence of a controlling hand after the discomfiture of his diplomats, like a caged tiger Nimeiri started to strike right, left and centre at his enemies. In August 1981 he sent two open letters to Hafiz al Assad of Syria and Gaddafi telling them to take their hands off Lebanon, to stop burning people and to side with Iraq or at least not to side with its enemy (*Al Sahafa*, 6 August 1981).

Nimeiri was not delegated by Iraq or the people of Lebanon to plead their cause. Countries who had more at stake in the Iraq–Iran war, e.g. the Gulf countries, have never arrogated to themselves this responsibility. They continued to maintain good working relations with Syria and laboured hard to belittle differences with Libya. To Nimeiri's advisers, however, who wanted to prove their worth by preparing virulent declarations which Nimeiri readily reads, such declarations make a noise. Nimeiri's name would be all over the news, as was General Amin's in his famous messages to Queen Elizabeth and President Nixon, advising him on Watergate. One question which those trusted advisers never posed to themselves was whether the Sudan deserved an Amin.

In December Nimeiri sent a very interesting message to Assad attributing the disasters (earthquakes) in Damascus to the regime's ungodliness. He wrote to Assad:

> The news of the disaster which has afflicted Damascus has been conveyed to us. God gives reprieve but does not forget. What has happened in Damascus is the result of your disregard for God's law and your attempt to extinguish the fire of the Qu'ran and the Light of Islam. Justice is the only way for establishing peace and the first principles of justice which God has decreed is the sanctity of human life and the futility of manslaughter without good cause and genocide without just trials. All these are against Islamic law. God our destiny is in your hands. If you will quicken your punishment at your will delay it (*Al Ayam* 4 December 1981).

Assad, of course, did not respond to this message. It could not have emanated from a sane person.

Later on we shall give another example of this peculiar aetiology of Nimeiri's, attributing natural disasters to human action.

In July 1981 Nimeiri arrogated to himself another task, speaking and acting on behalf of the Saudis. He told the Egyptian magazine *Al Musawwar* that the atmosphere is right to reconcile Egypt and the Arab countries and that his efforts in that direction would start with Saudi Arabia because it was the key to the 'moderate' Arab states and always works in the interest of the Arabs. Nimeiri never consulted the Saudis; they too were to be taken for granted. The Saudis, normally reserved and discreet in their utterances, rebuffed him flatly, saying that if the reports are true we think that it would be better for President Nimeiri not to trouble himself with this task which had already been dealt with by the Arab League (30 July 1981). Nimeiri was obviously looking for a role for himself, being more and more isolated. What he did not care to know was that the Saudis, who were trying to achieve a diplomatic feat by articulating an Arab position acceptable to all, following the Reagan plan on the Middle East, were certainly not ready to be identified with distracting initiatives that might be misconstrued.

The Saudi rebuff did not give enough of a lesson to Nimeiri so he went on meddling in the affairs of others, this time with Kuwait, again in the early 'eighties. When the Emir of Kuwait undertook a visit to some Eastern European countries Nimeiri found it necessary to disapprove publicly. He made a statement criticizing the visit and maintaining that he had better experience with the Communists, as if the Kuwaitis did not know what they were doing. Nimeiri never realized that in diplomacy silence is a language. Presidents and diplomats alike should know when and how to sign off. The Emir of Kuwait was not deterred. He went on with his scheduled visit.

On 21 December 1983 Nimeiri decided to provide President Mitterand with a Christmas present. He called the editor of SUNA and dictated to him a statement in which he accused the French of supporting Southern insurgents, attributing the report to a diplomatic friend in the French capital. What prompted this tirade was the decision of a French company to pull out of the Jongeli project in Southern Sudan because of the deterioration of the security situation. The decision was taken by the company and in no way reflected the official French position, nor was it evidence of French meddling in the internal affairs of Sudan. The following morning a leading article appeared in *Al Ayam*, the official SSU organ, in which President Mitterand was attacked personally. The French were enraged, for the attack came at a time when they were chairing the Club of Paris and doing more than anyone else to secure a good financial deal for Sudan. At the time they were also increasing their aid to Sudan and an arms deal was being negotiated between representatives of the two countries, a deal which was more in the nature of a grant. Fences were mended by MOFA and the Sudanese ambassador in Paris, who managed to concoct an explanation for their President's inexplicable behaviour. Whether the French believed them or not was immaterial, for they must have known by now that someone had become increasingly unbalanced. They could hardly blame the Sudan for that.

Adieu to Non-alignment

Non-alignment, of course, has become a dead letter but it is a mistake to think of Nimeiri, who was lurching to the right, as pro-Western, pro-American or pro-anything. 'Left' and 'right' presuppose a well considered policy. For Nimeiri decision-making is not a process of weighing actions and consequences but a more personal thing; his actions are dictated by his instincts rather than his mental faculties, whatever he has left of them. His personal security has become the main consideration. So personal insecurity led him to seek Western aid (military and intelligence) at all costs; at the cost of alienating his Arab friends, of angering his foes and of hurting and damaging national pride and the interests of his compatriots.

Nimeiri had reached a stage where he no longer cared about people's sensitivities. Independent Sudan is less than thirty years old and its people, with their long history of subjugation, are very sensitive and protective of their independence. In a press conference at which a large contingent of American journalists was present we had Nimeiri inviting the US to establish military bases on Sudanese soil. The public was incensed and General Khalil requested an explanation, noting that this contravened Sudan's established policy of non-alignment. Nimeiri denied having said anything to this effect, despite the fact that the statement appeared in American, European and Arab dailies and magazines. Radio

Monte Carlo embarrassed all by producing the statement recorded in Nimeiri's voice.

America in the eyes of the Arabs is Israel's arch ally, its source of power and the cause of their defeat. This is a truth that an Arab leader ignores only at his peril. Yet we find Nimeiri in 1983 inviting American troops into his capital as part of the rapid deployment exercises. Many Arab countries have military associations and even alignments with the USA. Their governments, however, are respectful of people's sensitivities to the American military presence. For example, the Egyptians had the sense and sensitivity to keep the troops away from the eyes of the masses and restrict joint exercises with them to the desert. Nimeiri did his best to ensure that the Americans were seen in Khartoum, his message (to his internal and external foes alike) being that he had strong friends behind him. Posing next to the American Awacs is perhaps the best example of his flag-waving and sabre-rattling. The show was not in the air base at Wadi Seidna, it was in Khartoum airport. A few of the ayatollahs of socialism, those unsleeping guardians of the revolutionary faith, were taken by Nimeiri on that ride; none of them came out against these excesses though all were still vaunting the National Charter and categorizing people into right and left. Non-alignment also went out of the window when Nimeiri instructed his ambassador at the UN to vote on the General Assembly resolution condemning the US intervention in Grenada. The Ambassador recalled Sudan's position condemning the Soviet intervention in Afghanistan. Nimeiri was not impressed. His diplomats could not tolerate this smirch on Sudan's name, they persisted. Even Reagan's staunchest ally, Mrs Thatcher, thought it necessary to distance herself from that episode. Nimeiri gave in; Sudan should abstain, but nothing more. In his company, apart from Western allies of the USA, was Zaire and Israel. To confound the world MOFA issued a statement deploring the US action in Grenada. Sudan by now had two foreign policies.

Africa Betrayed

But the principle of non-alignment was not the only casualty of Nimeiri's policy of mollifying and wooing the Americans in order to ensure their goodwill and support (for his personal security). For this support Nimeiri was prepared to pay any diplomatic price and abjure any alliance. In 1978–9 as chairman of the OAU he decided to go against the resolutions of the organization he himself was presiding over. Nimeiri's act of betrayal was not only against the OAU, it was against a time-honoured Sudanese commitment to African causes. Not even during the 'discredited' regime of the parties had the Sudan swerved from that path. Under the May revolution support for liberation movements and African causes was made into a revolutionary dogma; it was enshrined in the National Charter, repeated in the resolutions of the SSU and stipulated in the decrees creating MOFA. This policy was consistently abided by until the watershed year of 1978 and there is no lack of evidence to prove that.

Desirous of currying favour with the USA, Nimeiri decided to give way to American protests against the inclusion of the USA in the UN resolutions on apartheid. For years African countries have been singling out the USA and a few Western countries for condemnation of their policies in support of South Africa. Representations to MOFA were always made by the USA, as well as other Western countries, on this issue. Sudan's constant answer was that the decision was an African one to which we were tied. Sudan's voting record in the UN General Assembly was always in favour of OAU resolutions; indeed, Sudan has always been among the sponsors of those resolutions.

Come 1978, the year when the OAU held its first meeting on Sudan's soil and Sudan's President became for the first time the current chairman of that organization, and the situation had changed. Nimeiri's instructions to the Sudan mission in New York were unbending: no condemnation of the USA at any cost. The pleadings of his ambassador to the UN were met with a deaf ear. The ambassador who was called upon by virtue of his country's chairmanship of both the OAU ministerial council and its summit assembly, to play an effective role in mobilizing others was now put in the unenviable position of voting negatively against the resolution. He would have preferred to resign his post rather than do it, so he chose to absent himself from the meeting and so did all the members of the mission. The record of the resolution on apartheid 1978/33 paragraphs A to O showed it; Sudan was absent from the voting. The conscientious ambassador must have had a few sleepless nights. A few days later the ambassador went to the secretariat to change the record. The record reflects the following in a footnote: 'Later on Sudan advised the secretariat that it had intended to vote for the resolution.'

But all the wiles of diplomats were not enough to deter Nimeiri. In the following two years, 1979 and 1980, he could not tolerate any such nonsense from his ambassador. The position he had forced his diplomats to take showed the extent to which the President was recklessly willing to go to please the USA. Sudan has been a member of the UN apartheid committee since its inception. In that capacity Sudan invariably introduced the resolution of that committee to the General Assembly, and African, as well as other countries supporting African causes, sponsored it. 1979 was a different year, for the country that was the standard-bearer in the committee on apartheid had opted to abstain, on the instructions of the President, the current chairman of the OAU summit. The record of GA 1979/34 reflects that infamy. As for 1980 Nimeiri decided to carry his incursions into the UN General Assembly fourth committee. The issue now was the economic policies of South Africa. Sudan again, on Nimeiri's instructions, asked for separate voting to enable it to abstain on the paragraph referring to the USA. That again was a departure from Sudan's traditional position.

President Nimeiri, in his capacity as the OAU current chairman, undertook several trips in Africa. Following these trips he addressed the nation, vaunting his achievements as chairman. Speaking on his *Face the Nation* programme on 11 December 1978 about his meetings with African leaders and his visits to West and Southern African states he said.

I held various meetings with President Kaunda of Zambia . . . who gave me a detailed picture of the barbaric raids inside Zambian territories which were perpetrated by Smith's racist regime, which is threatening to launch new attacks with the help of South Africa. I have been made aware of the big sacrifice made and still being made by Zambia in its struggle for African liberation. During my meetings with the representatives of the liberation movements in Southern Africa I sensed the strong fighting spirit which reassures me that despite the enemy's barbaric and desperate raids, Africa is determined to continue the struggle until victory is achieved. . . . I have reiterated in the official talks I had and in my statements, the need for strong co-operation not only between the front-line states but also between these states and the liberation movement on the one hand, and on the other, all the members of the organization through the organization's general secretariat *through its current chairman*.

Indeed these last words were what Nimeiri wanted to convey. The OAU was to be treated like the government of Sudan as a personal estate exclusively run by the chairman. Unfortunately for Nimeiri, the OAU charter deals with four institutions, none of which is called the chairman. They are the assembly of heads of state and government, the council of ministers, the general secretariat and the commission on mediation, conciliation and arbitration. Nor do articles VIII and IX, relating to the assembly of heads of state and government envisage a role for the chairman as the master co-ordinator of the secretariat.

President Nimeiri's references to the role of the chairman are not what hurts, for they could be attributed to the ignorance of his speech-writers or his own megalomania and make-believe. However, the President's audacity was indeed unmatched when he went on tutoring Africans about the significance of solidarity and respect for commitments. Nimeiri's UN behaviour in 1978 and 1979 gave the lie to this posturing. The Sudanese had been taken for granted for a long time and now it was the turn of Africa to be taken for a ride. As to the beleaguered Sudanese diplomats who knew the inside story, they could not yet have recovered after having heard his *Face the Nation* address. Others, too, we recall, were equally dumbfounded, when they heard him admonishing the SSU in August 1979 for not doing much to promote the President's achievements in the course of his chairmanship of the OAU. Among these others, a few, like his ambassador to the UN, must then have mused and remarked: 'The President should have kept silent on his chairmanship of the OAU, for the less said the better.'

Denigrating his Past

The fact is, however, that Nimeiri was no longer able to relate his decisions and actions to broader aims, principles and commit-

357

ments. His actions were their own frame of reference. Foreign policy is not a branch of the science of politics but an instinct, mainly an instinct for survival. In 1983 Nimeiri surprised his Ministers when he announced that 'his friend', Master Sergeant Doe of Liberia, had sent him a letter informing him of his intention to resume diplomatic relations with Israel. Nimeiri wrote back, he told his Ministers, telling the Liberian Master Sergeant that 'We in Sudan believe that nations take the decisions best suited to their national interests. You should do the same.' This could hardly be the same President who travelled all over Africa and communicated with many an African leader enlisting their support for the diplomatic isolation of Israel.

When Minister Dafa Allah al Haq Yusuf retorted 'But Mr President we have regional commitments and we are not free to do as we please,' Nimeiri answered 'What commitments? . . . to the Arabs! The Arabs do not know what they want.' Sadat was equally unflattering to Arab governments, but he had the courage of his convictions and he paid the price for it. For Nimeiri it is a different ball game altogether. He is the President whose government was sitting in Arab councils at ministerial and ambassadorial levels, devising ways and means of aborting the new Israeli diplomatic inroads into Africa. Such a deliberate double-faced policy cannot be dismissed as the raving of a demented leader. It is sheer wanton betrayal on the one hand and cowardice on the other. Nimeiri, if he believed in what he told his Liberian friend, should have played a Sadat and defended Israeli initiatives in Africa. If he did not then there should have been a measure of consistency in his policies, these in the privacy of his own council as well as those in the glare of TV cameras inside Arab councils.

But that was not all. Nimeiri's surprises accumulate, for in 1980, during the UN Disarmament Conference held in New York, Iraq presented a resolution condemning Israel's nuclear policy. The resolution was to be put forward by a Sudanese, Mustafa Medani, who was chairing the Arab group. Medani found himself in the unenviable position of having to present the resolution on behalf of the Arabs and then abstain on it in the vote. The wires had already carried to him Nimeiri's instructions to abstain, in view of references to US support for Israel's nuclear policy. Medani contacted the Iraqi representative, asking him to modify the draft resolution to ensure unanimous Arab support for it. The USA has many friends in the Arab world, but none of them felt obliged to make that request. The head of the Iraqi delegation, Ismat Kittani, consulted his government and obtained its support. Iraq was intent on the condemnation of Israel at any cost. Medani communicated the 'happy' news to Khartoum, adding sarcastically: 'Reference to the USA was removed. Do you want us to do something about Israel too?' The resolution was later carried with no reference to the USA.

Nimeiri, in all his UN actions regarding Arab-related matters, was not only shaming his country, he was denigrating his own image, an image he had rightly earned by his steadfast support for Arab causes in his early years. That he did to the point of risking his life in Amman in 1970 to save the life of Arafat. But, in foreign policy as in domestic policy, Nimeiri's actions have been more and more influenced in later years by his personal fears and predilections.

Who needs Embassies?

When Nimeiri said that he wanted his foreign policy applied to the letter he meant it. This chapter is replete with examples. But to him the marginalization of MOFA was not enough. The institution has to be destroyed in the way domestic agencies were destroyed. The closure of over twenty embassies around the world, ostensibly for economic reasons, was only another ring in a chain. In the Arab world alone he closed the embassies in Algeria, Morocco, Jordan, Iraq, Qatar, Somalia and Oman, in addition to Libya and Syria, with whom Sudan had no diplomatic relations, for diplomacy would be conducted by the President personally through his advisers (the ones who wanted the Libyan ambassador extradited). For this to happen at the time when he was arrogating to himself a greater role in Arab affairs and playing the mediator, sometimes uninvitedly, simply did not make sense. In fact King Hussein of Jordan, who believed in a sobering role for Sudan in Arab diplomacy, sent his Foreign Minister, Murwan Qasem, to persuade the President against the closure of the Amman embassy. Sultan Qabus of Oman also pleaded with Nimeiri against removing his ambassador from Muscat. Both of them are staunch friends of Sudan. The answer in both cases was no, making even Nimeiri's friends come up with all kinds of guesses. None of them realized that Nimeiri's decisions, by now, could hardly be subjected to rational analysis. His future actions a few months later proved that.

The other embassies outside the Arab world which Nimeiri closed were Canada, Spain, Greece, Sweden and Holland in Western Europe and North America and Czechoslovakia, East Germany, Yugoslavia and Romania in the East. The closure of the embassies was Nimeiri's way of making economies with a deficit of 8 million dollars; the saving was a mere $2,000,000. Only a few months later Nimeiri decided singlehandedly to re-open some of those embassies: Oman, Qatar, Morocco, Romania, Iraq and Holland. The re-opening of only those embassies has cost a comparable figure. The closure of the embassies was made despite strong opposition from MOFA officials and advisers. Nimeiri never bothered to explain to his diplomats or political institutions what prompted him to take both actions. The flimsy argument on economies was exploded by the expense the country has incurred in re-opening a few embassies.

On the other hand, when set against the costs of Nimeiri's private visits, the so-called economies from closing embassies look even more droll. A stop-over in Europe on his way to the USA cost $1,000,000. The stops in Italy and France had to be private, as a request for an official visit was politely turned down by the Italians because they were receiving the Algerian leader Chedli Benjedid. The reason given for this *divertissement* of Nimeiri's was that he wanted to meet businessmen. For this purpose Nimeiri took with him a train of over a hundred people, fifteen of whom were of ministerial status. Benjedid, who was on a state visit, was accompanied by only three ministers and a few personal assistants. So there must have been another reason for closing twenty-two embassies. In our attempt to rationalize the irrational we could only see this wasteful and baleful decision as part of a process to emaciate institutions.

Sudan's foreign policy, therefore, after Nimeiri managed to gain a free hand in it, became as contradictory and inconsistent as its internal politics. His foreign policy bears the unmistakable imprint of his character, vindictiveness, megalomania, bullying and sloganeering. If these traits and tendencies alienated Sudanese diplomats and disheartened the loyal and faithful inside the Sudan, they also tarnished the country's image abroad, damaged its relationship with some friends and earned it the enmity of others. The country was made to pay dearly for the vagaries and freakish fancies of its leader. Diplomacy is 'forever poised between a cliché and an indiscretion,' Harold Macmillan told *Newsweek* (30 April 1956). That was, indeed, like Nimeiri's diktat diplomacy since 1978.

Epilogue and Prognosis

God help the country where informers thrive
Where slander flourishes and lies contrive
To kill with a whisper! Where men lie to live.

Archibald MacLeish

On 22 May 1983, a few weeks after his election for a third term, Nimeiri sent a circular to a number of personalities, mostly academics (university chancellors, vice-chancellors and professors). In the circular Nimeiri enquired indirectly why they had not sought an audience to congratulate him on his re-election, seek his goodwill and reassure him of theirs. The question was indirect because the circular consisted of a report on an incident which took place between the Abbasid Caliph Harun al-Rashid and one of his scholars, Sufyan al-Thawri. The circular was simply signed: 'To the Dear Brother so and so, with my best wishes, the President of the Republic'. In the story Harun asked Sufyan why he (whom he had befriended and treated like a brother), was the only one among the scholars not to visit him after he assumed the caliphate. Harun, history tells us, sought the friendship of scholars. Nimeiri, however, should have known better than to pose this question. The academics knew how he had treated their peers (e.g. Mohammed Hashim Awad). That alone should have dissuaded any academic from having anything to do with him. Nimeiri, inadvertently, included the scholar's fiery reply to Harun, in which he expressed in unequivocal terms his grievances against the Caliph, grievances which would certainly have been repeated by the academics had they been bold enough to reply, or rather, had they been sure that Nimeiri was magnanimous enough to accept them.

'Oh Harun,' Sufyan wrote, 'you have exhausted the Muslims' treasury against their will. . . . You have allowed yourself to be an oppressor and the Imam of the oppressors. . . . Oh Harun . . . you have drawn a curtain on your door [to conceal his activities] . . .

and you have dispatched your soldiers beyond the palace in which you are ensconced, to oppress the people. They [the soldiers] drink alcohol and punish those who drink, they commit adultery and punish the adulterer, they steal and amputate the hands of thieves, they kill and condemn killers to death. Should not these punishments be applied to you and them [the henchmen] before being applied to the people?' Sufyan repeated the familiar accusations of corruption raised by the sinful Caliph and his henchmen while paying lip-service to Islam and the Qu'ran.

As we said earlier, Nimeiri's attitude to the elite is ambivalent. He needs them and is aware that the modern state cannot be run without their talent and knowledge, but because of his lack of tolerance and inflated ego he will neither support their independence nor reconcile himself to the fact that they know better. Undoubtedly, Nimeiri had given Sudan's elite, the scholars and technocrats, the chance they long awaited; a chance to turn Sudan into a modern state (with all that implies in terms of institutions and organizations). At long last the elite thought that they were able to do what the traditional politicians of the Sudan could not do, either because of the divisiveness of the regime of the parties or the unwillingness of some of them to accept change, their interest lying in the perpetuation of the semi-feudal system that existed.

Nimeiri's action, however, was not wholly holy, for in his eyes this elite was paradigmatically apolitical. In his dealings with them Nimeiri played on their vanity (personal and ideological), selfishness and lust for power. That chance was soon to be taken away from them and their mission aborted at an early stage. The frustrated development programme has become a liability and an encumbrance on both the treasury and the people whose lot and standard of living it has been our aim to ameliorate. The revolution of May thus became a revolution of dis-May and despondency is no longer restricted to the academics who did not come forward and congratulate Nimeiri, for the feelings are ubiquitous.

The revolution has sadly gone beyond a revolution; politically and economically the Sudan today is in a more dire situation than the Sudan which Nimeiri inherited, or rather usurped, from the parties because he thought he could do better. Nimeiri has ruled the country for a decade and a half, longer than any President since independence. His record speaks for itself. Religion, which we thought we had incorporated into our body politic in a manner that takes account of the country's realities in both North and South has

363

been re-introduced as a political force in its ugliest and most hypo-critical form, a weapon of last resort. His religiosity is very suspect indeed, for not only has his brand of Islam put religion in a bad light, it has also alienated the pious elements in the country. Nimeiri's successors, consequently, will have the onerous task of weeding out all the noxious practices introduced by Nimeiri in the name of Islam. The family and clan ties that governed politics in the past and were broken by a system of meritocracy in the first Nimeiri era were replaced by a new one in the second Nimeiri era; the Nimeiri clan and its cronies. The President, none the less, con-tinues to denounce the so-called government by inheritance of the Mahdis and the Mirghanis. The old clique of notables, land-owners and religious leaders has been replaced by a cabal of fortune-hunters and obscure charlatans.

Furthermore, power is now more concentrated than ever before, and without challenge from the countervailing forces and checks and balances of a multi-party system, such as parliamentary oppo-sition, a free press and a general ability to express and communi-cate the dissenting viewpoint. Nimeiri has not only destroyed the achievements which earned the regime whatever popular support and legitimacy it had; he has also razed all institutions meant to share or check power. In the destruction as in the construction of these achievements Nimeiri was aided and encouraged by con-spiracies of silence, coalitions of convenience and political oppor-tunism. It is a sad commentary on our times that Nimeiri was largely assisted in this unwholesome endeavour by in-fighting within the institutions and competition among the ruling new class for Nimeiri's favour, thus building up his ego and facilitating his task of demolishing the institutions. Nimeiri wanted everybody at his beck and call, and effortlessly he managed that, the executive and legislative institutions acquiescing to his whims and the politi-cal leadership crouching ignominiously for his favour. In his on-slaught on the South, Nimeiri was assisted by the internecine struggle between the Southerners. So by playing one against the other, SSU people, opposition leaders and Southerners, he was able to ride all storms. He was also able to discard his adversaries easily, peeling them off one after the other, as one does the layers of an onion. Autocracy has taken fourteen years to marinate, seasoned by all manner of cajolement, intimidation and passionate perfidy.

Having said that, we must not underestimate the role Nimeiri has played and the negative contribution he has made, largely because of his basic limitations and rudimentary inadequacies. Nimeiri lacked both political vision and historical sense. He was further more a bully, a bully in dealing with his opponents, his RCC colleagues, his Ministers and aides and, as we have shown in the chapter on foreign policy, with foreign dignitaries and governments. Nimeiri's only purpose in life is to be number one and in his bid to stay at the helm he has not hesitated to destroy every single institution: Parliament, the SSU, government administration, the South, the Army and the judiciary, once they were thought to pose a challenge to his pre-eminence. In the process the whole country has been completely beaten to the ground, its people exhausted and its energies drained by his determination to divide and rule.

In spite of all Nimeiri's glowing claims of success the stark reality remains. To many of us the regime may have been everything in turn but nothing long. It simply could not deliver the goods it promised. On the other hand, Nimeiri's bullying nature, his unhistorical outlook and the other pernicious traits of his character, make him unqualified to lead the Sudan. By 1984 Nimeiri had everything that should disqualify him from office. In addition, Nimeiri has proved to be unable and unwilling to learn: the only things that seem to have sharpened are his divide and rule tactics, his deviousness and his total callousness, which has enabled him to survive for so long, outlasting all Sudanese Presidents, military and civilian. Of these, General Abboud enjoyed as much power as Nimeiri and, autocratic though he was, he had the decency to abdicate at the first sign of public discontent. Faced with the same sign Nimeiri did not hesitate to exploit religion and impose martial law in order to perpetuate his rule. The President did not pause to think of the implication of that decision on the economy, the morale of the people or the image of the country. It also did not dawn on him that what people expect from their President is not faith-healing, but rather an attempt to govern effectively and meaningfully. For faith-healing people turn to their religious leaders, not Presidents. Although no one expected Nimeiri to behave like President Senghor, i.e. abdicate at will, the fact remains that his rule was wanting by all regional and third world standards, save for those of the Amins and Bokassas. Sudan does not deserve either.

If Sudan is to come out of its morass, Nimeiri must go. Although there is nothing to make us believe that his removal by itself will take us back to what we called the years of promise, of one thing we are sure: the situation cannot deteriorate. Sudan has reached its nadir. Some of the achievements of the May revolution cannot be unmade but Nimeiri's regime must be stopped from taking an even greater toll and doing more damage. The *modus vivendi* that would emerge will probably be worse than the one which Nimeiri interrupted in 1969 but would certainly be better than the one he leaves. Nimeiri's recent policies and his unstoppable lawlessness, transgressing the constitution and changing laws and institutions at a whim, are all vindictive responses to people's criticism and disenchantment with his rule. Remorselessly, he did not hesitate to go to the extent of undoing his own achievements and institutions; it is all a revenge on history. Nimeiri has made believe that by opposing him, decrying his excesses and castigating his failures, people are not giving him what he deserves, as if tolerating him for fifteen years were not enough. For this reason he has gone on destroying institutions (making it hell for whoever will succeed him) and taking refuge in a mystical hope for success. Nimeiri's behaviour has become both foolish and dangerous, imposing a greater sense of responsibility on the Sudanese people to dislodge him.

Support for Nimeiri's rule comes mainly from outside the Sudan, i.e. the USA and Egypt. Internally his main supporters are the Muslim Brothers, who continue to be a marginal force in Sudanese politics. The Brotherhood is, by and large, a party of the urban elite (university students, civil servants, professionals etc.). However, the pull of traditional Islam continues to be very strong and the majority of the population owes its allegiance to the major politicized sects. That may explain why Nimeiri's choice fell on a minor apolitical Sufi sect. These sects, politicized and apolitical, have only succeeded in entrenching Islam in the Sudan through teaching and preaching rather than by punitive measures and coercion.

The Muslim Brothers have their own ulterior motives in supporting Nimeiri, for they think he is doing the dirty work for them, i.e. destroying the Communists, intimidating the non-Muslim Brother elite and imposing Shari'a on the Southerners. To the Muslim Brothers Islam is a weapon with which all cultural, political and ideological groupings and tendencies can be subdued. Once they succeed Nimeiri, so to speak, they would soon embark on redressing the balance to give Islam a better image. Dr Turabi, the Muslim Brothers' leader, was being less than honest when he said that the Brothers have decided to collaborate with the President in the aim of reforming the regime from within. 'We are opposed to all destabilizing tendencies which would lead the country into chaos and anarchy. This is why we take part in the defence of the regime whenever it is endangered,' he told *Le Monde*. Not only was he not forthright about the Brothers' motives, but he was overestimating their size and role beyond all proportion when he continued, 'The President knows it. No real plot against the government can take place if we stay on his side. Nothing can take place in this country without the Muslim Brothers' (*Le Monde*, 4 October 1983).

In fact the President knows something else, that the Sufi sects and the politicized sects are the ones that command the allegiance of the Muslim masses. He knows that the Brothers speak the language of the minority. This is why he sent two envoys to Sadiq el Mahdi in his prison cell (one of whom was Dr Turabi himself, the other the Minister of Energy, Sharif al Tuhami) in an attempt to gain his goodwill and secure his co-operation before he would be released. Nimeiri also made overtures to al Mirghani by deviously expressing the wish to call on him at the Id and visit the mosque of his father, a mosque which is still under construction.

The Muslim Brothers are grossly miscalculating, not only in assessing their political power but in their ability to make amends to the population. They do not seem to realize that they will never be absolved of the support that they have lent to Nimeiri's so-called Islamicization measures, particularly their support for the imposition of martial law and the outrageous constitutional amendments, e.g. the imamate, Presidency for life etc. We have given examples of al Turabi's very ardent, though tortuous, defence of constitutional amendments, martial law and emergency courts, describing them as the nearest thing to Islamic courts.

The Muslim Brothers (with Iran at the back of their minds) seem to forget that they are not the ayatollahs and mullahs of Sudan; if anything, it is the leaders of the traditional Sufi sects who should be compared to the ayatollahs in the power which they wield over the population. Turabi could not be the Khomeini of the Sudan, though perhaps its Bani Sadr, meeting the same fate as the latter. Khomeini's counterpart or not, al Turabi must remember that opposition to a Muslim Brother take-over will come not only from the traditional religious sects, the urban elite and the Southerners; other outside influences will be in play. For example, Egypt, which takes a special interest in the politics of Sudan will not allow such a take-over because it would upset the balance of power inside Egypt itself. The Saudis, for their part, would not like to see yet another fundamentalist upheaval on their western flank, for politics and economics in the kingdom are not a matter for the Saudi fringes with whom the Muslim Brothers are associated. These are political realities which politicians have to take into account whether they like them or not.

To say that the leaders of the traditional sects are Sudan's ayatollahs is not to say that Iran and Sudan are comparable or that what is happening now in Sudan is analogous to Iran's Islamic revolution. There are many differences:

1. Iran is Shi'ite and Sudan is Sunni; in theory as well as practice the role of the clergy (Ulema) in Shi'ite Islam has been greater than their role in Sunni Islam.
2. Iran has no sizable non-Muslim communities as Sudan does in the Christian and animist communities; communities, furthermore, which are related by faith and ethnicity to neighbouring countries whose help they can enlist.
3. Iran borders only one non-Muslim country whereas Sudan borders several. Religious extremism in Sudan would almost certainly adversely affect its relationship with its numerous neighbours.
4. Sudan has no economic resources comparable to Iran. She cannot afford to antagonize the West, Egypt or her neighbours across the Red Sea.

As for Nimeiri's outside supporters, the US administration, while realizing that his regime is not strongly based, is ready to support him as the devil they know. Nimeiri, President Reagan seems to think, is a bulwark against the spread of Communism in the Horn of Africa. His friendship is coveted nearly as much as that of Egypt. However, once an alternative emerges or once the American administration realizes that the threat of Communism has been exaggerated and that Nimeiri is no bulwark against it, they are bound to withdraw or at least qualify their support. Nimeiri is fully aware of the present American administration's paranoia about Communism, so he is playing the card of international Communism and 'Communist expansionism' as his ace. It is in this light that his tirades against the Ethiopians, the Syrian

Baa'th and especially Gaddafi should be seen, for all are meant to obtain more military equipment to fight his internal wars and subdue his ever increasing opponents. When the USA proved unwilling to supply the requisite arms (especially helicopters) which were essential for his anti-guerrilla war, he secretly ordered helicopters from Romania.

The American administration as well as the Egyptians no longer take Nimeiri's statements about imminent Libyan invasion at their face value and are no longer prepared, especially Mubarak's Egypt, to give him 100 per cent support. There is abundant evidence to show that Egypt has decided not to go to Nimeiri's help if an internal attempt is made by a Sudanese group to oust him. They have also refused to be drawn into the war in the South. Only in the case of foreign intervention would Egypt he expected to come to Sudan's (not Nimeiri's) rescue. The clearest expression of Mubarak's dismay came in his opening speech to the Egyptian Parliament in July 1983 when he said that he did not want to be more than a two-term president and that he does not want a *bay'aa* for life (Nimeiri was present at that occasion). Also, significantly, Mubarak talked about integration, describing it as a nexus between the Egyptian people and all sections of the Sudanese people.

President Reagan, on the other hand, has turned a deaf ear to the counsel of his advisers, diplomats and those acquainted with the Sudan scene. In effect several hearings on Sudan took place in the US Congress, e.g. the House Subcommittee on Africa (28 March 1984) and the Afro-American Institute luncheon on 21 May, chaired by Congressman Howard Wolpe, chairman of the African Subcommittee. The thrust of the statements made in these hearings was that the USA should not be dragged into Nimeiri's self-inflicted trauma, particularly in Southern Sudan. Nimeiri's reaction to these hearings was stupefying; Communist elements are now influencing elements in the US Congress, he said. President Reagan, however, continues to take the view that Nimeiri (the devil he knows) should be maintained until an alternative emerges in the Sudan.

The alternative the US administration is looking for is a man, not a system, which reveals a lack of trust in the Sudanese people's ability to choose their leadership. The USA knows better than anybody else that if Nimeiri has been kept afloat for the last few years, it was only thanks to its support for his personal security. Nimeiri's larger reason in life is no longer development, nation-building or seeking a place in the sun for the Sudan; it is only personal survival and the perpetuation of his rule at whatever cost. What makes the US (or rather President Reagan's) support for Nimeiri almost disrespectful to Sudanese sensitivities, is the way in which it shrugs off Nimeiri's Aminesque excesses and blunders. For one thing, in a country where a senator was denied the right to stand for election as a vice-presidential candidate (Thomas Eagleton in 1972) simply because he had, once upon a time, received psychiatric treatment, an American Nimeiri would have been deposited in a mad-house long ago. For another, the USA has every reason to know that the Sudan both deserves and is capable of producing better leadership; an Amin need not be rammed down its throat.

Factors like this will be taken in the balance of judgment by any successor to Nimeiri (including friends of the USA) when it comes to determining the nature, level and scope of relationship with that country. By any standard, faith in Nimeiri is no longer well founded. His total reliance on outside support is misguided, for outsiders support him as a rope a hanged man. The Sudan might look calm, but under its placid surface many hallucinating things are brewing. Sudanese passions always lie dormant, but suddenly they cascade mercilessly though they soon abate, all a reflection of the degree of tolerance of the people. History has it that the Sudanese are richly unpredictable and perhaps this is one reason why Nimeiri is paranoid and driven to excesses like the martial law which was meant to pre-empt reactions against him by the urban elite. At any rate the Sudanese who are both proud and discreet always keep their inner feelings to themselves; rulers who fail to understand this intrinsic characteristic of the people do so at their peril.

Sir James Robertson, the last British Civil Secretary during the colonial era, was once asked about the most difficult people to govern in the countries he served in, Palestine, Sudan and Nigeria. 'Without hesitation,' he said, 'it is the Sudanese. They are polite, good-natured and proud but you never know what they are up to. One thing is sure, however, even your *mursala* [messenger] who serves you politely and dutifully almost makes you feel that he is still a better man because, in the end, he will go to heaven and you will go to hell.'

What can one envisage as an outcome to this situation, to this deft balance of interests? The military is currently engaged in

fighting a raging war in the South and Nimeiri's henchmen are ter-
rorizing and arresting people of the North on suspicion of crimes
ranging from drinking alcohol to suspected intended adultery. The
level of intimidation and recrimination means that it is unlikely that
Nimeiri will be overthrown by a popular uprising, though, of
course, he might be assassinated.

Nimeiri came to power as a result of a military coup; he might
well be overthrown by another one. The catalyst for such an event
is likely to be the war in the South, as it was in 1969. The Army is in
a most untenable situation in the South, with its morale and
supplies running low while the Southerners' fighting spirit and their
determination to fight for their autonomy and cultural and religious integrity are running very high. By late September 1984
Nimeiri had backed down on his decision to dismember the South,
offering a return to the arrangement worked out in Addis Ababa.
The reversal was as whimsical as the original decision. Nimeiri, in
the utmost callousness, never felt that he owed an explanation to
his people in either the North or South as to the reasons for his
costly war, leading to the death of hundreds on both sides and the
serious economic lacerations suffered by the whole country. Precisely because of this cynicism Nimeiri's decision will impress
neither the Northerners nor the Southerners; a President who
declares war and peace at the drop of a hat is hardly to be trusted.
Nimeiri's recent decision may appeal to those who are looking for
all manner of face-saving devices for him, but cosmetic changes will
hardly resuscitate a regime already in the terminal ward.

The Army's reaction will not only be prompted by the war in the
South, for the general state of the armed forces is a cause of considerable frustration. The best indication of the unreadiness of the
Army was the bombing of Omdurman, allegedly by a Libyan
bomber. The incident not only came as a reminder of how dire the
Army's situation is but also of Nimeiri's fears and suspicions of his
officers. On the one hand, the bomber, if indeed it came from
Libya, penetrated miles into Sudanese territory undetected and
unintercepted. Days earlier Field-Marshal Nimeiri himself inspected the air base at Wadi Seidna and heard General
Mohammed Mirghani, the Air Force commander, praise Nimeiri's
efforts to maintain the position of the Air Force as a bulwark
against Sudan's enemies. He also heard him talk about the preparedness and eagerness of the 'sons of the Air Force' to answer
the call of duty. 'When national duty beckons them,' he said, 'they

371

will rise with the courage of men and the boldness of believers. The earth becomes too narrow for them so they glide in the skies warning against every mercenary and traitor in defence of the unity of the Sudan' (*Al Sahafa*, 12 March 1984). Nimeiri is not only the Supreme Commander of the Armed Forces, he is also the Minister of Defence, the Commander-in-Chief and the Chief of Staff. The incident should have shamed any honourable officer, let alone the one who was assuming all these powers and serving notice to the world that he was there to do what all his predecessors had failed to do. But Nimeiri, typically, discounts all considerations of accountability, honour and efficiency when it comes to himself. And when senior officers asked for an autopsy of the incident or a meeting with the President he refused, fearing a repeat of the 1982 confrontation with the Army. Instead, Nimeiri sent them a preacher to lecture them on *jihad* and morality. With his dismissal of the Chief of Staff and his assumption of the Army's chief command as well as the Ministry of Defence, Nimeiri was more than responsible for the unpreparedness of the armed forces. His reaction to the legitimate request of his officers not only revealed his cynicism but also his fear of the very forces he commands.

If the Army take power, as an establishment, such a move would not take Sudan back to 1969 but to 1958, to a militaristic dictatorship *à la* Abboud. The new junta would be nationalist and radical. Such a regime will not be long-lived on four counts:

1. Lack of popular support and participation.
2. Absence of civilian expertise to run state organizations and institutions.
3. Opposition of the traditionalist parties.
4. Mistrust in the South of Army rule.

Since the Army, as an establishment, has been emaciated by Nimeiri, it is more likely that the move will come from the bottom ranks; a Sudanese Doe or Rawlings might emerge to whom the multi-dimensional crisis of the Sudan can be solved by firing squads and confiscating property. One can also envisage another scenario whereby a civilian–military coalition (between a party and low- and middle-ranking officers) would seize power, not unlike the Baa'th that seized power in Syria in 1963, leading up to the militarization of politics and the politicization of the military. However, the cultural, ethnic and religious diversity of the Sudan militates against such one-party rule.

The third scenario is for the Muslim Brothers to try to stage a coup. There is some evidence that they have been amassing arms. Such an attempt is unlikely to achieve more than the Communist attempted coup of July 1971. The Army itself would almost certainly come out against the Muslim Brothers, the experience of July 1976 being a case in point. Such a move, on the part of the Muslim Brothers, would plunge the country into civil war, for unlike the July incursion the fighting would not be between civilian armed bands and the Army but would involve civilian elements on a large scale.

The fourth scenario is the come-back of the regime of the parties with either popular or military support, the former taking the form of civil disobedience. I dare say this would be welcomed. This might sound nonsensical in view of what I said in the first chapter about the parties, but the fact is that things as they stand now are so bad that going back to square one will be a move forward not backwards. One does not want another military dictatorship and a Doe or a Rawlings even less. One only hopes that the parties have learnt something (although one has a lurking suspicion that they have not). At any rate the parties would have to accept and resign themselves to the fact that there are some changes and achievements which took place during Nimeiri's years in office and are here to stay:

1. Southern autonomy based on the distinctiveness of the Southerners ethnically, religiously and culturally.
2. Regionalization, which has become a reality with the different regions accustomed to exercise certain powers and reluctant to give them up. They will fight any attempt to wrest power from them.
3. The role of the elite in government, for if the elite is not integrated into government the system will not work.
4. Development, which has become something of a creed.
5. In the sphere of foreign policy, a stable and confiding relationship with our neighbours, Egypt, Libya and Ethiopia (barring Nimeiri's recent excesses) and Saudi Arabia and the Gulf states, and genuine non-alignment, which was the order of the day in the mid-'seventies, when we established a good working relationship with the USA, the West and the Soviet Union, notwithstanding the events of July 1971. As far as our

relationship with Egypt is concerned, the policy of functional
and institutionalized co-operation should be maintained,
barring the vacuous sloganeering about unity which
characterized the early days of the May regime as well as the
regime of the parties, with all its undertones of political
blackmail.

As to non-alignment, the Communist Party would have to
respect the rules of the game were any pluralistic system to survive.
The Communists should realize that they cannot overplay their
cards, particularly in foreign policy, as they tried to do in 1969–70.
Non-alignment presupposes non-involvement in the global strategies of the superpowers. It also means being non-selective in the
condemnation of international lawlessness. Soviet intervention in
Afghanistan should be condemned as vociferously as the American
intervention in Vietnam and Grenada. They will also have to settle
for the fact that Sudan, in order to develop and modernize, would
have to work with the countries of the Western bloc as well as those
of the Eastern bloc, with the so-called conservative Arab states as
well as the so-called progressive ones.

Internally, playing by the rules of the game means that radical
groups should refrain from exerting pressure on duly elected
governments by resorting to extra-parliamentary means, e.g.
inciting riots, strikes and civil strife, either to destabilize or to frustrate governments.

The Arabists, by the same token, must reconcile themselves to
the fact that Sudan is also part and parcel of Africa, not only
because of its geographic position but also because a sizable
number of its citizens identify themselves with Africa. This identification should no longer be seen as a challenge to Arabism; the
new geopolitical realities in the region and the calls for Afro-Arab
solidarity should not remain mere slogans. They have to be a political commitment and a way of life.

The Southerners, in view of what has happened in 1983 and
1984, are quite justified in asking for greater guarantees for their
autonomy. Iron-clad articles, so to speak, will have to be entered
into the constitution for that purpose. On the other hand the
Southerners must relinquish any secessionist ideas that some of
them might be entertaining. The majority of the Northern
Sudanese and the Egyptians will not countenance such a move.
Egypt will come out with all its weight in support of the

Northerners, if need be, to ensure the unity of the Sudan. For Egypt what is at stake is the Nile, with many of the tributaries feeding the river as well as many of the Nile control works situated in the South. Apart from this consideration it is now a time-honoured principle of the OAU that the territorial integrity of states must be respected, and no African country would support attempts to dismember sister states.

The Southerners would also have to reconcile themselves to another fact: the Arab/Islamic cultural identity of the North. It will be the height of illogicality, if not political irresponsibility, to assert the cultural distinctiveness of the South while denying the same thing to the North. One of the greatest successes of the May revolution was precisely in this area, creating a *modus vivendi* between the two parts of the country, taking into account both the cultural and religious attributes of both.

It is evident that this scenario for the return to a multi-party system is replete with hypotheses and unresolved questions. One would hope, however, that Nimeiri's cynicism would not be matched by the parties' inability to learn from past errors and achieve a better national self-definition.

What about our claims for a one-party state? In a sense they are no longer just our own claims for all the traditional opposition forces have endorsed them, Sadiq el Mahdi and el Mirghani, who joined the ranks of the SSU becoming members of its Politburo, Sharif el Hindi, who signed the London declaration accepting the SSU as the only political organization in the country, and the Muslim Brothers, who are still hanging on. On the other hand, the Communists, who stood tenaciously against the SSU were not protagonists of pluralism between 1969 and 1971; if anything, they encouraged the destruction of the parties and, in their stead, sought to create a so-called national front based on organized labour and the urban elite, with the CP as the core of the movement.

The salutary lesson to be learnt from the SSU experience, i.e. Nimeiri's experience, is that one party imposed from the top would always degenerate into a one-man no-party rule. In effect even parties born out of political convulsions like wars of liberation would soon be washed out if they degenerated into one-man rule. That is a lesson we have learnt from the experience of Guinea under Sekou Touré and the way his omnipotent party was unceremoniously shipped into oblivion without a murmur from its supposedly widely based following.

Another lesson to be learnt is that people should never count on politicians who lack their own constituency. The only means for the political survival of such politicians must always be competing for the favour of the man at the top. When such a man is neither guided by history nor motivated by a higher purpose he will always end up surrounding himself with obsequious sycophants fawning on him, his megalomania increasing in the process. Eventually he will have no time for the people and the whole populace would become an expendable quantum, except when it comes to sloganeering in demagogic utterances.

Consequently, the third lesson to be learnt is not only never to trust a man that does not trust the people, but also never to trust a system that will produce a man who does not trust the people.

The reader might ask whether Nimeiri is likely to go back on his recent measures, reform his administration and make amends to his opponents, thus saving his neck. All observers of African politics are agreed that Nimeiri is perhaps the continent's master of survival. This is a result of his conspiratorial nature, his divide and rule tactics and the fact that he has no commitment to any principle (he was not joking when he said that there is no Nimeirism). All these traits of character have enabled him to make alliances and break them with great ease. Nimeiri throughout his many years at the helm has staged several coups against himself, so to speak, but this time his survival instinct has deserted him; he has landed himself in a cul-de-sac. To regain the South and the allegiance of the elite he would have to go back on many things, including his brand of Islam, and also accept a large measure of institutionalization. This would not be easy, for personal and non-personal reasons, the personal reasons being his illness and his queer religiosity, for religion now is a source of solace to him. Also he would still expect salvation in the nick of time by providential intervention; he has always made believe that his triumph in September 1975 and July 1976 was not because people died for his sake, it was all the work of a *deus ex machina*.

On the other hand Islam, unlike socialism and revolutionism, is a mass ideology in the Sudan and he cannot make a detour from it the way he did with socialism. All he can do is to retract some of his less palatable and more objectionable measures, as he did in the case of the constitutional amendments and in the case of the *zakat* law, the application of which he put off for one year, arguing that since it is a yearly tax it should come into effect at the beginning of the *hijra* year. What he could do, however, is to let Islamicization fade slowly into the background and go back to business as usual.

One must not forget, however, that Nimeiri's main reason for introducing Shari'a law was civil disturbance and public discontent about the state of the economy and the collapse of services. So Islamicization or not, Nimeiri's survival will ultimately depend on his ability to bring home the bacon so to speak. To rejuvenate the economy he has to resuscitate, or rather, rebuild the institutions and get rid of his valets, for the tragedy of the Sudan has been and still is mismanagement, corruption and disrespect for institutions. This he is unlikely to do. Those involved in corruption remain inviolable and continue to enjoy his grace. The political organization, the SSU, is now defunct; the very few bold souls with some residual fire were at last eliminated. In the economy irresponsibility was carried to its highest level with the abrogation and the reinstatement of the taxes that were the main source of government revenue without consulting economic experts. Parliament became a joke when it ratified the Presidential Decree on *zakat* (abolishing nearly all taxes) with applause, only to hear that the President had decided to re-instate them a few weeks later when he realized that his government was simply not going to have a budget without these taxes.

The Sudanese people have a high level of tolerance for many things, including inefficient governments, but this one beats them all. Nimeiri has been executing a successful political egg dance during his time in power. He was playing everybody against everybody and bluffing them all. In the process, not only the revolution of May, the SSU and the South have suffered; the whole of Sudan became Nimeiri's casualty. If only for this reason Nimeiri must go.

Postscript

Since the book was handed over to the publisher (Autumn 1984) the political scene in the Sudan has witnessed a number of manoeuvres on the part of the Leader Imam which are worth relating. The underlying themes, and the logic of action would, by now, be familiar to the reader; they are the actions of a desperate man who wants to remain in power by hook or by crook.

As far as the South is concerned, Nimeiri had pushed things beyond the point of no return. It is doubtful whether Nimeiri would be able (even supposing he wanted) to return to the 1972 *modus vivendi*. The solution of the Southern problem and the ending of the 17-year-old war, we recall, was achieved only after the credibility gap in North-South relations was bridged. The May regime, in its 9 June declaration, had promised to open a new chapter in North-South relations and, thanks to the activities of various African and world institutions and figures, the Southerners were persuaded to trust Khartoum.

Nimeiri, after his high-handed action in 1983, lost any credibility which the South might have placed in that regime. The SPLM is fighting for Nimeiri's demise and not merely for the return to the Addis Ababa agreement (i.e. the re-unification of the Southern Region etc.). Nimeiri's track-record (his erratic decision to divide the South and no less erratic decision to back down) made it difficult for any Southerner to place faith in him.

Early in October 1984 he announced his intention to annul his decree dividing the Southern Region before that very central leadership which had hailed his action in 1983; the annulment was received with no less enthusiasm than the 1983 decree. The annulment was as arbitrary and unsolicited as the decree itself. The incident is furthermore an illustration of the abdication of the central leadership of its role as policy framer. In making this decision he heeded the advice of the US administration (General Vernon Walters, Dr Chester Crocker, Mr Fairbanks). Similar advice from his Southern colleagues (e.g. Abel Alier, Clement M'boro and Bona Malwal) was dismissed; the latter two were even detained for venturing to advise him.

On the other hand, the situation on the battle-ground has increasingly deteriorated. The SPLA is no longer limiting its operations to Upper Nile (the Bentiu area); both Bahr al Ghazal and Equatoria are now engrossed in the fighting. Major cities like Bor (capital of Jongeli Province) and Yerol (Bahr al Ghazal) have already fallen into SPLA hands. All districts in Equatoria are now within firing reach of the rebel forces and all vital roads to Juba (the capital) are virtually cut. Western governments have already advised their nationals to vacate Equatoria.

It may be recalled that Equatoria is the region allegedly committed to the redivision of the South. President Nimeiri also suffered another humiliating defeat (political this time) when the SPLM exploded his much vaunted claims of a split in the Southern ranks. Early in October he named a three-man committee to undertake negotiations at Bentiu with so-called dissenting elements of the SPLM. A delegation, comprising the Governor of the province, local secretary of the SSU, commandant of police, national security representative (a Northerner) and a few other officials, was instructed to proceed to Bentiu and engage in negotiations with the 'dissenters'. The delegation fell into a SPLA trap. All the Southerners in this delegation declared over the SPLM radio their adherence to John Garang; the others were taken prisoner.

Nimeiri, failing to take the only honourable course to solve the Southern problem (indeed the Sudan problem), i.e. by abdicating, continued to delude himself by striving to divide the Southern front, bribe his way out and crush the insurrection. With the Army unable (and perhaps unwilling) to do that, his friends (the US and Egypt) able but unwilling to do it, he has no way but to resort to mercenaries and soldiers of fortune, a soldiery which he cannot finance.

In February 1984 Chevron stopped its operations in the South after three of its workers were killed by Southern rebels. Nimeiri called on Mrs Thatcher, in late September 1984, to help 'protect oil operations in Southern Sudan interrupted by rebel activity'. He wanted the British Government to 'help equip and train a mobile task force, drawn from the Sudanese army, to keep order and restore foreign confidence' (*Observer* 30 September 1984).

The prevailing conditions in the Sudan are optimal as far as Adnan Khashoggi is concerned. For there lies a country, whose President he knows, in a dire situation, unable to exploit its newly discovered natural resources: no oil company is willing to operate there. This dire situation, we recall, had proved to be a source of funds for Shahir Abdel Haq; now it is promising to take Adnan Khashoggi to even greater heights.

In October 1984 a joint venture company was formed, the National Oil Company (NOC), with Khashoggi's oil company Sigma holding 50 per cent of the shares. Sigma, a small oil company owned by Khashoggi, his brother-in-law Nayel al Assad and Michael Davis will assume total management of the NOC. People who know how Khashoggi's mind works are persuaded that what he is aiming at, with an agreement like this, is to enhance the value of Sigma's shares in the stock market.

He may also consider selling his share in NOC to Chevron or any other oil company before the Sudan falls into 'unfriendly' hands. Chevron will have a larger share (that was originally allowed by Sudanese institutions), Khashoggi will have an unearned increment and his Sudanese friends in the political doldrums or in exile will be assured of a pension for life. In fact, he has already approached a number of prominent Saudis, but they were all reluctant.

However, as things stand today, NOC, managed by Sigma, will take charge of petroleum exploitation, development and transportation in Sudan. It will also be involved in every processing industry connected with petroleum and gas. The company is furthermore empowered to deal with commodities such as sugar and cotton, which are Sudan's main (perhaps only) source of foreign currency, purchasing them free from fees and excise duties (an advantage over all public and private dealers on commodities).

The agreement also provides for the transfer of the following to the company: concessions, licences, leases, royalties, farmings-in, farmings-out and all other agreements and contracts under which

380

the Sudanese Government have rights relating to exploration and development of petroleum – e.g. agreements with companies undertaking petroleum exploration in Sudan, such as Chevron.

Additionally, the company will own all lands and interests in land (on-shore and off-shore) on which there are no contractual agreements with operators for exploration activity in the future. It will also own all petrochemical plants, pipelines, tanks etc. (in effect, abolishing the Ministry of Energy and the national petroleum corporation). NOC will also have access to all geological and geophysical data. (Khashoggi hurried to San Francisco on 5 October 1984 to meet Standard Oil president George Keller in order to gain access to their data on Sudan.) (*International Herald Tribune* 31 October 1984 and the *Financial Times* 31 October 1984.)

The reader will undoubtedly be anxious to know how many of his billions Khashoggi is committing in this *joint* venture company and the amount he is paying for the half-ownership of Sudan's known and unknown reserves of natural gas and oil. Nothing.

According to the agreement a fair value will be established, as at date of formation, by mutual agreement. The company has already been incorporated and its Sudanese chairman appointed, with no agreement in sight as to the price. However, NOC will also establish a finance company and Sigma agreed to arrange and obtain letters of credit and export guarantees for this company totalling in aggregate *up to $400 million*, guaranteed by Sudan and to be settled during a period of 8–10 years. Sudan will guarantee the loans through cotton advance sale contracts.

The Minister of Finance, who was not privy to the Khashoggi deal, put up a tough fight against the surrender of Sudan's cotton the Saudi tycoon, arguing that the Sudan with half a century's experience of dealing in cotton needs no advice from novices in this trade. The minister was soon to receive a Nimeiresque Christmas gift. He was dismissed on 25 December 1984. With him also went all the top executives of the Sudan cotton corporations, to be replaced by Army officers. Army officers do not answer back; they receive and execute orders. The President soon thereafter established a Supreme Economic Council under his chairmanship with Dr Idris as the rapporteur. 'The economic situation,' he said, 'requires his personal intervention.' Presidential intervention, as we have seen in Chapter four, is a euphemism covering up sensitive deals.

This deal should dispel any hope and faith the international monetary foundations, especially the IMF, might have had in Nimeiri. Nimeiri's Government had accepted the IMF and the World Bank's Paris Consultative Group's proposals for ending the underhand oil deals by creating a fund known as the 'oil pot', to which various countries, e.g. Saudi Arabia and the US – would contribute and which would enable Sudan to buy its oil on a competitive basis through international bidding. They have also cautioned Sudan against short and medium term commercial loans, particularly those obtained through the murky hands of middlemen (remember the $200,000,000 obtained by Khashoggi).

Although Khashoggi's company is putting next to nothing into the NOC, the arms dealer has promised to render the President a few services, recruiting and financing a task force for the South (what the US, the UK and Egypt were reluctant to do). The force is to be drawn from the Nuer tribe (the arch enemies of the Dinka), in addition to some foreign mercenary trainers (remember the Seychelles debacle). Nimeiri, to remain in power, is not only handing over to Khashoggi half of the Sudan's natural resources; he is also ready to dismember the whole country by playing tribe against tribe. This is the measure of desperation of the hero of national unity. The plan was only frustrated when his manoeuvres to divide the Southerners failed (the arrest of his negotiating team at Bentiu).

Another activity to which Khashoggi's support is enlisted is the intimidation of Sudanese opposition abroad, real and imagined, particularly in London. (Nimeiri mentioned 100 persons who should be 'put out of action'. In the name of the trade the message is very obvious.) It is evident that the Sudanese security agencies are reluctant to be engaged in shaky operations; a few examples are given in earlier chapters of their aversion to such activities. To this end a meeting was organized by Khashoggi in Khartoum, to which was invited the former CIA official and a former Reagan aide now an associate of Khashoggi. The two Americans listened attentively but were non-committal; however, they promised to report back to Nimeiri as to the best way to deal with his foes. (*Africa Confidential*, 31 October 1984.)

Meanwhile however, Nimeiri has been working on establishing a 'security fund' abroad. The Military Economic Organisation, upon the instruction of the President has deposited $600,000 – presumably its first commission on the Silk Cut deal – in a London bank for security purposes. This, we recall, is the corporation established to serve the armed forces (Chapter six). Article 95 of the MEO's Memorandum of Association stands on its own. The article stipulates that the NOC shall be audited by 'an internationally recognised firm'. We recall that in June 1984 Nimeiri ordered that the books of all national domestic banks be opened before the Auditor-General under the pretext of 'protecting public money'. In fact, what Nimeiri wanted then was to get out of these books a few names and certain figures. However, when sizable public funds and serious national interests are involved (such as in the NOC) which need the protection of the Auditor-General, Nimeiri gave in to Khashoggi's demands for an internationally recognised firm (i.e. one which he nominates).

But it is not only his own laws and directives that Nimeiri was prepared to bend and overlook, but also those of Allah. The relevant articles of the Presidential Order relating to the company's formation blatantly violate the laws on *riba* (interest) and the law on *zakat* (religious tithe). One article exempts interest by lenders from taxation (i.e. interest will be paid); another exempts shareholders, managers and contractors etc. from all personal taxes (i.e. the religious tithe not excepting).

The nature of the deal, its terms and the way in which it was concluded epitomises our analysis of what has gone wrong with the Sudan. Unable and unwilling to end the war in the South and wanting to stay in power at any cost, Nimeiri presented half of the known and unknown energy resources of his country, on a silver plate, to Khashoggi (the man who was responsible, among others, for the economy's *débacle*) in return for arms and security support.

The agreement which was drafted by Adnan's lawyers was signed hurriedly, without consultation. In fact the Minister of Energy, al Tuhami, was flown out of London on a private plane chartered by Khashoggi and brought back to London the same day, after signature, by the Saudi tycoon. On his return he was reported to have called on Khashoggi's London headquarters requesting more details on the deal and its follow-up; he was politely told, on instructions from Nimeiri, that his services were not needed. His role was to sign. In fact, neither his department (the Ministry of Energy) nor the Ministry of Finance nor the Bank of Sudan were represented at the talks that took place between Khashoggi and the Sudanese President.

This is not the first time that the Saudi billionaire has tried to carve himself a morsel of Sudan's national wealth with the assistance of Sudan's President. That was in the year 1973; the wealth in question – sugar; and the people involved – Tiny Rowland (Lonrho) and Osman Khalil.

The birth of the Kenana sugar project was more in the nature of a caesarean than a natural birth. Lonrho was chosen because of its long-time experience in the sugar industry and involvement in similar projects in the Continent (e.g. Mauritius). Objections were raised against our choice by many elements on the grounds of Lonrho's alleged ties with the South African and Smith regimes. I got Nimeiri to organise a meeting between Rowland and the objectors to allow the latter to make their case. No case was made and the go-ahead was given.

Khashoggi, with his eyes on the target production figure of 1 million tonnes, was quick to move and had the full backing of the President. Nimeiri organised a meeting between Khashoggi, Tiny Rowland and Osman Khalil. To help Rowland and Khalil to reach a sensible and rational decision, he chose his palatial Paris residence as a venue. The two were driven to the palace in Khashoggi's limousine. The two recall how they were shown into a splendid waiting room and how an usher appeared at regular intervals announcing that 'His Excellency' was coming. Half a dozen girls were placed in the waiting room in case 'His Excellency' took longer than expected.

Over a dinner where caviar was served like peanut butter and champagne like lemonade, Khashoggi attempted to make the two see sense. He wanted the three of them to acquire half of the Government's shares in Kenana, (60%) as well as beefing up the prices of the capital equipment for the project. Khalil, a Sudanese who had invested time and money in his country's development projects, would not have it. If you are keen, he told the Saudi wheeler-dealer, why don't we start a new Kenana? Lonrho, Khalil remembered, had already turned down the north-western Sennar project because they saw it as a purely Sudanese concern. Lonrho was interested in investing and making profit but not in depriving this poor country of its income.

'His Excellency' retorted that this was not his way of doing business. The two had foregone their opportunity to make a quick buck. They also had to make their own way back to the airport, in a taxi cab this time.

Nimeiri's aides who are grappling with the problems of the economy should have no second thoughts as to where whatever funds are arranged through Khashoggi should go. The President's priorities, notwithstanding what his bankers and economists say or agree to in Washington and Paris, are not the enhancement of production, the reduction of public spending nor the settlement of outstanding rescheduled debts (particularly those of international and regional development and financial institutions) that would help release more funds for development. His priority is to remain in power at whatever cost.

By late 1984 the economic situation has precipitously deteriorated. The IMF debt arrears reached 90 million SDR – more than half the total of arrears due to the IMF from debtor countries. The Club of Paris (which oversees the rescheduling of Sudanese debts) has served notice on Sudan that no further meetings would be envisaged in view of the country's inability to honour its obligations to creditors as they were determined in previous meetings.

The economic situation has been further aggravated by the drought of the previous two years, seriously affecting 4.5 million people according to World Food Programme reports (*Times* 22 January 1985). Needless to say that Sudan would not have been in this predicament had its plans for self-sufficiency in food and grain storage been carried out as envisaged. For months the Government was hiding from its own people the dimensions of this particular crisis while condemning the Ethiopian Government for its failure to feed its people.

Services, too, have not been saved from this deterioration. For example, in late December 1984 Sudan was completely cut off from the outside world (telephones and telexes) for ten days in view of the Government's inability to settle a trifling bill of about a quarter of a million dollars due to the international satellite system. The amount is less than half the sum made available by the President to his cronies of the Military Economic Corporation for their London operations (another example of Nimeiri's warped priorities).

To remain in power Nimeiri has also to keep the populace at bay. To do that, he transformed the judicial system (permanently this time) into an instrument of terror and intimidation. The emergency courts fulfilled this role for six months (April–September 1984) and, when their mandate expired, instead of renewing their term he chose to dismiss the whole of the Supreme Court and appoint in their place the judges of the emergency courts. Fouad el Amin's (a hard-liner amongst hard-liners) accolade was the Chief Justiceship. By this *tour de force* not only did Nimeiri turn the legal system in its entirety into an 'emergency court' but had the audacity to declare to the Sudanese people and to the world the end of the state of emergency.

In order to do this he had to repeal the 1983 Judiciary Act pertaining to the appointment of judges, which requires an active period of judicial service to qualify for serving on the Supreme Court. None of the judges he appointed qualified under this provision. Nimeiri's decision was finally challenged by both the judiciary and the Lawyers Association. The Judiciary Act, we recall, was intended to end the judges' strike and hailed as a judicial revolution. Article 4 of the Provisional Order which replaces the 1983 Judiciary Act reads: 'The administration of justice in the Democratic Republic of the Sudan shall be vested in one judicial body which shall be accountable for the discharge of its activities to the President of the Republic who has the power to overrule such decisions and issue such orders and regulations he deems necessary for the safeguarding of justice and the rule of law'. This article blatantly contradicts and violates the spirit of article 185 of the 1973 Constitution which reads: 'The administration of justice in the Democratic Republic of the Sudan shall be vested in an independent body which shall be called the judiciary.'

The ending of the state of emergency is not the result of a change of heart (for nothing in fact has changed, as we explained above) but rather the desire to dilute the extremist Islamic image which has come to be attached to the regime. The change was cosmetic. President Nimeiri, incensed by western criticism of his human rights record (particularly that emanating from the US) and the constant proddings of Egypt, decided to give a new look to his so-called Shari'a. He was to abide by those cosmetic changes as long as it would take to ensure the next wheat shipment from the US or the next photographic pose and joint declaration with President Mubarak which help serve notice on the world that Nimeiri is not isolated.

Part of this cosmetic surgery is also the removal of the Muslim Brothers from the prominent position which they have acquired during the past six months. Al Turabi has rendered the Imam a few services; in 1977, we recall, he joined the SSU and in 1978 he became Attorney-General. He was used as a countervailing force against the SSU old guard, the diehard secularists and those who still took the 'socialism' of those early years seriously. In recent years, al Turabi, 'the legal thinker', had placed his Islamic weight to support Nimeiri's 'unislamic' actions. The Imam saw in al Turabi a respectable Islamic figure who would lend legitimacy to his 'Islam', someone who would give the various 'unislamic' measures an Islamic dress.

Dr Turabi, however, continued to behave as if Nimeiri's accusations, e.g. calling the Muslim Brothers the brothers of Satan, were not directed against him. Early in November 1984 he attended a seminar on Islamic revivial organised by the UN University in Tunis. Turabi shocked the audience not only by defending Nimeiri's Islamicization measures but also by claiming that the Sudanese have never had it so good. Since the imposition of Shari'a, it is all milk and honey in Sudan, he claimed, the famines in the East and West, war in the South and the exploits of Adnan Khashoggi notwithstanding.

We have dwelt on the intentions and the motives of the Brothers above and on how they envisage themselves as Nimeiri's heir. What their activities in the last few months show is that they are working hard on getting a foothold in various key positions. This would give them a better bargaining position *vis-à-vis* Nimeiri and would put them in better stead when it comes to the battle for succession. This is what al Turabi calls 'change from inside' and what Nimeiri describes as 'Satanic infiltration'. Speaking to *Le Monde*, he described the Brothers as 'the brothers of Satan' and accused them of infiltrating (in true Satanic fashion) various state institutions with the aim of overthrowing the regime (*Asharq al Awsat* 6 October 1984).

Early in October 1984, before the central leadership of the SSU (as the body is called which every now and then forms an audience for the President), he attacked Turabi indirectly when he spoke of those who are taking advantage of Islamicization and posing as the champions of Islam. The Brothers, in fact, had put their full Islamic weight behind the President in his battle with the domestic banks. By encouraging the President to delve into the domestic banks the Muslim Brothers hoped to destroy those banks and get people to withdraw their money and deposit it with foreign Islamic banks whose confidentiality the Auditor-General cannot violate.

Physicists believe that for every particle in the universe there is an anti-particle with the opposite characteristics (charge, spin, mass etc.), the particle and anti-particle combine, annihilating and neutralizing each other and producing a wave of energy. Nimeiri has a similar belief. For every political animal there is an anti-political animal, so that if the two are brought together they will neutralize each other with the energy produced. The anti-Turabi that immediately sprang to Nimeiri's mind is Abul Gasim Ibrahim, whom Nimeiri appointed as Minister of Youth. (It is amongst the youth the Brothers are most active.)

But, whatever Nimeiri and Turabi think, the Sudanese view thinks differently. It came therefore as no surprise to many people that the Muslim Brothers were crushingly defeated in their main constituency (student unions) in early November 1984 – the first time in nearly a decade. That included the Islamic University at Omdurman. It took an Islamic revolution to defeat the Muslim Brothers.

With the situation in the South becoming more and more untenable, the economy continuing its precipitate fall and the trade unions more restive (the workers' trade unions joined the league of professionals with a litany of claims for pay rises in December 1984), the juggler had to come up with a new trick. Khashoggi has failed to deliver the goods (cash and arms or cash for arms); the tycoon rather than digging deep into his own coffer was shopping around the world financial markets to arrange loans for the Sudan. (Those markets knew better from the IMF and the Club of Paris.)

Nimeiri's new ploy was to have another go on national reconciliation. Towards the end of December he ordered the release of Sadiq el Mahdi and 24 of his aides. (Sadiq, we recall, was kept in prison, according to Nimeiri, because of his heresy and in order to save his life from the pious people of Sudan who would murder him, were he to be released.) He also ordered the release of other detainees including Mahmoud Mohammed Taha, the leader of the Republican Brothers, and Osman Khalil, the prominent Sudanese entrepreneur. The Communist detainees remained incarcerated. To save his neck Nimeiri was hoping to usher in yet another reconciliation attempt between the two major sects in the North (Ansar and Khatmiya) in order to use them as a countervailing Northern force against the South (the way he used the South against the North in the 'seventies). His overtures went unheeded.

Nonetheless, the SPLM was not to be completely discarded. In his major address on the anniversary of independence (1 January 1985) Nimeiri extended an olive branch to John Garang. The address was given at Juba, in which Nimeiri arrived unannounced and left a few hours afterwards by stealth. In that address Nimeiri called upon Garang to negotiate a peaceful settlement for the Southern problem. He stated that few things are not negotiable, i.e. the Constitution (which he sought to amend), the SSU (which he proposed to abrogate), the Addis Ababa agreement (which he violated) and the presidential system (which a few months earlier he wanted to turn into an imamate). Surprisingly he did not include Shari'a in his list of 'untouchable' subjects.

The President was badly advised, however, to choose the anniversary of independence as the occasion for declaring his new initiatives. Memories were still fresh in people's minds of his solemn commitment on a similar occasion in January 1984 not to introduce a Shari'a that goes contrary to the Constitution or jeopardizes national unity. Less than five months later Nimeiri did exactly that.

With this 'impressive' track record the President knew only too well that the SPLM would not fall into his trap. For this reason he sought the help of Tiny Rowland (Lonrho) as a contact with Garang. Rowland had more than one meeting with the Southern leader in December 1984 and January 1985, only to be told that there is no peace in the Sudan till Nimeiri packs up and goes. Typically, Nimeiri offered Garang the vice-presidency, responsibility for development of the South and a share of Sudan's oil to be allocated for Southern development. Garang was unbending, he saw in the proposition the good old Nimeiri who was trying to buy his way out through political bribery.

Those inside and outside the Sudan who saw in all these beguiling manoeuvres a genuine effort for reconciliation or an abdication of Nimeiri's confused religiosity were in for surprises. In fact, President Nimeiri in his attempt to promote his brand of Islam has overreached himself.

In December 1984 he undertook a state visit to China (probably to reinforce his socialist credentials). However, while out there, he opted to engage on a less earthly mission – converting the Chinese to Islam. Nimeiri was reported to have told his accompanying ministers that, in view of China's latter moves to 'abdicate' Marxism, he wished to introduce Islam to them. The President was advised by his Minister of Industry (Mohammed Beshir Wagie) not to follow this course, rather to attend to questions of immediate preoccupation to the Sudan – e.g. the economy; for this he was severely scolded. The minister was dismissed soon after his return to Khartoum. Nimeiri went ahead with his holy mission (initiating the

Chinese into Islam) and, needless to say, China was no less agnostic when the new Messiah left it. In fact, his Chinese interlocutors told him that theirs was not an abdication but a reinterpretation of Marxism.

Nimeiri was yet to take a deeper dive into barbarism. This time it was not through his misreading of the re-interpretation of Marxism, rather his reading of the ominous re-interpretation of Islam by those who are more learned and better respected by the Sudanese elite. Following his release from detention, Mahmoud Mohammed Taha (the leader of the Republican Brothers) decided to move to the assault against Nimeiri's brand of Shari'a. The Republicans, a peaceful and highly respected group, have been advocating a more progressive interpretation of Islam. Their support mainly comes from the educated sector of the population. Their leadership includes a number of university professors who are highly regarded by their peers.

For years the Republicans defended the Nimeiri regime for no reason other than the position it has taken against Islamic fundamentalists. They were allowed by Nimeiri freely to advocate their views on the modernization of Islam, which include equal rights for women and full respect for other creeds. Theirs was not a marriage of convenience with Nimeiri, rather an alignment with a regime which was committed to the same ideals they have striven for over the last forty years. Came 1983 and Nimeiri decided to espouse the fundamentalist cause, outdoing all his predecessors. The Republicans being faithful to their ideas and ideals, decided to stand up against this *volte-face*. Taha, with a number of his disciples, was arrested and kept in custody for over a year.

On their release the Republicans would not relent. On 25 December 1984, marking Christmas, they issued a policy statement calling for the repeal of the Shari'a laws and a halt to the war in the South. On those laws they said: 'These laws have jeopardized the unity of the country and divided the people in the North and South by provoking religious sensitivity which is one of the fundamental factors that aggravated the Southern problem. It is futile for anyone to claim that a Christian person is not adversely affected by the implementation of Shari'a. A Muslim under Shari'a is the guardian of a non-Muslim in accordance with the "verse of the sword" and the "verse of *jizia*" (respectively, calling for Muslims to use arms to spread Islam and impose a humiliating poll-tax on the subjugated non-Muslim believers). They do not have equal rights. It is not enough for a citizen today merely to enjoy freedom of worship. He is entitled to enjoy the full rights of a citizen in total equality with all other citizens. The rights of Southern citizens in their country is not provided for in Shari'a, but rather in Islam at the level of fundamental Qur'anic revelation – i.e. the level of *sunna*.'

The statement concluded with a call for:

1. The repeal of the September 1983 laws because they distort Islam, humiliate the people and jeopardize national unity.

2. The halting of bloodshed in the South and the implementation of a peaceful political solution instead of a military solution. This is the national duty of the Government as well as the armed Southerners. There must be the brave admission that the South has a genuine problem and a serious attempt to resolve it.

3. The provision of full opportunities for the enlightenment and education of this people so as to revive Islam at the level of *sunna* (the fundamental Qur'an). Our times call for *sunna* and not Shari'a. The Prophet, peace be upon him, said: 'Islam started as a stranger, and it shall return as a stranger in the same way it started ... Blessed are the strangers!! They said: Who are the strangers, O Messenger of Allah? He said: Those who revive my *sunna* after it has been abandoned.'

They also called for civil disobedience were Nimeiri not to pay heed to these calls. Words like civil disobedience are very ominous; they bring back memories of the overthrow of General Abboud. The Field Marshal would not tolerate this. So he ordered Taha and four of his disciples arrested and prosecuted for sedition, belonging to an illegal organization and heresy. Their trial lasted for a few hours and a death sentence was passed. This verdict was upheld by a so-called appellate court and later confirmed by the President. Nimeiri faced the nation to justify his decision to hang Taha, a 76-year-old man (Sudan's 'unislamic' penal code, which was repealed by Nimeiri, prohibits the infliction of capital punishment on persons above 70 years of age), to say that he was convinced beyond any reasonable doubt that Taha was an apostate; all his writings proved it. He also recalled that a similar verdict was passed against him in the mid 'sixties by the *Ulema* (Islamic jurists).

This was the same Taha who had been freely advocating his ideas for the last 15 years of Nimeiri's regime. The *Ulema* were then decried by Nimeiri as obscurantists. The President also castigated those of his aides who pleaded with him for mercy; he described them as weaklings and threatened to have them prosecuted. Nimeiri, by now, was assuming that people's minds and hearts are like his, immune to reason and devoid of compassion.

Nimeiri was not without supporters, however. There were the uprooted SSU types who stuck to him like glue, knowing which side their bread is buttered. There were also the Muslim Brothers, who were gloating over Taha's death – against all Sudanese and Islamic tradition of respect for the dead. (Taha with his incisive mind and mordant style has exposed, through his writings and preaching, the intellectual fallowness of the Muslim Brothers and won in the process many an adherent. Unable to face this intellectual challenge, the Muslim Brothers were only too happy to see Nimeiri doing the dirty work for them.)

Surprisingly, the Brother's leader, Dr Turabi, who was in Geneva when the verdict on Taha was passed, publicly declared that he was shocked by the decision and that Taha was an eccentric who should be left alone. In this we see two Turabis, the urbane intellectual who wants to endear himself to the elite and the political opportunist who is enthralled at the discomfiture of his opponents.

However, on the same day Taha appeared before his kangaroo court, Nimeiri decided to pardon Father Phillip Abbas Ghabbush and 208 of his supporters who were being tried for armed insurrection. Ghabbush is an 80-year-old cleric from the Nuba Mountains (Western Sudan); many of his accused supporters were non-commissioned officers in the Sudanese Army. In this action, as well as in his overtures to John Garang (once accused by Nimeiri of being a Marxist agnostic) one meets several facets of Nimeiri's multi-dimensional personality; in this case, the vindictive, the bully and the weak-kneed coward.

In pardoning Ghabbush, he was guided by considerations of the impact of his decision on the Nuba elements in the armed forces; in extending a friendly hand to the 'agnostic' from the South, he was looking for a face-saving device from the humiliating defeat on the battle-ground and, in hanging Taha, the harmless advocate of causes that were espoused and lauded by Nimeiri himself as late as 1980, we meet both the vindictive man and the bully. Taha's 'departure' from the ways of Allah was tolerated by Nimeiri as long as Taha had a good word for him; once Nimeiri was at the receiving end of Taha's peaceful criticism, the 'apostate' had to pay for his sins. On the other hand, Taha, who had no NCOs in the Army nor fighting men in the South, would be the most eligible person to be made an example of to the Northerners who are challenging Shari'a, i.e. Nimeiri.

President Nimeiri may have also thought that by pardoning a Christian priest he would appease his Western critics and get away with the murder of a non-violent Muslim scholar. It did not occur to Nimeiri that human rights, for many, know neither colour nor creed. He may also have thought that by harping upon Taha's so-called apostasy he would mollify his Muslim critics, notwithstanding the fact that he had tolerated for 14 years the man's caustic criticism of the established orthodox Islamic orders.

To Nimeiri's surprise the Western world's reaction was vehement. The US State Department called the execution a violation of human rights. The French press condemned the execution and described Taha as the Gandhi of Africa (*Le Matin* 21 January 1985, *Le Monde* 20 January 1985). The British press was no less fervent in their condemnation of the callous execution; in fact, three British parliamentarians organised a human rights meeting at the Grand Committee of the House of Commons (Wednesday 30 January 1985) to salute prisoners of conscience and pay tribute to Mahmoud Mohammed Taha (Dame Judith Hart, Cyril Townsend and David Alton.)

Tyrants are increasingly driven by their own lust for power to the point of self-destruction. Nimeiri, a bully through and through, having taken the country to the edge of the precipice, is not going to go over it alone; he is bent on taking the country along with him. His most recent action leaves no shadow of a doubt that the Sudanese are not only ruled by a cynic but also by a man who has completely run out of political strings.

What pains the heart, however, is not the cynicism of Nimeiri nor the barbarity of his vicars and judges but the unpardonable docility of those who want to inherit the earth after Nimeiri – the traditional forces. The voices of dissent against Nimeiri's criminal assault on a man and a group who espoused the cause of liberty, progress and national unity have come only from student movements and professional organizations: university professors, lawyers, judges etc. That the traditional forces take such an apathetic attitude towards such a monumental infringement of accepted standards in human decency by a toothless wolf does honour neither to their moral courage nor to their claim for leadership.

Postscript

As for the toothless wolf, he sealed his fate on 17 January 1985, the day Taha was hanged. No option is now left for him to undertake a navigated climb-down. His shall be a bloody one. One's only hope is that the right-thinking elements in the Sudan will muster their courage and apply their collective wisdom to see to it that he alone goes over the precipice rather than take the Sudan in his trail.

London February 1985

Index

395

401